The Grit, The Grumble, and the Grandeur:

Chicago to New Orleans

A Guide to Travel, Food, and Culture

By Scott Pfeiffer and Karolyn Steele-Pfeiffer

© 2022

Typesetting: Amy Pfeiffer

Cover Photo: Karolyn Steele, taken at the Shack Up Inn.

To our parents, who piqued our curiosity about the world, sparked our sense of adventure, and solidified our thirst for travel. Dream big.

Table of Contents

Key to Restaurant Price Guide: $ = cheap; $$ = mid-range; $$$ - splurge

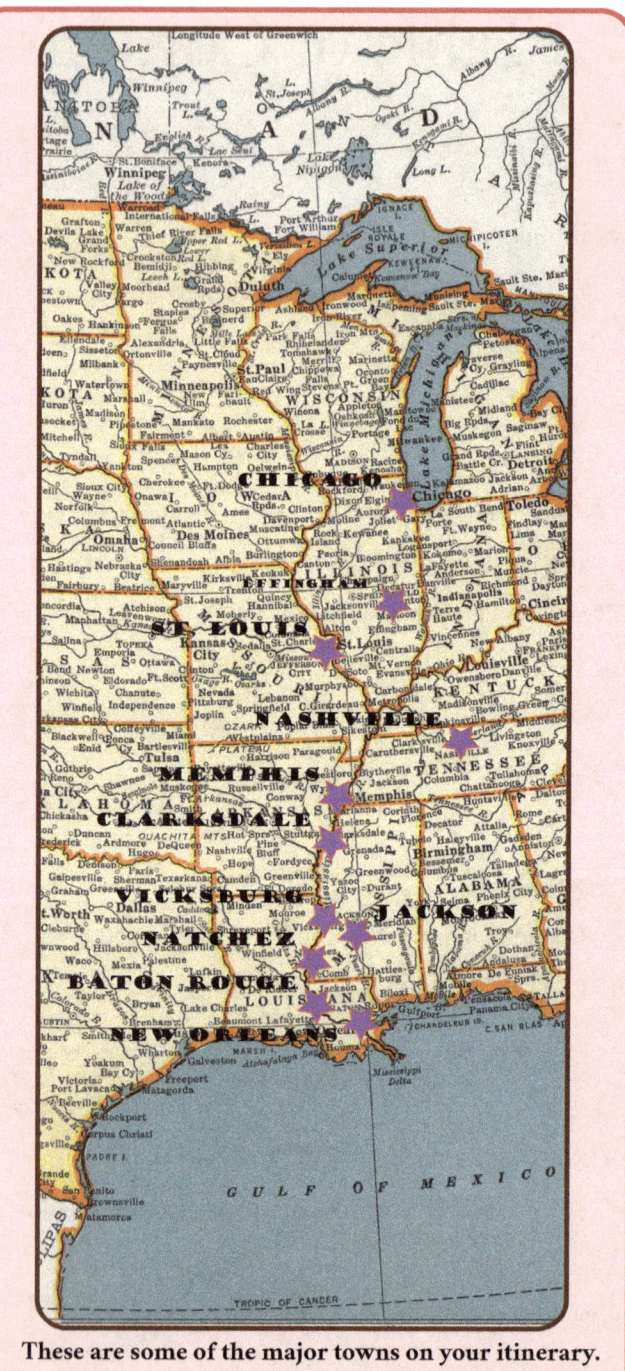

These are some of the major towns on your itinerary.

CHAPTER I

Introduction

Travel in the American South means tracing the roots of American music. At least, the way we do it. This guide is intended for people who are likewise interested in that connection with the past. If we lose our sense of history and memory, then we lose our true identity as Americans. We are keenly aware that history and memory can be lost. Preserving them is the motivation for this entire endeavor. There are forces in the culture who only profit from our forgetting. Forget the struggles and celebrations of people they'd as soon marginalize. Pretend there's no heritage of local, grassroots culture to pass along in the mass-culture age.

Part of it is just reminding ourselves of the side of American culture we love—the music, the food. Maybe that's the first step to ensuring that it survives.

Please allow us to introduce ourselves, then: we are Karolyn and Scott. We met online because of our mutual interest in travel.

— Karolyn: Scott commented on my picture of myself surrounded by Vietnamese children. I looked a hot mess because I had been building houses for them with Habitat for Humanity. I was wearing pigtails, a bandana, a men's white t-shirt stained with mud, and the biggest smile I'd ever had (up to our wedding day). Scott's comment was, very simply, "well done." I was perplexed. I had no idea why he was commenting on this particular photo, but I knew I had to respond. When I did, I learned that his mom was a nurse with USAID during the Vietnam War. Before I even met him, I knew that we would travel there together someday.

— Scott: I suppose I first commented on Karolyn's Vietnam picture because it showed she had a social commitment—that she was concerned about the world beyond one's own backyard, which is a rare quality. I had no idea at the time that we would honeymoon in Vietnam.

— I began to travel rather late in life: I was 38 when I took my first trip abroad, to Paris. I caught the travel bug right away. (Paris tends to be conducive for that virus!) When I commented on Karolyn's picture a few years later, I was in my early '40s. It was starting to feel like it was getting to be fairly late in the day, in terms of looking for a life partner—who would be a travel partner by definition. Actually, from our very first trip together (Morocco and Spain), we found that our combined experience and mutual interests, and perhaps our common age, made us a great traveling pair.

— Karolyn: I had traveled throughout the world before I met Scott, including backpacking through Europe solo for three months, hiking the Machu Picchu trail in Peru, and volunteering for Habitat for Humanity in Poland as well as Vietnam. I had been to New Orleans several times in the 90s, but I feel like I never truly engaged with the cultural side until I went with Scott.

And, in unison: For our book, we have drawn upon our own experiences and discoveries, while supplementing those with research. There are many fine books on our subject that have come before us. We've tried to synthesize these prior works and sources, combining our original insights while mining quotable nuggets. Hopefully, our reading and studying mixed with our lived experiences have produced a practical guide you can use.

Jazz and blues is an American invention, the great democratic art. Honoring those Southern roots through tourism is a way of (1) having fun; (2) tasting a lot of great food; (3) pumping money into depressed areas; and (4) keeping the best of our collective selves from drifting away. It's a way of acknowledging our common heritage, and keeping the places that birthed it afloat. Everything changes, but preservation of this culture is somehow related to preservation of our humanity, and that means honoring the grit, the grumble and the granduer of the South.

Turn the page. It's time to party.

CHAPTER 2

The Need for Speed - Why Drive Highway 61? (The "Long Cut")

If you're setting out on a Southern road trip from Chicago, as we do, you might well ask, why not just take I-55? It's faster.

We prefer to take legendary Highway 61. We're a bit romantic about it, actually. With a bit of imagination, the traveler conjures the ghosts and spirits of the blues heroes who traveled this road, through the very act of remembering them. Highway 61 is an emblem of folklore and of history, a symbol, a metaphor, with which every American should reckon.

Highway 61 runs through the Mississippi Delta, a place of monumental stories, some of which are legend, some of which are fact; some inspiring, many traumatic. It's a place that almost inevitably recalls the great maxim from John Ford's *The Man Who Shot Liberty Valence:*

"When the legend becomes fact, print the legend."

We've tried to do both, here.

"The legend" would include tall tales like Robert Johnson selling his soul to the devil at the crossroads in exchange for his musical talent—a myth to explain his rapid acquiring of almost magical chops on his instrument. "The fact" would include the tragedy of slavery, and the highway's historic role as the escape route for African-Americans fleeing Jim Crow during the Great Migration.

Traveling 61 is also a great way to connect with and support local culture, including the mom-and-pop restaurants still serving the kind of fare that sustained those who traveled this road in the past.

— Scott: Plus, there's this juke joint in Clarksdale, Mississippi on Highway 61 called Red's.

— Karolyn (ears perking up, having read of juke joints in Zora Neale Hurston's *Their Eyes Were Watching God*): Juke joint? Mmmmmmm. That's where the naughty happens. Take me there.

— Scott: If we leave now, we'll get there by sunrise.

— Karolyn: Highway 61 it is.

Party fingers, start dancing.

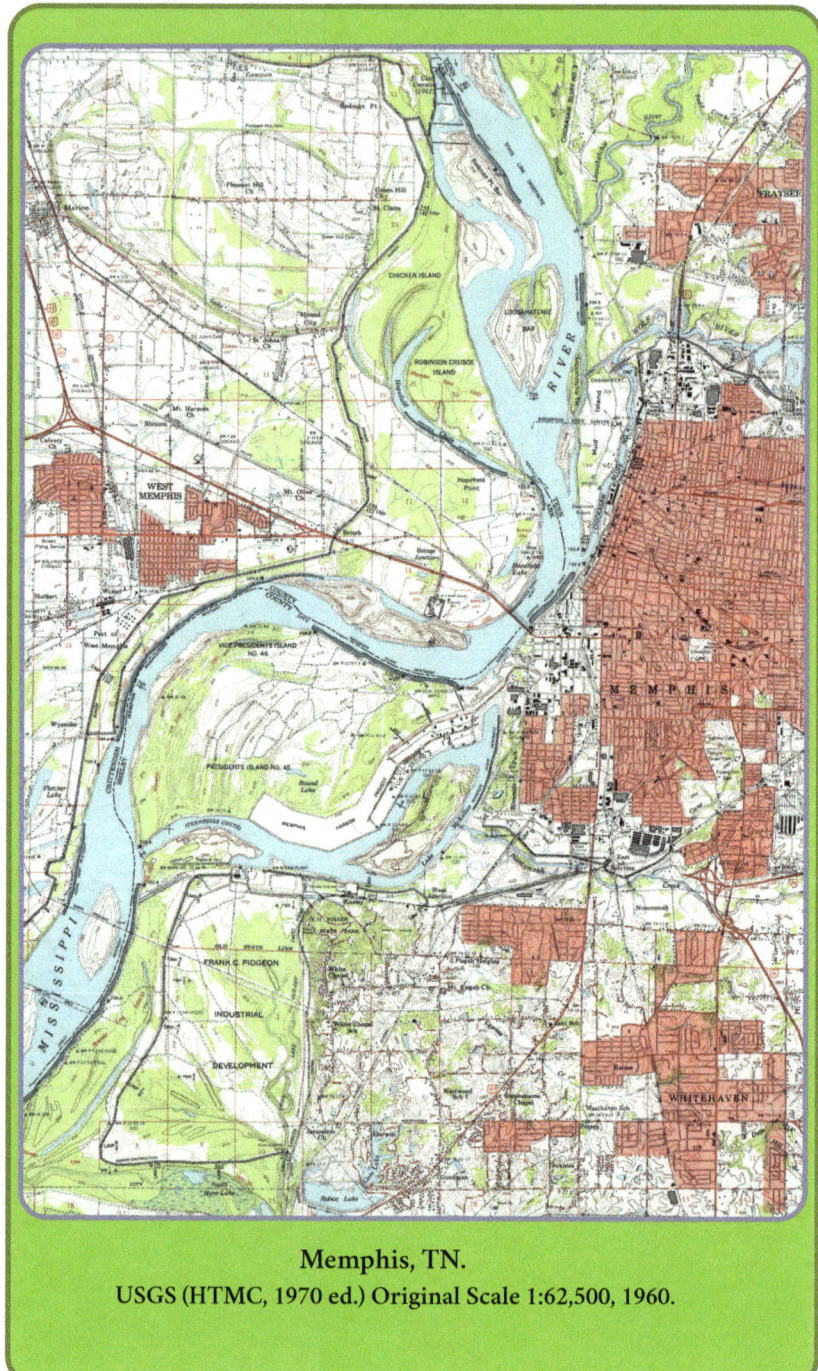

Memphis, TN.
USGS (HTMC, 1970 ed.) Original Scale 1:62,500, 1960.

CHAPTER 3

Memphis, Bluff City

Scott: Where to start with Memphis? It's the place of which Peter Guralnick has written, "Memphis, always a haven for eccentrics and individualists, is the only locale I know that actually boasts of its craziness."

Just think of the roll call: B.B. King, Elvis Presley, WDIA (the "Mother Station of the Negroes," the first Black radio station in the South), hipster R&B deejay Dewey Phillips, Sun Records and its founder Sam Phillips ("the man who invented rock 'n' roll," per Guralnick), Stax Records, Royal Studios. That's a pretty unbeatable musical and social history.

Not to mention Beale Street. Scott Barretta, writing in Living Blues magazine, summed up the significance of this legendary street: "For many decades Beale Street—the city's social, political and economic center for African Americans—was a first stop for thousands of Mississippians headed north in the Great Migration."

— Karolyn: Alright, hon, what do you want to start with?

— Scott: I think we should start with Sun Studio.

— Karolyn: Why?

— Scott: Sun Studio is one of the few places in the world—Cosimo Matassa's J&M Recording Studios in New Orleans is another—that can claim to be a birthplace of rock 'n' roll. It's where Jackie Brenston and His Delta Cats (really, Ike Turner's Kings of Rhythm by another name) recorded "Rocket 88," sometimes considered the first rock 'n' roll record, and where Elvis Presley recorded his first sides.

— Karolyn: They also need to go to Stax, where music and social change meet.

— Scott: Preach! The changes in the music were an organic reflection of social change. The music was an expression of the activity that led to change, and it also inspired the activists, bound them together.

— Karolyn: Okay, let's start by giving em', say, our weekend itinerary suggestions.

PLANNING YOUR TIME: ITINERARIES

First-timers' Weekend Jaunt

Day One:
Morning

Tour Sun Studios, one of the birthplaces of rock 'n' roll.

Afternoon

Have lunch at the The Four Way, for soul food and Civil Rights history.

Tour the Stax Museum of American Soul Music.

Evening

Have dinner at Rendezvous for BBQ, then hit Beale Street clubs.

Day Two:
Morning

Have breakfast at the Arcade, Memphis's oldest restaurant, then tour Graceland.

Afternoon

 Have lunch at Marlowe's for some Elvis-approved BBQ.

Tour the Memphis Rock 'n' Soul Museum.

Evening

Catch the march of the Peabody Ducks at 5pm, if you missed their 11am perambulation.

Drive or cab/Uber out to Wild Bill's for a true juke joint experience.

If you have more time, do Day One and Two of the basic Memphis itinerary, and then add the following.

Day Three:
Morning

Breakfast at the Beauty Shop, then stroll the Cooper-Young district.

Tour the National Civil Rights Museum.

Afternoon

Have lunch at Interstate Barbecue.

Tour W.C. Handy's Home.

Evening

Have dinner at Coletta's for Elvis' BBQ pizza.

Enjoy an evening at Ernestine & Hazel's, a classic dive.

Day Four:
Morning

Breakfast at Brother Juniper's.

Drop in at Lansky's, where Elvis and B.B. King picked up threads.

Afternoon

Have lunch at Gus's for hot fried chicken, or Bar-B-Q Shop for barbecue.

Tour the Blues Hall of Fame Museum

Evening

Go to Bar DKDC in the Cooper-Young district for small plates and live music.

SITES AND MUSEUMS

Sun Studio
706 Union Avenue
Memphis, TN 38103

Legend has it that Bob Dylan once walked into Sun Studio, kissed the floor where Roy Orbison and Johnny Cash once trod, and walked back out. That comes close to saying all that needs to be said. This is where men made history: Elvis, Jerry Lee Lewis, Carl Perkins, Charlie Rich, Howlin' Wolf, Ike Turner, B.B. King, and Bobby Bland all recorded here.

Elvis, Scotty Moore, and Bill Black may have been just fooling around when Elvis started belting out the blues song "That's All Right, Mama" in rockabilly style on the evening of July 5, 1954, the first of the recordings that would become known as the legendary Sun Sessions. (In other versions of the story, they'd rehearsed the moment for months.) When he heard the guys goofing around, Sam Phillips, the visionary Sun Records founder and owner—who hadn't thought much of the ballad Elvis had recorded for his mother, "My Happiness," one of two records Elvis cut the very first time he dropped in at Sun in '53—shot up out of his chair. Yeah, yeah, do that! he hollered.

They played "That's All Right, Mama" in a cross-cultural style not quite like anybody else. The b-side was a country song, "Blue Moon of Kentucky," done in a jumped-up tempo. Steeped in gospel, country, and rhythm 'n' blues, Elvis' record was too country for some, too Black for others—but it sounded great to many more. Even his sobriquets spoke to the black/white hybrid—was he the Hillbilly Cat, or the King of Western Bop? (As Peter Guralnick points out, these nicknames bespoke a "cultural schizophrenia," an inability to know what to make of him).

He wasn't the first white singer to play around with singing in a Black style, by any means, but these white southerners still broke a powerful taboo, experimenting with a musical miscegenation that would become the prototype for rock 'n' roll. The new music was met by violent resistance by white racist groups like the White Citizen's Council, who rightly recognized it as a threat to their idea of order.

To further bolster Sun's credentials as the birthplace of rock 'n' roll, the tune some consider the very first rock'n'roll hit was recorded here: "Rocket 88," by Ike Turner and his Kings of Rhythm (released under the name of singer/sax-man Jackie Brenston). The record actually came out on Chicago's Chess Records: Sam Phillips would sometimes sell Chess tracks recorded at Sun by Black artists like Turner and Howlin' Wolf.

Taking the informative, fun tour of Sun Studio is a quintessential Mem-phis experience. Your visit begins upstairs: enjoy the re-creation of Dewey Phillips' radio booth: Phillips (no relation to Sam) was the hard-partying deejay who first broadcast Elvis to the world. Exhibits honor lesser known performers as well: Rosco Gordon's music was played on New Orleans radio and thus went out to the Caribbean, where it influenced the islanders' music. In turn, of course, Jamaica influenced American music. There's an exhibit for Joe Louis Hill, a one-man band.

Examine the terrific photographs. We see deejay Nat D. Williams of WDIA, the historic Memphis radio station. With Williams' groundbreak-ing show in 1948, WDIA became the first station in the country to target an African-American audience. WDIA was a huge influence on Elvis, and Rufus Thomas and B.B. King once worked at the station.

Your visit winds up in the studio where the magic happened. You'll get to pose with an original Sun Shure 55 microphone which Sam Phil-lips donated, on the condition that it not be put behind glass but left out where people can enjoy it. The piano Jerry Lee Lewis played is here: look for his signature cigar burn on the keys. The spot Dylan allegedly kissed is marked in tape with an "X". Full disclosure: Scott got down on the ground and kissed it.

Sam Phillips created some of the most original popular music ever made. He prized non- conformity above all. In 1978, he told Guralnick, "I'm not saying go back to the fifties and this sort of thing. But if it could be worked—and it will be worked—to where just a few like Elvis could break out, then I would preach. For God's sake, *don't* let's become conform-ists—*please*. Just do your thing in your own way."

Cost and hours: (daily 10-6, adults: $15, children 5-11: free);
Tel. (901) 521-0664, Toll free. 800-441-6249;
website: https://www.sunstudio.com

Stax Museum of American Soul Music
926 E. McLemore Ave.
Memphis, TN 38106

Located in the "Soulsville" part of town, the Stax Museum of American Soul Music must be the world's finest soul music museum. Stax Records, founded by white siblings, Jim Stewart and Estelle Axton in 1957 and co-owned/run by Al Bell, a Black man, was a place where people were allowed to be themselves—or, even more importantly, who they wanted to be. As guitarist Steve Cropper testifies in the short documentary film which introduces your visit, Stax Records was *the* place in the '60's where Black people and white people came together to make music. (For Karolyn, this Cropper interview was one of the most moving aspects of the museum). It was a place of acceptance, he says, where color never came through the door—at least until Dr. King was assassinated. (Afterwards, Stax—and Memphis—were never the same). He speaks of it as a kind of idyll of community in diversity, where respect and gratitude and equality were mutually shared without hesitation—based soul-y on human talent. Listening to him speak, you can tell he still grieves what was lost. Cropper renders Stax's achievements on a personal, not historical, scale, but that doesn't reduce them so much as make them all the more poignant.

It's not too much to say that the Civil Rights Movement wouldn't have gone so far, so fast without the music made at Stax. Music was the movement's fuel and glue, and the museum does not hesitate to put Stax's music in the context of the Movement. Groups like the Staple Singers offered their audience solidarity, energy, and even analysis.

Today, this museum celebrates the spirit of Stax. Founded in 2003, it is a replica of the original Stax Records recording studios and offices, built *in situ*. Upon entering, you see a tribute from Led Zeppelin, a framed gift from Robert Plant which contains miniature reproductions of all of Zep's albums covers, acknowledging the "huge effect" Stax had on Zep— as if to say, we owe so much of what we did to you.

Further along, you can enter a Mississippi Delta church from 1906, which was disassembled at its original location and put back together in the museum, serving to reinforce the fact that soul music flowed out of the church and gospel music. This church is made up of all-original woodwork, including the pulpit and the handmade pews. Speaking of church influence, you'll see exhibits giving props to the "gospel quartets" (actually often comprising five members): the Dixie Hummingbirds, Five Blind Boy of Mississippi, Five Blind Boys of Alabama, Swan Silvertones, and the Soul Stirrers.

Next, we trace soul's roots in jump blues and the cotton field. A sidebar explains the importance of Chicago blues and Chess records and the world-historical migration from the Delta to Chicago by men like Muddy Waters and Sonny Boy Williamson II, who had worked in the cotton fields as sharecroppers. We also learn more about Ike Turner and "Rocket 88," cut across town at Sun.

Exhibits explain soul music's roots in jazz (Jimmy Smith's hard bop organ influenced Booker T. Jones), in vocal groups (the Five Royales' guitarist Lowman Pauling influenced Steve Cropper), and in country (many Stax artists listened to the Grand Ole Opry as kids)—not to mention Tin Pan Alley.

As it would so often as we trod in the footsteps of the giants of American music, a theme emerged as we walked these halls. Namely, the essence of American music is racial fusion—even in the years when the essence of America itself was segregation, by law in some places and by custom in others.

Major soul artists like Ray Charles and Otis Redding get their own exhibits. (Find the great photo of Otis sitting, quite literally, on the dock of the bay.) There's an exhibit for Rufus Thomas and his daughter, Carla. Rufus recorded for Sun Records as well as Stax. In fact, the museum made us begin to see Stax and Sun, as well as Beale Street, as parts of one unified Memphian whole—as pieces of one story, especially in the '50s and '60s.

There's an exhibit for Stax's competitors in soul, Motown. And you can't tell the story of Stax, or soul, without an exhibit for Atlantic Records. We learn about the "handshake deal" between Atlantic and Stax, which led to Atlantic artists recording at Stax—but also to Atlantic basically absconding with Stax's entire classic catalogue. Rather than fold up shop, though, Stax responded by announcing the "Soul Explosion": essentially, they would create an entirely new body of music virtually overnight, through an unprecedented outburst of creativity. The gambit worked.

There's some props for the Mar-Keys, the original Stax house band, which featured Booker T as well as future M.G.'s Donald "Duck" Dunn and Steve Cropper, not to mention the future Memphis Horns, Wayne Jackson and Andrew Love. Isaac Hayes and David Porter get their due—they're the songwriter/producer team who made a lot of the great Sam and Dave records. Note also the exhibit for two storied studios—Muscle Shoals Studio in Alabama, where Stax and Atlantic artists such as Aretha Franklin went to cut records with "the Swampers," a.k.a the Muscle Shoals Rhythm Section, and Rick Hall's FAME studio (also in Muscle Shoals), where that renowned group of musicians got their start.

Perhaps the main attraction of the museum is the near-exact replica of the legendary Studio A, where so many historic recording sessions took place. The studio was converted out of an old neighborhood movie theater, which Jim and Estelle renovated by hand. A sign explains: "Ironically, [Jim] Stewart refused to spend the money to have the theater's sloping floor leveled, which added to the concert hall feel and sound of the studio." That's one reason the records have that raw, live, exciting sound. The producers perched in the projection booth; for playback, they used the movie theater's old sound system.

In terms of musical instruments, you'll see Al Jackson, Jr.'s drum kit, Booker T's organ—the very one he played on "Green Onions"!—and Steve Cropper's and Donald "Duck" Dunn's guitars.

Other goodies your eyes cannot afford to miss: Isaac Hayes' spectacular gold-plated Cadillac, and the replica of the Soul Train dance floor, where Mavis Staples and the Staple Singers might inspire you to wield your best party fingers. Stop here and do the funky chicken.

The story of Stax's sinking is one of myriad factors—chief among them a bad deal with Columbia, who essentially refused to distribute Stax records. A morass of lawsuits and foreclosures sealed the company's fate. The original Stax studio was demolished in 1989.

Today, the Stax Museum honors the dream that Stax articulated at its best—its liberatory effect on the audience. It's a true testimonial to the power of music. The museum also runs the Stax Music Academy which mentors youth in music, many of them at-risk. As a side-note: back in the day, Memphis Slim lived next door to the studio, his home has been turned into a "collaboratory."

Cost and hours: (Tu-Su 10a-5p, closed M; adults: $13, Seniors 62+, Active Military, and Students with ID: $12, Children (ages 9-12): $10, Members, Children (8 and under): Free);

Tel. (901) 261-6338;

https://staxmuseum.com

Graceland
Elvis Presley Blvd.
Memphis, TN 38116

To go from visiting Sun Studio to visiting Graceland is quite a heady experience.

Think of Elvis as the shy teenager with the otherworldly voice singing the ballad "My Happiness," the demo he cut for his mom at Sun. Then consider the distance between where he started and Graceland, where tour buses carrying visitors from all over the world continuously roll up. See much more on Graceland under *Tours*.

Cost and hours: (Daily 9-4; mansion only tour starts at $42.50; "Elvis Experience" tour starts at $63; "Elvis Entourage" VIP tour starts at $102.50; "Ultimate VIP" tour starts at $180; various price points for children and seniors under each "plan";

Tel. (901) 332-3322; 800-238-2000, Toll-free in North America;

https://www.graceland.com

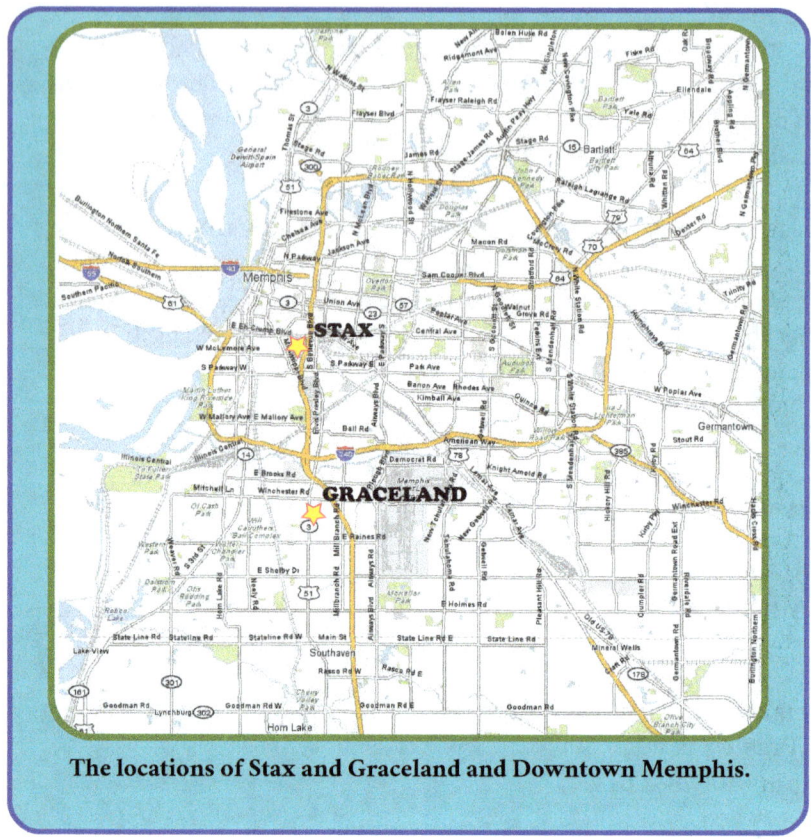

The locations of Stax and Graceland and Downtown Memphis.

National Civil Rights Museum
450 Mulberry St.
Memphis, TN 38103

This museum is a rich, powerful and rewarding experience. To walk through the history of the Civil Rights Movement heightens your appreciation for how each struggle and achievement built on the one that came before. In chronological order, you'll encounter exhibits about the bus boycott of '55-'56; enemies of the Movement like "Bull" Connor and J. Edgar Hoover; key organizations like the SCLC (Southern Christian Leadership Conference), SNCC (Student Nonviolent Coordinating Committee) and CORE (Congress of Racial Equality); the interracial Freedom Rides of 1961, including a replica of the Greyhound bus firebombed by a white mob in Anniston, Alabama; the Children's Crusade of 1963; and the passage of the Civil Rights Act of 1964.

An exhibit tells the story of how in 1966 Dr. Martin Luther King, Jr. brought the protest movement north "to take on black urban problems, especially segregation. Chicago seemed like the perfect battleground." A photo illustration depicts a march in Chicago's Marquette Park over housing discrimination.

You'll learn how freedom songs like "We Shall Overcome" continue to inspire uprisings around the world. "In 1989 alone," a placard reads, "the song was sung by those tearing down the Berlin Wall, standing up to the Chinese government in Tiananmen Square, and challenging apartheid on the streets of Johannesburg, South Africa." You'll see vibrant AfriCOBRA art by the likes of Barbara Jones-Hogu.

Above all, the museum makes you think of how far we've come, and how far we have yet to go. It is located, somewhat controversially, in the Lorraine Motel, where Dr. King spent his last moments before his assassination. Guests may stand on the balcony Dr. King stepped out onto on the fateful morning of April 4, 1968. To get there, you pass by the bedroom he slept in on his last night. We found it a powerfully moving experience to stand on this balcony, having seen it in history books. In many ways, Memphis has never the same.

Cost and hours: (Mon. 9-6, closed Tu, Wed-Sa 9-5, closed Sun; adults: $17, seniors 55+, college students with ID: $15, children ages 5-17: $14, ages 4 & under: free, museum members: free, active U.S. military: free);

Tel. (901) 521-9699;

https://www.civilrightsmuseum.org

Blues Hall of Fame Museum
421 S. Main St.
Memphis, TN 38103

This museum is run under the auspices of the Blues Foundation, which every year since 1980 has anointed a new set of inductees into the Blues Hall of Fame. If you're lucky, you'll get to meet Reed Marvinx, who volunteers at the Foundation and introduces guests to the collection, which you are then free to peruse at your leisure. Reed is a font of knowledge on music history and can also direct you to whatever good local music is happening.

Be sure to utilize the video touchscreen stations, which include especially well-curated and illuminating videos of Hall of Fame members performing live. In a nice move, producers who've recorded the greats have also been inducted alongside the musicians, as have authors who've expanded our understanding of the music. For example, Ralph Peer, who recorded "Blue Yodel" for Jimmie Rodgers and "Crazy Blues" for Mamie Smith, is an inductee.

The museum is chockablock with instruments played by Hall of Famers, including Robert Cray's Stratocaster, Albert Collins' Fender Telecaster, R.L. Burnside's Fender Squire Stratocaster, and a Gibson Custom Lucille guitar carried by Bobby Bland's son in B.B. King's funeral procession. You'll see a Hohner chromonica (chromatic harmonica) played by George "Harmonica" Smith, as well as Otis Spann's piano.

Also look for the hat worn by Big Walter Horton when shooting *The Blues Brothers,* and Sam Lay's reversible cape, painted cane and drumsticks. (Lay, the original drummer in the Paul Butterfield Blues Band, played his trademark "double shuffle" behind Little Walter, Willie Dixon, Howlin' Wolf and John Lee Hooker.) Stevie Ray Vaughan's Japanese "happi coat," is here, as well as a tape box for Bette LaVette's first album, recorded in '69 and never released (intriguing, that.)

Cost and hours: (W-Sa 10a-5p, Su 1p-5p, closed M-Tu, adults: $10, students age 13 to 18 with ID: $8, children age 12 and under are free);
Tel. (901) 527-2583;
https://blues.org/hall-of-fame-musuem/

Memphis Rock 'n' Soul Museum
191 Beale St.
Memphis, TN 38013

All roads led to Memphis for the rural Mississippi men and women who dreamed of making it big in music in the big city. This museum celebrates them. It offers a useful reminder that when we talk about Memphis music, we're largely talking about the music of rural Southern farmers and share-croppers. There are exhibits dedicated to Memphis legends like Bobby 'Blue' Bland and B.B. King, who, together with Junior Parker and lead singer Johnny Ace, started out in a band called the Beale Streeters.

You'll see Elvis Presley in a famous photograph with Parker and Bland taken at the WDIA Goodwill Revue, 1957. An exhibit honors trumpeter Wayne Jackson and tenor saxophonist Andrew Love, aka the Memphis Horns— who started as The Mar- Keys. Ike Turner's first piano is here, the one he used "to perfect the style that was used on 'Rocket 88'," maybe the first rock'n'roll hit. You'll see Al Green's stage outfits and the Hammond L-111 organ and Fender Jazzmaster guitar on which, in 1968, Mark James wrote "Suspicious Minds" for Elvis. Be on the lookout for Isaac Hayes's bejeweled piano watch.

Cost and hours: (daily 10-7, adults: $13, children 5-17: $10);

Tel. (901) 201-2533;

https://www.memphisrocknsoul.org

Center for Southern Folklore
119 S Main St.
Memphis, TN 38103

By way of introduction, Scott Barretta writes that the Center for Southern Folklore, founded in 1972 by Judy Peiser and William Ferris, "has remained true to its mission of documenting regional vernacular traditions. The Center features exhibits of area folk culture, serves downhome food, and offers regular concerts by artists including bluesman Daddy Mack (Orr), a native of Como." This valuable community center, led by a dedicated, knowledgeable and gregarious staff, also occasionally offers live blues at lunchtime by the likes of the Fieldstones. We met Ms. Peiser when we dropped in, and she couldn't have been kinder, personally showing us around, engaging us in conversation, and even sitting us down with lemonade to watch a blues documentary.

The Folklore Store is on the ground floor; upstairs you'll find Heritage Hall, with a stage and exhibits; this is where the live music takes places and films are shown. Even when nothing is happening, it's enjoyable to peruse the photographic exhibits upstairs.

You'll see pictures of Louis Dotson describing how to make a "one-string guitar" (also called a diddley bow) and Addie Burt describing how to make a bottle tree. You'll see a photo of embroiderer Ethel Wright Mohamed's needlework homage to the store her husband, a Lebanese immigrant, founded in Belzoni, Mississippi, in 1922.

There's an exhibit dedicated to the great Leland bluesman James "Son" Thomas, who was also a sculptor. (If you make it to the Highway 61 Museum in Leland, you can see his sculptures, as well as some by his son, musician/sculptor Pat Thomas, who continues his father's legacy). Over Labor Day Weekend, the Center hosts the well-regarded Memphis Music and Heritage Festival.

Cost and hours: (Mon-Fri: 11-6, Sat 2-11, Sun 2-8, free);

Tel. (901) 525-3655;

info@southernfolklore.com

W.C. Handy's Home & Museum
352 Beale St.
Memphis, TN 38103

Moved to Beale Street from its original location 10 blocks south, W.C. Handy's Memphis Home & Museum is a small shotgun house packed with history. A highly informed guide walks you through. Handy was the first man to write down and publish the blues, which had previously been a folk music—an oral tradition passed down from singer to singer. Bordello music, honestly. Handy lived in Memphis from 1905 to 1918, when he moved to New York. The home/museum is best appreciated in conjunction with our Mississippi Delta itinerary, which you'll find below. Our Delta itinerary will have you walking in Handy's footsteps in Tutwiler, the town where he "discovered" the blues in 1903—that is, he had a revelatory experience when he heard an unknown guitar player singing at the train station. We also take you to Clarksdale, where Handy lived at the time of his Tutwiler discovery, playing in the lucrative red-light district across the tracks.

Cost and hours: (summer, Tu-Sa: 10-5, winter Tu-Sa:

11-4; adults: $6, youth: $4);

Tel.(901) 527-3427, 901-522-1556;

http://www.wchandymemphis.org/wchandy.html

Al Green's Full Gospel Tabernacle Church
787 Hale Rd.
Memphis, Tennessee 38116

Bishop Al Green is pastor and founder of this house of worship. We turned up on a Sunday morning in hopes of getting our souls cleansed by the Reverend himself, but alas, illness prevented his appearance. This did not, however, stop his parishioners from catching the holy spirit. One can't help but get caught up in the regulars' faith, swept away in the intensity and glory and celebration in the gospel music. You'll see some beautiful hats, as well.

Cost and hours: (Sunday services begin circa 11:30a; free);
Tel. (901) 345-8040

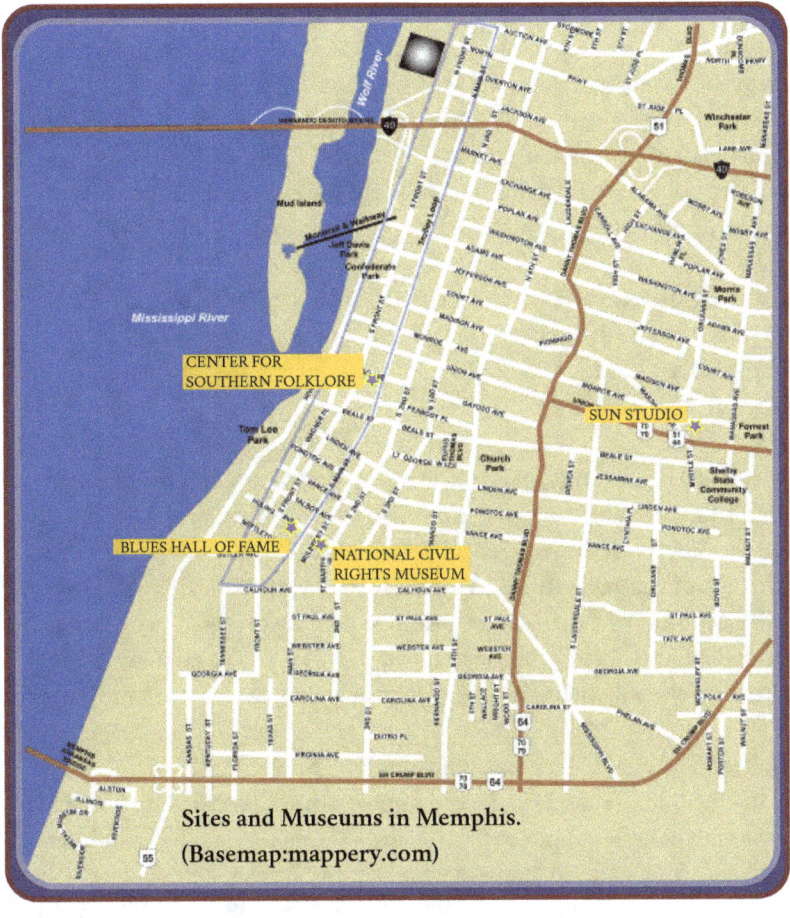

Sites and Museums in Memphis.
(Basemap:mappery.com)

Overton Park
1928 Poplar Ave.
Memphis, TN 38104

Memphis' public park, always open, is most notable for music lovers because it includes the Shell theater, where Elvis played his first professional concert on July 30, 1954. Free concerts *al fresco* still take place.

Memphis Minnie's Mississippi Blues Trail Marker and-
Gravesite
7564 Norfolk Rd.
Lake Cormorant, MS 38641

On your way out of Memphis to Clarksdale, be sure to stop here to commemorate virtuoso Memphis Minnie. It's about a half hour outside the city on Highway 61. Born in 1897, Memphis Minnie was one of the greatest blues guitarists. As *Living Blues* magazine wrote, in Memphis and Chicago "she adapted her masterful guitar technique to the electric era." She co-wrote "When the Levee Breaks," which Led Zeppelin brought to the world.

New Park Cemetery (Graves of Bukka White, Al Jackson Jr.,
and Rufus Thomas)
4536 Horn Lake Rd.
Memphis, TN 38109

At New Park Cemetary, pay your respects to great Memphis musicians Booker ("Bukka") White, Al Jackson Jr., and Rufus Thomas. The kind attendant we met when we stopped at the front office, Julie, who also helped us find some of the graves, told us that George "Mojo" Buford, who played harp with Muddy Waters, used to work here digging graves. She once asked him, why do you still work in the graveyard, when you're an international bluesman? He replied, "In order to know the blues, you got to work the grave."

Booker White was the great bluesman of "Shake 'Em on Down" and "Fixin' to Die Blues" fame. How he did ramble, from Clarksdale to Memphis and places farther afield. "Loved by all," says his gravesite. Al Jackson Jr. was one of the all-time great drummers who beat the skins for Booker T. & the M.G.'s and who died tragically, murdered at the age of 39. Rufus Thomas of

"Do The Funky Chicken" fame, recorded hits for Stax and Sun, and worked as a disc jockey at the trailblazing radio station WDIA.

— Scott: Well, that about does it for sites and museums. You could spend the whole day at the Stax Museum.

— Karolyn: I'd budget about three hours, and plan to return one day. We've got more on the itinerary.

— Scott: Fair enough. Now that they've done Stax, what's next, baby?

— Karolyn: Let's go to the Four Way!

— Scott: What is this Four Way, our readers want to know?

— Karolyn: Why, located conveniently down the road from Stax, Four Way is….

RESTAURANTS

Four Way Soul Food Restaurant
998 Mississippi Blvd.
Memphis, TN 38126

The moment you walk in, you know you're in more than a restaurant: you're in a Soulsville landmark. Southern hospitality begins at the Four Way. You're greeted with a smile as you peruse the walls dotted and decorated with mementoes and photographs from the restaurant's role in Civil Rights activism. In the pictures you'll see everyone from Martin Luther King, Jr. to Jesse Jackson, as well as the unsung folks who make up the grassroots movement. That includes the waitstaff, such as a charming young man we met who advised us of his plan to teach in the inner city of Little Rock, Arkansas. Why? Because he's following his passion for equality.

Irene and Clint Cleaves opened the Four Way Grill in 1946. Clint happened to be chauffeur to former mayor E.H. Crump, who liked his soul food. When Crump invited his friends to eat here, the Four Way became perhaps the only integrated eatery in Memphis. As Jennifer Biggs put it in the Commercial Appeal, as a restaurant "frequented by both black and white diners from the time it opened, it was an island of unity in a mid-century Southern city. It not only served civil rights leaders and activists, but politicians and entertainers; Elvis Presley took meals there. And of course, it was where Dr. King ate when he was in town."

On our first visit we met Willie Bates, the neighborhood man who bought the restaurant in 1996, when it fell on hard times and was shuttered by the state. His vision was to preserve the tradition and the passion. Mr. Bates has sadly passed away now, but his daughter, Patrice Thompson, keeps the legacy going.

Okay. So, the food. May we just say that it is so delicious that Karolyn hugged our server on our first visit?

— Karolyn: If you go to the Four Way and you do not order fried chicken, you are *not* respecting the Four Way. I don't care which sides you get. (Get the mac 'n' cheese.) But the fried chicken: juicy, piping-hot, and that crispy skin…ooh. Spices decorate every bit, and when you bite into it, it's like getting a facial: the steam bakes your face, causing it to burst into a beautifully effervescent sweat. You will gnaw every morsel off the bone. Do not try to restrain yourself. Screw the diet. This is worth it. No disrespect to Popeye's, but you can get that in any city. This is special. Wash it down with sweet tea.

— Scott: The turkey with dressing is a Thanksgiving party at any time of year, and you get to enjoy it with your new Four Way family. It's comfort food, giving you that warm tryptophan buzz. I like to go for a side of greens.

Now let's talk about the fresh-baked peach cobbler—because apparently you're not full yet. Our waiter had told us, "Don't you dare miss the peach cobbler." Upon inspection, the proffered concoction made our taste buds dance to its symphony of sweetness and flavor: cinnamon, warm peaches, peach glaze, vanilla ice cream, and crisp, buttery crumble. The peaches burst with flavor and you'd get these wonderful contrasting textures of crunchy and doughy crust. Save room, and if you don't, well—make room. Did we mention they have apple cobbler, as well?

The Four Way: it's not just the history. It's what continues to happen.

Cost and hours: (Tu-Sa 11a-7p, Su 10a-5p, closed M, $);

Tel. (901) 507-1519;

http://fourwaymemphis.com

Charlie Vergos' Rendezvous
52 S 2nd St.
Memphis, TN 38103

Down an alley across from the Peabody and down a flight of steps, you'll find Charlie Vergos' Rendezvous, the subterranean barbecue legend. Circa 1948, Charlie Vergos converted an old coal chute in the basement of the restaurant he co-owned with his brother into a smoker. Then, quoth the Rendezvous website, he "created a rub based on the seasoning from his father's unique Greek chili recipe and the cajun spices he discovered on visits to New Orleans. He added paprika to give it a more traditional barbecue color." The rest is history. There's fall-off-the-bone ribs, then there's stick-to-the-bone style. There's wet 'n' saucy, and then there's dry-rub. For 74 years (at present writing), Rendezvous has been *the* dry-rub, stick-to-the-bones Memphis experience. The ribs make you go atavistic as you primally gnaw every last reluctant, juicy morsel from the bone. If you're waiting for your name to be called, explore the upstairs area. We found framed sheet music for "The Memphis Blues" (1912) by W.C. Handy, "the first [published] blues song." There's also a real Wurlitzer jukebox. Consider picking up a shaker of that rub (and, yes, a bottle of sauce) on the way out.

Cost and hours: (Tu-Sa 11a-8p, closed Su and M, $);

Tel. (901) 523-2746;

https://www.hogsfly.com

Blues City Cafe
138 Beale St.
Memphis, TN 38103

The Blues City Cafe proffers tasty barbecue on Beale, albeit "fall-off-the-bone-style" ribs. Try the "Beale Street Throw Down": a platter with hickory smoked sausage and assorted cheeses (pepper jack is Scott's favorite), dill pickles, and peppers. The attached Band Box is a good place to hear some good, hot blues.

Cost and hours: (Tu-Th, M 4p-10p, Fr-Su 11a-10p, $);
Tel. (901) 526-3637;
https://bluescitycafe.com

Marlowe's Ribs
4381 Elvis Presley Blvd.
Memphis, TN 38116

Just down the street from Graceland, Marlowe's was one of Elvis' favorite rib joints. They feature cherry-wood-smoked barbecue as well as family recipes like homemake lasagna and Italian-style BBQ spaghetti. They even have a fleet of seven pink limousines on standby to whisk you to their front door.

Cost and hours: (Daily 4p-10p, $);
Tel. (901) 332-4159;
http://www.marlowesmemphis.net

The Arcade
540 S Main St.
Memphis, TN 38103

Speros Zepatos founded the Arcade in 1919. Whenever we're in town we always have breakfast at this historic diner, Memphis' oldest restaurant. Scott especially likes the country fried steak, though the "Eggs Redneck" is a "Travel Channel favorite." Your biscuits will be plucked fresh and warm from the biscuit drawer. Elvis ate at the counter here, and the peanut butter and banana sandwich on the menu pays homage. Fans of Jim Jarmusch's great film *Mystery Train* will feel like they stepped into the movie, since it was shot in the neon glow of this diner and the surrounding South Main Street environs. Speaking of which...

Cost and hours: (Su-Wed 7a–3p, Thu–Sat 7a-10p, $);
Tel. (901) 526-5757;
https://arcaderestaurant.com

Earnestine & Hazel's
531 S Main St.
Memphis, TN 38103

Just across the street from the Arcade, you'll find Earnestine & Hazel's, one of the candidates for "America's greatest burger dive bar." It's the kind of place that attracts superlatives, being also home to the storied "most haunted jukebox in America." More on that in a second, but first a bit of history.

Sisters Earnestine Mitchell and Hazel Jones were hairdressers who once ran a beauty parlor upstairs, then transformed the place when the building was bequeathed to them. As Susan Puckett writes, "During the civil rights era, [Earnestine and Hazel] turned the downstairs into a juke joint and served soul food." It was here that Stax artists would repair after a hard day of recording.

Upstairs, the sisters ran a brothel, Puckett goes on, "with a clientele that included many a bluesman who'd just stepped off the platform at Central Station. A photo of Howlin' Wolf with some of his admirers perched on his lap hangs on a wall. Supposedly, when the Rolling Stones dropped in, the ladies of the evening made such an impression it inspired their hit 'Brown Sugar.'"

The pride of Earnestine and Hazel's is the mysteriously perfect Soul Burger, invented by a man named Russell George, an R&B lover who took over the place in the early '90s. Back to Puckett: "Many locals declare it the best burger in the city. Dressed with yellow mustard, onions, and dill pickle slices (cheese is optional), this basic burger arrives in a plastic basket with the one side offered: a bag of Golden Flake potato chips. Whether it's the mysterious seasoning in the silver shaker that raises its flavor a notch or the dill pickle juice rumored to clean the flat-top griddle on which it's fried, it's hard to say."

Now, what was this we said about a haunted jukebox? Well, it seems the ghosts of those hairdresser sisters, Earnestine and Hazel, still inhabit the place. (They liked it so much, they never left.) According to legend, they amuse themselves by observing and eavesdropping on visitors to the bar, then commenting on their lives by, unbidden by any human hand, playing a slyly appropriate song on the jukebox —messages that speak to a specific visitor's needs. For some patrons, the songs have felt like a sign at a moment of personal crisis. When we visited, we challenged the sisters all night to send us one of these musical signs. We even needled them for not showing themselves. On our way out, after trying for hours to get the sisters to speak, Karolyn, on a whim, stopped at the jukebox, dropped in a bit of cash and punched in a random number. It would seem the sisters had grown tired of being baited: Which song did Earnestine and Hazel choose to to play, out of their entire library? The Beatles' "You Won't See Me."

Cost and hours: (M-F 5p–3a, Sat–Su 11a–3a, $);
Tel.(901) 523-9754;
https://earnestineandhazels.com

Coletta's Italian Restaurant
1063 S Parkway E.
Memphis, TN 38106

Coletta's invented barbecue pizza, much beloved by Elvis. This restaurant, founded in 1923, also makes a claim to be Memphis' oldest— though it would seem that the Arcade, establised in 1919, gets the title by simple mathemat-ics. In any event, Coletta's is a great old-school Italian place, festooned with pictures of Venice and Elvis memorabilia. The dedicated Elvis Room is something to see, a veritable shrine. When Elvis and Priscilla visited, this is the room where they'd eat: management would draw a curtain at the entrance so that Elvis could enjoy a furtive barbecue pizza—his favorite— in peace. Find the menu on the wall from the early '70s—the very one from which Elvis would have ordered. You'll note that barbecue pizza was only $1.75! One taste and you'll see why it kept the King coming back. Pizza topped with smoked pork shoulder in a tangy barbecue sauce—what's not to love?

Cost and hours: (M-Th 11a–10p, F 11a-11p, Sa 12p–11p, Su 1p-9p, $);
Tel. (901) 948-7652;
https://colettas.net

Dyer's Burgers
205 Beale St.
Memphis, TN 38103

Dyer's is a popular diner known for using the same grease to deep-fry their burgers and fries for over a century. As their website puts it, "Over the years, this famous cooking grease has been transported to our various Memphis locations under the watchful protection of armed police escorts, finally settling" at the current Beale Street setting. The burger is a delicious grease- bomb treat—just the thing to soak up a night of celebratory imbibing. Word of warning: the waitstaff is guaranteed a 20% gratuity for parties of two or more; with no reason to try, our server was disengaged and even a bit rude.

Cost and hours: (Daily 11a–10p, $);
Tel. (901) 527-3937;
http:// www.dyersonbeale.com

Lew's Blue Note Bar & Grill
341 Beale St.
Memphis, TN 38103

At the excellent website *The Delta Review* (http://thedeltareview.com), the author calls Lew's bacon cheeseburger the "best burger on Beale Street." You'll almost certainly see us there on a future research mission.

Cost and hours: (Th-Sa 12p-3a, closed Su-W);
Tel. (901) 577-8387;
https://lewsbluenotememphis.com

Central BBQ
147 E Butler Ave.
Memphis, TN 38103

Well-regarded BBQ with four locations, Central often tops polls of locals' favorite BBQ. We visited the location near the Civil Rights Museum. Good stuff, for sure, but it wouldn't be at the top of our list. That said, be sure to get the barbecue nachos, which are delicious.

Cost and hours: (M-Th, Su 11a–8p, F-Sa 11a–9p, $);
Tel. (901) 672-7760;
https://eatcbq.com

Jim Neely's Interstate Bar-b-Que
2265 S. Third St.
Memphis, TN 38109

The scrumptious fare at Interstate includes rib tips, ribs (beef and pork), and hickory- smoked pork (chopped or sliced), all of which comes slathered in tangy sauce. As Thrillist put it, Neely's "secret sauce is so delicious they can't keep bottles of it on the table lest they disappear. A large chopped sandwich with extra sauce is about as close to heaven as some of us may come." Dinners come with a choice of two sides (cole slaw, baked beans, or potato salad) and bread. Look for the barbecue spaghetti.

Cost and hours: (M-W 11a–10p, Th 11a-11p, F-Sa 11a-12a, closed Su, $);
Tel. (901) 775-2304;
http://www.interstatebarbecue.com

Payne's Bar-B-Que
1762 Lamar Ave.
Memphis, TN 38104

Payne's is another tantalizing subject for further research. As Ronald Payne told Thrillist: "Crispy and smoky bits in the meat and sweet 'n tangy dressings makes a chopped pork sandwich that stands out from any sandwich you've ever had."

Cost and hours: (Tu-Sa 11a–6p, closed Su and M, $);
Tel. (901) 272-1523;
http://www.interstatebarbecue.com

Bar-B-Q Shop
1782 Madison Ave.
Memphis, TN 38104

The New York Times' description of the Bar-B-Q Shop whetted our appetite: a "classic smokehouse that's known for ribs that can compel a moan," the restaurant features a "famous pulled pork sandwich piled with an extraordinary tasty coleslaw on Texas Toast," as well as baked beans that "might send you into the kitchen to ask what the secret is." We ordered the ribs and the pulled pork sandwich and we understood immediately why the sandwich is "famous." The baked beans especially are as wonderful as billed: smoky, spicy, and sweet. The day we visited they were baked by owner/chef Eric Vernon himself, who also waited on us—and he's a fun guy. Karolyn did, in fact, try to cajole the recipe out of him, but he wouldn't budge. (Hint: he's a huge Prince fan, so if you have any bootlegs, he just might budge on the recipe in exchange for a swap.) Next time we go, we'll order the barbecue spaghetti, which we were told by a local is a Memphis tradition. We recommend ordering the ribs wet: the bark is incredible, but the sauce puts it over the top. Fun fact: on the day we visited, Steve Earle was there grabbing lunch before his gig later that night. Last thing: the Times counsels: "for more 'bark,' order the rib tips, but be prepared for a mound of meat," and the tips are not always on offer.

Cost and hours: (M-Sa 11a–9p, closed Su, $);
Tel. (901) 272-1277;
https://thebar-b-qshop.com

The Beauty Shop
966 Cooper St.
Memphis, TN 38104

Over in the Cooper-Young district, the Beauty Shop is "a former beauty salon that purportedly coiffed that now famous sky-high beehive do for Priscilla Presley," quoth the New York Times. Scott had a delicious Eggs Florentine with fried oysters. Karolyn had a Thai Cobb salad with mango. Both were lovely. Have a Bloody Mary or a grapefruit Big Boy Mimosa to make it a truly jolly time.

Cost and hours: (M-Th 5p–9:30p, F 5p–10:30p, Sa 11a–2p, 5p–10:30p, Su 10a–3p, $);
Tel. (901) 272-7111;
https://www.thebeautyshoprestaurant.com

Bar DKDC
964 S. Cooper St.
Memphis, TN 38104

The name of this bar in the Cooper-Young District stands for "don't know, don't care." It's a good spot for live music, far from touristy Beale: we stopped in and saw Amy LaVere and Will Sexton. They're also known for their international small plates, which we'll have to go back and try some time. Their website advertises "global street food," with a menu that "reads like an global backpacker's food diary. Oaxacan Mexican to Shashlik from Israel. Spanish Tapas to the spices of the Caribbean. Plus, we change it up every five weeks." Sounds good to us. The Times recommends the crispy pork dumplings and the smokey bacon honey paddy, a Jamaican treat.

Cost and hours: (Temporarily closed, $);
Tel. (901) 272-0830;
http://bardkdc.com

Gus's World Famous Hot & Spicy Fried Chicken
310 Front St.
Memphis, TN 38103

Gus's is a spicy, white-paper-plate-style Southern classic. Scott had his first-ever fried green tomatoes here, and when we look back on our flushed-face photographs from our visit, we can see the evidence of the hot chicken having its happy effects. As Chicago Eater wrote (on the occasion of a Gus's franchise opening in Chi-town), "Gus's has developed a rabid cult fan base thanks to their chicken batter, a proprietary recipe that requires certain staff to sign non- disclosure agreements. With each surprisingly non-greasy crunch, the cayenne flavor expands, but not to sweat-inducing levels."

The detail we especially like: "[Proprietors Wendy] McCrory and her husband, Matt McCrory, have to take separate plane flights for insurance purposes due to their knowledge of the recipe." The couple carries on the legacy of founder Gus Bonner, who in turn preserved the original recipe of his mother Maggie and her husband Napoleon "Na" Vanderbilt, who opened Maggie's Short Orders in Mason, Tennessee in 1973. In 1984, Gus reopened under his own name. A big fan, Wendy McCory began working there, and she opened the Memphis branch in 2001. To eat like a local here, turn it up a notch by drizzling Louisiana hot sauce over your crispy breast—but only if you can take the heat. Allay your reddening cheeks with the essential white bread.

Cost and hours: (Daily 11a-9p, $);

Tel. (901) 527-4877;

https://gusfriedchicken.com/ downtown-memphis-tennessee-location/

The Majestic Grille
145 S Main St.
Memphis, TN 38103

If you're looking for a healthy bite in Memphis, the Majestic Grille is a good spot. Housed in an old movie palace from 1913, it offers big, lovely salads. Scott had salmon and Karolyn had chicken breast: both of these proteins arrived atop a bed of fresh greens. We did get some fried calamari on the side, but hey, it's still the South. Proprietors Deni and Patrick Reilly also conceive of the restaurant as a community/cultural center. On their website, they write: "Add to that the largest private movie screen in the city showing silent films & classic movies and you're center stage in an atmosphere that reclaims the cinematic glory of the dawn of the silver screen."

Cost and hours: (Tu-F Lunch: 11a-4p; Sa Brunch: 11a-2p, Dinner: 4p-9p;

Su Brunch: 10a-1p, $);

Tel. (901) 522-8555;

http://majesticgrille.com

McEwen's
120 Monroe Ave.
Memphis, TN 38103

McEwen's is a good place to find vegetarian-friendly food in Memphis. (Imagine that.) We actually met the owner, John Littlefield, at Bar DKDC on our last night in town. When we told him we were headed to Oxford, he told us about McEwen's sister restaurant in Oxford. We ended up eating there, and it was delicious, and indeed quite veg-friendly. (See our Oxford section.)

Cost and hours: (Lunch M–F 11a–2p; Dinner M–Th 5:30p–9p, F & Sa 5:30p–10p closed Su, $$);

Tel. (901) 527-7085;

http://mcewensmemphis.com

Huey's Burgers
77 S 2nd St.
Memphis, TN 38103

Their website proclaims Huey's the "home of blues, brews, and burgers since 1970." This family-run spot—another of Memphis' legacy restaurants—has several locations. It's been voted "Best Burger" by *Memphis Magazine*. Live music on Sundays.

Cost and hours: (Su-Th, 11a-1a, F-Sa, 11a-2a, $);
Tel. (901) 725-0770;
https://hueyburger.com

LBOE (The Last Burger On Earth)
2021 Madison Ave.
Memphis, TN 38104

Another contender for best burgers in Memphis, LBOE's menu proudly notes that their Benedict Burger (featuring a beef/pork-sausage blended patty over arugula, smoked Gouda, hardwood smoked bacon, poached egg, Hollandaise, paprika, and chives on a toasted brioche bun) was the 2017 World Food Championship Winning Burger. The menu also features enticing items such as the Mac-N-Cheeseburger.

Cost and hours: (Su-W, 11a-10p, Th-Sa, 11a-11p, $);
Tel. (901) 527-2700;
http://www.lboerestaurant.com

Brother Juniper's
3519 Walker Ave.
Memphis, TN 38111

It only took one visit for Brother Juniper's to become our favorite breakfast and brunch place in Memphis. Located outside of downtown near the University of Memphis, the restaurant is family-run since its roots in '60s San Francisco, when their forerunners served cheap coffee and cigarettes to the homeless and indigent of Haight Street. Scott's "Garden and the Lamb" omelet was packed with veggies, cheese, and gyro meat. Omelets come with home fries and coffee; get a side order of the cheesy grits, which are like puréed mac 'n' cheese. We left with a loaf of their homemade bread and a bottle of the house tabasco sauce. It's worth the trip.

Cost and hours: (T-Fr, 6:30a-1p, Sa 7a-12:30p, Su 8a-1p, closed M, $);
Tel. (901) 324-0144;
https://brotherjunipers.com

Jim & Samella's House
841 Bullington Ave.
Memphis, TN 38106

Phil Rosenthal went to Jim and Samella's House on his food 'n' travel program *Somebody Feed Phil*, which is a hoot. As the notes on the show's website proclaim, Phil and friends feasted on "fried chicken, waffles with apples and crown royal syrup, shrimp and grits, and the most amazing fried lobster tails you'll ever have."

Cost and hours: (Closed M-Th, F 11:30a-4p, Closed Sa, Su 12p-4p, $);
Tel. (901) 265-8761;
https://www.facebook.com/jimandsamellas/?ref=page_internal

Cozy Corner BBQ Restaurant
735 North Pkwy.
Memphis, TN 38105

Phil also dropped by Cozy Corner on the above-mentioned show, where, his website reminisces, Phil was "served some southern classics like barbequed cornish hen, smoked ribs, and a delicious bologna sandwich with homemade barbeque sauce."

Cost and hours: (Tu– Sa: 11a– 8p, Closed Su-M, $);
Tel. (901) 527-9158;
https://cozycornerbbq.com

Gibson's Donuts
760 Mt Moriah Rd.
Memphis, TN 38117

Gibson's Donuts was recommended to us by our new pal Reed, whom we met at the Blues Hall of Fame Museum. *(See above.)* He says their donuts are really something to experience, and one thing we've learned on our travels is to always trust locals.

Cost and hours: (Every day: 5a– 12a, $);
Tel. (901) 682-8200;
https://www.facebook.com/gibsonsdonuts/

Bryant's Breakfast
3965 Summer Ave.
Memphis, TN 38122

Another tip from our friend Reed, Bryant's Breakfast will have to be one of our subjects for future research on our next trip to Memphis. A tough job, but someone must do it. "Bustling, counter-serve eatery dishing out classic Southern breakfast & lunch fare," says Top Brunch Spots.

Cost and hours: (W-Su: 5a–2p, closed M-T, cash only, $);
Tel. (901) 324-7494;
http://bryantsmemphis.com

MUSIC, BARS, AND THE REST

Beale Street was historically the heart of Black Memphis and the Mem-phis Blues, from the days when W.C. Handy hit town at the end of the first decade of the century, through the '20s-'50s heyday when you might find the street's clubs featuring the likes of Louis Armstrong, Muddy Waters, Albert King, Memphis Minnie, B. B. King, Rufus Thomas, and Rosco Gordon.

So the first thing that should be noted about Beale Street is that it is not what it was in the '40s, obviously. The city forcibly relocated the Black neighborhood that was its lifeblood in the cause of "urban renewal," in an ongoing process that lasted until the mid-'70s. Today it's a blatantly touristic open-air liquor store—and fun enough, for all that. At a lot of these venues (and, frankly, at many of the places you'll see in this book) you'll see musicians who've got an "entertain the tourists" shtick going. Yet Beale still attracts some thoughtful blues travelers from around the world. The following is written with them in mind. First, we'll take you a few miles off the beaten path.

Wild Bill's Juke Joint
1580 Vollintine Ave.
Memphis, TN 38107

Memphis historian Robert Gordon calls Wild Bill's "the real deal" when it comes to what you want from an urban juke joint, and we second that notion. Just a 10-minute drive from downtown, Wild Bill's, opened by the late William Storey in 1993, is "where people come to dance, drink 40oz (two-pint) beers, and eat late-night chicken wings that reduce the belly's sloshing when you lie in bed." (Along with the wings, the menu features other grub, such as jumbo burgers.) Gordon's description of the room jibes with our experience: "The room glows with red Christmas lights and the memories of cigarette smoke." We'd add that the ambience is rounded out by the low ceiling, the small dance floor, and the long communal tables. When we were here on a Saturday night in July of 2014, we watched the musicians gather as we enjoyed a tasty sausage sandwich with a side of crinkle-cut fries—though we opted to wash it down with regular-old sized bottles of Bud Light. (The venue only sells beer; it's got a BYO policy to whatever other liquor you might like.) As the night wore on the room filled up with an integrated crowd of locals, regulars, and students, and the joint was soon heaving to the sounds of the rocking band. By visiting the late Mr. Storey's club, you keep alive the days when Big Lucky Carter, who passed in 2002, was the house guitarist. You're communing with ghosts, but you also may see Don Valentine, the last man standing from the original house band, the Hollywood All-Stars/Blues Busters. At Wild Bill's, you'll still find the kind of vibe that survives at Red's in Clarksdale, and precious few other places.

Cost and hours: (Fr-Sa 7a-12a; $)

Tel. (901) 409-0081,

https://wildbillsmemphis.com

Mr. Handy's Blues Hall Juke Joint/Rum Boogie Cafe
174/182 Beale St.
Memphis, TN 38103

The first time we visited Mr. Handy's Blues Hall on Beale Street, in 2013, we saw Brandon Santini and his band giving it everything they'd got. The lead guitarist, Jeff Jensen, was on fire, seemingly intent on picking up where Mike Bloomfield, Buddy Guy, or even Hendrix himself left off, leaping and thrashing like a shredding Tasmanian devil. On another good night here, Karolyn boogied with a new friend, an older, dapper African-American gent, while we grooved to a stirring performance by Queen Ann Hines. Perhaps you could call the Hall a simulated juke joint, but when the vibe is right, that's a distinction without a difference. Keep an eye out for Robert Kimbrough Sr., Junior Kimbrough's son, who occasionally plays here. Next door, the adjacent Rum Boogie Cafe displays two of the original signs from Stax Records. Dr. Feelgood Potts jams here on Mondays; also keep an eye out for Vince Johnson & the Plantation Allstars, a band steeped in the Chicago blues-harp stylings of James Cotton, Billy Branch, Carey Bell, and Junior Wells.

Cost and hours: (Su-Th 11am-1am, F-Sa 11a-2a; $)

Tel. (901) 528-0150,

https://rumboogie.com

B.B. King's Club
143 Beale St.
Memphis, TN 38103

The namesake club of perhaps the greatest artist in the history of the blues, B.B. King, this club is a good spot to catch some local flavor. We had a great night here once seeing Preston Shannon, the "King of Beale Street," who has since passed away. We won't forget his cover of Prince's "Purple Rain," which lifted the roof off the place. Photographs on the walls celebrate local legends like Laura Dukes, Ann Peebles, Furry Lewis, and Memphis

Slim. Tabletops are whimsically painted to look like, say, a Sun 45 of Elvis' "Mystery Train."

Cost and hours: (Su-Th 11am-11p, F-Sa 11a-12a; $);
Tel. (901) 524-5464
https://bbkings.com/memphis/

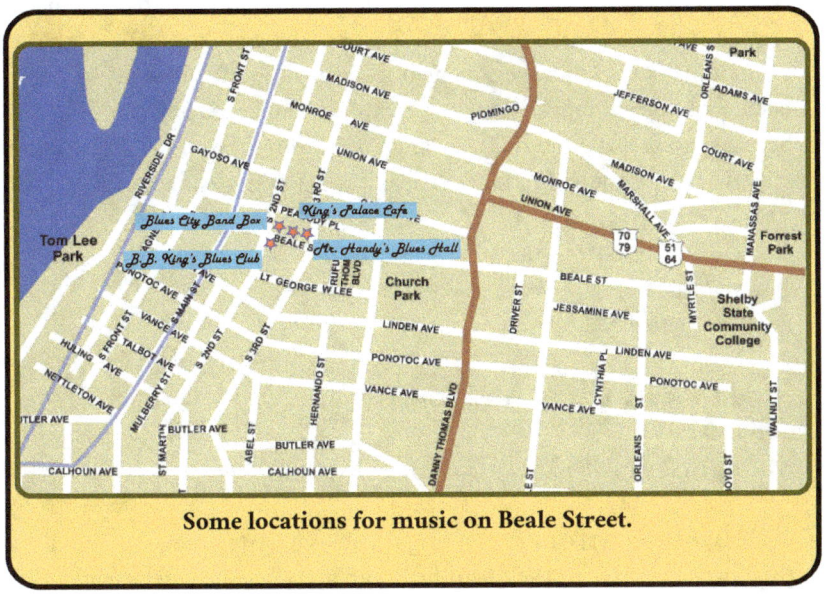

Some locations for music on Beale Street.

Blues City Band Box
142 Beale St.
Memphis, TN 38103

The Band Box is one of our favorite places on Beale. There's almost always some legit blues happening at the Box, the music hall of the adjacent Blues City Cafe restaurant. Look for living, passionate apostles of the blues such as Blind Mississippi Morris and Earl "The Pearl" Banks—86 years young and still rockin the blues.

Cost and hours: (Daily 11am-12a; $)
Tel. (901) 526-3637
https://bluescitycafe.com/music/

Railgarten
2166 Central Ave.
Memphis, TN 38104

Railgarten is an intriguing venue recommended to us by our pal Reed. Cedric Burnside often plays here, and it appears their calendar often features New Orleans bands, as well. Just read this bit from their website: "This isn't easy to summarize. Yes, we have 1.5 acres. Top-notch food? Got that too. Drinks? Beer, cocktails, you name it. A huge outdoor space to explore? Indeed. Railroad shipping containers? Duh. Of course. Live music? Oh hell yes. Secret spaces, surprises and games? Happy hunting. Your favorite Midtown friends, family and neighbors? Probably. It's Railgarten."

Cost and hours: (W-Th 4p-10p, F 11a-1a, Sa 11a-1a, Su 11a-10p, closed M-T, $);
Tel. (901)504-4342;
https://railgarten.com

King's Palace Cafe's Absinthe Room
166 Beale St.
Memphis, TN 38103

You're likely walking in Robert Johnson's footsteps here. Located above the King's Palace Cafe, the Absinthe Room was once the Black-owned Hooks Brothers photography studio. Johnson himself is believed to have trod these very boards in 1935. In fact, it's said that the great photograph of him in a pinstripe suit—you might have seen it on the cover of the 1990 boxed set "The Complete Recordings"—was taken here. (It's one of only two known photographs of him.) Climb the stairs, belly up to the bar and order an absinthe drink, which will come poured over a flaming sugar cube. Make sure to explore the warren of neon-bathed backrooms, where you'll find pool tables and posters for cinematic classics such as "How to Stuff a Wild Bikini" and "Red Line 7000."

Cost and hours: (Su-Th 11a-10p, F-Sa 11a-1a; $);
Tel. (901) 521-1851;
https://bluescitycafe.com/music/

Alchemy Bar
940 South Cooper St.
Memphis, TN 38104

A cocktail bar in the Cooper-Young district. Their Sparkling Pears quaff gets sparkling notices.

Cost and hours: (M-Th 4p-11p, F-Sa 4p-2a, Su 10:30a-2:30p and 4p-10p; $)

Tel. (901) 726-4444,

http://alchemymemphis.com

The High Point Pub
477 High Point Terrace Ste B
Memphis, TN 38122

This venerable joint turns 75 in 2022. It's got space for 25 folks. Only beer is served, but you may order pizza from the restaurant next door and they'll deliver it right to the pub. (Sounds like there's also lots of TVs with sports in your face, if that's your thing. Scott just barely tolerates it, when he's in the right mood).

Cost and hours: (T-Sa 5:30p-1am, closed Su-M, $);

Tel. (901) 452-9203;

https://www.facebook.com/highpointpub/?ref=page_internal

Memphis Music Records Tapes
149 Beale St.
Memphis, TN 38103

This is a terrific record store on Beale Street, where you can snatch up many classic albums reissued as budget CDs. It's open late, so you can even pop in while digesting your barbecue in preparation for some live music.

Hours: (M-Sa 10a-12am, Su 12p-10p);

Tel. (901) 526-5047;

https://www.facebook.com/pages/category/Movie---Music-Store/Memphis- Music-373173979494652/

A. Schwab Dry Goods Store
163 Beale St.
Memphis, TN 38103

The only remaining original business on Beale, still going strong after 146 years (at this writing), A. Schwab Dry Goods Store, established in 1876, is no ordinary store. As Steve Cheseborough notes, their slogan was, "If you can't find it at Schwab's, you're better off without it." The store began selling voodoo supplies when they noticed that people who bought blues 78s—three for a dollar—were also interested in voodoo. You've heard bluesmen sing about Mojo Hands? Well, at A. Schwab, you can actually get them. In fact, this is *the* place in Memphis to get your voodoo supplies—and the second floor is essentially an exhibit on voodoo/blues culture. You can not only get your High John the Conqueror Root, but, thanks to a display, you can read the fascinating tale behind it. (When you get down to New Orleans, you'll have more opportunities to learn about voodoo, a traditional Afro-Caribbean faith, via walking tours and some fine shops/community centers. See our New Orleans chapter below.)

Hours: (M-Sa 10a-12am, Su 12p-10p);

Tel. (901) 526-5047;

https://www.facebook.com/pages/category/Movie---Music-Store/Memphis-Music-373173979494652/

Lansky Bros., Clothier to the King
126 Beale St.
Memphis, TN 38103

Would you, in your dreams, like to be like Elvis and B.B. King? Then get your threads at Lansky Bros. A teenage Presley used to drop in at Lansky's when he was hanging out on Beale Street, then still the heart of the the Black musical community, who were largely the shop's clientele. Lansky's sold the hottest, hippest threads around to the likes of B. B. King, and Elvis thought he'd like to dress that way, too. The kid always was different. The shop's website tells a bit of the story: "Presley bought his high school prom outfit from the store—black pants, a pink coat and a pink-and-black cummerbund.

He bought the outfit he wore on one of his early 'Ed Sullivan Show' appearances at Lansky's—a plaid sport coat and pegged pants—and he bought his first gold-lamé jacket there." The white suit he was buried in also came from Lansky's, and was personally selected by Bernard Lansky, the man who'd also dressed him as a teenager. When Karolyn got Scott a snazzy shirt here with guitar buttons, he liked to imagine that the two Kings, Elvis and B.B., would've approved. (Carl Perkins, Bobby "Blue" Bland, and Isaac Hayes were Lansky's regulars, as well.) There's also a location inside the Peabody Hotel.

Hours: (M-W 12p-6p, Th 12p-8p, F-Sa 10p-9p, Su 11a-6p);
Tel. (901) 523-9782;
http://lanskybros.com

Memphis also boasts attractions we've yet to check out. We hope future editions of this book will feature entries on such subjects for further research as Loflin Yard, Rec Room, Crosstown Concourse, and Mud Island River Park. We also like the looks of the First Congregational Church. Once, when we were exploring in the Cooper-Young district, we spotted a banner promoting this congregation. It read: *"We've been called radical, liberal, progressive...we just thought it was Christian."*

TOURS & FESTIVALS

Graceland: The Home of Elvis Presley
Elvis Presley Blvd.
Memphis, TN 38116

One of the headiest experiences of visiting Memphis is to go from Sun Studios, where it all began, to Graceland—where the life (if not the story) ends. Think of that shy teenager with the otherworldly voice crooning the ballad "My Happiness" (the demo Elvis cut for his mom at Sun), and of those groundbreaking early singles with Scotty Moore and Bill Black. Then consider the distance—geographically a hop, historically an entire universe—between those beginnings and Graceland, where tour buses carrying visitors from all over the world continuously roll up. What began as a local lark became a dream the whole planet dreamed together.

Any pilgrim in search of American musical history, or America itself, must take a tour to see Graceland. Along with your group, you roll up to the estate in a shuttle bus, while listening on headphones to the provided audioguide.

— Scott: When Graceland first swam into my ken, I felt just like the poet fella, Keats, when he first looked into Chapman's Homer: "Then felt I like some watcher of the skies, when a new planet swims into his ken." I gazed with a wild surmise as the stately Colonial Revival home, built in 1939, hove up on the horizon.

As you enter, you see the Presley family dining room on your left. Passing through the living room, enjoy the colorful peacock-themed stained glass. Glimpse into the purple and pink bathroom.

The TV room amazes with its trifecta of boob-tubes, its mirrored ceilings and, yes, its porcelain monkey. After Elvis heard that Lyndon Johnson kept three TVs going at all times, he decided he'd do the same. (Part of us thinks they should've kept on display the one he famously blasted with a shotgun.) You catch a glimpse of his record collection over in the corner. Elvis was a student of all kinds of music, including classical. (He liked Monty Python, too.)

In the extraordinary downstairs Pool Room (not the wet kind, the kind you play on a table), the walls are festooned with a kind of folded drapery that shoots out from the center of the ceiling like a starburst. Back on the main floor, there is the Jungle Room, where the waterfall—yes, waterfall—trickles softly. Linger a bit to consider the green shag carpeting on the ceiling.

It's the details that make Graceland—which is cozier than you might imagine, and more personal than gaudy—an affecting emotional experience. You get a feel for Elvis' home life as you walk through the kitchen and see another TV on the counter (which, we learn, he always kept on, again Johnson-style). Later, in another building on the grounds, you listen through headphones to a snippet of Elvis' moving acceptance speech for the "Outstanding Young Men" Award. You could feel how this award, in particular, actually meant a lot to him.

You'll pass through temples housing iconic jumpsuits, gold and platinum records (the platinum ones are especially striking to the eye), posters from Elvis' notorious Hollywood career, and even the leather suit he wore in that legendarily galvanic '68 Comeback special. In one room, sofas are arrayed around a piano overseen, on a gallery level, by the King's pinball machines.

When you walk in Graceland—as so often when you tread in the footsteps of the giants of Southern music—you realize that people like Elvis were breaking down cultural barriers, sometimes just by implication. It's not as if they did it for ideological reasons; the rebellion was just inherent in what they did, in who they were.

Strolling the grounds, you'll see Elvis' private jet (the "Lisa Marie"), and wander past his kidney-shaped pool.

Finally, you come to the Meditation Garden, where Elvis rests alongside his mother, father, and grandmother.

— Scott: I'm not ashamed to admit I teared up when we got to the King's grave. I thought about how all he ever wanted to do was make people happy—and how that impulse may have been his undoing, in some ways. But how much happiness he brought nonetheless—and what a generous spirit.

As we pulled away in the shuttle bus, we observed the low wall around the grounds, the one Bruce Springsteen famously leaped over on that fateful night in 1976 when he snuck up and knocked at the door, hoping to meet Elvis, only to be politely turned away by a guard who advised him that the King wasn't home.

Other sites on the museum campus include the Elvis Presley Automobile Museum, where you'll see the iconic pink and purple Cadillacs, Lisa Marie's Mercedes-Benz 280SL, and a collection of some of Elvis' motorized toys— off-road vehicles in which he enjoyed scooting around the Graceland estate.

At the Elvis mall across the boulevard from Graceland, have a look at the exhibits in the shop devoted to the '68 comeback special if you cherish that unbelievably raw, dirty show. The exhibit makes a very creditable effort to put that concert in the context of the tumultuous year of 1968—a context of Vietnam and student revolts and the assassination of MLK. It underlines once again the extent to which Memphis was never the same after Dr. King's assassination.

Cost and hours: (Daily 9a to 4p; mansion only tour starts at $42.50; "Elvis Experience" tour starts at $63; "Elvis Entourage" VIP tour starts at $102.50; "Ultimate VIP" tour starts at $180; various price points for children and seniors under each "plan";

Tel. (901) 332-3322; 800-238-2000, Toll-free in North America;

https://www.graceland.com

Memphis Music and Heritage Festival

This fest takes place over Labor Day Weekend in September and is hosted by the Center for Southern Folklore. It all jumps off on Main Street between Peabody Place and Union; there are four outside stages and two stages inside the Center at 123 and 119 S. Main Street. The Everfest site describes this festival as a celebration of "the musical, artistic and cultural legacy of the Memphis area" with "eclectic performances, workshops and vendors. Multiple stages host musicians, dancers, poets, artists, speakers and more, and live music spans a variety of genres and includes artists from the local area and beyond."

Memphis in May International Festival

Taking place throughout the month of May, this festival includes a Beale Street Music Festival, headlined by major pop and rock acts, and a World Championship Barbecue Cooking Contest. Each year's fest features a salute to a specific country's culture—in 2022, the country honored was Ghana.

HOTELS

First, we should say that if you're on the road from Chicago to Memphis, we find Effingham is a conducive spot to stop if you can't drive straight to Memphis. There's several truck stops for breakfast; the TA used to have a Country Pride where, on our very first Southern road trip, we had good biscuits and gravy. It's gone now, but you should still find plenty of places to fill up. This hotel is perfectly adequate.

La Quinta Inn & Suites by Wyndham Effingham
1103 Avenue of Mid America
Effingham, IL 62401
(217) 540-1111
http://www.wyndhamhotelgroup.com

Now, back to sleeping in Memphis.

The Peabody Hotel
149 Union Ave
Memphis, TN 38103
(901) 529-4000
https://www.peabodymemphis.com

Not for nothing is the lobby of the Peabody Hotel referred to as "Memphis' living room." In 1935, David Cohn wrote, "The Peabody is the Paris Ritz, the Cairo Shepherd's, the London Savoy of this section. If you stand near its fountain in the middle of the lobby...ultimately you will see everybody who is anybody in the Delta." Elvis Presley signed his first contract in the lobby, on Peabody stationary.

Of course, we also have to cite Cohn's most oft-quoted line. In 1935, Cohn famously wrote that "The Mississippi Delta begins in the lobby of the Peabody Hotel in Memphis and ends on Catfish Row in Vicksburg." As Steve Cheseborough adds, Cohn "was not only defining the Delta's geographic limits, but also contrasting the lifestyles of those who sell cotton and those who work in the fields."

Cheseborough further notes that the Peabody "has an important place in blues history as a site of field-recording trips by northern record companies in the 1920s and 1930s. The companies would rent a room at a hotel in a southern city, then call for blues singers for auditions and on-the-spot recording sessions." In 1929, the likes of Furry Lewis and Big Joe Williams recorded live in guest rooms here.

Up on the roof, Sam Phillips and Marion Keisker—whom the world will greatly note and long remember as the first people to record Elvis Presley—once supervised musical broadcasts from the Peabody Skyway, where we've spent many a happy evening.

The Lobby Bar is a great place to get a cocktail: the Peabody Mint Julep is, as their cocktail menu boasts, a mid-South tradition, made with "Early Times Mint Bourbon, fresh mint and The Peabody's secret twist." Scott's favorite, the Peabody Punch, was mysteriously not on offer the last time we visited, perhaps due to COVID supply restrictions. At one time the Peabody's signature cocktail, it featured plenty of Jack Daniel's Tennessee Whiskey; hopefully, it will return.

Now then. When you hear the strains of John Philip Sousa's "King Cotton March," it can only mean one thing: the March of the Peabody Ducks is about to jump off! It all began in 1933, when manager Frank Shutt, after imbibing his fill of good ol' prohibition-era Jack Daniels on a winter hunting trip in Arkansas with a buddy (you've got to keep warm on those long cold nights), got back to the hotel late with live decoy ducks in tow. He decided he'd place them in the Peabody fountain for the night as a gag. In the clear light of morning he appeared in the lobby unsure of what he might find, only to see the ducks had stayed in the fountain, and the guests were loving them. The tradition caught on; it was formalized in 1940, when bellman Edward Pembroke (a former circus animal trainer, having run away to join the circus as a boy) taught the ducks the Peabody Duck March. The original Duckmaster, he held the position for 50 years(!). The current holder of that title, Brittany—you will know her by her red jacket—is the first female Duckmaster. (As she quipped to us, it only took 88 years and a global pandemic for that to happen.) Every now and then, the Duckmaster will ceremoniously hand over duties for the evening's march to one of the kids in attendance. The Peabody ducks march every day at 11:00 a.m. and 5:00 p.m., now and forever.

Don't miss the little one-room museum on the mezzanine level. You'll see fascinating memorabilia from the hotel's storied past, including Elvis' 1955 RCA contract and photos from the signing, and an exhibit for Frank Shutt.

KAROLYN'S TIP JAR

- Karolyn sez: At **Rendezvous**, consider holding the sauce. The ribs don't need 'em. I always get the charcoal-broiled half chicken, but for a good-value feast, get the combo platter with ribs and brisket. Scott always has to order the cheese 'n' sausage plate with peppers.

- At the **Arcade**, get the biscuits. They come hot 'n' fresh out of the biscuit drawer.

- Film scholar Scott pipes in: the **Arcade** was a part of the milieu of dark, crumbling romantic beauty explored in Jim Jarmusch's great movie *Mystery Train*. Watch for the scene where the man (Tom Noonan) tries to con Luisa (Nicoletta Braschi) with a story about a hitchhiker and Graceland.

- Ahem. Back to Karolyn: to see the Peabody Ducks, be sure to get there early. You might even be able to grab a seat at the bar. If you're staying at the hotel, don't miss a splash in the pool. If you're offered an upgrade, it's often a good idea to take them up on it. An upgrade can be about $40 per night, but it may include parking (a $20 value), so it works out to only about $20 more a night. An upgrade can also include turndown service; cookies and milk; tea and coffee; and even a complimentary cocktail.

- There's a security check to get into Beale Street, so bring your ID.

- Bring cash for Wild Bill's, as cards are not accepted.

The yellow star locates Clarksdale within Mississippi.

Map Source: mapofus.org

CHAPTER IV

Clarksdale

Clarksdale is our traditional Delta homebase, and it's really something special. Essentially, a handful of resident blues lovers have turned the entire town—a legend in blues mythology—into an open-air, living museum to its own blues heritage and culture.

Why is Clarksdale a legend? As former Mississippi representative Malcolm Mabry told author Roger Stolle, this town was once the "golden buckle on the Cotton Belt." As Stolle writes, "Blues—the art form that led to rock 'n' roll and so many other modern genres—most likely came together in the steamy fields of Mississippi's cotton plantations at the end of the nineteenth century and beginning of the twentieth. Most of Mississippi's earliest blues performers spent much of their time living on the region's cotton plantations, either performing fieldwork or trying to avoid it by entertaining the other laborers."

This is the town where Honeyboy Edwards used to spot Robert Johnson playing for tips on the streets, and where Wade Walton, the "blues-singing barber," cut Allen Ginsberg's hair while Harry Smith, editor of the classic *Anthology of American Folk Music,* looked on. Bessie Smith passed away here, at the Riverside Hotel, from wounds sustained in a wreck on the highway. When Muddy Waters journeyed to Chicago—where he plugged in the blues and changed the face of American music—he left from the train depot in Clarksdale, his hometown. W.C. Handy was living here when he "discovered" the blues in nearby Tutwiler in 1903—more on that below. (There's an empty lot and a historical marker where Handy's home once stood.) Ike Turner was born here; he may have been a monstrous man, but his band the Kings of Rhythm (who recorded as Jackie Brenston and His Delta Cats) made "Rocket 88" in Memphis, a contender for the first rock 'n' roll record.

There's more to the Clarksdale legend. As you roll down Highway 61 into town, you'll come to a "crossroads" that's really more of a T-junction between 61 and 49. In blues lore, Robert Johnson famously met the devil late one night and sold his soul in exchange for being able to play that otherworldly guitar. (Johnson's gift was actually more attributable to a lot of practicing than to Beelzebub. Still, the Delta is the land where legends, myths and history collide. If you're not at least a bit receptive to the former two, you're not really opening yourself to the experience.)

There's more than one crossroads that claims to be the "real" one—more on that later. In any event, this one is marked by a fun crossing-guitars sign, and Abe's Bar-B-Que is right across the street.

In Clarksdale you can still venture "across the tracks," literally, to The New World side of town. Historically, this was the Black neighborhood and the red-light district. This was where "the money flowed," according to W.C. Handy. "This led us to arrange and play tunes that had never been written down and seldom sung outside the environment of the oldest profession," he reminisced. "Boogie-house music, it was called."

Over at 133 Martin Luther King Drive, study the Mississippi Blues Trail marker, which describes the New World as a "breeding ground for ragtime, blues, and jazz music in Clarksdale's early days as a prosperous and adventurous new cotton town, when brothels here attracted both white and black clientele."

The now-defunct Red Top was the main juke joint in the neighborhood: historically, 4th Street (now MLK Drive) was the legendary street for jukes. On the Mississippi Blues Trail marker, find the photo of the afore-mentioned Wade Walton, the "blues-singing barber," playing harp in front of the Red Top, alongside guitarist/owner James "Smitty" Smith. Read about how, in the New World, "Jews, Italians, Chinese, Syrians, and Greeks owned various local businesses, as did some African Americans who lived here, including the Messenger family, which opened its first business on this block in the early 1900s." There's a lot of interest in that sentence—take the fact that there was once a large community of Syrian immigrants in Clarksdale and the Delta, for instance. Also, the Messenger family business to which it refers is Messenger's Pool Hall, opened in 1910 and Clarksdale's oldest continually operating business, and still hanging in there: once a place for sharecroppers to enjoy themselves after getting their pay, it still hosts the blues during Juke Joint Festival.

Also pictured is Dr. Aaron Henry's 4th Street Drugs. A little further down MLK Drive, at the site of his old drugstore, look for the Mississippi Freedom Trail marker for Dr. Henry, a noted local pharmacist who was also a "major early grassroots activist in the civil rights movement." The president of the local NAACP, he headed the Mississippi Freedom Democratic Party delegation to the '64 convention and led the Clarksdale store boycott campaign "during which he was arrested and his home and pharmacy firebombed."

To gaze upon a list of the musicians who were born in or around Clarksdale, or who regularly played its jukes and plantations, is to read a rollcall that echoes down the halls of blues and rock fame. Along with the above-mentioned Muddy Waters, Robert Johnson, Honeyboy Edwards, W.C. Handy, and Ike Turner, they include Sonny Boy Williamson II, Son House (a key inspiration for Johnson and Waters), Willie Brown (who played with Johnson), John Lee Hooker, Junior Parker, Sam Cooke, and Robert Nighthawk.

B.B. King, for his part, knew Clarksdale well. He'd often go live on the air with Early "Soul Man" Wright, one of America's first Black deejays, on Wright's pioneering blues programs on WROX radio.

This only scratches the surface of a town whose musical landscape also included Big Jack Johnson and his great juke-joint band the Jelly Roll Kings (with Frank Frost on keys and Sam Carr on drums), as well as Pinetop Perkins, the master boogie-woogie pianist. Today, bluesmen like Bill "Howl-N-Madd" Perry, Super Chikan, and Watermelon Slim carry on the Clarksdale tradition.

Clarksdale itself, as a town, often feels like a labor of love. It's dotted with people who chucked in what they were doing before—sometimes good white-collar jobs—to set up shop here and live in a way that expresses their love for this music. They are our kind of people. Walking the lanes of

Clarksdale, you'll feel an easy groove in the sleepy, warm air wafting off the Sunflower River. We think this town's gonna move ya.

PLANNING YOUR TIME: ITINERARIES

First-timers' Weekend Jaunt

Day One:
Morning/Afternoon

Head directly to the crossroads where Highway 61 meets 49, and have lunch at Abe's.

Tour the Delta Blues Museum.

Evening

Have dinner at Ground Zero Blues Club, and stay for live blues.

Day Two:
Morning

Have breakfast at Bluesberry Cafe, or Our Grandma's House of Pancakes.

Browse at Cat Head Delta Blues and Folk Art.

Afternoon

Have lunch at Hick's Famous Hot Tamales.

Browse at Hambone Art Gallery.

Head to the New Roxy for a drink.

Evening

Have dinner and a beer at Rust Restaurant in the Shack Up Inn, and stay for some live blues at the Juke Joint Chapel.

Head to Red's for a true juke joint experience.

SITES AND MUSEUMS

Rock & Blues Museum [CLOSED]
113 E 2nd St.
Clarksdale, Mississippi 38614

Sadly, this excellent museum officially closed on March 31, 2019. Watch this space to see whether it will reopen one day. The personal collection of Theo "Boogieman" Dasbach, a music-loving Dutchman, the museum memorably took visitors on a journey through "the evolution of America's music from blues, R&B, and rockabilly to rock 'n roll and soul," with a special emphasis on showing how our music "influenced people all over the globe." Dasbach put the collection together in his native Amsterdam and later brought it with him when he moved to Clarksdale. The man himself gave us a quick overview on the day we visited, before allowing us to look around for ourselves. Dasbach has been trying to sell the collection—which even includes Wade Walton's barber chair—as well as the building that houses the museum. With luck, an investor will take him up on it and the museum will open again.

Delta Blues Museum
1 Blues Alley
Clarksdale, MS 38614

The Delta Blues Museum's collection is beautifully *in situ*. The brick building housing the collection is the old passenger railroad depot, where Muddy Waters caught the train that whisked him to Chicago in 1943, where he'd electrify the blues. You'll see the instruments on which the greats created the music you love: guitars owned by Waters, John Lee Hooker, B.B. King, Big Joe Williams, Jimmy Burns, and Son Thomas. You'll see Super Chikan's homemade podium and a guitar crafted in his local workshop. Also on display are the original Three Forks sign (the grocery/juke where it's said Robert Johnson was fatally poisoned) and Clack Grocery sign (where Alan Lomax famously recorded Son House and his band).

The centerpiece and pride of the museum, though, is Muddy Waters' house. As the museum's website puts it, "The remains of the cabin from Stovall Farms where Muddy Waters lived during his days as a sharecropper and tractor driver are displayed in the gallery. Musicologist Alan Lomax recorded Muddy on the front porch of this shack for the Library of Congress in 1941." Also look for the life-size wax statue of Muddy, along with ZZ Top's 'Muddywood' guitar, which was crafted out of one of the cabin's timbers. Photos are not allowed.

Cost and hours: (M-Sa: 10a-5p, Closed Su; General admissions: $12, seniors 65+ or military: $10, children ages 6-12: $8, children under 6: free, students 17+: $8, Blues Society Members: $8);

Tel. (662) 627-6820;

https://www.deltabluesmuseum.org

Cat Head Delta Blues & Folk Art
252 Delta Ave.
Clarksdale, MS 38614

As the website proclaims, Cat Head is "your one-stop shop for everything Mississippi blues!" Grab an armful of the records you've long been hunting and enjoy the folk art at this combination music shop/gallery. Confirm your blues-traveling plans with Roger Stolle, the proprietor, if he's in the house. (You shall know him by his horn-rimmed glasses.) Roger is a one-man tourist information center and a tireless ambassador for Clarksdale and the blues. He's always got a tip or two. In fact, many of the signature Clarksdale festivals that bring visitors from all over the world are Roger's vision, and in many senses he's resurrected Clarksdale since moving here in 2002. During Juke Joint Festival, a canopied makeshift "stage" spills out of the Cat Head storefront as people prop chairs in the street, grooving to musicians jamming right on the doorstep. Roger has also written books (*Hidden History of Mississippi Blues*, with Lou Bopp) and produced films and records under the "Cat Head Presents" label. Their website features a handy music calendar.

Hours: (M-F 11a-4p; Sa 11a-5p; closed Su);

Tel. (662) 624-5992;

https://www.cathead.biz

Old Greyhound Bus Terminal
1604 N State St.
Clarksdale, MS 38614

As a symbol of the Great Migration, the Greyhound Bus Terminal makes for an evocative stop. From 1936, the bus station's streamlined Art Moderne (that is, late Deco) design, with its rounded corners, is meant to evoke movement and the "sleek aerodynamics of the buses that served its transportation system," in the words of the National Register of Historic Places. The Clarksdale station's architect is unlisted, but William Strudwick Arrasmith designed some 50 of these, including the one in Jackson.

Hours: (M-F 7a-5:30p, 7:45p-8:30p; Sa 11a-5p, 4:30p-5:30p; Su 4:30p-5:30p, 7:45p-8:30p);
Tel. (662) 627-7893

Deak's Mississippi Saxophone & Blues Emporium
13 3rd St.
Clarksdale, MS 38614

The proprietor at the Saxophone & Blues Emporium is our friend Deak Harp, a local musician who plays a fiery gumbo of North Mississippi Hill Country/Chicago blues. Don't miss a chance to see him live: he leaves everything on the floor. Deak comes by his mastery of blues harp (harmonica) honestly: he paid his dues playing with Chicago's James Cotton, one of the greats. He also plays the diddley bow (homemade one-string guitar) and electric guitar. Deak's harmonica shop is just down the street from Ground Zero, where he can make you a custom harmonica, repair your harp or offer lessons. He's got CDs and t-shirts, as well.

Hours: (M-F 11a-5p, Closed Sa-Su);
Tel. (217) 218-2194;
http://deakharp.com

RESTAURANTS

Abe's Bar-B-Que
616 North State St.
Clarksdale, MS 38614

We always know we're really back in the Delta when we step into Abe's. You'll find it across the way from the crossroads, where Highway 61 meets 49. (Go ahead and imagine it's the Robert Johnson one—it's fun). Lebanese immigrant Abraham Davis started the place in 1924—in fact, there are still grape leaves, a Lebanese tradition, on the menu. Today his son, Pat Davis Jr., carries on the tradition. Tuck into some hot tamales to get started—Scott likes 'em smothered in chili 'n' cheese. Scott's advice: at least one person in your party must order the towering, mighty "Big Abe" sandwich.

Karolyn's tip: don't leave without taking a bottle of sauce with you.

Hours: (M-Sa 10a-8:30p; Sa 11a-5p; Su 11a-2p);
Tel. 662-624-9947;
http://www.abesbbq.com/index.html

Hicks' Famous Hot Tamales & Banquet Hall
305 South State St./HWY 61
Clarksdale, MS 38614

On the occasion we visited Hicks Famous Hot Tamales, we roused founder and proprietor Mr. Eugene Hicks himself, who greeted us warmly. "Eugene and Betty Hicks have been rolling bundles of meat and masa for more than 40 years," wrote blues journalist Scott Barretta a few years ago; as of this writing, they've been doing it for closer to 50 years, and Mr. Hicks is close to 78.

It's worth reading the oral history taken by the Southern Foodways Alliance in 2005: "Eugene Hicks, born in 1944, has been making hot tamales since 1960. Acy Ware, who peddled tamales on the streets of Clarksdale, gave Hicks his recipe. In 1970, Hicks opened his first restaurant. The recipe has changed a bit over the years as he has experimented with different meats and spices. Hicks has never committed a recipe to writing, though. He works alone to cook and spice the meat, keeping the secrets to himself. What is no secret, though, are the custom devices and ingenious methods of production he has created. As a result, Hicks can produce ten times the amount of hot tamales that could be made by hand."

(Speaking of the Southern Foodways Alliance, we should take a moment for a round of applause for this project and its co-founder and director, John T. Edge. They do important work to document, study, and preserve Southern food.)

Along with the incendiary hot tamales, which cry out to be washed down with a cold Bud Light, the rib tips combo comes slathered in a BBQ sauce so zingy and good that we bought a styrofoam cup full of the stuff for the road.

Hours: (M-Th 11a-6p; F-Sa 11a-9p; closed Su);
Tel. (662) 624-9887;
http://www.hickstamales.com/

Our Grandma's House Of Pancakes
115/117 3rd St.
Clarksdale, MS 38614

At this family-run diner, expect tasty breakfast/brunch fare, such as homemade pancakes, hashbrowns, and omelets, served at an unhurried pace. Karolyn enjoyed her pancakes with honey and fresh berries.

Hours: (M, W-Su 7a-2p; Tu 7a-1p);
Tel. (662) 592-5290

Bluesberry Cafe, Bakery & Deli
235 Yazoo Ave.
Clarksdale, MS 38614

The Bluesberry Cafe offers "breakfast, lunch, soups, sandwiches, and the blues." The time we dropped by for breakfast, Scott enjoyed his pork chop with grits and Karolyn enjoyed her eggs. What's more, we dug digesting our grub to the strains of live blues, as is one of the Bluesberry's attractions on Saturday and Sunday mornings. Be prepared to linger, as service is at Delta speed. (That's not a putdown: it is what it is). For more about the Bluesberry Cafe, see our entry under "Music."

Hours: (M 6p-11:30p; Sa-Su 8a-1:45p);
Tel. (662) 627-7008

Delta Amusement Blues Cafe
348 Delta Ave.
Clarksdale, MS 38614

We're never quite sure if this place is truly open. If they are when you're in town next, we've heard good things about the hamburger steak.

Hours: (maybe M-Sa 8a-2p; closed Su);
Tel. (662) 627-1467

The Stone Pony
226 Delta Ave.
Clarksdale, MS 38614

No, this Stone Pony is not the Asbury Park club where Bruce Springsteen got his start. (*That's what Scott thought at first, too!*) Rather, it's our go-to pizza joint when in Clarksdale. We usually eat here at least once a visit.

Hours: (Everyday 5a-9p);
Tel. (662) 624-7669

Ground Zero Blues Club
387 Delta Ave.
Clarksdale, MS 38614

Ground Zero is a tremendously fun music venue which also slings reliably tasty Delta cooking, such as hot tamales and fried green tomatoes. In case you feel "fried" becoming a bit of a motif here, Karolyn likes the grilled catfish salad. There's also sandwiches, burgers, tacos, and (yes) fried chicken. Ground Zero is a great way to start an evening, taking in dinner and staying for live blues. After a few hours here, you can also stroll across the way to Red's to top off the night. If you're lucky you'll get to exchange banter with the sassy bespectacled Tameal, who goes by the nickname "T", who used to be a waitress and is now the club's booking manager. Karolyn loved her when she was our server! Engage her: she's got stories to tell. Also see our entry for Ground Zero under the "Music" and "Hotel" sections below. (Yes, this joint's got the trifecta.)

Hours: (M 11a-2p; otherwise closed due to COVID-19; typical hours: M-T 11a–2p; W–Th 11a–11p; Fri-Sat 11a–2a; closed Su);
Tel. (662) 621-9009;
https://www.groundzerobluesclub.com

Ramon's
535 Oakhurst Ave.
Clarksdale, MS 38614

The Clarksdale town website describes Ramon's as "Italian food with a southern tradition (the fried shrimp is a must)." We're intrigued.

Hours: (Tu-Sa 5p-9:30p; closed Su-M);
Tel. (662) 624-9230;
https://www.facebook.com/EatRamons/

Yazoo Pass Expresso Bistro Bakery
207 Yazoo Ave.
Clarksdale, MS 38614

The Yazoo Pass offers "downtown coffee, pastry, breakfast and bistro fare," says the Clarksdale town website. The lunch menu features scrumptious-looking sandwiches and burgers.

Hours: (M-Sa 7a-9p; closed Su);
Tel. (662) 627-8686;
https://www.yazoopass.com

The Ranchero (BBQ, Steaks, Seafood)
1907 N. State St.
Clarksdale, MS 38614

This "Clarksdale tradition for decades," according to the Clarksdale town website, keeps rather eccentric hours—see below. It appears that about half the time they're open for dine-in, half the time for carry-out. The town site describes the Ranchero as offering a "Southern menu with Italian choices. Good raw oysters, salad bar, lunch specials and more"—and "BBQ, steaks and seafood" are right there in the name. Sounds good to us. When we followed up with the Visit Clarksdale folks—very helpful (https://www.facebook.com/VisitClarksdale)—we were advised to call beforehand, just to confirm they're open.

Hours: M-F: 11a-2:30p (Dine-In), 2:30-6:30p (Carry-Out); W: 11a-2:30p (Dine-In) 2:30-5:30p (Carry-Out), Sa: 11a-2:30p (Dine-In), 2:30-5p (Carry-Out), closed Su;

Tel. (662) 624-9768;

http://www.theranchero.com

Levon's Restaurant & Bar
232 Sunflower Ave.
Clarksdale, MS 38614

Levon's is "a New Orleans style dining experience," quoth the Clarksdale town website, while on their own site, Levon's describes themselves as offering a "creative and innovative Southern cooking style" with "a constantly evolving seasonal menu, a full bar and original cocktails." Along with changing specials, menu fixtures include gumbo, buffalo shrimp, penne filet pasta and a "succulent" Angus filet. Patrons may dine inside/outside or get takeaway/curbside pickup.

Hours: (W-Sa 4p-"late"; closed Su-T);

Tel. (662) 302-6474;

https://www.levons.net

Domino's Pizza
640 Desoto Ave.
Clarksdale, MS 38614

What's this doing here? Isn't the whole point to support local, independent places, not national ones? Yes—but hey, Domino's is a useful fallback. Many is the time we've stopped for takeout here on the way back to the Shack Up Inn from downtown. We rate the Clarksdale Domino's an extra tasty and convenient outpost of this franchise. Maybe it's something local in the sauce, or it could just be the ambience (of the town, not the franchise itself, which is, of course, just like every other).

Hours: (M-Th, Su 10:30a-12a; F-Sa 10:30a-1am);

Tel. (662) 624-7669

Shady Nook
16774 Highway 61 N.
Clarksdale, MS 38614

This is a truck stop on the north side of town, which is reputed to serve up some pretty dang good soul food. We're always up for convenience store fried chicken!

Hours: (Everyday 5a-9p);
Tel. (662) 621-1525

MUSIC, BARS AND THE REST

Red's
398 Sunflower Ave.
Clarksdale, MS 38614

Red's is one of America's few remaining authentic juke joints, literally located "across the tracks." Passing the grill on which every so often something's cooking, step inside and immerse yourself in a womb of red neon and Christmas lights. Explore a decor that could be described as "funky ramshackle." We like to amuse ourselves by counting all the neon "notes" on the walls. How many can you find? Or, look for the moving poem for Big Jack Johnson by Dick Lourie, framed on the wall. Belly up to the bar and grab a jumbo Bud Light. There's a convivial vibe, a mix of locals and travelers who've come to hear the blues and have fun. A cool side note: Red's used to be "Levine's Music Center" once upon a time, and it's where Ike Turner and his Kings of Rhythm bought the instruments on which they played "Rocket 88," the tune we keep mentioning as the first rock 'n roll song.

Presiding over it all is cantankerous old Red. The gruff exterior conceals a heart of gold: get him talking, as Scott did one night when he found himself sitting next to the great man during a break between sets, and he might regale you with tales of all the great jukes and bluesmen you've already missed—as well as some little-known joints you might still visit before they disappear. Once, we saw him curl up on a recliner in front of a TV in the corner and nod off while watching "Baywatch," even as a bluesman a few feet away filled the club with loud electric blues. (Presumably, he was dreaming sweet blues dreams).

We've had so many great nights here. We were lucky enough to see the late, great Delta bluesman Leo "Bud" Welch, a man of tremendous dignity who appeared dressed in a natty suit. It was January 29, 2016. (Scott: I know because he autographed and dated my CD in gold sharpie, in a careful, shaky hand.) It's always a good night when Mark "Muleman" Massey is playing. (His anthem "She's Hongry" is a personal favorite of Karolyn's.) Pork Chop Willie is a great North Mississippi Hill Country band we discovered at Red's—except they're from Manhattan! Led by singer-guitarist Bill Hammer and violinist Melissa Tong, often backed up by members of the Kimbrough family, they certainly play with your preconceptions about what a blues band can be. Take it from us, though—they're a joy. Anthony "Big A" Sherrod always tears the place up. He's especially fun on nights when "Ms. Judy," one of his biggest fans and thorns in his side, is in the house. She's known for backing her thang up to his fiery blues and giving him plenty of sass in equal measure.

Anybody who's ever spent an evening at Red's knows the blues is most assuredly a *living* music. Bring cash: this juke don't take credit cards.

Hours: (12p-2a everyday);

Tel. (662) 627-3166;

https://www.facebook.com/pages/Reds-Blues-Club/163702543685722)

Ground Zero Blues Club
387 Delta Ave.
Clarksdale, MS 38614

Co-owned by Morgan Freeman (who hardly needs an introduction) and Clarksdale mayor Bill Luckett, this club was clearly set-designed with adjectives like "funky" and "gritty" in mind, but over the years the mise-en-scène became the reality. To put it another way, if any of the graffiti was ever the work of a set designer, it's long since been covered by the etchings of real blues lovers. Look for local heroes like Bill "Howl-N-Madd" Perry and James "Super Chikan" Johnson. We once heard a 17-year-old Christone "Kingfish" Ingram, a prodigy if ever there was one and now a Grammy winner, blow the roof off the place with a finale of "Purple Rain." A few day later, we heard the news of Prince's death. When we did, the first thing we thought of was how Kingfish had used that song to bring us home. Bottom line: have a great time at Ground Zero, but then do head across the tracks to Red's for a dose of the original inspiration. (Also see entries under the "restaurants" and "hotels" sections.)

Hours: (W-Th 11a-11p; F-Sa 11a-12a;Su 11a-3p; closed M-T)
Tel. (662) 621-9009;
https://www.groundzerobluesclub.com

Juke Joint Chapel at Shack Up Inn
001 Commissary Cir Rd.
Clarksdale, MS 38614

The densely decorated Juke Joint Chapel is the live-music hall of the Shack Up Inn. At this Chapel, you can sip a Southern Magnolia IPA and order grub from the adjacent Rust restaurant kitchen, all while listening to impassioned performers like Deak Harp, who stokes the spirit of the blues with his electric diddley bow. Take a spin: you'll see a panorama where a semiology of the blues meets pure eccentricities. Gazing toward the rafters, you'll see a dangling, upside-down model of an airplane looking about 100 years old, while nearby is the famous picture of Johnny Cash flipping the camera the bird. See if you can find both the big boll weevil (bane of Southern life for its propensity to eat cotton) and Santa, somehow making an appearance from the North pole. (Hint: the former is hanging out over the quilt.) Notice the poster-sized photo of Bob Dylan from the *Street Legal/ Live at Budokan* era. Speaking of the great man, look closely behind the bar and you'll see a bumper sticker on which one "B. Springsteen" expresses the kind of patriotism we can get behind. His quote reads: "bob dylan is the father of my country."

Hours: Live music every F and Sa night from 8-10p, with occasional live music at other times; call or check the website.
Tel. (662) 624-8329;
https://www.shackupinn.com

New Roxy
363 Issaquena Ave.
Clarksdale, MS 38614

The New Roxy is an old movie theater repurposed into a nightclub, live music venue, art gallery, and theater in the New World District (historically

Clarksdale's Black neighborhood). It's a convivial, multi-level place, fun to explore. We fondly recall seeing local keepers-of-the-flame like the late Robert "Bilbo" Walker and Terry "Harmonica" Bean here. Out front, don't miss the Mississippi Blues Trail marker honoring Clarksdale native Sam Cooke. In fact, sitting in the New Roxy, you can't help musing once again on all the great musical artists who were natives of Clarksdale or who lived and performed in the area. As you sit at the bar nursing a beer, let those names rattle around in your mind: Son House. Ike Turner. Junior Parker. John Lee Hooker. Muddy Waters. Pinetop Perkins. Sam Cooke. Bukka White. Robert Nighthawk, and his son Sam Carr (drummer for the Jelly Roll Kings).

Hours vary;
Tel. (662) 313-6220;
http://www.newroxy.com/

Bad Apple's Blues Club
349 Issaquenna Ave.
Clarksdale, MS 38614

This hole-in-the-wall juke used to be Club 2000—during Juke Joint Festival, we once caught the great Bentonia bluesman Jimmy "Duck" Holmes here—and we're so happy to see Sean "Bad" Apple has turned into his own place. If you haven't heard him sing Junior Kimbrough so sweetly, you'll want to soon.

Hours: (Everyday 3p-6:30p);
https://www.facebook.com/badapplebluesclub/

Bluesberry Cafe
235 Yazoo Ave.
Clarksdale, MS 38614

Festooned with local and international flags, the Bluesberry Cafe is another of Clarksdale's labors of love. One memorable stormy night we ducked into the Bluesberry, taking shelter with a roomful of other blues fans. As we all sat dripping and warming up, we were treated to the sounds of Ron Parks and Gypsy Blue, an all-star band comprised of ace local sidemen like Billy Earheart of the Amazing Rhythm Aces on keys and Heather Crosse—best known for fronting her own band, Heavy Suga' & The SweeTones—on bass. Come for breakfast and blues on Saturday or Sunday mornings, or drop by on Monday evenings, which often feature Italian food. Be sure to have a look around the place, which displays the owner's personal collection of posters and memorabilia. Check out the framed copy of "Mersey Beat" newspaper from January 1962, where the headline announces, "Beatles Top Poll!" Again, don't be in a hurry—oft times, the proprietor himself is doing the cooking.

(As a side-note, did you wonder about that flag which advertises New Orleans' version of the running of the bulls—"San Fermin"? That's a NOLA tradition where, instead of bulls, runners are chased down the streets by the Big Easy Rollergirls, who hit them with foam-filled plastic bats and attempt to run them through with the plastic horns attached to their helmets.)

Hours: (M 6p-11:30p; Sa-Su 8a-1:45p);
Tel. (662) 627-7008

Hambone Art & Music
111 E 2nd St.
Clarksdale, Mississippi 38614

This art gallery is a showcase for owner and blues-singer-turned-painter Stan Street's paintings of blues icons and New Orleans scenes, and it doubles as a music venue and pub, as well. We've seen Terry "Harmonica" Bean here, and Scott found himself bellied up next to Watermelon Slim at the bar here one memorable evening. (He's quite a guy.) Since 2007, Street has thrown the Hambone Festival on the premises over Halloween weekend.

Hours: (Tu-Sa 11a-5p; closed Su-M);
Tel. (662) 403-8810;
http://stanstreet.com/gallery/

Messenger's
133 Martin Luther King Blvd.
Clarksdale, MS 38614

Messenger's Pool Hall opened in 1910, making it Clarksdale's oldest continually operating business, and has been family-owned ever since. A sign posted outside runs down the menu: "Bar-B-Q Sandwiches, Rip Tips, Burgers, Hog Maws, Polish Sausage." We've always been intrigued by that "hog maws" bit.

Hours: (Tu-Sa 3p-12a; closed Su-M);

Tel. (662) 483-1674;

https://www.facebook.com/pages/Messengers-Pool-Hall/389813951050381

Wade Walton's Barbershop
317 Issaquena Ave.
Clarksdale, MS 38614

Wade Walton (1923-2000) was the "blues-singing barber" who cut the heads of Ike Turner, Sonny Boy Williamson II, and Honeyboy Edwards. He'd do more than cut your hair, though—he entertained you, as well, playing an acoustic guitar behind his back or blowing his harp. If you'd like to see something fun, look up footage on YouTube of him playing the blues with his razor and strop (https://youtu.be/r8uu26uGGbU or https://youtu.be/_dnih8yQh50). Walton's barbershop is now more a landmark than it is a functioning building, though during Juke Joint Fest there's music out in front.

Historically, Walton's barbershop was a cultural hub (the original shop was over on 4th Street). For decades, and especially during the blues revival of the '60s, young (often collegiate and white) blues pilgrims would call on him at his barbershop for information and introductions to the Clarksdale blues scene, of which he was something of a documenter, recording local musicians for record companies. There's an anecdote we like about two such young student-seekers who once called on Walton, as chronicled on the Mississippi Blues Trail signpost in Walton's honor: "On a return trip [to Clarksdale] in 1961, the students were jailed, but after concluding that they were indeed in town to record blues, not to agitate for civil rights, a State Sovereignty Commission investigator dismissed them as 'crackpots'."

Hopson Commissary
1 Commissary Rd.
Clarksdale, MS 38614

Like the Shack Up Inn, which is next door, the Commissary was a building on the old Hopson Plantation, now converted into this fun, atmospheric music venue/bar, densely and flamboyantly appointed with memorabilia and flags. Walk through this world of Christmas lights and cotton plants, and you'll pass, more or less randomly, old drums, a vintage coin-operated horse "kiddie ride," a duck decoy. We had some Happy Hour vegetable soup at the Commissary once, and even that had ham hocks in it: hey, it's the South! Slight caveat: the live music isn't always blues. One night when we were there it was a rock cover band featuring local teenagers/frat boys—and there was a cover charge for that!

The Hopson Plantation is an important historical site for being the first Southern farm to cease manual sharecropping by replacing farmers with mechanized cotton planting, picking and baling during the '30s and '40s—thus kicking off a process that accelerated a Great Migration already in progress, as former farmers moved to big cities to find work. (As Trevor Smith notes in the online Mississippi Encyclopedia, by the '20s many Black ex-sharecroppers had already moved to northern cities like Chicago in the Great Migration, causing plantations increasingly to rely on "day laborers and seasonal migrant labor.") Hopson is also where bluesmen like Pinetop Perkins worked and lived; he was a tractor driver here in the 40s. (See more on all this below.) Often on weekends, the place is booked for wedding receptions.

Hours: (M-Tu: 5p-7:30p, W: 5p-12a, Th-F: 5p-7:30p, Sa: 5p-1a, closed Su);

Tel. (662) 624-5756;

http://hopsonplantation.com

TOURS AND FESTIVALS

Movie History Bus Tour Trolley

Offered as part of the Clarksdale Film Festival, your guide on this fun and informative movie history bus tour is Robert Birdsong. Exploring movie history in Clarksdale means exploring the grand part of town where Tennessee Williams grew up, which we'd never seen (and frankly, which we didn't even know existed). Rolling past Tennessee Williams Park, our trolley arrived in this mansion district. Birdsong told us that during the annual Tennessee Williams Festival, plays are performed on these grand porches and one can wander the neighborhood from play to play.

As we rolled through the historic neighborhood, Birdsong pointed out where the real-life characters who inspired Williams' plays and movies lived. We saw the **Cutrer Mansion** (109 Clark Street), which Birdsong told us was the real-life "Belle Reve," the lost ancestral manse for which Blanche and Stella pine in *A Streetcar Named Desire*. Jack Cutrer was a bit of a rascal from the sounds of it; according to Birdsong, he knew "everybody in movies," all the B-western actors like Kit Carson and Lash LaRue. His wife was Blanche Clark Cutrer, the daughter of Clarksdale's founder John Clark.

Birdsong pointed to the neighborhood spots where the models for Maggie the Cat and Baby Doll and *The Glass Menagerie's* Amanda Wingfield once played and walked. A bully who beat Williams up he would later cast as a homosexual in *Cat on a Hot Tin Roof*. If you squinted, you could almost see them.

Back in "The New World," historically the African-American side of town, Birdsong took a break from movie history to devote a good deal of time to talking about Aaron Henry, a local pharmacist who was also head of the Mississippi branch of the NAACP, and who rode with the Freedom Riders in '61. Henry was also a founder of the Mississippi Freedom Democrats, and as we lingered in front of the site where his pharmacy once stood, Birdsong told us the story of Henry's struggle to get the Freedom delegation seated at the '64 Democratic Convention, instead of the proffered all-white delegation. Henry went on to serve in the Mississippi House for 14 years (1982-96).

Back on the trolley, we passed an empty field; Birdsong evoked the days when this ground hosted "tent shows." He passed around a photograph of such a show, which boasted attractions such as Bessie Smith in person and the 1937 film *The Prisoner of Zenda*.

The tour took us past the town's historic movie theaters. As we passed the New Roxy, Birdsong talked about how they could show more risqué films there because it was on the Black side of the tracks. It was fun to get Birdsong's perspective, as someone who'd grown up in Clarksdale and who presumably could still recall segregation. You could just picture him sneaking across the tracks to see a film that might be a little too juicy for "prim" audiences.

(As an added point of interest, our trolley rolled past the ship-shaped building along the Sunflower River that once housed blues scholar Jim O'Neal's record company, Rooster Records. It's never clear to us what, if anything, that building is used for today).

Taking this tour provided a dramatic, see-it-with-your-own-eyes illustration of the historic hierarchy of Southern life. These grand mansions, churches, and schools for the "cotton-rich" were just a few minutes away from the crumbling, funky part of town where blues tourism happens today—and yet worlds away from where, historically, the broke, pushed-down, Black cotton-pickers lived and worked: the very people who made the whites' lavish lifestyle possible. Even today, the contrast between the two worlds is acute.

To enquire about Robert Birdsong's tours, send him an e-mail at Mississippimojo@yahoo.com.

Quapaw Canoe Company
291 Sunflower Ave.
Clarksdale, MS 38614

For over 40 years, John Ruskey, the owner of Quapaw Canoe Company, has been a river guide on the Lower Mississippi and its tributaries. Aside from his flagship location in Clarksdale, Ruskey has also opened Quapaw outposts in Vicksburg, MS and Helena, AK, any of which can help you set up your canoe or kayak adventure. We have yet to try this, because we have learned from bitter experience that we are congenitally unsuited to either of those modes of transportation! You may have seen Ruskey on Anthony Bourdain's *Parts Unknown*, which profiled him in connection with the admirable apprenticeship program for youth which Quapaw runs for underprivileged communities in Mississippi and Arkansas.

https://www.island63.com/clarksdale.cfm

The Clarksdale Film Festival

This fest bills itself as "great Southern films, music documentaries & more." To give you a sense of what it's like (and perhaps also give you some ideas for appropriately themed films to see in preparation for your own trip), we offer Scott's report from the January 28-30, 2016 Clarksdale Film Festival. It picks up with the intrepid couple rolling down Highway 61 towards Clarksdale, the "home of the blues," having just done Muddy Waters' journey in reverse—Chicago to Clarksdale, instead of the other way 'round.

We had three nights in town, and we meant to fill our days with film, music, and barbecue (three of our favorite things). Of course, the first thing we did upon hitting Clarksdale was make it over to Abe's to savor some good ol' barbecue.

The following journal is narrated from Scott's point of view:

The question on my mind was, would seeing films about Southern music and culture *in situ*—that is, in their original context, culturally and otherwise—alter both the experience of Southern traveling *and* how we might otherwise experience the films? Would the movies enhance what we were experiencing out in the streets of Clarksdale, and vice versa?

Thursday, January 28, 2016

Every evening there was a reception in the lobby of the Delta Cinema. Trays were piled high with meats and cheeses, peppers and garlic-stuffed olives. Free box-wine flowed, and while cheap wine may be a false economy, no one was complaining. In a corner near the popcorn counter, the Delta bluesman Terry "Harmonica" Bean regaled us with stories and songs. (In fact, Bean spends almost as much time telling stories as he does playing music. They're good stories, including reminiscences of his father, who'd been a sharecropper, and the influence he had on Bean's music.) He jammed on traditional down-home blues like "Got Love If You Want It," as well as Hill Country blues—the distinction of which from Delta Blues we would learn later, from one of the films on the bill at the festival. The Delta's lobby is appointed with real movie theatre seats, bolted in for just this sort of live performance/reception.

From the lobby, we repaired into the cavernous, shambolic old theater. Owner Bruce Elis needs $70,000 to "go digital" (as I gleaned another day when I overhead Roger Stolle, owner of Cat Head Delta Blues & Folk Art, discussing the matter. It sounds as though Stolle, a tireless booster of Clarksdale and the Delta blues, is considering helping spearhead a drive for these funds). For now, though, the theater is dank and smells of mothballs; its stillness is occasionally shattered by the roar of some kind of dehumidifier or air conditioner. The jerry-rigged digital projector is propped up on a theater seat. In short, it's a funky place.

Up on the screen, the first film of the festival (for us, at least) kicked in. It was **Crossfire Hurricane** (2012), a superb Rolling Stones documentary directed by Brett Morgen. We watched it up until the death of Brian Jones and the advent of Mick Taylor, before hunger pangs compelled us to hie over to Ground Zero, where we tucked into some catfish and fried pickles. The film features footage of the unbelievable violence that greeted the Stones wherever they played during their initial tours in the mid-60s. Riots broke out. They were part of the incendiary zeitgeist of the '60s, the general rejection of the older generation's values and their "petty morality."

The film's spine is audio-only interviews done with the Stones on the occasion of their 50th anniversary. Crucially, no cameras were allowed. Thus, we hear but do not see the Stones; the film finds a creative way around becoming just another "talking heads" music doc. The archival footage has the effect of illustrating their memories, and the montage accelerates with an almost centrifugal force, spinning around a nucleus of incredible live footage of the band at its peak. Keith's guitar roars like a Concorde, Charlie kicks hard and fast. As Keith says of the band's twin rhythm/lead-guitar attack, when you get two guys playing guitar together and they do it right, it can sound like an orchestra. Anyone who loves rock 'n' roll must respond to this film.

Theo "Boogieman" Dasbach, founder of the local Rock & Blues Museum (since closed—see our entry above) had been on hand to introduce the film. Dasbach's love for music is contagious. He'd brought along items from his own cherished Stones collection, and he spoke passionately about what this band had meant to him as a kid growing up in the Netherlands. He brandished an original edition of the single "It's All Over Now"—that title had felt pretty cataclysmic at the time, he told us. He held aloft a copy of the band's first album, wishing to emphasize for us that the Stones's early material—before they moved to originals—was *all* blues and R&B.

Later that evening at Ground Zero, we caught a blues-jam open mic with David Dunavent, during which Clarksdale elder-statesman Josh "Razorblade" Stewart, who has since passed away, sang a few numbers. A talented teenage band from Iowa was in town, thrilled to be in Clarksdale and playing at Ground Zero. They'd won some kind of regional blues-band challenge. Coincidentally and encouragingly, both bands that night had female drummers. In fact, a teenage guitarist commented from the stage that until that night, he'd never even seen a female drummer, except for the one in his band. We were served by our favorite server, Tameal, who treated us to a beer flight *gratis*. [2022 editor's note: today she is the venue's booking manager]. I found I liked the Lazy Magnolia Southern Pecan. It would become my quaff of the trip.

Friday, January 29, 2016

After a pleasant morning spent in our rocking chairs on the porch of the Cadillac Shack, we made our way back to the Delta Cinema, parking once again in our favorite spot along the Sunflower River.

Despite the heroic efforts of boosters like Stolle, Clarksdale remains an economically depressed area. We were reminded of that during a moment in our first film of the day, **Cheesehead Blues: The Adventures of a Dutchman in the Delta**. It's a documentary which happens to take as its subject our friend from the previous evening, Theo Dasbach, and the story of how he came to open his Rock & Blues Museum in Clarksdale. In the film, there's a moment when Dasbach is showing a visitor from abroad around Clarksdale, and they encounter a homeless, mentally ill woman while doing a bit of site-seeing out at the mythic crossroads of Highways 61 and 49. As Dasbach advises his nonplussed friend, in America "the first thing they cut is education." It doesn't take much to see that a lot of our economic and social problems are, in fact, down to lack of education. ("How many is in a half dozen?" we would later overhear a woman ask her lunch companion at Hicks' Tamales).

Cheesehead Blues was made by Dasbach's fellow Dutchman, Jan Doense. I mused on how Europeans often seem to appreciate our American musical heritage more than we do ourselves—but then, that's an old story. (Think of the Stones and their generation: as Bob Dylan has noted, it took the British to reawaken Americans to our own roots). It also occurred to me that, having come from the Low Countries, Dasbach would find the Delta country around Clarksdale comfortingly familiar. Indeed, I've been to the Netherlands; driving down Highway 61 through the marshy wetlands, it seemed easy to believe it might remind Theo of what I'd seen of his homeland.

Cheesehead is populated by colorful local characters like Super Chikan and Watermelon Slim; it was fun to see our Clarksdale "friends" up on the big screen, including Stolle, "Red" Paden (proprietor of Red's, of course) and even the gent who'd checked us in at the Shack Up Inn. The film walks you through Theo's museum, as well [ed. note: which gives it extra value, now that you can't visit it yourself]. It takes on an added layer of interest when it shifts to talking to blues women like Chicago's own Liz Mandeville.

After the film, we wandered down Sunflower Avenue alongside the river in search of legendary Hicks' Tamales. Passing the historic Riverside Hotel, we followed Sunflower Avenue until it hit highway-like State Street, whereupon we crossed a bridge over the river and found Hicks'. At first we found the door locked, but then Eugene Hicks himself, who's been at it since 1960, opened the door and and greeted us warmly. Shortly we were tucking into some of the hottest tamales we've ever had, as well as an order of rib tips slathered in sauce so zingy we could only lament they don't bottle the stuff. No matter, Mr. Hicks could improvise: we bought a styrofoam coffee-cup full of sauce for the road!

After lunch we wandered over to the New Roxy, in front of which stands the Sam Cooke Mississippi Blues Trail marker. It's across the tracks once traversed by the Yazoo and Mississippi Valley railroad, in the historically African-American side of town dubbed "the New World"—the one-time red light district. The current owners of the New Roxy have converted this old movie theater into a kind of loft, with a ground-floor bar and screening area under a mezzanine. It's still under construction, with multiple levels and rooms to explore. Peek out one door and you arrive in a partially open-air concrete lot running up to a stage, with all sorts of funky things strewn about—bicycles, pink flamingoes, old space heaters. It's a bit like a Southern amphitheater.

We enjoyed two films at the New Roxy that afternoon. **Very Extremely Dangerous** (2012) was already about a half-hour in when we arrived. I sidled up with another Lazy Magnolia Southern Pecan (thanks again for the tip, Tameal!) as the film (or DVD, in this case) rolled. America loves its outlaws, or at least its Wild West characters, and **Dangerous** features a lulu: Jerry McGill. (As if to illustrate the point, I needed only gaze up to see hanging from the loft a tapestry of the pistol-packin' mama herself, Annie Oakley, pointing her six-shooters at me). The film, an unflinching, unforgettable spectacle, is a portrait of '70s-era "cowboy" McGill, a sometime Memphis musician, one-time running buddy of Waylon Jennings, and full-time maniac. It's a disturbing portrait of a true wild man—drug-fueled, gun-waving, irredeemable. It incorporates footage of the young McGill, as charismatic as a Rolling Stone, shot by the great Memphis photographer William Eggleston, and culled from the raw footage he titled *Stranded in Canton*.

I won't forget the spectacle of the elderly, frail McGill cooking up his (prescription!) drugs, then shooting up in the backseat of the car on the way to this hospital, his head bobbing maniacally on his wrecked frame. Eggleston's unflinching aesthetic must have influenced the filmmakers, Paul Duane and Robert Gordon. But then there's that footage of a club gig towards the end of McGill's life, where he plays heartbreakingly, beautifully.

Next up was **You See Me Laughin': The Last of the Mississippi Hill Country Bluesmen** (2002), which profiles the distinctive drone of the artists who hail not from the Delta but from the hills in the northern part of the state. The film follow the young founders of Fat Possum records, blues lovers Matthew Johnson and Peter Redvers-Lee, through the North Mississippi hills, as they valiantly attempt to track down and record aging bluesmen. For some of these musicians, it was their first time making proper albums, even though they were at relatively advanced ages. These are relatively unsung figures like Asie Payton, Johnnie Farmer, and T. Model Ford, who tells the horrifying story of how he only has one nut—his daddy beat him between the legs—and also of the time he killed a man in a knife fight.

We meet CeDell Davis, who plays with a knife due to a childhood bout with polio which left his hands mangled, and whose startling music initially sounds out of tune until you get used to it. Davis was championed by the late blues critic Robert Palmer, who shepherded Davis's recordings for Fat Possum. In fact, Palmer was a bit of a compass for the Fat Possum guys; he also produced Junior Kimbrough's excellent album "All Night Long" for the label. Some of the most memorable sequences in the film take us to Kimbrough's storied juke joint, the late, lamented Junior's Place.

While Fat Possum always struggled, they had a hit with R.L. Burnside's album with the Jon Spencer Blues Explosion, "A Ass Pocket of Whiskey"; Burnside gained an even higher profile when a couple tracks from his album "Come On In" (a collection of remixes) was used in "The Sopranos." Iggy Pop is on hand to wax rhapsodic about Fat Possum artists like Kimbrough, although he confesses to still being a bit baffled by Cedell Davis's tunings. In fact, Iggy loved Kimbrough's music enough to invite the man to tour with him in the mid-90s. **You See Me Laughin'** celebrates a too-often unsung corner of the blues world. [2022 editor's note: As for Fat Possum, they're still out there, boasting a limited roster of terrific acts putting out terrific albums, including important new voices like Buffalo Nichols.]

From the New Roxy we strolled back over to the Delta Cinema for what was becoming a habit I didn't want to break: hors d'oeuvres-time in the lobby. This night, the cheese 'n' sausage was digested to the exciting Hill Country-influenced blues of Sean "Bad" Apple. Having just come off the documentary about hill music, it was eerie to hear Bad Apple cover Junior Kimbrough's "All Night Long," with its keening "Junior, I love you...." refrain. He played us a little R.L. Burnside, as well.

We then shuffled once again into the theater for a screening of Hank Bedford's 2015 narrative feature, **Dixieland**. A faded, wilted American flag is the signifier of the state of the American dream in this poetic, powerful drama, a portrait of how some marginalized Americans live today. Interweaving its fiction with interviews with real-life poor people, the film features Chris Zylka as an ex-con called Kermit, just sprung from jail for running his mom's sleazy boyfriend (Brad Carter) out of her hot tub with a shotgun. Riley Keough, Elvis' granddaughter, plays the young woman who lives next door. Her gaze is fascinating, with all that history haunting her cheekbones; she has no choice but to wear it. Faith Hill, the country star, is memorable as Kermit's young mother. Steve Earle is on hand as a crusty uncle who lives around the way, and who owes the local drug dealer money. In Pearl, Mississippi—where you grow up fast, where there's little employment—pole dancing constitutes work if you are a woman, and drug dealing is good business if you're a young man. Kermit should know that when your criminal peer proposes "one last job," it never ends well.

Over post-movie pizza at the Stone Pony, we were regaled by singer/songwriter Taylor Bailey. Next, we beat it over to Red's Blues Club, where we caught a treasure of a set by 83-year-old Leo "Bud" Welch. We happened to run into the writer/director of **Dixieland**, Hank Beford, at Red's, and we told him we thought he'd made a powerful piece.

Saturday, January 30, 2016

After a good Southern breakfast at the Bluesberry Cafe (I still recall that pork chop fondly), we wandered back to the Delta, where we saw a terrific film about the Rev. Gary Davis, **Harlem Street Singer** (2013). This revealing documentary is important for establishing Davis as a true original, as well as a beloved teacher to a generation of guitarists (Bob Weir, Jorma Kaukonen). An innovative picker who never played a song the same way twice, he played like no one else. Listeners couldn't pigeonhole him. Was his music blues or gospel or ragtime? His spectral songs were covered by the Dead ("Death Don't Have No Mercy" and "Samson and Delilah") and the Stones ("You Gotta Move," though they might have been doing Mississippi Fred McDowell's version.)

When Peter, Paul and Mary recorded Davis's "Samson & Delilah," they insisted that the Reverend get paid, even bringing him in to sign an affidavit attesting that he'd written the song. Amusingly, there was initially a hiccup when Davis insisted he had not written the song so much as it had been revealed to him by God. Thereafter, and for the rest of his life, he was set financially—Peter, Paul, and Mary's records made good money—making him one of the relatively few instances of a blues great being rewarded monetarily in his own lifetime.

The film's footage of Davis performing, including stretches of his appearance at Newport '65, are a spine-tingling delight, but the emotional climax is a warm recording session celebrating Davis's music, and organized specifically for the film. It features guitarist Woody Mann (a co-producer of the film) and the stirring voice of Bill Sims Jr. Actually, for me, Sims Jr. was the great discovery of the whole Fest. I made a note to purchase immediately any album made of this music (and I found this session had been released under the name of the "Empire Roots Band"). Sims Jr. sings Davis's music gorgeously, and the session scenes depict the joy of musicians discovering the music together, reminding me of *Once*. [2022 editor's note: Sadly, Mr. Sims passed away in 2019. Do look him and his music up].

After the film we repaired to the lobby once again for my by-now favorite ritual: hunkering down over that table groaning with trays of meats and cheese and free-flowing wine. Sean "Bad" Apple was once again laying down the reception's music, and both real and would-be musicians who happened to be passing through would ask him if they could sit in and wail. This night's supplicants included a whimsical gent wielding a melodica, which tickled Bad Apple to no end. It seemed to mark the first time either of us had ever seen that instrument used as a blues harp. (On Thursday night, we'd see this same man take the stage at Ground Zero as part of open mic-jam night, where his melodica stylings again delighted all in attendance. What's more, we met a young girl who'd drawn skillful copies on her shoes of John Tenniel's drawings from *Alice in Wonderland*, which I've always loved).

We clambered back into the theater to see **America's Blues** (2015), a new documentary by Patrick Branson and Aaron Pritchard which seeks to show the impact of the blues on nearly every facet of American life, with a particular focus on its influence on American literature, especially on the language of Langston Hughes and Ralph Ellison. It features some interesting commentators making provocative points: Lonnie Johnson's biographer Dean Alger theorizes that the birthplace of the blues might actually have been New Orleans, not the Delta; Jimbo Mathus from Squirrel Nut Zippers has some interesting things to say, and I always enjoy hearing from Terrence Blanchard. To their credit, Branson and Pritchard underline America's ugly history of vitriolic opposition to "race mixing" (we see protestors carrying placards calling it "communism"). Admirably, they devote attention to blues women like Samantha Fish and Chicago's own Sharon Lewis. Also admirably, they bring hip-hip into the mix, enlisting Drumma Boy, and country music as well—Jimmie Rodgers is shown singing "Blue Yodel."

That evening we stayed in at the Shack Up Inn, where we ate at the Inn's restaurant, **Rust** (good pulled pork sandwich and fish tacos), which shares an open area with the Juke Joint Chapel, the Inn's live music venue. We ate at the lip of the stage as we rocked to the sounds of that night's act, Frankie Boots, a gregarious and talented two-man band: a guitarist and a stand-up bassist, who also plays a nice trumpet. We got to chatting with them after the set and we told them we thought they'd go over big in New Orleans. We then wandered next door to the Hopson Commissary to hear more music, which turned out to be a fun rock cover band. Karolyn requested, and they played, a nice version of "She Talks to Angels" by the Black Crowes.

The Clarksdale Film Festival is a thoughtfully organized, immersive experience. The answer to that question I posed near the beginning of this report—would the Southern-themed films enhance our experience of the South, and vice versa—turned out to be a resounding "yes." The films enriched our travels and our understanding of the blues, while our daily Delta explorations added a patina of personal experience to how we viewed the films. In one of the fest's films, we had heard a man lament the "Disney blues," worrying that this music might become essentially a "novelty" form, a bit like traditional New Orleans jazz (a characterization I'd dispute, by the way). He meant a music that, while it may be beautiful, was no longer a living language. At least as practiced in Clarksdale, though, the blues is alive.

The Clarksdale Film Festival takes place the last weekend of January; for more information, go to https://www.clarksdalefilmfestival.com

JUKE JOINT FESTIVAL

As the late Anthony Bourdain once said, the Delta is "a whole 'nother planet." One great way to experience this "other world" is Juke Joint Festival, held annually in mid-April. The fest is your best chance to see all of the still-living musicians we've been discussing here, as you move among all the venues listed above, and more—the whole town becomes a site for live music. (We once even saw Christone "Kingfish" Ingram in a cavernous bank lobby.) It's especially important since competition from casinos has had a disastrous impact on Mississippi juke joint culture for decades now. As a gentleman tells Peter Guralnick in his book *Lost Highway: Journeys and Arrivals of American Musicians*, "I don't care what you say, you get the best music in the world in these little juke joints and holes in the wall, because this is where they always sing from the heart."

There are special events. For example, at the 2016 fest we attended a live radio show at the New Roxy, where we got to hear journalist and documentary filmmaker Robert Gordon read from his essay about hanging out at Junior Kimbrough's legendary juke joint—and not quite being able to bring himself to taste Kimbrough's moonshine. That was followed with performances by the Yalobushwhackers, Lil Poochie, and the late Robert "Bilbo" Walker, who passed away in 2018. The fest also features attractions such as Monkeys Riding Dogs: "actual organ-grinder monkeys riding border collies and herding sheep."

Do make your hotels reservations early for Juke Joint Fest: blues travelers come from all over the world for this one.

Juke Joint Festival takes place annually in mid-April; for more info, go to:
https://www.jukejointfestival.com

Sunflower River Blues and Gospel Festival

Typically held in the second weekend of August and dating back to 1988, the Sunflower River Blues and Gospel Festival is a subject of further research for us. We always love a reason to go back to Clarksdale. For more information, head to http://www.sunflowerfest.org.

Deep Blues Festival

The Deep Blues Festival is typically held in mid-October at the New Roxy. For more information, go to https://deepbluesfest.com.

HOTELS

Shack Up Inn
001 Commissary Cir Rd.
Clarksdale, MS 38614

Just a few miles outside of town, there couldn't be a more inspiring or atmospheric way to sleep in the Mississippi Delta than the Shack Up Inn. The grounds look much the same as they did when this was the working Hopson Plantation, a cotton farm for over 120 years, from 1852 to 1972. Wander amid the junkyard chic of the grounds: you'll see rusting trucks, fading Coca-Cola signs, and dusty bottle trees gleaming when the setting sun hits them just right, all deep blues and emeralds. (These trees were meant to keep ghosts bottled up.) As the hotel's website proclaims, you will see "authentic sharecropper shacks, the original cotton gin and seed houses and other outbuildings." You'll stay in either the cotton gin or one of the stand-alone shacks. Nice touches abound, such as the prop guitars you may borrow from the reception desk; it's fun to sit on the porch of the Cadillac Shack, pretending to play. There's still a cotton patch out front. Wander out and touch the fateful cotton, reflecting on the days when "cotton was king" of economics and culture.

Strolling the grounds, you'll notice one of the first mechanized cotton pickers, manufactured by International Harvester. Indeed, Hopson was a testing-ground for this game-changing machine, beginning to experiment with it in 1935 and finally bringing it online in 1944. Hopson had been a technological innovator even before, introducing the tractor as early as 1914; seminal blues pianist Pinetop Perkins, a key member of Muddy Waters' '70s band, drove a tractor here. Machines took over the fields, largely replacing manual cotton pickers, as Hopson hastened on the end of the sharecropping era. By 1950, Hopson was completely mechanized.

Sure, there's a certain irony involved in sleeping and partying at a plantation. Still, we prefer to think of the Shack Up as a monument to the people who lived and loved here, and to blues music as the life force—not just an expression of the farmers' misery, but also of their fiery joy and steely core. This funky, gritty hotel offers a window onto the environment that inspired people to have the blues in the first place, but also a monument to their resiliency, and the music-making that allowed them to steal a bit of fun and enjoyment from an exploitative system. When you're in the Juke Joint Chapel (the Inn's concert venue) and an inspired musician like Deak Harp has got your bones howling with the electricity of the blues, you'll feel the spirit shoot straight through you.

At the Shack Up Inn, you may feel the spirit of the blues wafting by in the breeze blowing through these old plantation grounds, if you happen to be rocking on your porch at just the right time, the sun on your face. The people who run the joint, Bill Talbot and Guy Malvezzi, are great characters, too.

(Cotton Gin Rates: 2-night minimum stay on weekends. Sunday thru Thursday $80, $100 on weekend nights; 1 bedroom Shacks Rates: Sunday thru Thursday $85, $100 for weekend nights. Festivals, holidays and certain weekends have an added room charge. You must be 25 or older to rent a room, though international tourists traveling with kids are welcome. Check in starting at 3pm, check out 11am;

Tel. (662) 624-8329;

https://www.shackupinn.com

The Riverside Hotel
615 Sunflower Ave.
Clarksdale, MS 38614

On the banks of the Sunflower River, you'll find the historic Riverside Hotel. "The Riverside Hotel, set behind a broken Schlitz sign and a blues marker noting its history as the hospital where blues singer Bessie Smith died from injuries sustained in a car wreck, is homey, hospitable and filled with nostalgia." That's Susan Puckett saying that: we've never stayed here ourselves. The Riverside was converted from an African-American hospital into a hotel in 1943; in the ensuing years, as their website puts it, it was "one of the only African American hotels in Jim Crow Mississippi" and thus "played host to a Who's Who of blues and R&B legends including Duke El-lington, Muddy Waters, Howlin' Wolf, and Sam Cooke. Others, including Ike Turner, Sunny Boy Williamson II, and Robert Nighthawk, liked the place so much they moved in." The room where Bessie Smith died is now a shrine. Ike Turner dreamed up and developed "Rocket 88" in Room #7.

(For information about rates and reservations, call Zee at 662-624-9163 (home) or 662-645-3152, or fill out a form at the hotel's website, http://www.riversideclarksdale.com)

Ground Zero Blues Club
387 Delta Ave
Clarksdale, MS 38614

This blues nightclub and restaurant (see our entries above) also has spacious, nicely appointed rooms available upstairs. We stayed in one in 2015. It was an enormous, rather elegant loft-style apartment with a small kitchen and everything you need to do some cooking. In the one nod to the grit downstairs, fun graffiti decorates the doors of each apartment. Grab a sharpie and make your mark. If you see some scrawling saying "Scott & Karolyn's Love Nest, Southern Road Trip '15," that's us! Don't worry about the noise level if you're one of those people who needs a good night's sleep, as you cannot hear the music coming from below. You'll probably be down there anyway, though, won't you?

Tel. (662) 621-9009;
https://www.groundzerobluesclub.com

The Squeeze Box
108 E 2nd St.
Clarksdale, MS 38614

This is a new place in town. The New York Times writes: "The Squeezebox, a former downtown storefront, has just opened as a guest suite where the décor includes a gold-painted parking meter, a lamp with a zebra-patterned shade and a flute as a base and an X-ray table converted into a headboard with images of blues men."

Tel. (732) 740-6155;
https://www.visitclarksdale.com/blog/lodging/squeeze-box

KAROLYN'S TIP JAR

- E-mail Roger Stolle ahead of time (roger@cathead.biz) with any questions about your Clarksdale trip. He's whip-smart on Delta culture and history. In our experience, he'll almost always get back to you within 24 hours with more info than you'd ever hoped for.

- Make your hotel reservations for Juke Joint Festival early and make them often. Otherwise, you might not be able to get into any hotels in Clarksdale. When this happened to us, we found a port in the storm, so to speak, at the Isle of Capri Casino Hotel in nearby Lula. (https://www.isleofcapri-lula.com/, (610) 241-1626). The Shack Up Inn is more our style, but it sufficed.

- Don't leave Abe's without bringing home a bottle of sauce with you.

- When you visit Hick's Famous Hot Tamales, be sure to knock on the door or call if they appear closed. Sometimes they're just in the back.

- Don't miss the Sunday Blues Brunch at the Bluesberry Cafe.

- There are no alcohol sales in Clarksdale on Sundays.

- The Shack Up Inn admits no kids, but dogs seem to be allowed. *(That's just the right mix, if you ask us.)*

- Scott interjects: when it comes to tasty treats, do not miss Kim's pork rinds, a justly revered local snack. *(Ugh!, ripostes Karolyn).* And if you're in the mood for something sweet, Sweet Magnolia Ice Cream is made right here in Clarksdale.

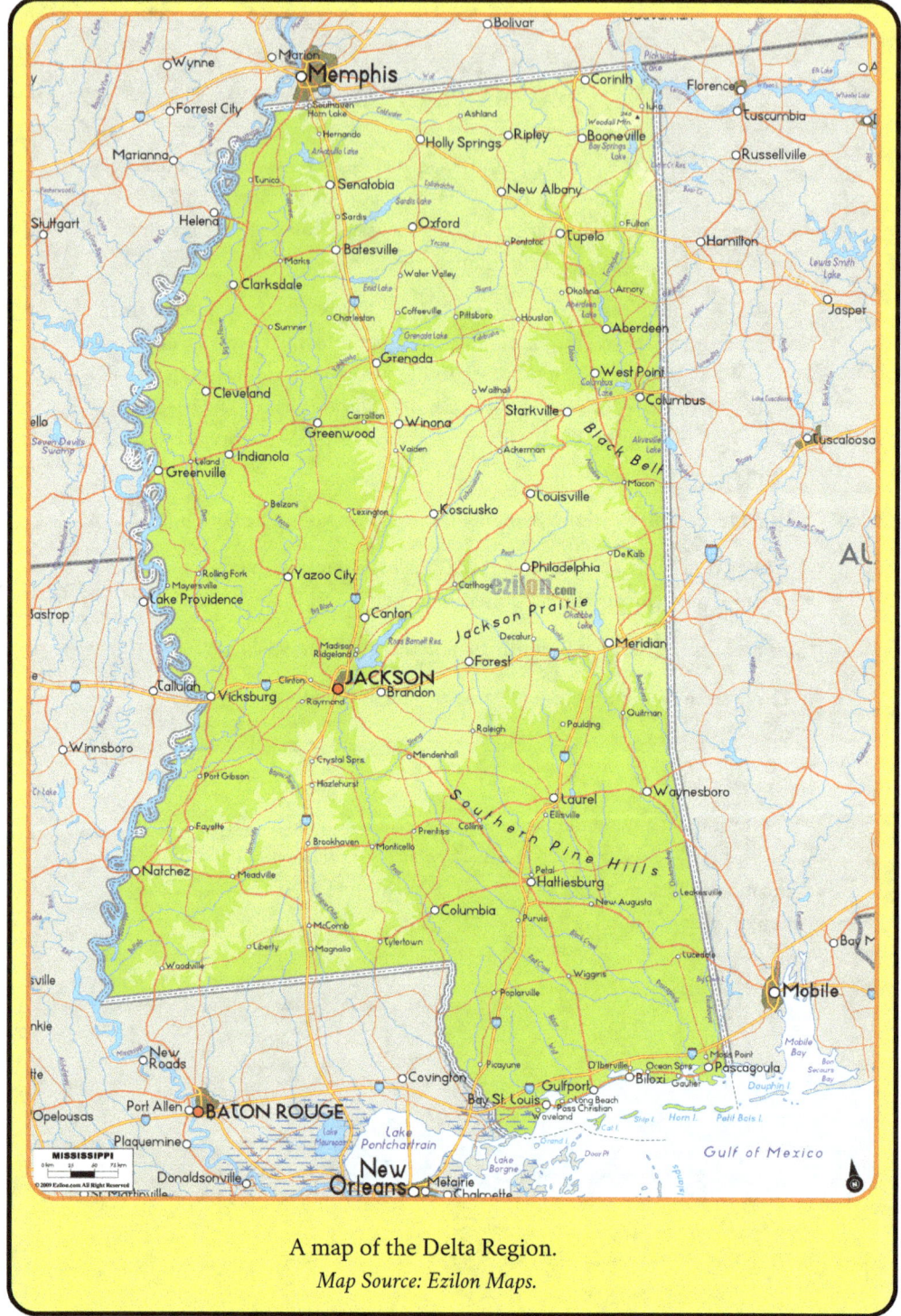

A map of the Delta Region.
Map Source: Ezilon Maps.

CHAPTER V

Delta Exploring

Characterized by its flat, dark, rich alluvial soil ideal for cotton-growing, the Mississippi Delta is defined as the area located in between the Mississippi and Yazoo Rivers. The key towns of the Delta are Clarksdale, Greenville, Cleveland, Indianola, and Greenwood. We like to think of the region as more or less a triangle, with Clarksdale as the northern tip, Greenville as the western lower point, and Greenwood as the eastern lower point. Highway 61 connects Clarksdale to Leland; Greenville is just west of Leland. On the western side of the triangle, Cleveland is in the middle between Clarksdale and Leland. "The raggedy 37-mile stretch of 61 between Cleveland and Clarksdale is as evocative as any section of the Blues Highway," wrote Richard Knight in his groundbreaking book on Highway 61.

Highway 82 runs between Greenville and Greenwood, forming the bottom side of our triangle. It is this stretch that is considered the very heart of the Delta, with Indianola in the middle. From Greenwood, Highway 49E takes you back up to Clarksdale, forming the eastern side of our triangle.

We typically make Clarksdale our home base for Delta exploring, but we've found that Greenville also makes a good hub. Known as "the Athens of the Delta", it's also a great town for American literature. As Susan Puckett puts it, the town "prides itself on its homegrown literary talent," which includes noted authors William Alexander Percy and his nephew Walker Percy. William Alexander, a lawyer and poet, wrote *Lanterns on the Levee: Recollections of a Planters' Son* (1941), whereas Walker penned the celebrated novel, *The Moviegoer*, as well as works that spoke to his abiding interests in matters such as linguistics, the nature of faith, and human nature, such as *Message in a Bottle*. (Scott heartily recommends both of those.) Actually, Puckett notes, the Percy family was Delta aristocracy. William Alexander's father, LeRoy Percy, was one of the foremost cotton growers and Southern Democrats—a U.S. Senator who also ran law practices and plantations. (As an interesting sidenote, William Faulkner used to stay periodically at William Alexander's house, where Walker lived as a boy after his parents died. Walker remembered Faulkner's visits years later).

Other illustrious writers to hail from Greenville include Shelby Foote, Hodding Carter, David Cohn, Angela Jackson, Ellen Douglas, and Julia Reed.

As we've had occasion to mention a few times now, when you explore the Delta, a key year to keep in mind is 1903. This was the year W.C. Handy had a "Eureka!" moment when, while waiting for a train in Tutwiler, he chanced to overhear a fellow traveler playing "the weirdest music" he'd ever heard. While strumming his guitar, this man held a knife to the strings, Hawaiian-style. Handy was hearing a familiar technique, deployed in an idiosyncratic way. This incident is often referred to as Handy's "discovery" of the blues; it might more accurately be described as his discovery of, well, slide guitar. (What's more, it was really but one incident in Handy's larger tour of Mississippi, its plantations and levee camps, which he'd undertaken for purposes of making a survey of Black folk music.) Still, 1903 is a key date—in a sense it's the date the father of the blues "conceived," if you will, because Handy went on to become the first to write down and publish music based on the folk techniques he'd discovered, and recordings of his compositions such as "Memphis Blues" were some of the very first blues hits. By codifying the music he popularized it, bringing blues to the world.

It was also around 1903 when Handy had another revelatory moment while performing with his dance band in Cleveland, when he temporarily ceded the stage to a local band. Their galvanizing performance further demonstrated for him "the beauty of primitive music," which he seemed to admire and condescend to in equal measure, and which he would later popularize by incorporating its techniques into his own, "sophisticated" compositions. Relatively recent research by Elliott Hurwitt unveiled the previously-unnamed leader of the local band in question as one Prince McCoy—though Handy had mentioned McCoy's name in the initial manuscript of his memoir, the name was mysteriously excised from the published version, perhaps because Handy didn't want any historical competition for the title of "Father of the Blues." McCoy turns out to be quite an interesting figure. No recordings of his music exist, but he was a member of the traveling Maxey's Medicine Show band, playing in Cleveland, Greenville and environs. In fact, Handy's composition "Memphis Blues" (1912) was probably based on a version he heard McCoy play that night in 1903. So was his take on "Winding Ball," a number both Handy and his friendly rival Jelly Roll Morton played, and the authorship of which was a matter of contention between them. As it turns out, they both probably got it from McCoy! Check out McCoy's Mississippi Blues Trail marker, when you're passing through Cleveland.

Enjoy the Delta! It's more important than ever to support the surviving remnants of the culture. Casinos have been wiping out juke joints for decades now; the local joints can't compete with free booze and music give-aways. However, the casinos can't compete with the richness of the experiences you'll find elsewhere.

PLANNING YOUR TIME: ITINERARIES

Day One
Morning

Head out from Clarksdale to Tutwiler to see Sonny Boy Williamson's grave; the site of the train station where W.C. Handy "discovered" the blues; and Emmett Till funeral home.

Head to Dockery Plantation, one of the birthplaces of the Delta Blues.

Afternoon

Eat lunch at the Country Platter Restaurant in Cleveland.

Head to Leland to visit the Highway 61 Museum.

Drive down Nelson Street in Greenville.

Evening

Return to Clarksdale and grab a pizza at the Stone Pony.

Go hear some live music of your choice in Clarksdale (see above).

Day Two
Morning

Head to Quito to see one of Robert Johnson's three graves, then drive over to Moorhead to see the railroad tracks "where the Southern cross the Dog."

Afternoon

Head to Indianola and eat lunch at the Blue Biscuit.

Visit the B.B. King Museum and Delta Interpretive Center.

Evening

Back in Clarksdale, have dinner at Ground Zero Blues Club while enjoying some music.

If you've still got the energy, head to Red's.

Day Three
Morning

Drive out to Holly Ridge to see the gravesite of Charley Patton.

Stop in Leland to see the Exhibit of Jim Henson's Delta Boyhood/Birthplace of Kermit the Frog.

Afternoon

Have lunch at Sherman's Restaurant in Greenville.

Head into downtown Greenville to see the Mississippi River levee. Walk the Blues Walk of Fame on Walnut Street.

Evening

Eat at Doe's Eat Place in Greenville.

Head over to the Walnut Street Blues Bar.

Day Four
Morning

Visit Stovall Plantation.

Head over to Rosedale. Have lunch at the White Front Cafe.

Afternoon

Head to Greenwood, about an hour's drive.

Stop at the bridge spanning the Tallahatchie River to observe the Mississippi Country Music Trail marker commemorating Bobbie Gentry.

Pay your respects by taking a moment to look out over the Tallahatchie River, into which murderers dumped Emmett Till's desecrated body.

Across the Tallahatchie bridge, head down Money Road to find another one of Robert Johnson's three graves at Little Zion Missionary Baptist Church.

Evening

Your choice of live music in Clarksdale.

To help with your Delta Exploring, we'd like to offer this expanded guide to our itinerary suggestions above, in the form of a chronicle of our own experiences. There are many ways you could group the below attractions, depending upon whether Clarksdale or Greenville is your home base. This itinerary includes options for both. Depending on where you're staying, it might make more sense for you to group Rosedale with the Tutwiler/Dockery day, or visit Quito while you're down in the Greenwood area. On the day you're in Greenville, you could drive down Nelson Street on the same day you explore Walnut Street and eat at **Doe's Eat Place**. You could even do Holly Ridge on the same day you do Indianola. For Day Four, there's a little over an hour's drive between Rosedale and Greenwood, but you could break up the drive by stopping at Dockery, or by dropping in on some of the other sites and restaurants we've listed below. Have fun!

DAY ONE, MORNING: TUTWILER AND DOCKERY PLANTATION

Intrepidly, we set out to explore the Mississippi Delta, the flat and fertile cotton lands where the blues began—"the most Southern place on earth," according to Richard Knight in his book *The Blues Highway: New Orleans to Chicago*. "No music," he writes, "better reflects its environment."

We began by heading down Highway 49E from Clarksdale toward Tutwiler. Down a lonesome stretch of road, near the woods in a small cemetery, we found the grave of Sonny Boy Williamson II (the stage name of Rice Miller, 1910-1965), perhaps the greatest harmonica player in the history of blues. (It's either him or Little Walter.) Sonny Boy's sisters, who died in a fire in 1995, are buried nearby.

We'd never have found Sonny Boy without the aid of a kindly old fellow who happened to be tending the first graveyard we came to, which we explored in vain. Noting our poking about, this fellow asked if he could help us. We explained our mission: we were looking for Sonny Boy Williamson's grave. "He's not here," the man explained, then gestured out over the fields in the direction of the correct, and much smaller, cemetery, out behind Whitfield Church. (This same gent would turn up later several times as we explored Tutwiler, tailing us to a certain extent, perhaps, but with the avowed intent of making sure we didn't get lost).

The grave of Sonny Boy Williamson and the W.C. Handy Train Station.
Tutwiler, MS. USGS, 1:24,000, 2018.

If you'd like to plug the coordinates of Sonny Boy's grave into your GPS or Google, the location is N 34° 01.108' W 90° 27.464'. The address reads as 6-2 Prairie Road, Tutwiler, MS 38963. Also, we offer this link to a Google Map referencing the grave: **https://www.google.com/maps/place/ Whitfield+Church/@34.019449,-90.458953,160m/data=!3m1!1e3!4m5!3 m4!1s0x0:0x38f3ac8dc997b164!8m2!3d34.0194485!4d-90.4589533?hl=en-US.** (Thanks to the Mississippi Blues Travelers website for the coordinates and the link).

Tutwiler has another claim to blues fame. It's where W.C. Handy "discovered" the music in 1903 at a since-demolished train station. After paying our deep respects to Sonny Boy Williamson, we hopped back in the car and drove over to this next historical site. The GPS location of the MTB marker at the site is: N 34° 00.871' W 90° 25.919' . You'll approach via Second Street: cross the railroad tracks and look for the murals.

As we parked and approached the site where the train station once stood on foot, Cristen Barnard's murals beckoned us on. (One of the murals even offers a map to Sonny Boy's grave...see if you can spot it. If the directions above don't work out for you, you could always attempt to use this map). While the station's no longer standing, the tracks are still there.

On the fateful day in question, Handy was waiting for a train when a man sat down next to him. In Handy's own words, as recounted by Richard Knight, the "lean, loose-jointed Negro commenced plunking a guitar...His clothes were rags, his feet poked out of his shoes. His face had on it some of the sadness of the ages. As he played, he pressed a knife on the strings... and the effect was unforgettable." As Knight surmises, "W.C. Handy had discovered the blues." Enjoy Barnard's murals, which depict the scene of this fateful meeting. They make for a fine photo opportunity, as well.

As Knight further narrates, the bluesman went on to sing the line "Goin' where the Southern cross the Dog" which, Handy discovered, referred to the point where the Yazoo & Mississippi Valley railroad (nicknamed the 'Yellow Dog') crossed the Southern railroad in Moorhead. Later, we will take you to Moorhead to visit this very site for yourself.

As we stood musing, the old gent who'd helped us back at the graveyard pulled up. "Just wanted to make sure you didn't get lost on these back roads," he said. He tipped us off to one more thing we shouldn't miss. Right around the corner, he said, stood the site of the Tutwiler Funeral Home where, in 1955, Emmett Till's desecrated body was prepared to be sent back to Chicago. A white man, our new friend spoke of Till in an almost apologetic manner, though he'd only been five years old when it happened. He struck a reflective tone—as though he wished there were something he could have done. He looked on and swept the dirt with his feet. Those farmers, he said, came in the middle of the night and dragged him out, and they tortured that poor boy—"and that's the true story." (As if there'd ever been some other narrative that needed countering. Maybe if you grew up white in the south, there had been. Our new friend indicated as much when he added that "some will still fight" this truth). Thanking him again and bidding him farewell, we strolled around to the former site of the funeral home, today just a brick husk. We read the sign erected there, a memorial to Till that is part of the Civil Rights Driving Tour. We got back into the car with our friend's words still resonating, thinking about history and memory.

Getting back on 49W and then heading west on Highway 8, just outside of Cleveland we pulled up to our next destination, the Dockery Plantation (229 Hwy 8)—the site many scholars identify as the birthplace of the Delta blues, to the extent that such a thing is even possible. Note the cotton gin of Will Dockery's old plantation overlooking the Sunflower River, still emblazoned with the family name. Charley Patton's father moved the family to these farms in 1897. Over to you, Richard Knight: "Charley Patton grew up here learning at the feet of Henry Sloan who played a rhythmic guitar style which Patton later developed into blues. That contribution is hard to underestimate. Robert Palmer, in his definitive book *Deep Blues*, claims, '... he [Patton] inspired just about every Delta bluesman of any consequence. He is among the most important musicians twentieth century America has produced.'"

As we strolled about on the big porch, we liked to imagine Patton playing for a crowd assembled for a hard-won Saturday night's entertainment. Helping to set the mood were speakers playing piped-in Delta blues, a nice touch. It was amazing to think about what had gone down here: not only did Patton learn from Sloan, but he in turn taught Howlin' Wolf—right here! Pops

Staples grew up here, too. As Steve Cheseborough writes in *Blues Traveling: The Holy Sites of Delta Blues*, Pops' "beautiful guitar playing is based on the downhome Delta blues." These giants grew up inhaling this atmosphere, and they exhaled out a universe of beautiful music.

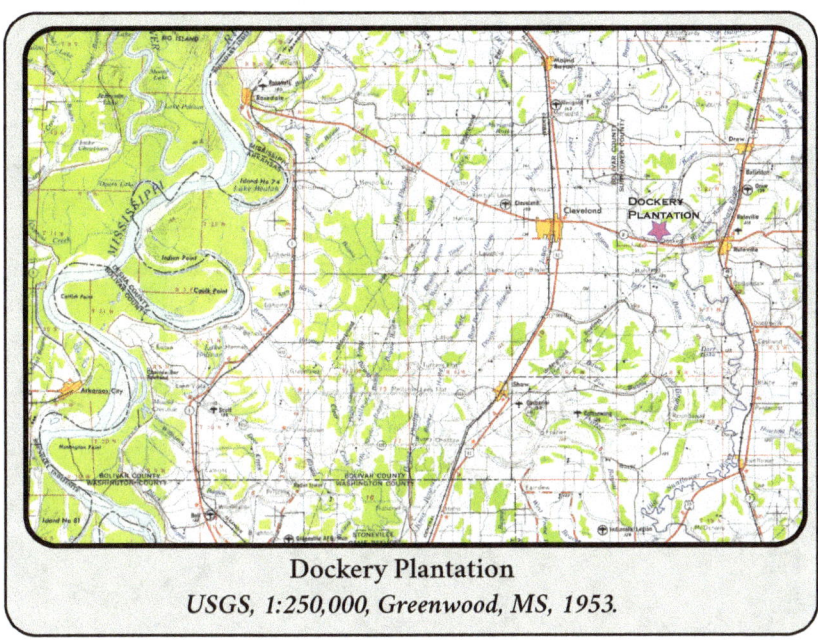

Dockery Plantation
USGS, 1:250,000, Greenwood, MS, 1953.

Strolling the grounds, you shouldn't miss the great old filling station down on the corner (note the old-school "Coca-Cola" Dockery sign), which is in the process of being preserved. The Baptist Church across the way served the plantation's Black workers.

At our next stop, the Highway 61 Blues Museum in Leland, you'll see a model of the Dockery Plantation. It's fun to examine it after you've been to the place itself. Look for dollhouse-size versions of the filling station, church, cotton gin, and even the porch where you've been dreaming your blues reveries.

DAY ONE, AFTERNOON: LELAND AND GREENVILLE'S NELSON STREET

We're going to continue exploring the deep Delta, the area between Greenville and Greenwood, immersing ourselves in the incubator of the blues. This land was as much a birthplace and crucible for this music as New Orleans' Congo Square was for jazz and funk

Get back on Highway 61 and head south towards Leland, our next stop, where we'll visit the Highway 61 Blues Museum (307 North Broad Street), which restricts its focus to musicians who hail from in and around this region. Just outside of Greenville, Leland was described as the "hellhole of the Delta" by Collier's in 1908 for its Saturday night saloon scene, when as many as 10,000 people from the plantations in the surrounding countryside would converge here. As a sign in the museum shows, the Washington County Anti-Saloon League proclaimed Leland's moral problems were the result of "blind tiger booze, crap shooting, and kept women." No wonder people flocked here.

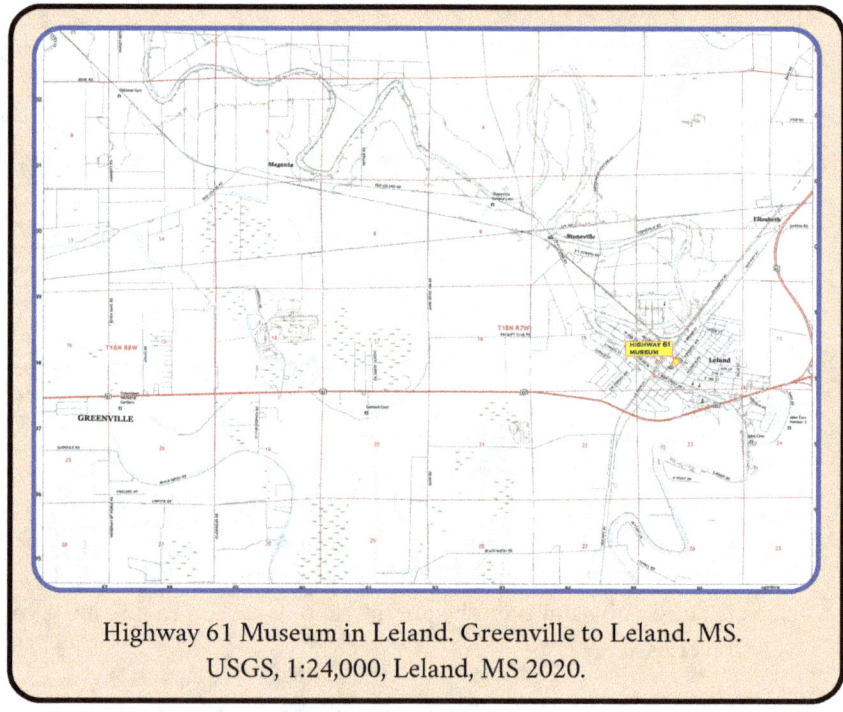

Highway 61 Museum in Leland. Greenville to Leland. MS.
USGS, 1:24,000, Leland, MS 2020.

After you explore the museum, be sure to knock around town a bit. There are several Mississippi Blues Trail markers to find. Your easter egg hunt might include finding the marker for James "Son" Thomas, which is right in front of the museum, so that's easy. Then, right across the street, check out the marker for Johnny Winter. Where 3rd Street meets Main, you'll find the marker commemorating the "Corner of 10 and 61," a street corner where musicians once busked. It's also where passengers on the "Planter," a train that ran daily from New Orleans to Memphis, would alight to eat dinner and listen to blues musicians. Over at 411 Main, find the marker for the soulful Chicago bluesman Tyrone Davis ("Can I Change My Mind," "Turn Back the Hands of Time," and "Turning Point"), who grew up here.

Nearby, look out for the mural showing B.H. ("UG") McGee playing guitar with James "Son" Thomas. Known for his entire life by the unusual sobriquet of "UG," Ben Humphrey McGee had been a gunner in the Marine Corps Air Force during WWII; his family owned Pantherburn, one of the oldest and largest cotton plantations in the Delta. James "Son" Thomas worked on the plantation, and McGee apparently liked to sit with him and jam on the blues a bit.

On the south wall of the building at the corner of 4th and Main Streets, find the "Highway 61" mural depicting local blues legends by Cristen Barnard, whose murals we'd also admired in Tutwiler. She was the "Tom Sawyer" behind this huge painting, which she created in 2000 along with Jay Kirgis and a cast of locals. Its cast is restricted to bluesmen born within 25 miles of Leland. Find Boogaloo Ames, Jimmy Reed, Little Milton, Eddie Cusic, Willie Foster, James "Son" Thomas, and brothers Johnny and Edgar Winter, all of whom are clustered around the Highway 61 highway sign.

On the south wall of the building located on the corner of 3rd and Main is a mural dedicated to B.B. King, who hailed from Indianola. (We'll head that way tomorrow.) Also at 3rd and Main, on the west wall, there's a mural depicting "Delta Dancing" at Lilo's Italian restaurant out on Highway 82, a tradition which apparently still goes on. (We hope to get to join in, someday). Boogaloo Ames is shown pounding out a tune with "Doc" Booth on sax, as happy guests dance. Back when Ames was alive, he'd play at Lilo's with a young Eden Brent. Theirs is quite a great Mississippi story, incidentally, the friendship between the old Black master pianist who mentored the young white female prodigy. We understand there's a film about it, *Boogaloo and Eden: Sustaining the Sound* (1999).

The newest mural honors Jimmy Reed, who was born on Dunleith Plantation, just northeast of Leland (there's a MBT marker for him out there). You'll find this work, again by Barnard and Kirgis, on the wall of Stovall's on the Creek at the corner of Broad Street and South Deer Creek Drive East.

Lastly, you might want to check out the MBT marker for Ruby's Night Spot, one of the most happening blues clubs in the '40s and '50s, owned by Ruby Edwards, who also ran Club Ebony over in Indianola, which we'll visit later. It's over at the site where the club once stood on McGee Street, near the intersection with Dean Street. From Main, head across the railway tracks on 3rd Street, take a right onto Railroad Avenue, and then a left on McGee.

We should mention that Leland is also the "birthplace of Kermit the Frog." The wonderful Jim Henson, inventor of Kermit and the other Muppets, grew up here. There's a museum in town dedicated to Kermit and Henson's Delta boyhood.

Back at the Highway 61 museum, we'd learned more about Nelson Street in Greenville, just west of Leland on Highway 82, and its storied place in blues lore. It's been called "Mississippi's most infamous and blues-drenched street." Unfortunately, as Roger Stolle—fount of blues knowledge and proprietor of the funky Cat Head Delta Blues & Folk Art shop in Clarksdale—would later observe to us, the only reason to go down to Nelson Street today is to score some crack. It's very sad.

Still, we had to roll over and take a look for ourselves. We viewed the historic street from a rolling car, and, much as we hate to say it, it's probably a good idea that you do the same. You can still enjoy the street's murals from the window. Linger as long as you can at the mural for Milton Campbell, better known as Little Milton, who had a hit record with "Annie Mae's Cafe," inspired by The Flowing Fountain, the legendary Nelson Street club owned by Perry Payton. Willie Love's hit "Nelson Street Blues" is an homage to the famous area, and the street certainly has the blues today. It's sad, considering the area's former glory, but it's a familiar story. With all the jobs gone, you'll see men hanging around the corner, trash riddling the streets of what was once a thriving community.

We burned up Highway 61 back to our home base in Clarksdale. As a sidenote, at some point you'll probably find yourself passing through Duncan, in between Cleveland and Clarksdale on Highway 61 (278). The town's blues marker is worth a stop: hopping out of the car to have a look, we learned Duncan is the birthplace of Anthony "Big A" Sherrod, whom we'd seen rock at Red's in Clarksdale the night before. The marker traces the journey of Duncan-born bluesmen to Clarksdale and then on to northern towns like Chicago. Jimmy Reed worked on a plantation here, and Charley Patton's daughter, Rosetta, lived here.

Back at the Shack Up Inn in Clarksdale, a gorgeous sunset drew the day down. As the sky burned over our shack, the Red House, I thought of a line from a Jesse Winchester song: "the sky was red from off towards New Orleans."

That evening found us over at the Hambone Gallery, catching a set by Terry "Harmonica" Bean. Before he began a song, he'd tell us a story about learning at his grandfather's knee, and then he'd demonstrate for us how his father and grandfather used to play it. In this way, Harmonica Bean is a living link to a departed generation of Delta and Hill Country bluesmen.

Scott got to hang with local hero Watermelon Slim, who was out that night enjoying the music himself. He's a certifiable cool cat.

— Scott: As an experience, meeting Slim is kind of like what I'd imagine meeting Tom Waits would be like.

DAY TWO, MORNING: QUITO AND MOORHEAD

The next day we set out for Quito, a town near Greenwood so small it's not even on the map. On the way we passed the junction of Highways 82 and 49E, the general area where the Three Forks Grocery juke joint once stood. That's where it's believed Johnson played his last note, jamming with Sonny Boy Williamson II until, as legend has it, the owner of the joint poisoned him. It seems the man objected to Johnson's dalliances with his wife.

Our destination was Payne Chapel, whose cemetery contains one of Robert Johnson's three graves. To get there, you'll get off 49E at 82 and head west a bit, then head south on winding Highway 7 about three miles, passing through Itta Benna. You'll cross a bridge: there won't be a sign for Quito. Turn west onto a dirt road across from the cotton gin with a "HE Hardwick-Etter Ginning System" sign. In about a block you'll come to Payne Chapel. (Technically, the address is 32830 Co Rd 167, Itta Bena.)

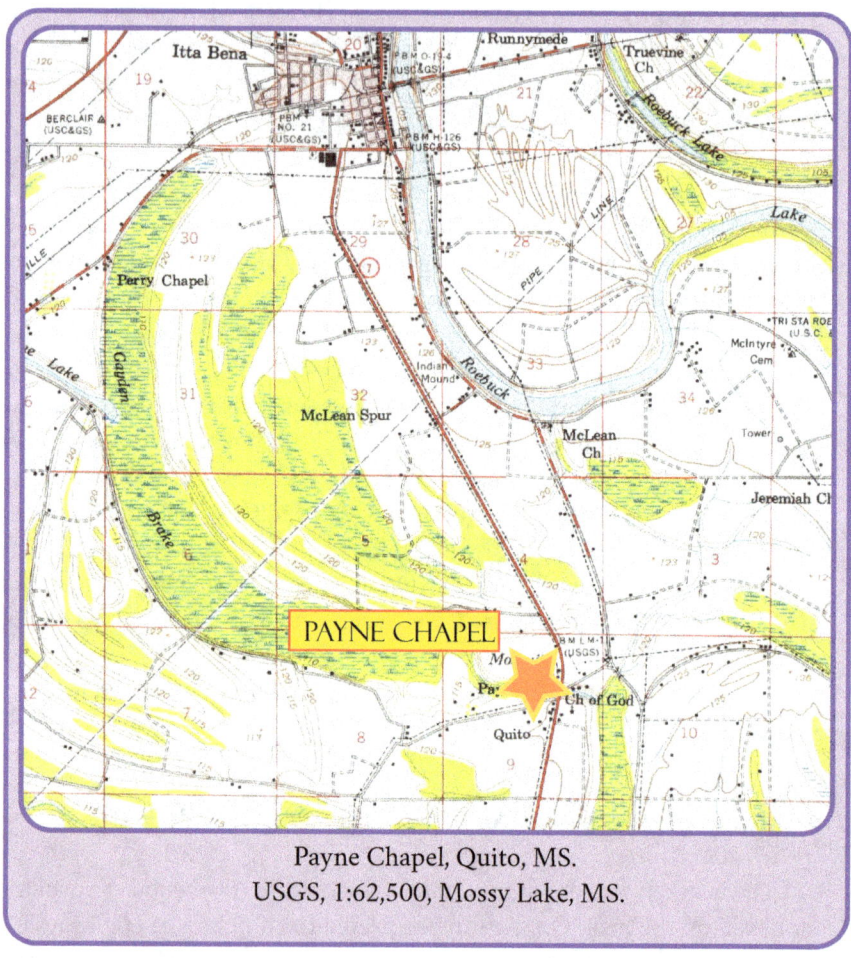

Payne Chapel, Quito, MS.
USGS, 1:62,500, Mossy Lake, MS.

We wanted to see this grave, though it's generally accepted that Quito is not where Johnson's really buried. His true resting spot is likely Little Zion M.B. Church, north of Greenwood. (We'll get there; see below.) Still, since no one knows for sure, it's fun to visit all three sites. You're soaking up the atmosphere of Johnson's stomping grounds, in any event. You're seeing where the music comes from.

Next up on our tour is Moorhead, where we'll visit another much-sung spot in blues lore. Head back up Highway 7 to 82, then turn west onto Highway 3, which you'll take for about 13 miles into Moorhead. Highway 3 becomes Olive Street, which you'll take over to Southern Avenue, where you'll see a railroad crossing sign. Hang a right onto Southern and you'll see the railroad crossing and the state historic marker.

Recall a detail from yesterday when we visited the former train station in Tutwiler, where W.C. Handy overheard a fellow traveler, in 1903, singing that he was "goin' where the Southern cross the Dog." This gentleman was referring to the intersection of the Southern Railroad and the Yazoo Railroad (a.k.a the "Yellow Dog"), right where we're standing in Moorhead. (In 1900 the "Y.D" was incorporated into the Yazoo and Mississippi Valley Railroad).

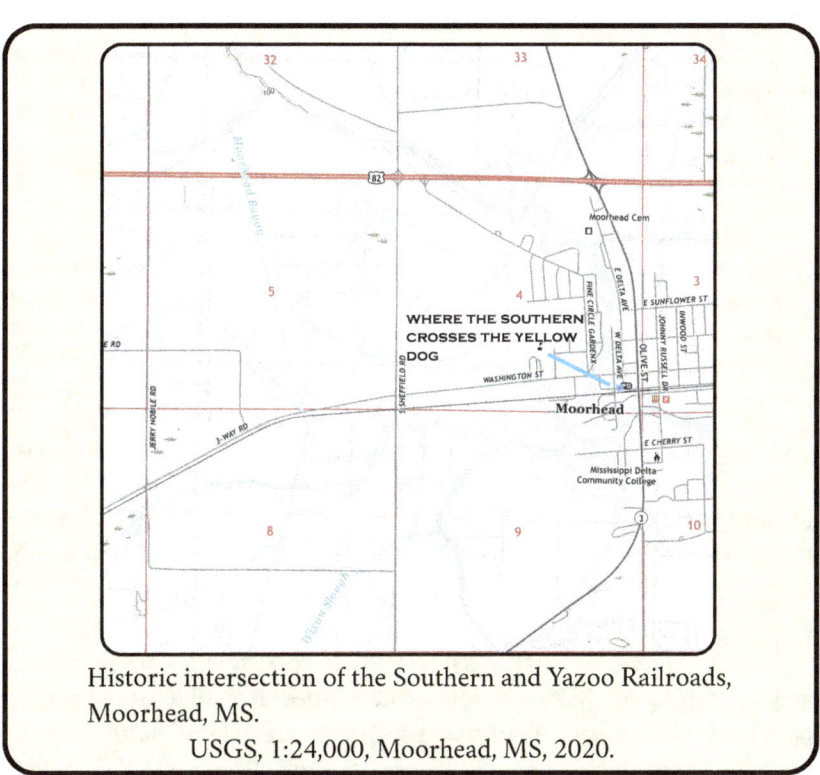

Historic intersection of the Southern and Yazoo Railroads, Moorhead, MS.
USGS, 1:24,000, Moorhead, MS, 2020.

As Steve Cheeseborough notes, Handy thought the line about "goin' where the Southern cross the Dog" too good to lose, and incorporated it into his own "Yellow Dog Blues." Blues masters who've sung about this legendary crossing are legion, including Charley Patton ("Green River Blues") and Big Bill Broonzy ("Southern Blues").

Why was this junction so important? On the one hand, thanks to its railroad crossing, Saturday nights in Moorhead became the place to be in the '30s. Peruse the Mississippi Blues Trail marker: "As local resident Jim Harrison recalled: 'A few white folks and many, many black folks came to town to celebrate the end of a hard week of manual labor. They shopped, socialized, and generally turned the town into a mini-Mardi Gras.'" The railroad junction also took on a larger meaning, as a metaphor for escape, and not only a metaphor. Simply put, in Jim Crow days, if a Black person could get to the train station in Moorhead, he or she had a shot at getting out of Mississippi.

Spend some time with the MBT markers at this historic site. Look for the one for Johnny Russell, the Moorhead-born country signer who wrote "Act Naturally".

DAY TWO, AFTERNOON: INDIANOLA

Get back on Highway 82, which, running between Greenwood and Greenville, cuts right through the heart of the Delta. Head west for about 15 minutes and you'll be in Indianola, B.B. King's hometown, where we'll visit the **B.B. King Museum and Delta Interpretive Center** (400 2nd St.). It's a handsomely appointed and smartly curated museum. You'll wend movingly through King's storied life. It makes for a stirring visit and a great warmup for Memphis. For our guide to your visit, see our entry below.

After your visit, hop back in the car and head over to the corner of Church and Second Street. This was the curb where little B.B. used to sit and play for passersby, when he was too small to get into the nightclubs. Imagine Church Street at its peak: Sonny Boy Williamson II, Louis Jordan and Count Basie used to jam in its clubs, as did Jay McShann's band featuring no less than Charlie Parker. As a busker, little B.B. noticed that he received compliments when he played gospel, which was one thing, but he got cash tips when he played blues, which was quite another. Blues it is, he decided. Imagine his trajectory from this corner to the greatest concert halls in the world.

Do you see the hand and footprints in the concrete on the corner? "On June 5, 1986, King placed his footprints, handprints, and signature in the sidewalk where he used to sing," writes Steve Cheseborough. While you're here, don't forget to enjoy the MBT marker and the painting of Lucille, King's sobriquet for his beloved black Gibson guitars. It is the work of Indianola musician Bobby Whalen.

Stroll or drive over to nearby Hanna Ave. to find historic **Club Ebony**, est. 1948 (head south on Church, turning left onto Clay St., then right onto Hanna Ave). Almost every year since 1968, B.B. played Indianola's annual outdoor Homecoming concert in remembrance of slain Civil Rights activist Medgar Evers. Afterwards, he'd play a set here at Club Ebony. In 2008 B.B. bought the club from Mary Shepard, who, true to her name, shepherded the club for 34 of its most storied years. (Shepard had actually bought the place from King's one-time mother-in-law, Ruby Edwards, back in 1974). We were gladdened to note that Club Ebony apparently still hosts occasional live blues.

DAY THREE, MORNING: HOLLY RIDGE, CHARLEY PATTON, AND GREENVILLE'S WALNUT STREET

The town of Holly Ridge is in between Leland and Indianola on Highway 82. (From 82, take the Holly Ridge turnoff which goes a mile north into town. After turning left on Main Street, you'll shortly come upon New Jerusalem M.B. Church, where Patton sang. Another 0.2 mile down, just past Holly Ridge Gin, is the cemetery.) Charley Patton, the father of country blues, rests here, under a huge Delta sky. What we owe him can scarcely be measured. As you pay your respects to one of the greatest American musicians of the twentieth century, play back your memories of your recent visit to Dockery Plantation, where Patton grew up. Study his Mississippi Blues Trail marker. Nearby, bluesmen Asie Reed Payton and Willie James Foster also rest.

Next up, let's head over to Walnut Street in Greenville to check out the Blues Walk of Fame and the Mississippi River Levee. To get to Walnut Street, get back on 82 and head west for about 20 miles, take a right onto S. Washington Ave., and a left onto Walnut.

Historically, the legendary blues street in Greenville is Nelson Street, but the music stopped ringing out there long ago. Today, the avenue you want for live blues is Walnut Street. Go down there even before the clubs open and you'll find the Blues Walk of Fame, celebrating famous names and local heroes both. At some cost to his back, Scott was able to bend over and espy plaques in the brick walkway celebrating the following names, some of whom we've been talking about: Jimmy Reed, Johnny Winter, B.B. King, Charley Patton (the "King of the Delta Blues"), James "Little Milton" Campbell, Jr., R.L. Burnside, Eden Brent, Abie "Boogaloo" Ames, Walter Horn, Jr. (aka "Mississippi Slim"), Calep Emphrey, Jr., George "All Nite" Allen, and Sam Chatmon. See how many you can find.

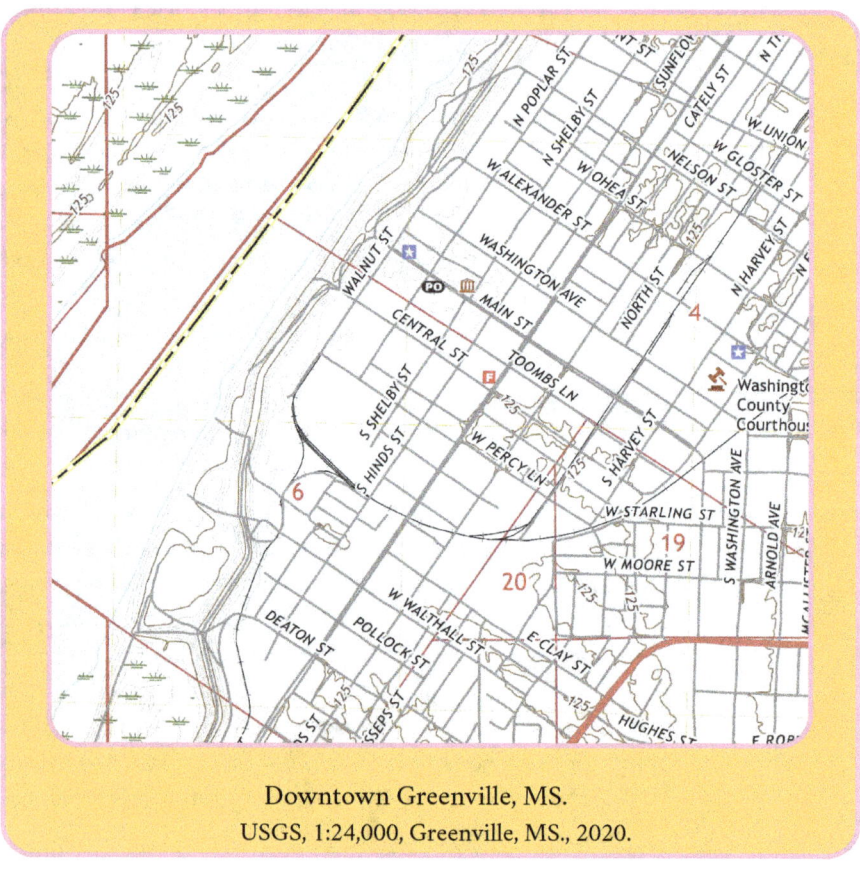

Downtown Greenville, MS.
USGS, 1:24,000, Greenville, MS., 2020.

While you're on Walnut Street, you can also scramble up onto the banks of the Mississippi River Levee. (Technically, this body of water is Lake Ferguson, an oxbow lake—that is, a curved "lake" that forms when the meander part of a river, in this case the Mississippi, gets sealed off from the main thrust of the river).

Atop the levee, study the markers describing the Mississippi River & Tributaries Project. In 1927, Greenville was submerged in water for months when the levee broke near Mound Landing. As Susan Puckett writes, "The Great Flood of 1927 has been called the worst natural disaster in the nation's history, with societal and economic repercussions that linger today." In its wake the Project raised the levee, fortified its banks and shortened the river. These improvements proved strong enough here to contain the great Mississippi River flood of 2011, which elsewhere proved devastating. Compare river stages between the floods of 1927 and 2011: the river rose slightly higher in 1927, but the 2011 flood carried more water.

Here is a fun fact for you to contemplate: the Mississippi River levee system is both longer and taller than the Great Wall of China.

Nearby, look for the marker honoring the site of the former offices of the Delta Democrat Times, the newspaper edited by Hodding Carter. The marker is named for his memoir, *Where Main Street Meets the River*. As Richard Knight writes, "Greenville has long been seen as one of Mississippi's more progressive towns. Back in the forties Delta Democrat Times editor Hodding Carter Jr won the Pulitzer Prize for his editorials against racial prejudice."

DAY FOUR, MORNING: A VISIT TO ROSEDALE

Rosedale is the essence of the heart of the Delta. "Lord, I'm going to Rosedale, gonna take my rider by my side. We can still barrelhouse baby, 'cause it's on the riverside," sang Robert Johnson in "Traveling Riverside Blues" (1937). Some say Rosedale is the true site of Johnson's mythic crossroads, where Highway 8 and Highway 1 intersect. There's a restaurant there now called **Leo's Market**, which is also the headquarters of the **Crossroads Blues Society**.

Now, the town of Beulah, on Highway 1 just south of Rosedale, is where they shot the crossroads for the famous Ralph Macchio film. We spent a fruitless afternoon once driving through farmland in Beulah, looking for this crossroads, but found nothing satisfying, even though we were using Steve

Cheseborough's directions. Let us know if you find it. By the way, Highway 1 is an atmospheric way to get to Rosedale from Clarksdale, with the wending Mississippi always at your side, or if you're coming up from Greenville.

There's not much here anymore, but there is beauty in its crumbling buildings; the history hangs in the air, waiting to be breathed in. Find the burnt-out remnants of the storied juke joint **Bug's Place** over at 515 Bruce Street. You'll see that it's jukin' days are behind it. Bruce Street, by the way, is named for Blanche K. Bruce, an ex-slave who became a U.S. senator in 1874(!). As recently as 2009, when Steve Cheseborough put out his book *Blues Traveling*, Bug's Place was open and serving beer. Sad to see it's only a ghost, now. Still, treading in the footsteps of Robert Johnson is like knocking around in London in the places where Shakespeare trod. Do be sure to drop in on the **White Front Cafe** ("Joe's Hot Tamale Place") to taste the recipe of the late Joe Pope, "the high priest" of tamale making. *See our entry below.*

DAY FOUR, AFTERNOON: A TRIP DOWN MONEY ROAD

Just north of Greenwood, we'll take a detour down Money Road to visit another one of Robert Johnson's graves. (This is the one many historians agree is the "real" one.) We'll stop at the edge of the Tallahatchie River in observation of the murder of Emmett Till, the event some historians credit with giving birth to the Civil Rights movement.

This detour down Money Road was inspired by Rosanne Cash's fine, haunting album *The River & the Thread*, which was in turn inspired by her own road trip through the South. The album finds Cash reckoning with the past and her own roots, searching for the intersection of the land with personal and historic memory.

If you're coming down 49E from Clarksdale, get off on 82 (musing again on how this juncture is likely the site of Johnson's poisoning in 1938) and head east to Greenwood. Coming into Greenwood, get off 82 on Park Ave. and head through town to Grand, where you'll hang a left.

You'll come to the Tallahatchie River and the famous bridge, or rather its modern iteration, immortalized in Bobbie Gentry's song. We refer, of course, to that Southern Gothic legend, "Ode to Billie Joe." Gentry's voice was as warm and Southern as peach cobbler and fried chicken. Pull to the side of the road, step out of the car and observe the Mississippi Country Music Trail marker commemorating Gentry's mysterious hit. *Why* did Billy Joe MacAllister jump off the Tallahatchie Bridge?

As you gaze out over the Tallahatchie River, observe a moment of silence for Emmett Till. It was into this river that murderers dumped his desecrated body—shot, mutilated, gouged. This was the murder that sparked the Civil Rights Movement. Till's mother insisted on an open casket so the world could see what the killers had done to her boy. The shocking, unspeakable sight, shown to the world in photographs, was the spark that ignited the world-historical movement. Think about how, in some real sense, the banks of this river are the birthplace of the Civil Rights movement. Pay your respects and get back into the car.

Over the bridge, Grand becomes Money Road. As we rolled over the bridge headed toward the cemetery, we were thinking of Emmett Till and Robert Johnson all the way. In Rosanne Cash's song "Money Road," she sings about Till and Johnson, respectively: "A lonesome boy in a foreign land, and a voice we'll never understand/One lies in the Zion yard, and one sleeps on the river bar/Neither one got very far, out on Money Road."

When you reach the Mississippi Blues Trail Marker, turn into the Little Zion Missionary Baptist Church, where Robert Johnson rests out in the humble cemetery, near the big tree. Think about this short stretch of Money Road that connects these two seminal post-Reconstruction American lives.

We'll leave you with a few other important Delta sites which we intend to explore in the future:

Next time we're exploring in between Clarksdale and Cleveland, we could check out the former site of **Po' Monkey's** in Merigold, just south of Shelby. The dilapidated building is apparently out in a field, more or less. Quoth Wikipedia: Po' Monkey's "was founded in the early 1960s and was one of the last rural juke joints in the Mississippi Delta. It ceased operating after the death of operator Willie "Po' Monkey" Seaberry in 2016." Mr. Seaberry ran the juke for 50 years, and a pilgrimage there still seems worthwhile.

Merigold is also home to the "world-famous" McCarty's Pottery, started 60 years ago in an old mule barn.

We still need to explore West Helena, Arkansas, which is an extension of the Delta for all intents and purposes.

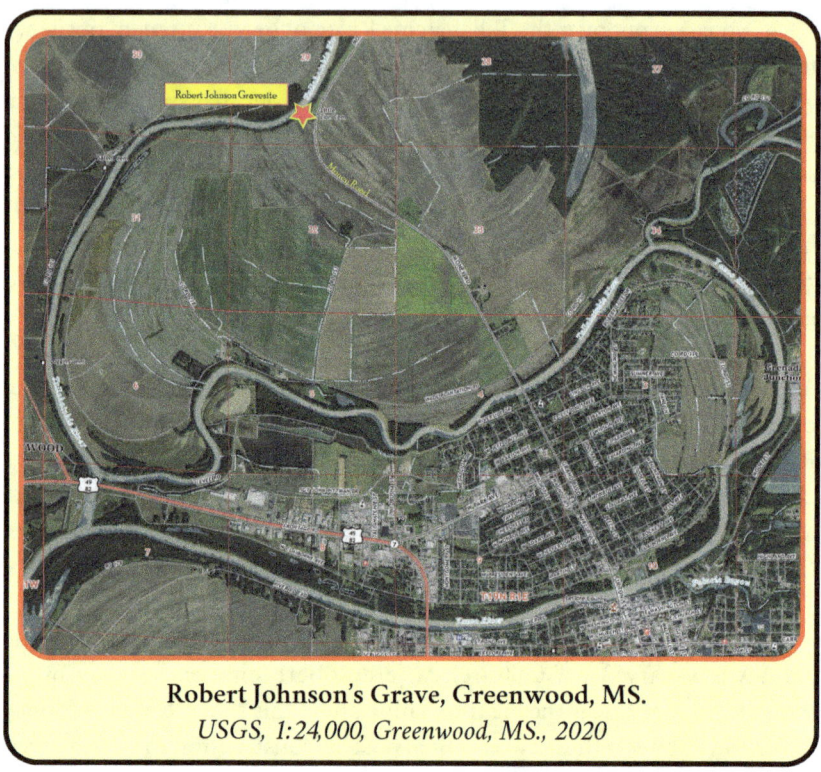

Robert Johnson's Grave, Greenwood, MS.
USGS, 1:24,000, Greenwood, MS., 2020

We also must spend more time in Greenwood (and Itta Bena, the microscopic town it encompasses) and environs. For example, Avalon, a town about 12 miles north of Greenwood, is the site of Mississippi John Hurt's grave. We also need to visit Morgan City, about 10 miles southwest of Greenwood. (This is the site of the third gravesite for Robert Johnson, the only one of the three that we haven't visited, which can be found at the Mount Zion Missionary Baptist Church near town.) If you then keep going southwest from Morgan City you'll come to Bezoni, where you'll find **Mama's Dream**

World, a stitchery museum showing the "Delta way of life." Keep going another 70 miles or so south and you'll come to Vicksburg, the "southern tip" of the Mississippi Delta. It'd be worth investigating whether anything is still shaking on Catfish Row.

SITES AND MUSEUMS

Stovall Plantation
4146 Oakhurst Stovall Rd.
Clarksdale, MS 38614

Just outside of Clarksdale, you'll find Stovall Plantation, where Muddy Waters (the artist who first turned Scott on to the blues) grew up. As you gaze out over the fields, try to picture Muddy driving a tractor across them. It was here also that he saw Son House perform—an experience which inspired him to put his harp aside and pick up the guitar. In his time off, Muddy would go into Clarksdale and play in the Fourth Street juke joints. It was on Stovall Plantation, as well, that Alan Lomax, under the auspices of the Library of Congress, caught up with Muddy in 1941 and made his historic recordings. Read the MBT marker describing the sharecropper's cabin where Muddy was born. If you visit the Delta Blues Museum in Clarksdale, you'll see Muddy's restored childhood home itself, which once stood right here on Stovall Plantation. Find the plaque, which contains a quote from Eric Clapton that says it all: "Muddy Waters' music changed my life, and whether you know it or not, and like it or not, it probably changed yours, too." What are the hours? The farm is always open, of course. Free, as well.

B.B. King Museum and Delta Interpretive Center
400 2nd St.
Indianola, MS 38751

In this handsomely appointed and smartly curated museum, you'll wend movingly through B.B. King's storied life. In an early room, study the huge image of Beale Street printed onto the wall. This strip has changed a lot since this picture was taken, but you can still visit the **King's Palace Cafe**.

We start at the beginning. (Actually, if you wish you can go back even further than the beginning, as the museum traces the African roots of blues and gospel. Using headphones, you can listen to recordings which demonstrate key concepts of African music, like polyrhythms and syncopation.)

After King's mother's death in 1935, his father moved him out to the edge of the Delta. However, in 1938 he hopped on his bicycle and rode back to Indianola—back to the heart of the Delta. He had people there, and he could find work in the cotton fields. Saturday night on Church Street—another one of those streets that ring out in blues lore—was the stuff of legend. As a youngster, Riley King (the future "B.B.") would sit on the curb and play for passersby. He'd sneak peaks through the door of the Jones Night Spot and glimpse the likes of Count Basie and Louis Jordan in full flight. The club's owner, John Jones, also opened the historic Club Ebony, just a block or two off Church. You'll see an exhibit displaying signage and a bar stool from the Ebony's heyday. Actually, the place still exits. To visit, see our guide to Indianola above.

A funny story we learned at the museum: B.B. arrived in Memphis in 1948 virtually penniless, hoping to work at Black-operated WDIA with Nat D. Williams (legendary disc jockey, teacher, and host of the famous Amateur Night at Beale Street's Palace Theater). Arriving at the station, B.B. eavesdropped as the boss informed Williams that his show had a new sponsor: a "tonic" called Pep-Ti-Kon. Glancing B.B.'s way, the boss said, say, can you write us a jingle? Indeed, said B.B., and right on the spot he came up with a tune extolling this miracle product's wonders. You're hired!, cried the overjoyed boss. A video installation shows B.B. being interviewed late in life, when he was still happy to sing the Pep-Ti-Kon jingle that got him his first big break. It's catchy. (*Wonder what was actually in that stuff?*)

Moving through King's developing life from his origins onward gave us a new appreciation of what it meant for him to make it on Beale Street. From there, of course, he went on to transcend all narrow demographic categories to become an international ambassador of the blues and one of the greatest musicians America ever produced. To finish your visit, stroll out onto the museum grounds and pay your respects at the great man's final resting place.

Cost and hours: T-Sa 10a-5p, closed Su-M; Members free, Adults 18+ $15, Over 60 Years $12, Students (with valid ID) $10, Children (5-17) $10, Children under 5 free;

Tel. (662) 887-9539;

https://bbkingmuseum.org

Highway 61 Museum
307 N Broad St.
Leland, MS 38756

Johnny Winter sang about the "Leland Mississippi Blues," and the Highway 61 Blues Museum is the place to learn about it. It restricts its focus to musicians who hail from in and around Leland, such as the legendary Jimmy Reed. The museum's walls are lined with striking photographs capturing the area's culture, such as a baptism at Moon Lake in 1995. Just as memorable are the portraits of area performers, many of whom went on to be key players in Chicago blues, like Little Milton, Sunnyland Slim, harmonica master Sonny Boy Williamson II (Rice Miller), and Howlin' Wolf (whose crack Chess band in Chicago was led by Greenville saxophonist Eddie Shaw). Some of these went on to international fame: Wolf toured Europe, where he became a hero to Eric Clapton and the Rolling Stones. Look for the terrific photo of Sonny Boy Nelson, one of the foremost proponents of early Delta Blues in the '30s, from late in his life (1993), depicting him with his third wife Lois Nelson, who's playing a guitar. Find the one-stringed diddley bow, the improvised instrument on which many Delta musicians got their start.

Local bluesman James "Son" Thomas also practiced as a sculptor, and the Highway 61 Museum boasts several of his clay sculptures. You'll also see works by his son, Pat Thomas, who carries on his father's legacy of practicing as both a musician and a sculptor—clay skulls, animals and "gypsy men." (As a card notes, Pat reckons these possess supernatural power.)

Don't miss the sculpture assemblage by Jay Kirgis. Look closely—the wax figure inside represents an African griot (history storyteller), which symbolically represents Robert Johnson. Painted panels tell the mythological tale of the crossroads. You'll also learn more about Nelson Street, the onetime entertainment center and "cultural center of the African-American community" in nearby Greenville. Be moved once again by the story of pianist Boogaloo Ames, a fixture on Nelson Street in its heyday, and Eden Brent, the prodigiously talented young white woman he tutored. There's even an exhibit for Jimmie Rodgers, the father of country music. "America's blue yodeler" recorded a song called "MS Delta Blues," and was an avowed influence on B.B. King, Little Milton, and Howlin' Wolf.

Cost and hours: 10a-5p M-Sa, or by special appointment; we believe the admission is $7;
Tel. (662) 686-2063 or (662) 686-2004;

http://www.highway61blues.com/highway_61_blues_museum.htm

An Exhibit of Jim Henson's Delta Boyhood/Birthplace of Kermit the Frog
415 SE Deer Creek Dr.
Leland, MS 38756

We haven't been here yet, but we're going to make sure we visit next time we're in town. The exhibit is located on the Bank of Deer Creek, the birthplace of Kermit the Frog. "Where we celebrate the spirit, the genius, and the legacy of Jim Henson," proclaims their website. "We provide a place where both old and new fans can join in the celebration of Jim Henson's creativity. The exhibit includes educational displays, videos, memorabilia, a welcoming staff, and a gift shop."

Cost and hours: No admission fee, donations appreciated; Contact the venue for tours and hours.
Tel. (662) 686-7383;

https://www.birthplaceofthefrog.com

Sunflower County Freedom Project
120 Delta Ave, PO Box 701
Sunflower, MS 38778

This is perhaps a project to know about rather than a site to visit. The Delta Review writes: "Sunflower, which was an historic battleground in the Civil Rights Movement (the legendary Fannie Lou Hamer was from nearby Ruleville), is home to a Student Non-violent Coordinating Committee offshoot called the Sunflower County Freedom Project, which has taken over the row of historic buildings along the railroad downtown."

It's a mentorship program for at-risk young people that works on shaping them into "leaders in the Mississippi Delta" in the tradition of Hamer, "the spiritual leader of the freedom struggle in Mississippi." We encourage our readers to check out the work of this important project. Their website is: http://www.sunflowerfreedom.org.

Emmett Till Interpretive Center
120 N Court St.
Sumner, MS 38957

The former Tallahatchie County courthouse where Emmett Till's killers were tried for murder (and acquitted—"not guilty," though guilty) has been turned into this interpretive center. It is a "permanent memorial to Emmett Till and an educational site about the fight for civil right in Mississippi." As the Civil Rights Trail website puts it, visiting the Center offers "a unique opportunity for reflection on one of the most notorious and violent incidents of the Civil Rights Movement…The center prides itself on its approach of using storytelling and art to foster an environment of healing and reflection."

Cost and hours: 10a-5:30p M-F; guests are encouraged to use the "book now" feature on the website to request a time and date for your visit. It's unclear whether there is an admission fee: perhaps a donation;

Tel. (662) 483-1231;

https://www.emmett-till.org

Grammy Museum in Cleveland
800 W Sunflower Rd.
Cleveland, MS 38732

This is a subject for further research for us; we list it here just so you're aware it's there. The Grammy Museum apparently offers such salutary programs for youth as a weeklong summer day camp whose end goal is the campers creating a recorded production. The kids learn about various aspects of creative endeavor, from the technical details of recording to education about performing. For inspiration, they study works by Mississippi artists featured in the Museum, and teach the kids about the "influence of Mississippians on American music and our cultural heritage." What's more, campers "will receive instruction on recording techniques, music production, and live performance techniques. Aspiring songwriters will sharpen the skills of their craft while exploring song structure, harmony, melody, lyric writing and, where applicable, vocal technique." This all sounds great, and we salute the endeavor.

Cost and hours: T – Sa 10a–5p, Su 12p–3p, Closed M); Adults: $14.00, college students: $8.00 (18 years and older, valid ID required), seniors: $12.00 (65 Years and Older), youth: $8.00 (Under 18 Years), military: $12.00 (valid ID required); groups: $12.00 per person (10 or more persons), student groups: $6.00 per student (10 or more persons), children: free (Under 5 Years), members: free;

Tel. (662) 441-0100;

https://www.grammymuseumms.org

RESTAURANTS

Kathryn's on Moon Lake
5770 Moon Lake Rd.
Lula, MS 38644

You'll find Kathryn's on your way from Memphis to Clarksdale. The timing's just never been right for us to get here, but it looks nice. Put it on your itinerary and maybe we'll see you there.

Cost and hours: $$, F– Su 5p–10p; $$;
Tel. (662) 337-0022;
https://www.kathrynsonmoonlake.com

Country Platter Restaurant
700 Ruby St.
Cleveland, MS 38732

This delightful soul buffet is where Scott tried his first smothered pork steak and had his first taste of blackberry cobbler. Both were as scrumptious as they'd been in his dreams. Karolyn had fried chicken (*of course*), sweet potatoes, beans, and rice and gravy.

This room has a rich history. As Amy Evans writes, "Before it was the Country Platter, the building was home to Lily Robinson. It was also home to Lily's Cafe. Robinson lived in the back of her house and served meals in the front. In the 1960s Lily's Cafe literally fed Mississippi's Civil Rights Movement. SNCC (Student Nonviolent Coordinating Committee) members nourished their bodies and their souls in between registering black Mississippians to vote. Martin Luther King Jr held secret meetings after hours, making history and eating well. For many, Lily Robinson is right up there with Delta civil rights icons Amzie Moore and Fannie Lou Hamer as a soldier of the movement in Cleveland." Nuff said.

Cost and hours: Su–F 7a–6p, Sa 7a–7p; $;
Tel. (662) 846-7051;
https://country-platter-restaurant.hub.biz/

[Distressingly, as we were going to press, we received word that the Country Platter may be permanently closed. Call before you go.]

The Senator's Place
1028 S. Davis Ave.
Cleveland, MS 38732

A classic soul-food place which Scott and Karolyn have yet to visit. When Anthony Bourdain was there, here's what he ate: classic Southern soul-food buffet of collard greens, fried okra, mac 'n' cheese, lima beans, red beans, neck bones, rice and gravy, and a piece of fried chicken. Sounds like good eating to us. The joint is owned by Willie Simmons, a longtime state senator.

Cost and hours: T–F 11a–2p, Su 11a–5p, Closed M and Sa); $
Tel. (662) 846-7434;
https://www.facebook.com/thesenatorsplace/

[Just as distressingly as above, as we were going to press we discovered that another classic, the Senator's Place, may now be permanently closed. Call before you go to confirm].

Delta Meat Market
15 Cotton Row
Cleveland, MS 38732

As seen on *Somebody Feed Phil*, the Delta Meat Market is described by Phil as a spot where owner Cole Ellis puts "his modern twist on southern cuisine."

Cost and hours: T–Sa 10a-6pm, Lunch: T–F 10:30a–2p, Dinner: W–Sa 5:30p-9p, Brunch: Sa 9:30a-3p; $$,
Tel. (662) 444-6328;
https://www.deltameatmarket.com

White Front Cafe
902 Main St. Route 1
Rosedale, MS 38769

White Front Cafe is also known as Joe's Hot Tamale Place, after original proprietor Joe Pope, "the king of Delta tamale makers." As Robert Johnson sang in 1936, "They're red hot!" This cafe is still serving what are, in our humble opinion, the best tamales ever. Why? It has a bit to do with the real corn shucks, but it has even more to do with Mr. Pope's secret recipe, itself adapted from a recipe a friend of his picked up from a Mexican migrant in the '30s. Joe passed away in 2004; when we dropped by the cafe, we met his sister Barbara, still making tamales in this little white clapboard store. As Susan Puckett writes in *Eat Drink Delta*, after Joe died, "for seven years, Barbara Pope helped her ailing older brother fill and roll tamales. Not until the week before his death did he share the recipe with her and their sisters."

Ms. Pope was so sweet to us. When Karolyn got a spot on her shirt, she even helped her clean it.

The White Front Cafe is also the site of the first *culinary* marker on the Mississippi Blues Trail: the "Hot Tamales and the Blues" marker. While you're here, you must take a few moments to study it. It explains the fascinating story of hot tamales in the Delta.

It reads, in part, "Made of corn meal and meat, the tamale was a staple in the diet of Mexican migrant laborers in the Delta and became a popular item of local culture." As Scott Barretta writes of hot tamales in a corroborating passage elsewhere, this "Delta delicacy is thought to have originated with Mexican laborers who were brought to the Delta during harvest season, initially during WWI." Back to the marker: "Another wave of Mexican migration to the Delta came with the onset of WWII, when the federal government started the Bracero Program to regulate and address labor shortages resulting from many local workers' being drafted or moving north for wartime industry jobs."

The story can't help but cause one to reflect that what truly makes America great is *precisely* immigrants—our mix of cultures. The story of the humble hot tamale, as you'll read, begins with Mexican migrant laborers and includes Native Americans; Lebanese; Chinese; Italians; and African-Americans.

Tamales were a workers' food: as the marker goes on to say, a "major appeal of tamales to laborers was that they would stay warm during the day because they were wrapped in cornhusks and bundled tightly. They were sold at street vendors, stands, groceries, restaurants, and blues clubs including Ruby's Nite Spot in Leland."

Tamales were quickly embraced by African-Americans (the foremost keepers of the tradition today) and Italian-Americans, who added their own recipes and family traditions. As the marker notes, "Whereas tamales in Mexico are usually steamed, tamales in the Delta are often simmered and served with the cooking water, with countless variations."

While it's on the subject of Mexican migrant laborers in the Delta, the marker takes the opportunity to explore the intersection of Latin music and the blues. Early Texas bluesmen probably saw parallels between themselves and the Mexican street singer, the toreador or guitarrero. Look for the bit about accordionist Valerio Longoria, the "son of migrant farm workers" who "was born in Clarksdale in 1924, and later became a major innovator in conjunto music in south Texas." The picture near the upper right corner of the marker shows a Mexican boy playing guitar on the steps of a railway station. Mexican families lived on plantations during the cotton picking season in the years (beginning in the '20s) when African-American farmers moved away with the Great Migration.

The marker runs down the Latin beats found in many popular songs to which we've long been accustomed to tapping our toes: the habanera in "St. Louis Blues" (W.C. Handy had been to Cuba with a minstrel troupe in 1900, where he picked up the beat; he also owned a Mexican guitar), the Afro-Cuban clave in Bo Diddley's music, and the rumba and mambo in songs by

Fats Domino, Professor Longhair, Ray Charles, Louis Jordan, B. B. King, Muddy Waters, and Jimmy Reed.

Cost and hours: T – Sa 11a–6p, Su-M 10a-2p; $;
Tel. (662) 759-3842;
https://www.southernfoodways.org/interview/joes-hot-tamale-place-a-k-a-the-white-front-cafe/

Airport Grocery
3608 US-61
Cleveland, MS 38732

On Highway 61 you'll find the Airport Grocery, which Susan Puckett aptly describes as "a rambling structure built of unpainted wood from a nineteenth-century house and decorated with antiques and old signage inside and out. Its roots go back to the Depression." On your way in, notice the "Hot Tamales" sign. Airport Grocery proudly uses Joe Pope's recipe, and his technique, for their own tamales. Pope, as you'll recall, was the great man behind the White Front Cafe in Rosedale. (It turns out Airport Grocery owner Jonathan Vance's grandfather was friends with Pope, and Pope thought enough of him to share his top tamale secrets with the Vances.) Aside from the tamales, Scott recommends you try the catfish hoagie.

It should be noted that the current location of the Grocery is not the original one out on Highway 8, where the late harmonica legend Willie Foster recorded his 1999 album, appropriately titled *Live at Airport Grocery*. Rather, this Grocery is in the building that once housed Vance's other restaurant, the Shanty. Susan Puckett writes, again aptly, that the "atmosphere at the latest incarnation of Airport Grocery conjures a Deltafied version of T.G.I. Fridays." Still, look closely and you'll find cool artwork like Wild Bill's "My Blues Legacy."

Cost and hours: M-Sa 11a-10p, Su 5-9p, Happy Hour 5p-7p; $$;
Tel. (662) 843-4817;
https://www.airportgrocerycleveland.com

Lillo's Italian restaurant
Hwy. 82 East
Leland, MS 38756

Lillo's has been operating since 1948. The great tradition here is "Delta Dancing," which in the halcyon days was accompanied by live music pre-formed by the the late pianist Boogaloo Ames and his young mentee, Eden Brent. Apparently, this tradition lives on: their site boasts "Entertainment every Thursday, and on the 2nd and 4th Sunday nights."

Cost and hours: W-Th 4:30p-9:45p, F 4p-9:45p, Sa-Su 4:30-9:45p, Closed M-T); $;
Tel. (662) 686-4401;
https://www.facebook.com/Lillos-Family-Restaurant-410143365342/

Blue & White
355 US-61
Tunica, MS 38676

Established in 1924, the Blue & White is the home of the "Big Blue" break-fast, which of course Scott had to order when we were there: waffle, donut, hash-browns, ham, and eggs your way. We were a bit distracted during our visit: we'd suffered a crack in our windshield on the way, and Karolyn had to spend most of breakfast on the phone lining up an appointment for a local repair. Still, we tasted enough of their cooking to be able to vouch for what it says on the website: "In the kitchen you will find a grandmother cooking side by side with her daughter-in-law and two of her grandchildren as she passes down a seventy-year-old tradition of true Southern style cooking. Serving great food along with true Southern hospitality was and still is the driving force behind everything we do at the Blue and White."

Cost and hours: Everyday 11a-10p; $;
Tel. (662) 363-1371;
https://blueandwhiterestaurant.com

Highland Club
462 Highland Rd.
Chatham, MS 38731

The Highland Club was seen on *Somebody Feed Phil*. As the program's website proclaims, Phil and friends feasted on "fried catfish, hush puppies, rotisserie chicken, and even some alligator!"

Hours unavailable at press time. Try calling (662) 839-6223.

Lusco's
722 Carrollton Ave.
Greenwood, MS 38930

As their website boasts, Lusco's Restaurant has been serving up "wonderful" steaks, poultry and authentic seafood dishes in Greenwood for 80 years now. We look forward to the day when we can be the judge of that with a personal visit. When Anthony Bourdain was here, here's what he ate: the special salad with Italian vinaigrette, steak, shrimp, onion rings, and the "world famous" whole pompano.

Cost and hours: Open F and Sa nights only. Dinner service begins at 5:30p. No reservations taken after 8:30p; other times see telephone number below. $$;
Tel. (66) 219-0085;

http://www.luscos.net

Giardina's
314 Howard St.
Greenwood, MS 38930

Located in the posh Alluvian Hotel, Giardina's is a Delta institution, founded in 1936. Aside from a dining room opening onto a courtyard, Giardina's also preserves the Delta tradition of private booth dining.

Cost and hours: M-Sa 5p-10p, Closed Su; $$
Tel. (662) 455-4227
http://www.thealluvian.com/giardinas

The Crystal Grill
423 Carrollton Ave.
Greenwood, MS 38930

Writer Aliyah Veal reports enjoying the burgers and fries at the Crystal Grille. It's also known for its dessert, she notes: good cheesecake, and they sell lemon meringue pies with filling "a mile high."

Cost and hours: Su, Th 11a-9p, M-W Closed, F-Sa 11a-9p; $;
Tel. (662) 453-6530
https://www.crystalgrillms.com

Drake's BBQ
1906 Leflore Ave.
Greenwood, MS 38930

When reporter Aliyah Veal asked about good places to eat in Greenwood, a local told her, "We have a couple barbecue places, but Drake's is my favorite. It's kind of a small place, but really good." That's good enough for us.

Cost and hours: M–Sa 11a–7p, Su 12p–5p; $;
Tel. (662) 374-5202
https://www.facebook.com/DrakesBBQ/

The Crown
112 Front St.
Indianola, MS 38751

We stopped at this homespun restaurant when we were in Indianola to see the B.B. King Museum and Delta Interpretive Center. We tried the Catfish Allison, a poached catfish fillet gratineed with Parmesan cheese, butter, and green onion sauce. It had a yummy nutty, buttery flavor. The Crown describe itself as a "Delta tradition that generations of Mississippians and their guests have enjoyed," having opened in 1976 "in the cotton field north of Indianola, dripping Southern hospitality." The round loaves of hot-from-the-oven bread are a nice touch.

Cost and hours: T-Sa 9a-4p, Closed Su-M; $$;
Tel. (662) 887-4522
https://www.facebook.com/The-Crown-110879078973817/

Blues Corner Cafe
226 Church St.
Indianola, MS 38751

The Blues Corner Cafe is also known as the Cozy Corner Cafe. Look for it when you're in Indianola.

Cost and Hours: M 12a-1a; F 11a-11:59p, S-SU 12a-1:00a and 11a-11:59p, T-Th-Closed, $;
Tel. (662) 887-6400;
https://www,facebook.com/Blues-Corner-Cafe-1800842533482401/

The Blue Biscuit
501-503 Second Street (Corner Pershing & Second Streets)
501 2nd St.
Indianola, MS 38751

The Blue Biscuit is located right across from the B.B. King Museum. The "biscuits and barbecue" dish sounds amazing: pulled pork placed between the halves of four buttermilk biscuits. Yes, please!

Cost and hours: M 11a-2p, F-Sa 11a-2p and 5p-11p, Su 5p-10p, Closed T-Th; $;
Tel. (662) 645-0258
https://www.facebook.com/The-Blue-Biscuit-32123963542/

Chillie's Package Store
2002 Highway 82 E.
Greenville, MS 38703

The shop to get your wine to enjoy with your Doe's Eat Place steak. See next entry!

Cost and hours: M–Sa 10a–10p, Closed Su;
Tel. (662)335-1941
https://www.chilliespackage.com

Doe's Eat Place
502 Nelson St.
Greenville, MS 38701

Doe's may look ramshackle; in fact, it's the only place we've ever eaten where a fella with a sidearm and handcuffs watches over your car while you dine. (For an explanation of why this should be, see our description of Nelson Street, above). However, Doe's has the awards to prove it's considered one of the very best steakhouses in America. It's worth the risk—which really isn't that serious, anyway.

A bit of background: in *The Blues Highway*, Richard Knight writes, "Doe Sr. started the business in 1941 after the 1927 flood had destroyed his grocery on the same site. He was a white man but ran a honky-tonk for blacks in the front of the building and a restaurant for whites out back." Knight goes on, "[Doe's] steaks and hot tamales quickly became famous so Doe closed the honky-tonk and focused on the restaurant. Despite its humble appearance, Doe's has a huge following of discerning steak fans."

As you enter, you pass the giant stoves where the magic happens. You are then ushered into the kitchen to your table, almost as if you're in someone's home. (Doe's brings new meaning to the term "open kitchen.") We would counsel you to start with the tamale trio and chili, as well as Aunt Florence's famous iceberg lettuce and tomato salad. (Word of warning: the latter comes swimming in lemon vinaigrette dressing, which Scott found glorious; it was decidedly not Karolyn's bag. Still, we wouldn't advise asking for the dressing "on the side" as you would at a more conventional restaurant: the essence of this salad is the heavy dressing.) You also must get an order of fries, which are cooked in steak drippings for added deliciousness. The jumbo broiled shrimp are another must: glorious.

Presumably, you've picked up some bottles of wine from Chillie's (see prior entry) on your way to Doe's. Enjoy a Saltine cracker and a sip of wine in between bites of tamale, as you anticipate your steak. While you enjoy the splendor and true Delta ambience of the Doe's dining room, you might reflect, Hey, it was good enough for President Bill Clinton!

The true star at Doe's, though, is the porterhouse. Since they've been cooking steaks since 1941, let's just say they know what they're doing at this point. "Baby" Doe himself cooked our steak.

There's a spirit at Doe's that seems rather to have been lost in our polarized times.

In *Eat Drink Delta* Susan Puckett writes of one Clarke Reed that he was "credited with masterminding the modern Mississippi Republican Party after a century of one-party Democratic rule...Just as legendary is his love of food and drink—and his enthusiasm for hobnobbing regularly with politicians and reporters of every stripe, usually at Doe's Eat Place. Hodding Carter III, a liberal Democrat who was then editor of Greenville's Delta Democrat-Times, was one of his best drinking buddies."

Anthony Bourdain famously ate here. What did he eat? Precisely the meal we've outlined above: the classic Delta dinner comprised of Doe's famous salad, hot tamales, fries, shrimp, porterhouse steaks, and no dessert. Bourdain wasn't a dessert guy, but even if you are we'd bet you don't have room.

Nearby on Nelson Street is historic St. Matthew's, the first African Methodist Episcopal church in the Delta. It's close enough that you can stroll over safely and have a look at it without straying too far down Nelson.

Cost and hours: M-Sa 5p-9p, Closed Su; $$;
Tel. (662) 334-3315
https://www.doeseatplace.com

Sherman's Restaurant
1400 S Main St.
Greenville, MS 38701

This venerable Greenville restaurant had fallen on hard times when it was featured on Gordon Ramsay's *24 Hours to Hell and Back* in an episode which aired in July of 2018 (and was filmed in November 2017). When we visited, the place was back on its feet and serving solid dinners. Karolyn had some blackened seafood that was fine. Scott had spaghetti and meat balls which hit the spot, a side of finger-tempting fried dill pickles, and some good tamales.

Cost and hours: T-Th 11a-1:30p and 5p-8:30p, F 11a-1:30p and 5p-9p, Sa 5p-9p Closed Su-M; $$;
Tel. (662) 332-7297
https://www.shermans.restaurant

While we're on the subject of Greenville and tamales, we should mention that Greenville is officially known as "the Hot Tamale Capital of the World." Here are some other spots in Greenville to know about when you're looking for tamales and good Mississippi cooking: **Jack's Hot Tamales** (1112 E Alexander St, Greenville, MS 38703); **Hot Tamales Heaven** (1427 MS-1, Greenville, MS 38701); and **Delta Lunchbox** (1298 Hwy 1 N Greenville, MS 38703).

Walnut Hills
1214 Adams St.
Vicksburg, MS 39180

Walnut Hills is a classic restaurant in Vicksburg, at the "southern tip" of the Mississippi Delta.

Cost and hours: M, W-Sa: 11a–9p, Su 11a–2p, closed T; $$;

Tel. (601) 638-4910

https://walnuthillsms.com

MUSIC, BARS, AND THE REST

You'll notice that some of the places listed below may be closed, and others may be simply legends. We list them here because sometimes jukes close and then reopen, and in other cases for pure historical interest.

The Walnut Street Blues Bar
128 S. Walnut St.
Greenville, MS 38701

The Walnut Street Blues Bar is still tending the flame. When you're down by the levee, drop in.

Cost and hours: T–F 5p–2a, Sa 6p-2a, Su 12p–3p, Closed M-Su); $;

Tel. (662) 378-2254;

https://www.facebook.com/WalnutStreetBluesBar

Spectator's Pub and Eatery
139 S Walnut St.
Greenville, MS 38701

Spectator's is across the street from the Walnut Street Blues Bar. We had a drink here once, and we met some nice local characters.

Cost and hours:T–F 5p–2a, Sa 6p-2a, Su 12p–3p, Closed M-Su); $;
Tel. (662) 335-3334
https://www.facebook.com/spectators.greenville/

Do Drop Inn
1110 South Lake St.
Shelby, MS 38774

The Do Drop is one of the legendary jukes—a shotgun shack, we understand—though it's unclear whether they still feature music on weekends, or even if they still exist. (Their Facebook page hasn't been updated since 2016). A lot of the old spots, like **Boss Hall's** in Leland and the **Subway Lounge** in Jackson, just aren't there anymore. It's worth checking into, though. (Shelby is only about 22 miles south on Highway 61 from Clarksdale.) Let us know what you discover.

Cost and hours: F– Sa 5p–3a, Closed Su-Th;
Tel. (662) 902-7542;
https://www.facebook.com/Do-Drop-Inn-278203332535041/

Windy City Blues Cafe
Shelby, Mississippi 38774

The only information we have about the Windy City Blues Cafe is that it was once across the street from the Do Drop Inn *(see above)*. It was another institution in Mississippi's historic juke circuit. Again, it's not clear whether they're extant. If you're in Shelby, why not go over and check it out.

Club Black Castle
118 Front St.
Ruleville, MS 38771

In Ruleville (just east of Cleveland) the great blues street was Front Street—which had the memorable sobriquet "Greasy Street." The Black Castle was one of the legendary Greasy Street jukes, but we believe it's doing hip-hop shows now. Next door was the **Main Event** club, another venerable juke. Whether these clubs are still in operation, or still blues club, is tough to determine. If you're interested, try checking with Roger Stolle or driving by.

Cost and hours: Everyday 8p-2a; $;
https://www.facebook.com/CLUB-BLACK-CASTLE-111860158844751

Mitchells Lounge
401 W. Johnson St.
Greenwood, MS 38930

There was a juke here as recently as 25 years ago. (Their name's never listed with an apostrophe; we're just reproducing the original mistake here. English teacher Karolyn wanted you to know!) If you're in Greenwood, drive by and at least see the site where it once stood.

People's Choice Lounge

We're not even sure what Mississippi town the People's Choice is meant to be in. It's one of those names you hear bandied about. We list it here on the off chance we'll find it one day, or perhaps one of our readers will.

TOURS AND FESTIVALS

Sylvester Hoover's Delta Blues Legend tours
214 Young St.
Greenwood, MS 38930

"Hi, my name is Sylvester Hoover," proclaims the website for Delta Blues Legends tours. "Join me for an unforgettable journey through the history of the Blues. I designed the tour to give visitors to the Mississippi Delta an intimate Blues experience like none other in the world. You can walk the same path as Robert Johnson and other blues greats, visit historical sites that tell the story of the Blues, and most importantly, the people who played the Blues and the people who lived it. Look around on my site to get an idea of what the Delta Blues Legend Tours is all about. Thanks for visiting and hope you can join me real soon in the Delta!" We've long considered taking this tour; we've heard good things. A future edition of this book may include our experience with it. Or, poke around the site yourself. If you take the tour, let us know what you think!

Cost and hours: M–Sa 2p to 6p; $75 per adult, children < 5 yrs. free; Tel. (662) 392-5370

https://hoovertours.homestead.com/home.html

HOTELS

Belmont Plantation
3498 Highway 1 South
Greenville, MS 38701

Just outside of Greenville, the Belmont Plantation—the "last antebellum mansion along the river"—makes an evocative and atmospheric home base for Delta exploration. Dr. William M. Worthington built the house between 1855 and 1861. As the Belmont's site relates, the stately manor is "a blend of the prevailing Greek Revival and Italianate styles of the day." In order to become the fine B&B it is today, the Belmont Plantation survived both the Civil War and the 1927 flood, when the levee broke and the house took on nine feet of water on its first floor. Starting in the '40s it was a hunting lodge for 50 years, and you can still see the vestiges of that era in the mounted deer heads. Joshua Cain, a builder and preservationist who fell in love with the place in 2015, is responsible for the consummate restoration you see before you today. Explore the beautiful formal rooms, including a music room and a library, with their soaring fourteen-foot ceilings. We stayed on the second level, and the ceilings are just as high up there. We enjoyed having a read out on the screened back porch.

As the plantation's website notes, "Inside, Belmont features some of the finest decorative plaster work in Mississippi. Local lore holds that German plaster artists were stranded in Washington County when the Civil War started; having no means of escape and no other work, they whiled away the war years by carving intricate molding and ceiling medallions into Belmont's plaster...Another version of the story behind the Belmont's decorative plaster work relates that Dr. Worthington met a group of Italian carvers on a boat trip to New Orleans and convinced them to return with him to Belmont. Regardless of its origins, the decorative work in Belmont rivals the finest interiors of Natchez or Columbus."

The innkeeper/hostess is a kind, jovial lady. She related to us how the property's roaming cat came to be known as "Dollar General"—because they found him down at the Dollar General, of course. When we broached the subject of our being bitten by mosquitoes, she at first feigned being scandalized: why, we don't have skeeters! She then produced some small boxes for which she offered the following explanation which became something of a catchphrase with us: "There are three things I believe in: Jesus Christ our lord and savior, the Belmont Plantation, and these here natural skeeter traps." (While these are somewhat effective, we'd advise a backup bug spray of your own.)

[Editor's note: As we went to press, we learned that (1) the Belmont is under new management; and (2) it has attracted controversy for tastelessly listing a slave cabin as a luxury bed-and-breakfast on Airbnb. When we stayed at the Belmont in 2018, we were aware of said cabin, having observed it as we strolled the grounds, but we were under the impression that it had been a sharecropper's shack. It did not appear to be occupied. For what it's worth, Airbnb removed the listing, and the new owner has apologized, saying it was the former owners who marketed the cabin as slave quarters. According to CNN, he vows that "he is working to find experts who can help him identify people who have lived and were enslaved on the Belmont Plantation to provide an accurate account of history."

The issue of turning plantations into charming hotels will continue to be a fraught one, and we will ultimately defer to feedback from our African-American readers to determine if we continue to list them. It is our hope that if approached mindfully, a stay at a plantation can be an immersion in the history and culture of the South, an exercise of conscious memory, but that means acknowledging both the beauty and the horror of these properties. What seems clear is that thoughtful people will continue to wrestle with these contradictions.]

Tel. (901) 652-1390
website: http://www.belmontplantation1857.com/home.html

Alluvian Hotel
318 Howard St.
Greenwood, MS 38930

Throughout the Delta, a night or two at the plush Alluvian Hotel in Greenwood is renowned as a luxurious treat. Giardina's restaurant is here, as well. *(See our entry above.)*

Tel. (662) 453-2114, 866-600-5201 toll free;
e-mail: thealluvianhotel@thealluvian.com;
https://www.thealluvian.com

KAROLYN'S TIP JAR

- Before you explore the Delta, bone up on your history of names like Robert Johnson, Emmett Till and Medgar Evers. See the Appendix.

- When it comes to cemetery exploring, be sure to wear sturdy shoes. Do not wear open-toed shoes because you might wade through ankle-deep grass. Watch out for snakes!

- Bring a gift for your bluesman whose grave you are visiting. He might like a beer, some whiskey, or some smokes.

- A few tips on food. When you're in the Delta, if you're not a breakfast person, consider skipping that meal. You'll save room for the day's feast! If you are, then consider skipping lunch—the breakfasts pack a punch. *(Scott, we must note, looks askance at skipping any meal.)* Pack granola bars.

- Also, bring floppy hats, big hats, baseball hats, visors, anything to prevent sunburn. I am an extremely fair person. The sun kills me every time if I do not have my hat. Hats, hats, hats. Especially in the summer—you can get away without a hat until, say, mid-April, but mid-April through September, bring a hat.

- Another thing: when you're eating in the Delta, do keep in mind the theme of cultural diversity we've been trying to hammer again and again. Remember the words from the Mississippi Blues Trail marker in Rosedale, the one about hot tamales. Even the humble tamale was a product of the interweaving culinary traditions, cultures, and foodways of Mexican migrant laborers, indigenous American Indians, Anglo- and African-Americans, and immigrants of Lebanese, Chinese and Italian origin.

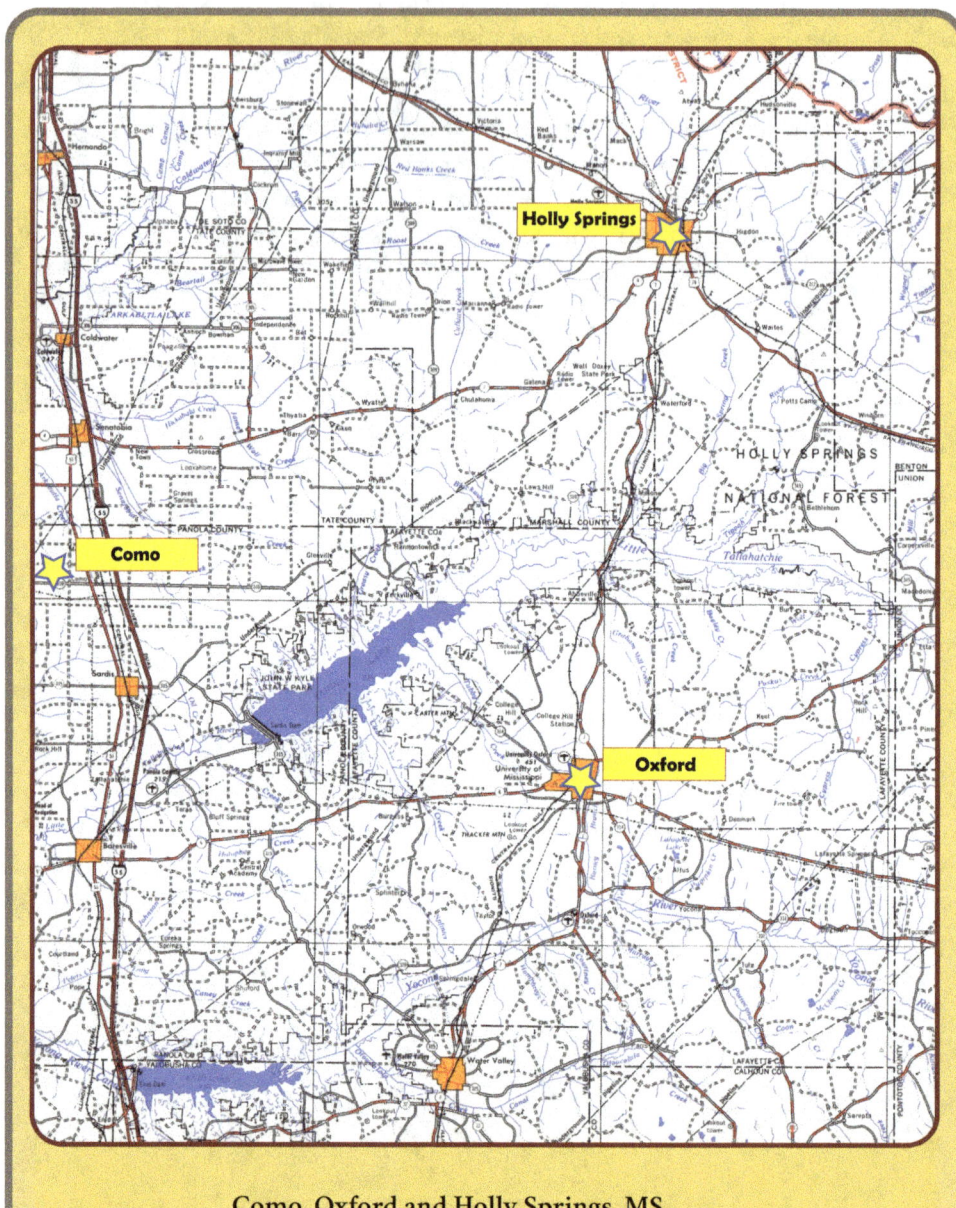

Como, Oxford and Holly Springs, MS.

USGS 1:250,000. Tupelo, MS. 1984.

CHAPTER VI

Mississippi Beyond the Delta

(North Mississippi Hill Country, East Mississippi, and Jackson Area)

It's at this point that we should say, since we haven't said it before, that we find an old-fashioned sat-nav, or GPS, absolutely essential for our travels in Mississippi. The one we use is the Garmin brand. You pop it right onto your windshield and it directs you right where you need to go. It's brilliant. You can use your phone as well, of course, but we actually prefer the sat-nav—it seems to be more accurate than the phone, as well. If you've got one, you won't need our directions below for following our suggested itinerary. Just enter the address we've provided and the sat-nav will do the rest. Still, just in case you need some extra guidance, we've provided occasional steps on how to get from place to place.

For this chapter, we'll start with a general itinerary for how you might plan your journey through these three regions, all rich in blues lore and history: (1) the North Mississippi Hill Country, (2) East Mississippi, and (3) the Jackson Area. Then we'll break each region down by restaurants, sights/museums, music, tours/festivals, and Karolyn's tip jar. This itinerary assumes you are heading out from Memphis or Clarksdale.

PLANNING YOUR TIME: ITINERARY

Day One
Head out towards Oxford (North Mississippi Hill Country).

Pass through Holly Springs. Visit Aikei Pro's Record Shop.

Head out to Chulahoma to see the Chewalla Rib Shack, the log cabin that was once Junior Kimbrough's juke joint.

Pay a visit to Junior Kimbrough's grave in Hudsonville (481 Kimbrough Chapel Rd).

After paying your respects, drive on to R.L. Burnside's grave in Harmontown/Como (Co Rd 511, Como).

If you have extra time in the Senatobia/Como region, see Jessis Mae Hemphill's grave (3000 US-51) and Fred McDowell's grave (Hammond Hill M.B. Church, 3785 Hammond Hill Rd).

Head for Oxford, your home base.

Have dinner at Bouré.

Day Two
Morning
Get breakfast at Big Bad Breakfast

Tour Rowan Oak, William Faulkner's home.

Pay your respects at Faulkner's Grave at St. Peter's Cemetery.

With extra time, tour Burns Belfry Museum, an African-American history museum in Burns Methodist Episcopal Church.

Afternoon

Get lunch at McEwen's Oxford

Drive over to the University of Mississippi ("Ole Miss") campus to see the Civil Rights Monument/Freedom Trail Marker for James Meredith on University Circle. Look for the MBT marker for "Living Blues" magazine at the Center for the Study of Southern Culture.

Drive back to the city center. Knock about on Courthouse Square. Stop in at Square Books (classic local bookstore) at No. 160 and End of All Music Record Store at No. 103a. Look at the MBT marker on Courthouse Square dedicated to the Lafayette County "hill country" blues tradition.

Dinner

Happy hour and small plates at City Grocery.

Day Three
Morning

Leave Oxford, visiting Tupelo (East Mississippi) on your way to Jackson.

See Elvis' birthplace in Tupelo. At this site, also see the Assembly of God Church, explore the museum in the main building, and climb the overlook.

Afternoon

Have a picnic on the grounds of Elvis' birthplace.

Visit the Tupelo Hardware store in downtown Tupelo where Gladys bought Elvis his first guitar.

Drive on to to Bentonia.

Evening

Eat dinner at Bentonia Bugs

Head to the Blue Front Cafe for some live blues. (Or, depending on timing, go to the Blue Front before dining at Bugs.)

It's still a 40-minute drive to Jackson, your home base.

Day Four
Morning

Head to Farish Street, Jackson's historic blues street, to see the MBT market sites (Trumpet Records, Alamo Theatre, H.C. Speir's Speir Phonograph Company).

Take a spin across town to see the MBT markers for the King Edward Hotel and Ace Records.

Afternoon

Have lunch at the Big Apple Inn.

Visit the Mississippi Civil Rights Museum.

Evening

Have dinner at Saltine.

Day Five

On the way out of Jackson, stop at the MBT marker for the Subway Lounge.

Stop in Hazlehurst, Robert Johnson's birthplace. See the MBT for Johnson at the train station and visit the Mississippi Music Museum, located in the train station.

Visit the Robert Johnson monument in Hazlehurst town square, which includes a brick for H.C. Spier, Jackson record-store owner. (100 Caldwell Dr.)

That's about it for this itinerary, which assumes you'll be heading on from where it leaves off to New Orleans. If that's the case, consider stopping to eat at Mr. D's Old Country Store (8801 US-61, Lorman, MS). It's about an hour west of Hazlehurst, or about one-and-half hours southwest of Jackson. Then you've got about another three hours until NOLA.

NORTH MISSISSIPPI HILL COUNTRY

(OXFORD, HOLLY SPRINGS, COMO, ETC.)

The Mississippi Blues Trail is particularly rich through the towns of North Mississippi Hill Country.

In the Oxford/Holly Springs area, visit the stomping grounds and final resting places of R.L. Burnside and Junior Kimbrough, known to blues connoisseurs as two of the foremost exponents of the rich musical traditions of this region.

In fact, Kimbrough is considered the father of Holly Springs/North Mississippi Hill Country Blues, though he preferred to call his music "Cotton Patch Soul Blues." Charlie Feathers said of him, "Junior Kimbrough is the beginning and end of all music"; that quote is inscribed on Kimbrough's gravestone. To visit his resting place, make a pilgrimage to 481 Kimbrough Chapel Rd. in Hudsonville, right outside of Holly Springs. From Holly Springs you'll drive 10 miles north on Highway 7. When you see Bolden's Grocery, turn left on Clear Creek Road, then take another left onto Kimbrough Chapel Rd. The graveyard will be on your left.

Rediscovered late in life, R.L. Burnside recorded popular records for Fat Possum (as did Kimbrough) and became a favorite in Oxford/Ole Miss. His music is not for the fainthearted. Burnside's grave is behind the Free Springs CME Church in Harmontown, outside of Holly Springs. On the day we visited, there was a note attached to his heart-shaped gravestone wishing RIP "from a fan from Cuba." To get there, get back on Highway 7 and drive 10 miles west on Highway 310. When you see the sign for Free Springs United Methodist Church, turn south. However, you're going to pass that church and continue straight about a half mile until you find Free Springs CME Church.

It's also fun to pass by The Chewalla Rib Shack in Chulahoma, a nearly 100-year-old log cabin where Junior Kimbrough used to rock back in the heady days of the '80s and '90s. It's east of Holly Springs. Kimbrough hosted blues, ribs and moonshine nights at this makeshift juke joint every week before moving on to establish his own juke (which has since burned down). Blues lovers came from far and wide to get their blues 'n' barbecue on. The owner of the cabin, Mr. Sammy Grier, who painstakingly moved it log by log from its original site out in the woods, lived in the house next door. Probably still does.

To get there from R.L. Burnside's grave, head back on Highway 310 and Highway 4 to Holly Springs. Hang a right onto J M Ash Dr. to Highway 178, which you'll take to Higdon Road. Continue to 2644 Higdon. It's not open to the public, so you'll just be able to look at it from the road. It's the small, red-stained log cabin just past the big log, modern house.

If you pass through Senatobia, you may visit Jessie Mae Hemphill's grave. She was a pioneering guitarist and a drummer in the fascinating fife and drum tradition of the Como/Senatobia region. It's about 43 miles west of Holly Springs on Highway 4, at Senatobia Memorial Cemetery. In Como, you can visit the final resting place of master slide-guitarist Fred McDowell, the man who famously proclaimed "I do not play no rock 'n' roll." It's about a 10-minute drive from Jessie Mae Hamphill's grave. Get on Highway 51 headed south and take a right on Hugh Taylor Road, which becomes Tate-Panola Road. Stop at the intersection with Hammond Hill, where you'll see Hammond Hill M. B. Church and its small cemetery.

Then there is Oxford. For the literary, it is, of course, the land of William Faulkner. This book isn't really about literature, but Faulkner is as telling of the South as is blues and jazz, so we'll make an exception and talk about him.

In terms of MBT markers, there's one for "Living Blues" magazine at the Center for the Study of Southern Culture on the campus of the University of Mississippi (Ole Miss). On Courthouse Square in the center of Oxford, you'll find a Blues Trail Marker for Lafayette County and its "hill country" blues tradition. (Lafayette County, of course, is the inspiration for Faulkner's fictional Yoknapatawpha County.) The sign gives props to R.L. Burnside and other hill country artists, along with Oxford's Fat Possum records and blues scholars like William Ferris and Robert Palmer. It also tells the story of Oxford's biggest rhythm and blues band of the '60s, the Checkmates.

SITES AND MUSEUMS (NORTH MISSISSIPPI)

Rowan Oak Museum
916 Old Taylor Rd.
Oxford, MS 38655

Rowan Oak was William Faulkner's estate for more than 40 years. Curated by Bill Griffith, the antebellum house was Faulkner's home from 1930 until his death in 1962. The house itself was still closed for COVID when we visited in 2021, but the grounds were open. We would've loved to have seen the study where he famously wrote the outline for "A Fable" right onto the walls. Still: reason to go back. It's fun just to stroll the grounds: it doesn't get much more Southern Gothic. Faulkner renamed the house Rowan Oak after the Rowan Tree, a symbol of security and peace. Make your way on the walkway lined with eastern red cedars up to the stately Greek Revival house, built by General Sheegog in the 1840s. Stroll through what remains of the antebellum circle garden, originally a maze garden. (Faulkner believed the ghost of Colonel Sheegog's wife would haunt the house if he messed with her garden, so he never altered its condition.)

Note the servants' quarters, which Faulkner built on the foundations of an 1840s structure. This was the home of Caroline Barr ("Mammy Callie"), who died in 1940 at the age of 100. She was the Faulkner family nurse (what was called a "mammy" at the time) for generations and had cared for Faulkner since he was a baby. Her death hit him hard.

Karolyn also wants you to know about the friendly ghost of Mr. Faulkner who still inhabits the house. She called on Mr. Faulkner to move the drapes in an upper window to show us he was still there, and the drapes moved and then stopped. He was quite accommodating, because she asked him several times just to make sure, and he continuously moved them. (Don't ruin our fun and tell us it was an air conditioner.)

Cost and hours: we're advised the house is now once again open to the public. Hours are Tu–Sa 10a–4p and Su 1–4p (it's open until 6p in June and July). Closed M, except in June and July, when it's open from 10a-6p. The grounds are open from dawn to dusk. $5 (cash only) house admission for visitors 12 and over.
Tel: (662) 234-3284
http://www.themetimeradio.com/cat/themetime/season2/

William Faulkner's Grave
St. Peter's Cemetery
Oxford, MS 38655

Pay your respects to the breakthrough American novelist, William Faulkner. His grave can be found by going to the corner of Jefferson and N 16th St. and walking straight out into the cemetery. (You'll see a marker for him, as well, telling you that his grave is just 20 steps away.) The day we visited, someone had left a bottle of Writer's Tears whiskey: a brilliant gift. Hours and cost? Free and always open.

Square Books
160 Courthouse Square
Oxford, MS 38655

The classic local bookstore. Scott always says the two things a proper neighborhood has to have are a good record store and a good book store. Oxford's Courthouse Square has both: Square Books and End of All Music records (see below). As a framed handbill notes, on July 7, 1962, Square Books closed between 2:00 and 2:15pm in observance of the death of William Faulkner.

Hours: M-Sa 9a-8p, Su 9a-5p;
https://www.squarebooks.com

End of the World Records
103a Courthouse Square
Oxford, MS 38655

Terrific record store, and it is just that: it's all vinyl. Climb up the stairs. An image of R.L. Burnside on the door bids you come inside. The knowledgeable clerk can help you find whatever you need.

Hours: Su-M 1p-5p, T noon-6p, Th-Sa noon-7p;
https://theendofallmusic.com

Burns-Belfry Museum & Multicultural Center
710 Jackson Ave. E
Oxford, MS 38655

Burns-Belfry is an African-American history museum in the historic Burns Methodist Episcopal Church. From their website: "Professionally-designed exhibits present an overview of African American history from Slavery through Civil Rights. Other exhibits narrate the history of the old Burns Church, including a 10-minute video. A special exhibit on 'African Americans in Lafayette County' installed for Black History Month continues."

Cost and Hours: Su 1p to 4p, W-F 12p to 3p, closed Sa, M-Tu; Admission free but donations appreciated;
Tel: (662) 281-9963

http://www.burns-belfry.com/index.php

Civil Rights Monument in Honor of James Meredith
University of Mississippi — Ole Miss
University Circle
University, MS 38677

On the Ole Miss campus, visit the powerful Civil Rights monument in honor of James Meredith, who in 1962 became the first African-American student to enroll at Ole Miss even as segregationists rioted, unleashing bloody havoc. Nearby, a Mississippi Freedom Trail Marker honors Meredith. While you're here, gaze upon the Lyceum, the historic building (completed in 1848) where Meredith enrolled. It's the only survivor of the five original buildings of the university. Play Bob Dylan's "Oxford Town," even if only in your head. As for cost and hours, it's free and always open.

Center for the Study of Southern Culture
University of Mississippi — Ole Miss
Sorority Row and Grove Loop
University, MS 38677

In the Barnard Observatory building on the Ole Miss campus, the center is devoted to the academic study of southern culture, as its name would indicate. As well as being a school, it houses the Blues Archive, the largest public blues collection in the world, but it's mainly of use for researchers. Today, it produces "Living Blues" magazine, among many other endeavors such as radio programs, books, conferences and symposia. Look for the MBT maker out front for "Documenting the Blues."

Cost and hours: M-F 8a-5p, free admission,
Tel: (662) 915-5993
http://southernstudies.olemiss.edu/

The Chewalla Rib Shack
2644 Higdon Rd.
Chulahoma, MS 38635

A log cabin that was Junior Kimbrough's original juke joint, is still standing in Chulahoma outside Holly Springs. It's not open to the public, but it's a scenic drive to get there and it's fun to see the site where so much went down. To get there, see our directions above.

Aikei Pro's Record Shop
125 N. Center St.
Holly Springs, MS 38635

This is a bit of a legendary North Mississippi spot. It's the vision of WWII veteran David Caldwell, a local character (and friend of the late Junior Kimbrough) who's apparently still knocking about. The interior is apparently stacked with teetering piles of records on every surface, but also filled with piles of old stereo equipment and whatever else strikes Caldwell's fancy. Kind of an emporium of wonders, apparently. It was closed the day we stopped by. Hours? Who could ever say? Try showing up during regular business hours. (We heard from a local that if Mr. Caldwell isn't around, just ask someone in the street if he's eating over at the Copper Kettle, where he apparently can often be found.) There's no phone, either.

The Ida B. Wells-Barnett Museum
220 N Randolph St. #2412
Holly Springs, MS 38635

A museum dedicated to Ida B. Wells-Barnett, the great suffragist and social-justice investigative journalist—who was active not just in Holly Springs, where she was born, but in Memphis, Chicago, and New York, too. Her focus was on anti-lynching and she co-founded the NAACP. The Ida B. Wells-Barnett Museum is located in Holly Springs next to Rust College, which she attended, and which we passed on our travels.

Cost and hours: By appointment M-F 10a-5p, Sa 12p-5p, Adults: $10 Children (12 and under): $5,
Tel: (662) 579-5747 (to schedule a tour)
http://idabwellsmuseum.org

RESTAURANTS (NORTH MISSISSIPPI)

City Grocery
152 Courthouse Square
Oxford, MS 38655

City Grocery is chef and owner John Currence's flagship restaurant. We had a good time here at happy hour, eating and drinking at the bar upstairs—Karolyn declares their scrumptious chicken wings the best she's ever had. Friendly bar-staff, and if you eat upstairs, you can dig the paintings by self-taught Southern artist Lamar Sorrento. Look for Black Elvis! Anthony Bourdain was filmed having drinks and finger food here, as well.

Cost and hours: Lunch Tu-Sa 11:30a-2:30p, Dinner Tu-Sa 6p-10p; Bar Hours M-Sa 4p-until ?; Closed for lunch & dinner Su and M; Reservations recommended for the dining room: $$,

Tel: (66s) 232-8080,

https://citygroceryonline.com/city-grocery/

McEwen's Oxford
1110 Van Buren Ave.
Oxford, MS 38655

Two cool things about McEwen's: the first, and the coolest, is that it used to be a furniture store owned by Scott's late Aunt Lou's grandfather! Second, in a twist of fate, on the night before we had lunch here, we'd happened to meet the restaurant's owner, John, in a Memphis bar. We told him of our plan to journey to Oxford the next day, and he told us he had a restaurant there. (He also owns McEwen's in Memphis.) The third thing to know about McEwen's is that the food is really good. Karolyn enjoyed the farmer's plate, which changes every day: on this day it was broccolini, fried okra, tomato and asparagus salad, and a minestrone soup with local veg. All farm-fresh, simply but perfectly cooked and seasoned. Here, you can get the veggies your body has been craving.

Cost and Hours: Sunday Brunch 10:30a-2p, Lunch W-F 11a-2p; Dinner W-Sa 5p-9p, Closed M & Tu; Reservations recommended for dinner; $$:
Tel: (662) 234-7003;

https://mcewensoxford.com

Bouré
110 Courthouse Square
Oxford, MS 38655

Bouré is part of John Currence's City Grocery Restaurant Group (see above), which also includes City Grocery, Snackbar and Big Bad Breakfast. You can't go wrong with any of his places. Currence is from New Orleans and cut his teeth training at Mr. B's Bistro (one of our NOLA favorites).

Cost and hours: M–Th 11a-10p, F–Sa 11a-10:30p, Bar Hours M–W 4p-12a Th–F 4p–1a, Sa 12p-1a; $$; No reservations, walk-in only;
Tel: (662) 234-1968;
https://citygroceryonline.com/boure/

Big Bad Breakfast
719 N. Lamar Blvd.
Oxford, MS 38655

The Big Bad is one of Oxford's favorite breakfast spots, part of John Currence's restaurant group.

Cost and hours: M 7:30a-1p, Closed Tu, W-F 7:30a-1p, Sa-Su 8a-2:30p; $;
Reservations not accepted. Walk-in only;
Tel: (662) 236-2666;
https://bigbadbreakfast.com/locations/oxford-mississippi/

Taylor Grocery and Restaurant
4A Depot St.
Taylor, MS 38673

We stumbled upon Taylor Grocery while looking for Rowan Oak. It has the grit and atmosphere of a ramshackle roadside diner from another age. They're apparently renowned for their catfish. We'll have to get back here one day.

Cost and hours: Th-Su 5p-9p ("Give us a call to see what the crowd is like."); $;
Tel: (662) 236-1716;
https://taylorgrocery.com

MUSIC, BARS AND THE REST (NORTH MISSISSIPPI)

Proud Larry's
211 S Lamar Blvd.
Oxford, MS 38655

Proud Larry's is a restaurant by day and one of Oxford's favorite music venues by night.

Cost and hours: M-F 11a-9p, Sa 11a-midnight, Closed Su; $;
Tel: (662) 236-0050;
https://www.facebook.com/proudlarrys/

Rooster's Blues House
114 Courthouse Square
Oxford, MS 38655

On the Square, Rooster's is "Oxford's only dedicated blues venue" that often features the likes of Mark "Muleman" Massey, one of our faves. Food is served, as well.

Cost and hours: M-Tu 2:30p-12a, W-Sa 11a-midnight, Su 11a-9p: $;
Tel: (662) 236-7970;
https://www.facebook.com/roostersblueshouse

Taylor Grocery and Restaurant features live music along with food on Saturdays and Sundays. (See entry above).

TOURS AND FESTIVALS (NORTH MISSISSIPPI)

Othar Turner Memorial Picnic & Goat Roast
8647 US-51
Coldwater, MS 38618

Traditionally held in late August in Senatobia, and now apparently taking place in Coldwater, MS, this fest dedicated to Othar "Otha" Turner sounds intriguing. It's a two-day family fife-and-drum picnic which its website bills as an "annual blues and roots music 'festival' started by fife-legend Otha Turner" running from "late afternoon till late at night." Acts who have appeared in the past include Otha's granddaughter Sharde Turner & the Rising Star Fife & Drum Band, Blue Mother Tupelo, and "many more." "Often Kimbroughs, Burnsides and others perform. Goat (and 'regular') BBQ available."

Price: Free, Website: https://www.facebook.com/goatpicnic

The Kimbrough Cotton Patch Soul Blues Festival
Kimbrough Estates
2478 Hwy 7 North
Holly Springs, MS 38635

Robert Kimbrough Sr.'s annual festival was traditionally held in late September in Chulahoma, about 10 miles west of Holly Springs, at a VFW hall called the Hut. It was near the site of his late father Junior Kimbrough's infamous juke joint, **Junior's Place** (that's the one he established after leaving the Chewalla Rib Shack.) The festival is an attempt to recreate the heady days at that century-old ramshackle juke, which burned down in 2000. Besides Robert Kimbrough Sr. and other sons of Junior Kimbrough, featured performers often include Duwaye Burnside, one of the late R.L. Burnside's son (he had 14 kids), and Cedric Burnside, one of his grandkids (he had 35 of those). You may also see Earl "Little Joe" Ayers, an original member of Kimbrough's band. Mark "Muleman" Massey plays here, as well. In 2022 the fest took place in the new address above, in May instead of September. Doubtlessly, many such fests will come back in slightly altered form after COVID. We should be glad if they come back at all.

Tel: (662) 471-0846;
e-mail: robertkimbroughsrblues@yahoo.com;
https://kimbroughcottonpatchsoulbluesfestival.com

HOTELS (NORTH MISSISSIPPI)

Hampton Inn Oxford Conference Center
103 Ed Perry Blvd.
Oxford, MS 38655

This soulless business hotel makes for perfectly acceptable accommodations.

Tel: (662) 234-5565.
https://www.hilton.com/en/hotels/oxdeahx-hampton-oxford-conference-center/

KAROLYN'S TIP JAR

- Get the wings at City Grocery.

- Definitely don't miss Square Books: it's one of the great bookshops.

- Talk to the ghost at Mr. Faulkner's house.

EAST MISSISSIPPI (TUPELO)

Located two hours east of Clarksdale, Tupelo is where Elvis Presley was born. The reason to visit is, of course, to explore Elvis' early influences. Our itinerary assumes you're coming from Oxford, and that you'll continue on to Jackson. It's about a 50-minute drive to Elvis' birthplace from Oxford. You'll take US-278 E to MS-6 E/E Main St in Tupelo. Hang a left onto Elvis Presley Dr.

After you leave East Mississippi, you'll be headed to Bentonia, and on to Jackson. (See next section).

SITES AND MUSEUMS (EAST MISSISSIPPI)

Elvis Presley Birthplace
306 Elvis Presley Dr.
Tupelo, MS 38804

Visit the two-room house where Elvis was born in 1935 (and where his identical twin, Jessie Garon, was stillborn). The house, which is *in situ*, was built by Elvis' father, grandfather and uncle. If you've been to Graceland, it's quite something to compare that homey mansion, where Elvis ended up, to the two-room shotgun shack where he began. It'll take you a matter of seconds to see the entirety of it. Look for the markers nearby: Elvis' birthplace features both a Mississippi Blues Trail marker and a Mississippi Country Trail marker, honoring Elvis' revolutionary blend of country and blues. (He blended other forms as well, but those are the big two.)

The Assembly of God Church where Elvis' family worshipped when he was a boy has been moved to the grounds of the park. After you see the house, step inside: Elvis was immersed in Southern gospel right here in this church in the '40s. He was especially influenced by the adamant style of guitar-playing Pentecostal preacher Brother Frank Smith, who taught him some basic chords. Elvis grew up to be a great gospel singer, of course: in fact—and we hadn't realized this—the only three Grammys he won were all for gospel music. Your visit to the church is accompanied by an immersive, if amateurish, film experience. While we're on the subject, be sure to skip the extremely amateurish film playing under the marquee in the main building, which purports to dramatize Elvis' early years.

However, do save some time to look through the unexpectedly rich museum, which contains an interesting collection, including some of Elvis' toys and memorabilia, donated by a woman who was a close personal friend. Outside, be sure to peep the 1939 green Plymouth, the vehicle the Presleys used to beat it out of Tupelo in the dead of night when Elvis was 13, one step ahead of their creditors. They were Memphis-bound, looking for a better life.

To conclude your visit, climb up to the overlook in the hills above Elvis' boyhood home. The 'Becoming' statue on the overlook symbolizes Elvis' transformation from the boy he was when he roamed these hills into the world's beloved entertainer.

Hours and costs: M- Sa: 9a-5p, Su 1p-5p; Cost: There are cheaper rates available if you just want to see one or two of the three attractions. We're just going to give you the rate for our recommended grande ticket, where you get all three. Costs Adult Grande $20, Senior Grande Age 60+ $15, Child Grande Ages 7-12 $10, Children Ages 7 and under free.

Tel: (662) 841-1245;

https://elvispresleybirthplace.com

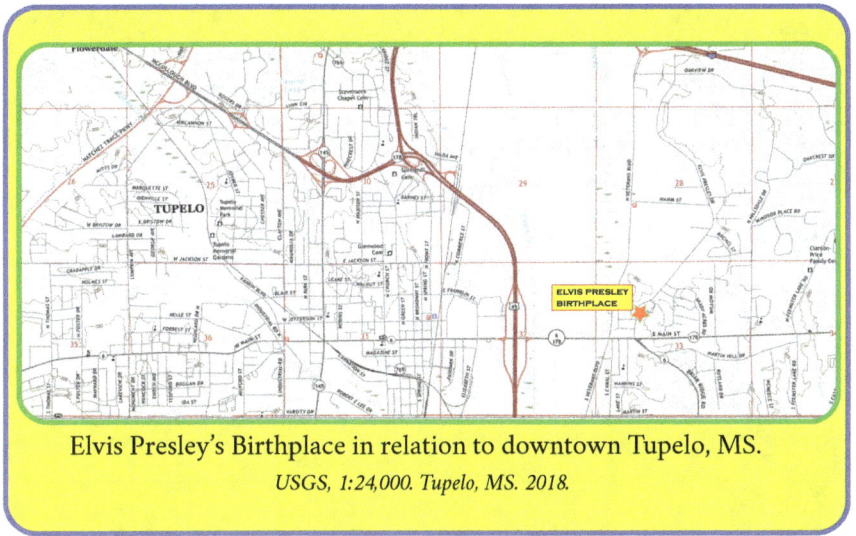

Elvis Presley's Birthplace in relation to downtown Tupelo, MS.
USGS, 1:24,000. Tupelo, MS. 2018.

Tupelo Hardware
114 W. Main St.
Tupelo, MS 38804

While you're in town, go down to Main Street to see the hardware store where Gladys bought Elvis his first guitar in 1946, for $7.75. The hardware store still looks very much like it must have on the day Elvis and Gladys stopped in. A plaque outside describes how easily Elvis could have come away from the hardware store on that fateful day with a bicycle or a rifle, instead of a guitar. And then where would we be?

Hours: M-Sa 8a-5p, Closed Su;
Tel: (662) 842-4637;

https://tupelo-hardware.myshopify.com

RESTAURANTS (EAST MISSISSIPPI)

Blue Canoe
2006 N Gloster St.
Tupelo, MS 38804

At the Blue Canoe you'll find pub grub, over 100 types of beer, and live music. There's music every night, starting at 9:30p on weekends and 7:30p midweek.

Cost and Hours M-Th: 3p-12a F: 3p-1a Sa: 2p-1a, Closed Su; $; e-mail:
Tel: (662) 269-2642;
https://www.bluecanoebar.com

MUSIC, BARS AND THE REST (EAST MISSISSIPPI)

Blue Canoe. See above!

TOURS AND FESTIVALS (EAST MISSISSIPPI)

Tupelo Elvis Festival
108 South Broadway St.
Tupelo, MS 38804

Held in early June, the Tupelo Elvis Festival features an Ultimate Elvis Tribute Artist competition (dueling Elvis impersonators!), concerts by former winners, interviews with special guests with special Elvis knowledge or connections, and a Gospel Sunday performed by more Elvis impersonators (er, Tribute Artists). There's even a Running with the King 5K. What fun!

Tel: (662)841-6598,
e-mail: INFO@TUPELOMAINSTREET.COM,
https://www.tupeloelvisfestival.com

KAROLYN'S TIP JAR (EAST MISSISSIPPI)

- When you visit Elvis' birthplace, bring a picnic lunch to eat on the grounds. When we there in July, the temperature was just right—82, with a light breeze. There are several tables set up for your use.

JACKSON AND ENVIRONS

(HAZLEHURST, BENTONIA, NATCHEZ, ETC.)

You've done Tupelo, and now you're headed for Bentonia. You'll come in on Highway 49, taking either Bentonia exit. You'll find the Blue Front Cafe literally across the tracks (as you may have noticed by now, railroad tracks often separated Black and white neighborhoods). It's perfectly safe—we'd tell you if it wasn't.

Enjoy your time, keeping in mind that it's a 40-minute drive to Jackson, where you'll be spending the night.

Spend some time knocking around in Jackson, the capital of Mississippi, the next day. Farish Street was once Jackson's equivalent of Memphis' Beale Street—a blues Mecca, as well as the heart of the Black business and entertainment district. Sadly, today, like Greenville's Nelson Street, it's pretty desolate. Still, a lot of musical history went down on this street, and you can still stroll up the street to see the excellent **Mississippi Blues Trail** (MBT) markers which tell the rich tale.

While you're in town, be sure to see the inspiring Mississippi Civil Rights Museum.

On our way out of town, we'll stop at the MBT marker for the Subway Lounge, a now-vanished juke joint, and we'll stop in Hazelhurst, Robert Johnson's birthplace.

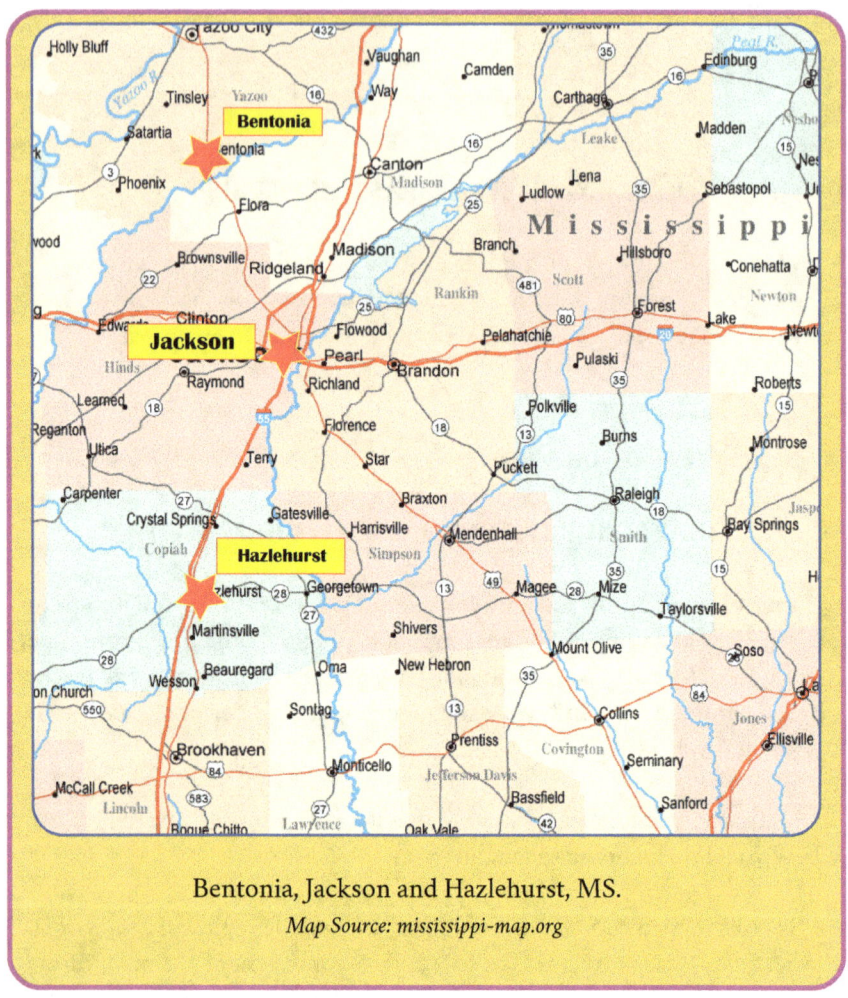

Bentonia, Jackson and Hazlehurst, MS.
Map Source: mississippi-map.org

SITES AND MUSEUMS (JACKSON AREA)

Mississippi Civil Rights Museum
222 North St #2205
Jackson, MS 39201

Jackson should be very proud of its Civil Rights Museum. It's intense, impressive, and necessary—quite beautifully done. For blues lovers, there's an exhibit for Sonny Boy Williamson's "Mighty Long Time" and "Nine Below Zero," recorded at Jackson's Trumpet Records, and Sammy Meyers' "You're So Fine" and King Edward's "The Things I Used to Do," recorded at Ace Records. Music lovers will also learn about the music of the struggle, as an exhibit traces the roots of "We Shall Overcome," one of the movement's most popular freedom songs in the 1960s, to early 20th-century African American spirituals.

If you've been following our itinerary, you've just recently visited the Ole Miss campus in Oxford, where we saw the powerful Civil Rights monument to James Meredith and visited the Lyceum—where, unleashing bloody havoc, an armed and furious white mob rioted when Meredith showed up to register for admission. That makes the museum's exhibits for Meredith all the more powerful. You'll see how Gov. Barnett whipped up the racist crowd at a football game in Jackson the day before Meredith's admission. You'll see how students and white supremacists fought the federal marshals tasked with protecting Meredith. (In fact, federal marshals ended up escorting Meredith his entire year on campus.)

What's more, now that you've been to Clarksdale, you will appreciate the commemoration of Clarksdale's Aaron Henry, state NAACP president, and Vera Pigee, who organized the Clarksdale boycott of white businesses.

Special attention is given to Fannie Lou Hamer, the Congressional candidate and Civil Rights activist who co-founded the Poor People's Campaign and the Freedom Farm Cooperative. There's an exhibit recalling how Hamer and Dick Gregory proposed an airlift of 20,000 turkeys from the heart of Chicago to Mississippi, during a particularly fraught time for the movement.

COFO was the Council of Federated Organizations, a federation of all the national Civil Rights organizations active in Mississippi, including SNCC (the Student Nonviolent Coordinating Committee). (According to Hamer, the SNCC kids made a decisive difference in the Mississippi struggle.) The Freedom Houses were a kind of movement community center/school staffed by COFO. Among other brave and courageous acts, COFO staffers Michael and Rita Schwerner opened a Freedom House in Meridian. You might know Michael Schwerner's name: he was one of the three Civil Rights workers murdered in Mississippi during the Freedom Summer. There's an exhibit detailing the plot to kill Schwerner (whom the killers called "Goatee"), known as the Queen Bee of the movement. A great man, by all indications.

Look for the exhibit on performers who boycotted segregated performance venues in Jackson. Yay, cast of "Bonanza" and Original Hootenanny USA troupe.

Special sections honor writers, teachers and artists, such as author Anne Moody, who wrote "Coming of Age in Mississippi," and the great historian Staughton Lynd. If you were one of his students, he considered a huge part of your education to be your real-world experience out in the Freedom Schools. Florence Mars, who flouted local racist customs, wrote "Witness in Philadelphia" about Schwerner and the other two murdered Civil Rights activists (James Chaney and Andrew Goodman). Illustrator Tracy Sugerman gets a remembrance.

The Mississippi Civil Rights Museum is a powerful and inspiring reminder that people died fighting for these rights. (Rights that are now under fire: as one exhibit shows, the only real "election fraud"—then as now—is perpetrated by the rightwing against voting rights for Black people.) Your visit will leave you with the overwhelming conviction that we can't go back. We've come too far.

Cost and Hours: Tu–Sa 9a–5p, Su 11a–5p, Closed M; Adult: $15, Youth (ages 4–22): $8, Senior (ages 60+) or military: $13, Children under 3 years: free, Admission is free on Su;

Tel: (601) 576-6800;

https://mcrm.mdah.ms.gov

Now let's have a walk down Farish Street and look at the MBT markers. It's free, and you can do it anytime.

MBT Marker for Trumpet Records
309 N. Farish St.
Jackson, MS 39202

At this site was Lillian McMurry's husband's furniture store, which also sold records. One day in 1949 she was blown away after she put on a copy of Wynonie Harris' "All She Wants to Do is Rock." A white woman, she fell in love with blues and increasingly turned the furniture store into a blues Record Mart. Next, she founded Trumpet Records, becoming the first to record Sonny Boy Williamson and Elmore James. (She also became Sonny Boy's lifelong producer and manager.) Eventually the McMurrys even opened Diamond Recording studio, right here at 309 Farish.

MBT Marker for the Alamo Theatre
Intersection of N. Farish/East Hamilton St.
Jackson, MS 39202

Like many historic Black theaters, the Alamo featured a legendary talent show (Otis Spann and Dorothy Moore were winners) and a gospel show; Lillian McMurry from down the street at Trumpet Records would attend these shows to scout talent. It was a movie theater, as well. The theater was restored in '96, and shows occasionally still happen there. Next door, enjoy the facade of Peaches Cafe (no apostrophe), for decades a beloved neighborhood soul food restaurant. It's gone now too, sadly.

MBT Marker for H.C. Spier
225 N. Farish St.
Jackson, MS 39202

The marker is located at the original site of H.C. Speir's Speir Phonograph Company. Aside from selling and assembling phonographs, Speir was a great talent scout and artists' representative. Without him a lot of the historic recordings made by Victor, Paramount and Vocalion wouldn't have happened. He "discovered" Charley Patton, Tommy Johnson, Skip James and Willie Brown. Robert Johnson bought his guitar strings here, and his seminal recordings might not have happened without Speir's recommendation. Speir also had a career in real estate and loved gardening, especially sunflowers.

Nearby, the **Big Apple Inn** (509 N Farish St.) still manages to hold on (see our entry below). Sonny Boy Williamson II and Elmore James lived upstairs. The Big Apple is famous for its own invention: pig-ear sandwiches! The restaurant was closed the day we dropped by; Karolyn was truly disappointed we didn't get to try the pig ears. (Not!) Hey, B.B. King and Bobby Bland loved 'em.

Next, hop in your car and plug the address below into your Garmin or phone. We're going to see a few more markers.

MBT Marker for The Hotel King Edward
235 West Capitol St.
Jackson MS 39201

The Hotel King Edward was once Jackson's equivalent of the Peabody in Memphis. Bluesmen recorded here, just like at the Peabody. H.C. Speir, for example, set up blues recording sessions here for OKeh records in 1930. Bo Carter, Robert Wilkins, Joe McCoy, Isaiah Nettles, and the Mississippi Sheiks, among others, all recorded and/or performed at the King Edward. Imagine catching the gig mentioned on the MBT marker: Houston Stackhouse and Robert Nighthawk, with country star Jimmie Rodgers!

MBT Marker for Ace Records
W Capitol St & N Roach St.
Jackson, MS 39201

Just down the street from the King Edward marker on Capitol Street (you'll be able to spot it from there), find the MBT marker for Johnny Vincent's Ace Records. Interestingly, they initially released mainly records by New Orleans artists. Earl King's "Those Lonely, Lonely Nights" (which was recorded over at Trumpet Records back on Farish Street) was a big hit when released by Ace.

MBT Marker for Subway Lounge
Dr Robert Smith Sr. Pkwy.
Jackson, MS 39203

When you're ready to leave Jackson on your way to Hazlehurst, stop at the MBT marker for the much-lamented Subway Lounge, the underground midnight-to-whenever juke joint in the basement of the old **Summers Hotel** (est. 1944). Jimmy King opened it in '66 and was still running it when it closed in 2003. The place was torn down in 2004. To get there, head south on 51/N. State St. and hang a left onto East Pearl Street, which becomes Dr. Robert Smith Sr. Pkwy. Pass the traffic circle and you will see the marker coming up on your right. When you're done reading the marker, get on Highway 55 heading south to get to Hazelhurst.

MBT Marker for Robert Johnson
Hazlehurst, MS 39083

About 30 miles south of Jackson, on your way from Jackson to New Orleans, stop at the MBT marker for Robert Johnson. As man and as myth, he embodies the blues. He was born just north of Hazlehurst at the intersection of 51 and Highway 28. Enjoy the train station, which looks just like it did when it was built in 1925. There's no doubt Robert Johnson played at this train depot as he rambled in the '30s. Try to pick up on his vibrations still in the air.

Mississippi Music Museum
138 N. Ragsdale Ave.
Hazlehurst, MS 39083

Hazlehurst is the birthplace of Robert Johnson. In that sense, the "other" or "real" crossroads is where Highway 28 meets 51 just north of town—as an ornamental sign outside this museum denotes. Dr. Jim Brewer, the curator of this museum—which is located in the old train depot—makes it a point to highlight the contributions of Johnson's teacher Ike Zimmerman (also spelled "Zinnerman"), who taught Johnson to play guitar in that amazing way that sounded like two people playing at once. (In that sense, you could even argue that the "real" crossroads is a cemetery in nearby Beauregard, where Zimmerman and Johnson used to meet to practice.) The museum also offers an exhibit, the "Mississippi Music Experience," at the Iron Horse Grill in Jackson.

Hours and cost: Thu 10a-3p, F 10a-2p, closed Sa-W; Free admission, but donations accepted;
Tel: (601) 894-5601

RESTAURANTS (JACKSON AREA)

Saltine
622 Duling Ave. Ste 201

Jackson, MS 39216

We didn't know what to expect when we tried Saltine: it turned out to be one of the best meals we've had on our Southern travels. A dozen oysters were plump and refreshing. The fried oyster po'bao was a delightful bite that will satisfy your want for something fried yet fresh. The salmon was delicious, as was a dish of blackened blackfish—the first time Karolyn had tried that particular seafood—with crab butter sauce, Brussels sprouts, and roasted potatoes.

Cost and hours: M-Th 11a-9p, F 11a-10p, Sa 11a-10p, Su 10:30a-9p; $$;
Tel: (601) 982-2899;
https://jackson.saltinerestaurant.com

Big Apple Inn
509 N Farish St.
Jackson, MS 39202

We've yet to eat at the Big Apple Inn, still located on Farish Street, the historic blues strip in Jackson—see our comments on the restaurant's historical importance above. It was sadly closed on the day we dropped by. For his part, when Anthony Bourdain visited, he ate tamales and "smokes and ears". "Smokes" are smoked sausage sandwiches; "ears" are pig's ear sandwiches. Now, don't you want to visit? Well, it's on *our* list. The joint is owned by local character Geno Lee.

Cost and hours: Tu-Sa 8a-9p, closed Su-M; $:
Tel: (601) 354-9371;
https://www.facebook.com/BigAppleInn/

Hal and Mal's
200 Commerce St.
Jackson, MS 39201

Offering music-themed Southern food, Hal & Mal's certainly sounds like our kind of place. Their website calls it "the most-talked-about upscale honky-tonk in all of Mississippi, where art is made, music plays, and folks gather to share community and celebrate the very best of Mississippi's creative spirit."

Cost and hours: Tu–F 11a–9p, M 5p–midnight, Closed Sa–Su, "Hours are for the Kitchen. The Bar stays open UNTIL. Our closing hours depend on what shows we have going on"; $;

Tel.: (601) 948-0888;

https://halandmals.net

Iron Horse Grill
320 W Pearl St.
Jackson, MS 39203

The Iron Horse Grill features a Mississippi Music Experience Museum which was co-conceived by Dr. Jim Brewer of the Mississippi Music Museum in Hazlehurst (see our entry above), who also founded the Mississippi Musicians Hall of Fame in Clinton, MS. They also have a very robust live music calendar (see below). Oh yes: they're a restaurant, too: burgers, fajitas, steaks, fish, etc.

Hours and cost: M–W 11a–9p, Thu 11a–10p, F–Sa 11a–11p, Su 10:30a–3p, Happy hour M–F 3p–6p. To tour the museum, call events manager Kila Milner at 601-398-0151 and she'll help you schedule a time;

http://www.theironhorsegrill.com

Bentonia Bugs Crawfish
203 Pritchard Ave.
Bentonia, MS 39040

Highly recommended, Bentonia Bugs is just down the road (across the railroad tracks) from the **Blue Front Cafe**. Scott had a steak that wasn't just kissed by the grill: it was *made love to* by the grill. The comeback sauce was delicious, the first time we'd had it. This sauce is to Mississippi cuisine what remoulade is to Louisianan food, but even zingier. Bentonia Bugs is a family-friendly spot with live music in the back. "Bugs" is Southern for crawfish, in case you looked askance at that name—it's short for "mudbugs."

Hours and cost: F-Sa 5p-10p, Closed Su-Th; $;
Tel: (662) 571-4342;
https://www.facebook.com/bentoniabugs.crawfish/

Mr. D's Old Country Store
8801 US-61
Lorman, MS 39096

On the Blues Highway in the little town of Lorman—about an hour south of Vicksburg and about 45 minutes before you get to Natchez—you'll find the Old Country Store, colloquially known as Mr. D's. It is the home of a legendary all-you-can-eat buffet, heaping with ribs, greens, dirty rice, corn on the cob, potato salad, macaroni and cheese, corn muffins, and, crucially, fried chicken that is in serious competition for the title of best in the world. (Its chief competitor being Dooky Chase's…and the Four Way Grill. And Lil' Dizzy's. We'd better stop.) This chicken is the family recipe of host and owner Arthur Davis. When we were there, Mr. Davis even serenaded us with a love song. As Karolyn gushed of his chicken, "It's the first time the inside [the meat] is even better than the outside [the skin]!" In any case, if you're like Scott you consider "all you can eat" a challenge—yet do be sure to save a bit of room for the peach cobbler with vanilla ice cream. ("To die for," exclaims Karolyn.)

Though primarily a restaurant, Mr. D's is also a real, functioning country store, or "crafts mall." It's been there for over 130 years, and was once a place to pick up work boots and cotton. Today, it's replete with James Brown bobble-heads, caps, Raggedy Ann dolls, and much more. (Apparently, you can also sample Mr. Davis's fried chicken at Wingo's in Vicksburg.)

Cost and hours: Open everyday from 10a to 4p, and sometimes until 6p on Sa; $;
Tel: (601) 437-3661;
https://www.facebook.com/oldcountrystorelorman/

Wingo's
5164 Hwy 552 EXT
Lorman, MS 39096

Arthur Davis of Mr. D's Old Country Store opened Wingo's, so you know their wings have got to be good. His sons apparently manage the Wingo's shops, while he holds down the fort at Mr. D's. There's a Wingo's in Vicksburg, as well, at 3046 Indiana Ave, Vicksburg, MS 39180 (Tel. 601-631-8171).

Cost and hours: M-F 11a-midnight, Sa 11a-2p, Su 5a-midnight; $;
Tel: (601) 631-8170;
https://www.facebook.com/theoriginalwingos/?ref=page_internal

MUSIC, BARS AND THE REST (JACKSON AREA)

Blue Front Cafe
107 W Railroad Ave.
Bentonia, MS 39040

20 miles northwest of Jackson on the way to Baton Rouge, you'll find the Blue Front Cafe, a storied juke established in 1948 and run today by Jimmy "Duck" Holmes—recently nominated for a Grammy for his album "Cypress Grove"—who keeps the Bentonia tradition alive. The Bentonia tradition is a unique School of the Delta Blues (though Bentonia is not actually in the Delta) with a tuning all its own, a haunting minor-key style perfected by the likes of Skip James and Jack Owens. The form's supernatural vibes influenced Robert Johnson.

Like James, Holmes learned to play this music directly from Henry Stuckey, who pretty much originated, or at least developed, the Bentonia style during the first World War. He'd often learn from jamming with Owens, as well. Today, Holmes returns the favor by teaching young guitar players the Bentonia tradition.

When we stopped by, we just missed the man himself but got to chat with some locals. We'll get back, and when we do, it's likely Mr. Holmes will be there, still keeping the tradition alive.

Cost and hours: M-Th 12p-8p, F-Sa 12p-10p, Su 1p-7p;

Tel: (662) 528-1900;
https://www.facebook.com/bluefrontcafeblues/?ref=page_internal

Hal & Mal's
200 Commerce St.
Jackson, MS 39201

Hal & Mal's is a live music venue as well as a restaurant. (See our entry above.) It's closed on the weekends, peculiarly, but there's typically live music Tuesday through Friday, with Tuesday evenings being a jazz night.

Iron Horse Grill
320 W. Pearl St.
Jackson, MS 39203

Jackson's Iron Horse Grill has a robust music calendar as well as a full menu. (See our entry above). There's music on most Thursdays, Fridays and Saturdays, jumping off around 6 or 7pm. Clarksdale's Bill 'Howl-N-Madd' Perry plays occasionally.

Smoot's Grocery Lounge
319 N. Broadway St.
Natchez, MS 39120

Natchez is about an hour-and-40 minute drive south from Vicksburg. One day we'll get down that way, and when we do we'll likely head to Smoot's. From their website: "Smoot's Grocery Lounge is located on the corner of Broadway Street and High Street. A restored Juke Joint, Smoot's is in the historical heart of downtown Natchez, overlooking the Mighty Mississippi, facing the riverwalk along the bluff." Sounds great. There's live music most nights. While not a restaurant, they do feature a fish fry on Sundays.

Cost and hours: Th 6p-10p, F 5p-until ?, Sa 1p until ?, Su 12p-6p; Closed M-W; $;
Tel: (601) 431-5530 or (601) 807-1161;
https://www.smootsnatchez.com

Juke Joint
1911 Government St.

Ocean Springs, MS 39564

Should you ever find yourself down around Biloxi and the Gulf Coast, this imaginatively-titled spot could be an intriguing prospect. Tuesdays it seems are open-mic comedy nights, whereas Thursdays are given over to karaoke. Saturdays feature bands, and Sundays feature an "open jam" at 10p. There's a kitchen, as well.

Cost and Hours: M-Sa: 7p-till late; Su noon-till late for all you can eat crawfish; bands on Saturdays require a ticket, which you can get at the door;
Tel: (228) 215-0506;
https://www.msjukejoint.com

TOURS AND FESTIVALS (JACKSON AREA)

Bentonia Blues Festival
107 W Railroad Ave.
Bentonia, MS 39040
- and -
Holmes' Farm at 313 Wilson-Holmes Rd.
Bentonia, MS 39040

The Bentonia Blues Festival, created by Jimmy "Duck" Holmes in 1972, takes place annually around the third Saturday in June at Holmes' Blue Front Cafe and the Holmes Family Farm. In 2022, guests included Bobby Rush and R.L. Boyce.

Cost and Hours: Takes place over three days, with music usually starting around 2:30p and continuing long into the night; Admission is free, but donations are welcome and appreciated;

Tel: (662) 528-1900;

https://www.facebook.com/BentoniaBluesFestival and https://visityazoo.org/bentonia-blues-festival/

HOTELS (JACKSON AREA)

Homewood Suites by Hilton Jackson Fondren Medical District
2815 N. State St.
Jackson, MS 39216

Another impersonal, forgettable business hotel offering perfectly accept-able accommodations. Scott always hopes the breakfast buffet will feature the greasy sausage patties for which he has a mysterious predilection.

Tel: 1-800-CALL-HOME;

https://www.hilton.com/en/hotels/jantyhw-homewood-suites-jackson-fondren-medical-district/

That's about it for Mississippi. From here, we'll move on to Louisiana. Still, there's more Mississippi to explore, if you're so inclined. We haven't even been to two ports along the Mississippi River, Vicksburg and Natchez. Look for us on the road, doing research!

KAROLYN'S TIP JAR (JACKSON AREA)

- Sunday nights at Saltine feature the special dollar-oysters and half-off bottle of wine. As there are very few restaurants open on Sundays, it is a great spot.

- The Mississippi Civil Rights Museum is one of the only spots open on Sunday, and admission is free on that day, as well.

- At Mr. D's Old Country Store, skip all sides—go directly to the fried chicken. Well, maybe you can dabble a bit. Really, you shouldn't miss the mac 'n' cheese. Okay—just don't fill up on bread! Also, if you ask nicely, Lil D (one of Mr. Davis's son) may even sing for you, at your table.

- When it comes to cemetery exploring, be sure to wear sturdy shoes. Do not wear open-toed shoes because you might wade through ankle-deep grass. Watch out for snakes!

- Bring a gift for your bluesman whose grave you are visiting. He might like a beer, some whisky, or some smokes.

CHAPTER VII

On the Road in Louisiana's Cajun Country

Past the seductive beauty of the Big Easy, Louisiana is all about nuance, possibility within the boundaries imposed by climate, landscape and, in many places, poverty. Over all, it is flat, hot and wet. But it is there—in the interstices between the limited *real* and the spiritual *perhaps*—that the masterpieces of Louisiana literature unfold. I love these places: small towns, weedy railroad tracks, bridges over bayous leading to wetlands that give way to the oil rig-dotted Gulf of Mexico. There are no signposts, no big photo opportunities. Just a unique and, for me, magical way of being in the world. — *Jennifer Mose*

Here we highlight attractions on the road from Mississippi to New Orleans, with a focus on French Louisiana, one of the most fascinating regions in the United States. This southern part of the state—west of New Orleans, east of Lake Charles—is where the French-speaking Acadians who migrated from present-day northeast Canada settled in the 1700s. The British carried out the Great Expulsion of the Acadians from what is today New Brunswick, Prince Edward Island, Nova Scotia, Quebec, and Maine during and after the French and Indian Wars (*1754-1763*).

Though Louisiana was actually Spanish at the time, it had once been a French territory, beginning in 1681, so there was a culture and community there for the Acadians.

It's still an evocative land of French Catholicism, zydeco, and gumbo—the forces of homogenization haven't quite wiped that away yet. Sadly, some features of local life such as the Zydeco Hall of Fame in Opelousas are no longer there—it burned down in 2017. (Opelousas is the birthplace of zydeco, and swamp pop, too.) We've listed places and people that are tending the flame of the culture, keeping it alive. It's heartening to see how many are still out there.

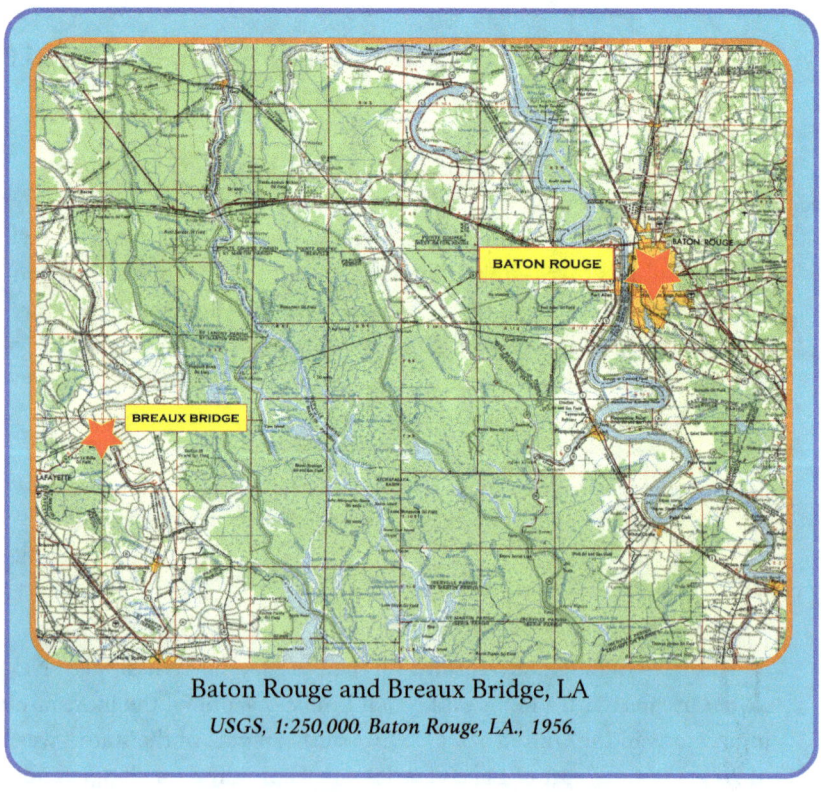

Baton Rouge and Breaux Bridge, LA

USGS, 1:250,000. Baton Rouge, LA., 1956.

If you're just passing through, see our first itinerary. On the other hand, if you'd like to sojourn in Cajun Country, aka Acadiana, our second itinerary is for those spending a night or two. We like to make our home-base the town of Breaux Bridge, the "crawfish capital of the world."

For extra credit, attend a parish dance in one of the dance halls between Eunice and Opelousas. There used to be about 1,600 of them; now there are about 30. If you can't find one in Cajun Country, don't despair: at Rock 'n' Bowl in New Orleans, people still come from all over southern Louisiana to dance on Thursday zydeco nights, keeping alive the tradition that was once such a staple of Louisiana life.

Hopefully, these experiences will evoke for you that magical land of Louisiana literature of which Moses speaks—think James Wilcox, Walker Percy, Tennessee Williams, Kate Chopin, John Kennedy Toole, Ernest Gaines.

ITINERARIES

Itinerary One (For those just passing Louisiana)

- Visit the Whitney Plantation in Wallace, Louisiana on a drive between Mississippi and New Orleans. You could do our "Andouille Sausage Crawl" in LaPlace before or after visiting the plantation—it's just 20 minutes away.

—or—

- If you're staying overnight in Baton Rouge, spend an evening at Teddy's in nearby Zachary. Then, in the morning, visit the Whitney Plantation on your way to New Orleans.

Itinerary Two (for Cajun Country sojourners)

Day One
Morning
Make your way to Breaux Bridge, Louisiana.
Check into Maison des Lion.
Afternoon

Get lunch at Glenda's Creole Kitchen Restaurant.
Visit the Living History Museum and Folklife Park at the Vermillion Performance Center.
Evening
Have dinner at Poche's Market, Restaurant & Smokehouse.
If it's a Saturday, head to La Poussiere Cajun Dancehall.

Day Two
Morning
Take the Cajun Country Swamp Tours.
Afternoon/Evening
Have lunch at Johnson's Boucaniere
If it's a Sunday, head out to Whiskey River Landing (*zydeco dancing and food trucks*) or Cajun Country Lounge & Dancehall (*live Cajun music and BBQ*).

The next morning, pull out of Breaux Bridge and head towards New Orleans. It's about 126 miles, about a 2-hour drive. On the way, you could visit the Whitney Plantation and do our "Andouille Sausage Crawl" in La-Place. (Attractions such as The Dew Drop Inn in Mandeville and the Abita Mystery House in Abita Springs probably make more sense as day trips from New Orleans. Whereas Teddy's Juke Joint works best if you're staying the night in Baton Rouge.)

SITES AND MUSEUMS

Whitney Plantation
5099 Louisiana Hwy 18
Wallace, LA 70049

The United States has never truly had a reckoning with slavery—not like, say, Germany has with its dark past. Located 48 miles north of New Orleans off of River Road, on the west bank of the Mississippi River, the Whitney Plantation museum is a step in that direction. It is—rather astonishingly—the first slavery museum in America. Evocatively situated amid the sugarcane fields of "Plantation Alley," it was founded by John Cummings, a wealthy white attorney who spent 15 years and $8 million of his own money on the project. While there are a handful of other plantation museums in

Louisiana, not one is even attempting to offer the eye-opening experience of the Whitney.

David Amsden, who profiled the Whitney for the New York Times, makes a key point: "Forty-eight years after World War II, the United States Holocaust Memorial Museum opened in Washington...One hundred and fifty years after the end of the Civil War, however, no federally funded museum dedicated to slavery exists, no monument honoring America's slaves." Amsden quotes historian Eric Foner: "It's something I bring up all the time in my lectures... If the Germans built a museum dedicated to American slavery before one about their own Holocaust, you'd think they were trying to hide something. As Americans, we haven't yet figured out how to come to terms with slavery. To some, it's ancient history. To others, it's history that isn't quite history."

At the beginning of the tour you are given a lanyard with a badge inscribed with the name of an enslaved child—similar to the approach of the Holocaust museum, where each guest wears a lanyard with the name of a specific victim of the genocide. This helps visitors to personalize the experience: you come to identify with "your" child. In fact, the Whitney tour is especially powerful for highlighting the experiences of enslaved children, which are largely drawn from the memories of elderly ex-slaves themselves, as told to FDR-era researchers with the W.P.A.'s Federal Writers' Project. As you stroll the grounds, in Amsden's words, you are "surrounded by dozens of ghostly sculptures of child slaves [by Woodrow Nash]" that Cummings commissioned to represent these reminiscing men and women "as they would have looked when enslaved." (In fact, Cummings eventually plans to install a speaker system near the slave cabins, where the W.P.A. recordings will play on a loop, "allowing visitors to hear the voices of former slaves while staring into the type of homes in which they once lived.")

Our guide pointed out instances where what we were seeing had been arranged for impact instead of historical accuracy. For example, the slave quarters would never have been in the sightline of the main house, as they are at the Whitney. (Interesting, isn't it? Out of sight, out of mind.) The grounds are arranged so that the memorials and buildings, some reconstructed from other sites, tell a narrative and speak a larger truth about slavery beyond these specific grounds.

You'll see an iron slave pen brought in from Gonzales, Louisiana and a Baptist church founded by freed slaves in 1867 which was moved here from a neighboring parish. You'll see a restored blacksmith's shop where a slave named Robin worked for 40 years; this is also where Tarantino filmed the scene in *Django Unchained* where Django, played by Jamie Foxx, was branded by his owners. Vats for cooking sugarcane are arrayed around the grounds; they get smaller as each step of the refinement into crystal sugar was performed. Railcars in the distance transported sugar cane to the mills. You'll take a spin through the main house, which features hand-painted walls and ceilings.

Perhaps the most powerful memorial is the "Wall of Honor." After finding old court documents which provided the names of 354 slaves who worked on the plantation before emancipation, Cummings had their names engraved into Italian granite to create this Wall. Reading the names is a powerful experience. Laura Rosanne Adderley, a Tulane history professor specializing in slavery, puts it powerfully: "Like Maya Lin's memorial [to Vietnam veterans in Washington, D.C.], the Whitney has figured out a way to mourn those we as a society are often reluctant to mourn."

At the time we visited, there were plans for what the NYT calls the "Whitney's most provocative memorial," which may be completed by the time you visit: a memorial "dedicated to the victims of the German Coast Uprising, an event rarely mentioned in American history books. In January 1811, at least 125 slaves walked off their plantations and, dressed in makeshift military garb, began marching in revolt along River Road toward New Orleans. (The area was then called the German Coast for the high number of German immigrants. In fact, during the slavery era the Whitney Plantation was owned by the Haydels, a family of German immigrants.) The slaves were suppressed by militias after two days, with about 95 killed, some during fighting and some after the show trials that followed. As a warning to other slaves, dozens were decapitated, their heads placed on spikes along River Road and in what is now Jackson Square in the French Quarter."

The ghosts of slavery haunt the present. As Amsden writes, America's "longstanding culture of racism and racial tensions—from the lynchings of the Jim Crow-era South to the discriminatory housing policies of the North to the treatment of blacks by the police today—is deeply rooted" in slavery. A visit to the Whitney can help Americans face facts.

Cost and hours: Open W-M, Visitor Center: 9:30a-4:30p, Tours: Ground open at 10a, with last entry for a tour at 3p. (Visitors that arrive after 3p should expect an abbreviated visit.); Adult $25, Child (6-18) $11, Child (Under 6) Free, Seniors (62+) $23, Military/Student Discount $23, Exhibits within Visitor Center free to the public; Tel: (225) 265-3300;

https://www.whitneyplantation.org

Abita Mystery House
22275 Hwy 36
Abita Springs, LA 70420

45 miles north of New Orleans across Lake Pontchartrain is the Abita Mystery House (also knows as the UCM Museum, pronounced "you see 'em museum"). It's a truly eccentric collection of folk art and much else, put together by John Preble—the kind of place that must be seen to be believed. Just one of its attractions, to set the mind wobbling: the prospect of seeing Darrell, the half-alligator, half-dog "dogigator."

Cost and hours: 10a-5p everyday; $5 if over 5 yrs old; Tel: (985) 892-2624; email: john@johnpreble.com; https://abitamysteryhouse.com

Abita Brewery
21084 Hwy 36
Covington, LA 70433

Abita beer *is* the taste of New Orleans for us. Karolyn's favorite is the strawberry lager, while Scott likes Purple Haze and Amber. The tours are about 30 minutes and you get four 4-ounce tastes of this fine elixir. The brewery is located in Covington, just a 10-minute drive from Abita Springs.

Cost and Hours: Guided Tour Hours: Th 1p & 3p, Fr-Su 12p, 1pm, 2p, & 3p; $10 and you can bring folks under 21 for free; Self-Guided Tour Times: M 12p-5p, Th 12p-5p, F-Su 11a-7p (self-guided tours are free but don't come with any tastes); Tap Room Hours: M 12p-6p, Tu-W: Closed; Th 12p-6p, Fr-Su: 11a-8p; Tel: (985) 893-3143;

https://abita.com

RESTAURANTS

Poche's Market, Restaurant & Smokehouse
3015 Main Hwy #A
Breaux Bridge, LA 70517

When you want barbecue in Acadiana, head to Poche's! It's a good deal: we got a chicken plate with dirty rice and a rib plate featuring five of the biggest ribs we'd ever seen, all for around $20. Plates comes with two sides. Enjoy the mounted-deer-head decor.

Cost and hours: Su 6a–6p, M-Sa 4–8p; $;
Phone: (337) 332-2108 or 800-3POCHES;
https://poches.com

Glenda's Creole Kitchen Restaurant
3232 Main Hwy # 31
Breaux Bridge, LA 70517

Glenda's is a Creole/Cajun restaurant serving plate lunches. The menu changes daily, and features such yummy items as smothered porkchops, stuffed turkey wings, and spaghetti 'n' meatballs.

Hours and cost: Su-F 10a-2p; Closed Sa; $;
Tel. (337) 332-0294;
https://www.facebook.com/Glendas-Creole-CreoleCajun-Restaurant-Catering-159514480749925/

Johnson's Boucaniere
111 St. John St.
Lafayette, LA 70501

Johnson's Boucaniere is an absolute treasury of smoked meats—just in terms of sausage, they've got pork, garlic pork, mixed beef and pork, and turkey. They've also got pork tasso, turkey tasso, beef jerky, smoked meat sandwiches, boudin, and BBQ. It's making our mouths water to think of it.

Cost and Hours: W-F 10a-3p, Sa 8a-3p, Su 10a-2p; $;
Tel. (337) 269-8878;
https://www.johnsonsboucaniere.com

"ANDOUILLE SAUSAGE CRAWL"

In LaPlace, Louisiana, the "Andouille Capital of the World" (about 30 miles northwest of New Orleans), you should hit up the following three sausage shops. See how much World Famous Andouille Sausage you can eat!

First up:

Bailey's Andouille
513 W. Airline Hwy.
LaPlace, LA 70068

At Bailey's, a happy and plush mascot-sized sausage greets you as you step inside! Step past the anthropomorphic wiener to the counter. As the Bailey's site notes, their sausages are "stuffed with fresh garlic and a special blend of spices which are slowly smoked over a pecan wood fire."

Hours: M-F 8a-5:30p; Sa 8a-5p (Sept.-March), 8a-3p (April-August); Su Closed); $;
Tel. (985) 652-9090;
http://www.baileysandouille.com

Right next door, you'll find:

Jacob's World Famous Andouille
505 West Airline Hwy.
LaPlace, LA 70068

Since 1928, Jacob's World Famous has been covering all of your needs when it comes to sausage, smoked turkey necks, hog head cheese, and smoked ham hocks.

Hours: M-Sa 8a-6p, closed Su; $;
Tel. (985) 652-9080, Toll Free: 1-(877)-215-7589;
e-mail Original@JacobsAndouille.com;
https://www.cajunsausage.com

Down the road apiece, you will find:

Wayne Jacob's Smokehouse
769 A West 5th St.
LaPlace, LA 70068

Not to be confused with the afore-mentioned Jacob's, Wayne Jacob's is "Home of Andouille Smoked The Old Fashioned Way!"

Hours (during ongoing renovation): Restaurant: Mon-Fri, 11a-2p; Smokehouse Country Store: 7 days a week, 9a-2p; $;
Tel. (985) 652-9990;

https://wjsmokehouse.com

MUSIC, BARS, AND THE REST

Teddy's Juke Joint
17001 Old Scenic Hwy.
Zachary, LA 70791

One of the last of the old-school juke joints, Teddy's can be found in Zachary, a town just north of Baton Rouge. The drive is dark and lonely, but as you approach, the twinkle of Christmas lights and sounds of the blues puts you at ease.

Step inside: the interior is dense, festooned with Christmas lights. Records and masks hang from the ceiling. You're greeted with the conviviality of a party. There's dancing and, buried deeply in the bluesy mise-en-scene, you may spot Teddy himself, or at least his Cheshire cat grin. He'll be seated centrally, like some kind of savior of all that is holy (*or not*) in a juke joint. In between sets of live music Teddy spins records, narrating the music in his own inimitable fashion. The beer and hospitality runneth over. There's a kitchen, as well.

On the night we were there, Selwyn Cooper & the Sharecroppers were rocking the joint, and the great Eden Brent dropped by to tickle the ivories. This was the first time we'd seen her, and we were blown away by her virtuoso boogie-woogie runs. After all, she learned at the knee of the Abie "Boogaloo" Ames himself, one of the greats of Greenville's Nelson Street—indeed, the "Mozart of the Delta."

Cost and Hours: Teddy spins records "most nights" at 8pm—definitely on Sundays, Mondays and Thursdays, and some Saturdays if there's no band. There's an acoustic circle every Wednesday at 7p. Tuesdays and Fridays generally feature a blues jam at 7p—Tuesday's jam is led by Dewayne & Company, Friday's by Doug Brousseau and the River City Allstars; No cover charge that we recall, but do tip the band; Kitchen is $;

Tel.(225) 892-0064 or (225) 658-8029;

e-mail: teddysjukejoint60@yahoo.com;

https://teddysjukejoint.com

Tabby's Blues Box and Heritage Hall Red Stick Social
1503 Government St.
Baton Rouge, LA 70802

An exciting recent development is the reopening of Tabby's Blues Box and Heritage Hall, originally founded by "the late Baton Rouge blues legend Tabby Thomas," as the Hall's website puts it. His son, bluesman Chris Thomas King, has revived Tabby's inside a cavernous entertainment hall called the Red Stick Social (103 years old). (Chris first revived his father's idea of the "Hoodoo Party" in January 2020, and we all knew what happened just a couple months later: the COVID-19 pandemic.) The new joint is only a block away from the location of the original club in the historic Black entertainment district. The original Tabby's was a true incubator for Louisiana blues. It certainly looks like all the people involved in the new venture intend it to be a place that honors culture and history.

Cost and Hours: Red Stick Social is open M-W 4p–10p; Th 4p–12a; F-Sa 11a–12a; Su 11a–10p;
Tel: (225) 223-6637;

https://redsticksocial.com

Dew Drop Jazz & Social Hall
430 Lamarque St.
Mandeville, LA 70448

Located in "the heart of Old Mandeville, Louisiana," the refurbished Dew Drop now hosts around 12 traditional jazz concerts a year. Why is that such a big deal? The roots of the Dew Drop go back to 1885, when it was established on the north shore of Lake Pontchartrain as the meeting hall for a newly-formed mutual-aid society. (The Black community often formed such "benevolent associations" to fill the gap left by the insurance industry, which refused to serve them.)

Among other community functions, the hall also served as a performance space. Quoth the Dew Drop's website: "The hall on Lamarque Street, unpainted and nestled in a grove of ancient live oaks, is now considered the world's oldest virtually unaltered rural jazz dance hall. It was built the same year that scholars agree was the year of the birth of traditional jazz in New Orleans."

During its heyday in the '20s and '30s, legends such as Bunk Johnson, the Fritz Brothers Band, Papa Celestin, Buddie Petit, Buddy Mandalay, and Kid Ory played here. Most crucially, Louis Armstrong played here before he ventured into the wider world as New Orleans's "jazz ambassador," and returned to play here occasionally even after attaining international fame in the '30s and '40s.

We'll leave the last word with the Dew Drop itself: "While at the Dew Drop many attest to feeling spirits of former jazz greats who played in the building at the turn of the century. With the large shutters thrown open and fans sitting on ancient church pews, spirited jazz bands transport audiences back in time to the early years of America's most enduring cultural gift to the world—traditional New Orleans jazz."

Cost and hours: Concerts Sa 6:30p-9:30p; Admission to each concert is $10 at the door (no advance tickets are sold);
Tel. (985) 264-7401;

http://www.dewdropjazzhall.com/home.html

Pont Breaux's
325 W. Mills Ave.
Breaux Bridge, LA 70517

[Pont Breaux's is now permanently closed, which is very sad—the reasons, it seems, were rising food costs, short-staffing, and the death of patriarch Randy Leblanc. We're still including the entry we'd prepared, just on the off chance that someone may revive it one day, and also to memorialize our happy evening of crawfish and Cajun country dancing. When we lose something like Pont Breaux's, we lose a bit of local life and landscape; by writing about it we can keep the memory of it, at least, alive.]

At Pont Breaux's, you'll find crawfish, country dancing and Cajun music nightly. On the night we visited, we caught Jay Cormier & Cajun Country, who play impeccable, danceable Acadian-country. Jay sang in plaintive French and the steel guitarist played sweetly.

It's a restaurant as well as a music hall: it was here that Scott had his first-ever crawfish boil. (Breaux Bridge, after all, is the "crawfish capital of the world.") He was struggling mightily with his "joeys" (our sobriquet for crawfish, for some reason—not sure of the provenance) when an older gentleman approached. We'd noticed him earlier—we'd admired the grace of his Cajun jitterbugging with his wife. They'd clearly been doing it all their lives. "I can stand it no longer," he proclaimed. With that, he proceeded to teach Scott how to efficiently pop the shell off a crawfish. As this anecdote may demonstrate, Point Breaux's is your perfect evening in French Louisiana. (Now that we've conquered crawfish, on our next visit we'll have to tackle some country-dance steps.) On the way out, a sign lists famous visitors. Scott was chuffed to see that the list included Bob Dylan and David Byrne.

Next, we'll list a few of the still-extent Zydeco/Cajun Dancehalls. Get to one if you can.

Cajun Country Lounge & Dancehall
9708 Church Point Hwy.
Church Point, LA 70525

The Cajun Country Lounge & Dancehall features live music every weekend. On Thursday there's an open Cajun jam session, and every Sunday afternoon consists of live Cajun music from 4p to 7p and a "real charcoal BBQ." What's more, there's "daily plate lunches, full menu & seasonal boiled crawfish," as their website puts it. "We are a smoke free dancehall located in the heart of Cajun Country in Church Point, LA. We support local upcoming artist and work hard to keep our Cajun and country culture alive. We have a fully stocked bar with frozen drinks and a variety of beer and liquor… We have a large dancefloor with tables and seating to dine in and enjoy the entertainment." It sounds divine, doesn't it? (Must be 21 to enter.)

Cost and hours: M-Sa 10a-2a, Su 10a-12a; $;

Tel: (337) 684-9101;

https://cajuncountryloungecp.com

Whiskey River Landing
1365 Henderson Levee Rd.
Henderson, LA 70517

Whiskey River Landing, as they say themselves, is "the place to be on Sunday afternoon! Allons Danser!" According to Cajun Country chronicler John 'Pudd' Sharp, this joint features some of the most popular zydeco/Cajun bands in the region. To get there, "a long ride south down Henderson Levee Road leads to a wooden sign emblazoned with a red, white, and blue accordion. It beckons you up and over the levee, revealing the Atchafalaya Basin." The dancing jumps off at 3p. They sell buckets of beer and there are often food trucks out front.

Cost and hours: The dancing starts at 3p on Sundays.

Tel: (337) 228-2277; $;

https://www.facebook.com/WhiskeyRiverLanding/?ref=page_internal

Vermilion Performance Center
300 Fisher Rd.
Lafayette, LA 70508

Along the banks of Bayou Vermilion in Lafayette is the Vermillion Performance Center. It contains a Living History Museum and Folklife

Park, similar to Europe's open-air folk museums, where vanishing aspects of Cajun Country life and history are recreated, many of which go back to the 1700s and reached a peak during the Civil War. You'll find a typical Southern Louisiana village with various styles of historic buildings and a "garden of healing plants." Arrayed around the grounds are master craftsman and artisans demonstrating traditional techniques for cooking, spinning cotton, weaving, and woodworking, as well as playing Cajun and Creole music. Vermilionville also boasts a popular dancehall. As John 'Pudd' Sharp writes, "The bands on the schedule are all crowd favorites–Creole legend Goldman Thibodaux, Swamp Pop crooner Warren Storm, zydeco headliners like Geno Delafose and French Rockin' Boogie, classic Cajun groups like the Ray Abshire Band, as well as extremely popular younger groups like Bonsoir, Catin, The Revelers and Soul Creole."

Cost and Hours: The Living History Museum and Folklife Park is open Tu-Su, 10a-4p; adults (ages 19 – 65): $10; senior citizens (age 65+): $8, students (ages 5 – 18): $6, children (under 5): free; The bal du dimanche—or Sunday dance—takes place in the dancehall in the Performance Center from 1p-4p weekly; Admission $10, includes a self-guided tour of the Vermilionville Living History museum. You may come early and get lunch at the La Cuisine de Maman restaurant, which features an all-you-can-eat Sunday Buffet. You know how Scott feels about all-you-can-eat.

El Sid O's Zydeco and Blues Club
1523 N. Saint Antoine St.
Lafayette, LA 70501

The names of those who have played at El Sid O's ring out in zydeco lore: Clifton Chenier, Buckwheat Zydeco, Rockin Dopsie, John Delafose, Beau Jocque, and Nathan & the Zydeco Cha Chas. Nathan Williams (leader of the Cha Chas) is actually the brother of El Sid O's owner Sidney Williams—a mean accordion player himself. Many of these greats play at the hall's annual Thanksgiving food drive show, a longtime tradition. El Sid O's is a great place to see zydeco dancing, and to give it a whirl yourself. The kitchen (Sid's One Stop) serves plate lunches, and there's $2 drink specials on Friday and Saturday till 11p.

Cost and hours: F and Sa 9p-2a, closed the rest of the week; $;
Tel: (337) 237-1959;
https://www.facebook.com/ElSidos/

186 | PFEIFFER, STEELE-PFEIFFER

La Poussiere Cajun Dancehall
1215 Grand Pointe Ave.
Breaux Bridge, LA 70517

La Pousserie lives on, restored and repaired after a devastating tornado thanks to a benefit concert held by a coalition of musicians who love the place (Jackie Callier and the Cajun Cousins, Geno Delafose and French Rockin Boogie, Cheryl Cormier and Cajun Sound, High Performance, Walter Mouton and the Scott Playboys, and Steve Riley and the Mamou Playboys). This dancehall has been around since 1955: the music remains Cajun, Country, and Swamp Pop. There's dancing and music every weekend, on Saturday at 8p and on Sundays at 2p, when Jackie Caillier, Ivy Dugas and the Cajun Cousins are the regular band. There's also occasional special Friday shows, often featuring Geno Delafose & French Rockin Boogie or Dylan Aucoin and the Judice Ramblers.

Cost and hours: Sa-8p-11p; Su 2p-5p; occasional F shows at 8p; closed the rest of the week; It appears there is no cover charge but for reservations you can call or text 337.332.1721, or message them on their FB page: https://www.facebook.com/LaPoussi ereCajunDancehall/?ref=page_internal

For even more information and background on zydeco dancehalls you can still visit, such as Paul's Playhouse in Sunset, the Blue Moon Saloon and Grand Street Dancehall in Lafayette, Fred's Lounge and Holiday Lounge in Mamou, and the Southern Club outside Opelousas, read John 'Pudd' Sharp's excellent article Dancehalls of Cajun Country at https://www.lafayettetravel. com/things-to-do/trails/dancehalls-of-cajun-country/. It does our heart good to see the culture being nurtured like this.

TOURS AND FESTIVALS

Cajun Country Swamp Tours
1209 Rookery Rd.
Breaux Bridge, LA 70517

To get out onto the bayou on a boat, drifting among the cypress trees and the Spanish moss, is an experience not to miss when you're in Acadiana—like taking a gondola ride through the canals when you're in Venice. We recommend Cajun Country Swamp Tours. Along with numerous close gator sightings, we saw a lot of colorful fauna and wildlife on our journey through the swamp: an egret, an owl, and a mama hawk feeding her babies, just to name a few. Afterwards, Karolyn used the metaphor of 'gardener' to describe our guide Shawn; he had a gardener's sense of stewardship and care for the environment.

Cost and Hours: Tours last 1 1/2 hours and leave from Lake Martin Rd & Rookery Rd., Louisiana 70582; boats go out everyday at various times, usually around 9a, 10:45a, 12:30p 4:30p, 6:30p; $25.00 per seat;

Tel. (337) 319-0010;

https://www.cajuncountryswamptours.com

HOTELS

Maison des Lion Bed & Breakfast
(formerly Maison des Amis Bed & Breakfast Inn)
111 Washington St.
Breaux Bridge, LA 70517

Maison des Lion is our recommendation for your home on the bayou in French Louisiana (we knew it as Maison des Amis, when it was under different ownership). Located about 126 miles west of New Orleans in Breaux Bridge, the "crawfish capital of the world," this b&b is a cozy and well-appointed place. (We recall the poetic inscription on the painting in our bedroom: "Only the moonlight could properly illuminate the words he wrote to her.") During our stay, we had the whole place to ourselves except for an extraordinarily friendly kitty who liked to drop by and play. It's located on the banks of Bayou Teche, with an expansive and verdant landscaped garden spreading down to a gazebo and boardwalk right on the water's edge. To sit relaxing on a rocking chair in the gazebo, sipping a drink and looking over the bayou, is the very definition of "the good life." We couldn't have been happier with the place. They even have a recording of H2O waves—if, ironically, you have trouble sleeping in so much silence.

At the time we went to press, the new owner, Tressie Jordan, had not had a chance to update the b&b's website/social media. You may reach her at 1-954-263-9307 and she will set you up.

Renaissance Baton Rouge Hotel
7000 Bluebonnet Boulevard
Baton Rouge, LA 70810

You know the drill by now. This hotel got all the soul and charm of your typical chain—the kind of place that's short on local flavor but good on convenience. It's a perfectly acceptable place to sleep if you're staying overnight in Baton Rouge. We enjoyed sitting outside and sipping a cocktail on the terrace while gazing at the palm trees and the full moon. The flaming decorative bowls were a nice touch.

Tel: 225-215-7000;

https://www.marriott.com/en-us/hotels/btrbb-renaissance-baton-rouge-hotel/over-view/

KAROLYN'S TIP JAR

When the spirit moves you, dance. Even if you can't do it well. Ask a stranger to teach you.

CHAPTER VIII

New Orleans: The Big Kahuna: From BBQ Shrimp to Ya-Ka-Mein and Back Again

"Liberation is a place most of us visit temporarily and some of us strive to bring humanity toward; it's both a destination and moments of joy and solidarity."—King Oliver

❝ The street has the beat. The beat embodies the rhythm, the rhythm embodies the culture."—Herlin Riley

❝ It is better to live here [in New Orleans] in sackcloth and ashes than to own the whole state of Ohio." —Lafcadia Hearn

❝ New Orleans is the city where imagination takes precedence over fact."— William Faulkner

How do we love thee, New Orleans? Can we even count the ways?

At the grandest level, New Orleans is the cradle of American music—our greatest contribution to the world. (What else?) It's where "jazz and funk began, where American cultural immortality launched itself and still sings all night if it's not busy in bed," in the great words of Rebecca Snedeker and Rebecca Solnit in their indispensable book *Unfathomable City: A New Orleans Atlas*. At the most basic level, New Orleans gives you permission to be yourself, as we once heard a DJ on local radio station WWOZ put it.

What you want is to experience that culture up-and-moving—alive and kicking—and that means you want live music. Which in turn means you want Frenchmen Street in the Marigny neighborhood. Lined with one great music venue after another, it's a street where the air is always dancing with rhythm and melody. Our recommended hotel, Lamothe House, is quite literally right around the corner from Frenchmen. In fact, one way we know we're really back in town is when we hear the stentorian sounds of a brass band playing on the corner of Frenchmen/Chartres from the porch of Lamothe's Creole guest cottage, calling us out the door and down into the streets. (At least, all of the above *used* to be the case. Enough of this is true that we're still keeping it: Frenchmen's still great. Still, now we have some caveats, which we'll get to later.)

Roots run deep here. Musicians often come from a background in which playing is a family tradition: Danny Barker, Wynton Marsalis, Leroy Jones, and Tuba Fats, to name just a few, are products of musical legacies. Jon Batiste, former bandleader on *The Late Show with Stephen Colbert*, hails from a long line of musicians, including saxophonist/arranger Harold Battiste and Lionel Batiste, legendary bass-drum/kazoo player/singer with the Treme Brass Band (and all-around local character).

Often, great musical families are also great cooking/restaurateur families. At Li'l Dizzy's, for example, you used to be able to order a delicious dish called "trout Baquet"—it has since been supplanted by the "catfish Jourdain"—which was an homage to the Baquets, the esteemed local family of restaurateurs/musicians who founded Li'l Dizzy's. The Baquets have deep roots in the Creole culinary tradition as well as in jazz history: Achille and George Baquet were clarinetists in the seminal early New Orleans jazz scene. (Dean Baquet, incidentally, is the executive editor of the New York Times—the first Black man to have that role.)

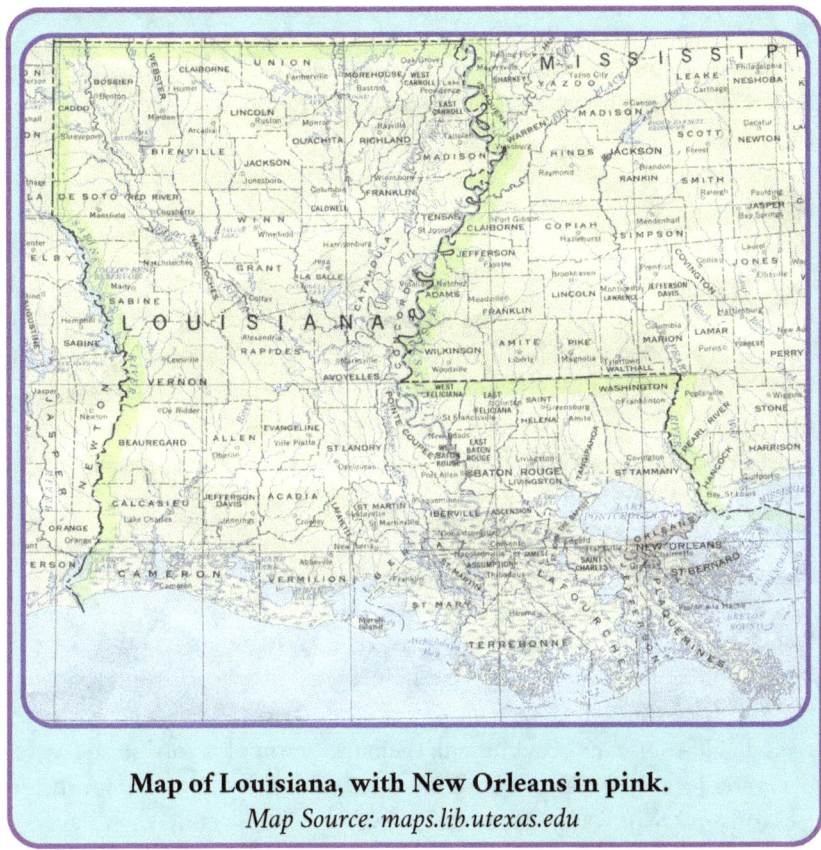

Map of Louisiana, with New Orleans in pink.
Map Source: maps.lib.utexas.edu

Perhaps what we love most about New Orleans is the way that everything that's wonderful about it—the music, the food, and the architecture, too—is a product of cultural fusion. It all came out of the melting pot, and didn't our civics books used to tout that metaphor as the most American of all notions?

What are the ingredients of the gumbo in that fiery pot? New Orleans is both the northern tip of the Caribbean-Latin American south *and* the most European of American cities—in the 1800s, it was the "opera capital of North America." Cuba's Santiago is considered New Orleans' sister city, and many New Orleanians can trace their cultural and ancestral roots back to that island. The Fodor's guidebook puts it concisely: "Springing from colonial origins, New Orleans was born of a unique blend of people (Creoles, escaped slaves, Jeffersonian Americans) and influences (France, Spain, the Caribbean)."

The story of this "unique blend" is continuously fascinating. Bone up on the history before your visit. The town was founded in 1718 as a French colony, a convenient seaport on the Gulf of Mexico. It became part of the United States in 1803, with the Louisiana Purchase. There are endlessly fascinating byways to explore from there.

Let's just take the story of Haiti's profound influence on Louisiana, which extends to its politics, people, religion and culture. How'd that happen? Today's Haiti was once France's Saint Domingue—this Caribbean island was Louisiana's parent colony. Between 1791 and 1803, an anti-slavery revolution rocked the island, during which thousands of refugees, including free people of color and white colonists—sometimes bringing along the people they enslaved—arrived in New Orleans.

The Haitian Revolution was a Black slave-led uprising against French rule which transformed Saint Domingue into Haiti in 1804—a nation ruled by ex-slaves who had freed themselves. (The French then had the nerve to insist upon reparations for their slaveholders' lost property (!), thus shackling the country in debt forever, but that's another story.) The refugees who arrived in New Orleans brought with them the "germ of revolt," in the words of planter Joseph Pontalba, whose stately apartment buildings famously line Jackson Square. It was a "germ" he believed would infect his own slaves.

How can you, too, get infected with this "germ," catch an echo of this culture of revolt and liberation? Participate in a second line parade! Why would you want to do that, you ask? Because it's exhilarating to take over the streets to a brass band accompaniment. While the roots and context of this celebratory parade tradition are in the city's African-American neighborhoods, a second line is wonderfully inclusive—people from every walk of life participate. You'll be dancing in the streets. If you've never taken part in the reclaiming of public space by a community too often marginalized by a conformist society—well, in short, you should. (See more in our section on second lines.)

Of course, you could also come down for New Orleans' local version of the worldwide Carnival season of celebration—popularly known as "Mardi Gras." See more about that in our entry under "festivals."

We can tell you about it, but it's best you walk the streets and experience it for yourself. Feel the warm Caribbean wind in the palm trees. Taste the Jamaican and Haitian flavors. Groove to the Latin and Afro-Cuban habanera and clave rhythms. Dig the rumba and mambo beats undergirding the music of local favorites like Fats Domino and Professor Longhair. As Jelly Roll Morton once said, we wouldn't even have New Orleans blues and jazz without the influence of the "Latin tinge."

New Orleans' vibes are hypnotic, drawing you in—asking you to witness and experience her pain, her glory, and everything in between. It is the embodiment of resilience and renewal—especially after Katrina and Covid-19. It is America's most important city. (There, we said it.)

In short, it is the Birthplace of Jazz, and it is Where the Culture Lives Today.

PLANNING YOUR TIME: ITINERARIES

The essence of New Orleans is live music. That's one reason COVID was so devastating. In our recent visits, we've witnessed the joys of the city coming back to life.

Depending on what night of the week it is, supplement the itineraries below with your choice of evening music. If it's a Monday, say, you could see John Boutté at **d.b.a.** (618 Frenchmen St., 70116; https://dbaneworleans.com) at 7pm if he's in town; if not, you could see The New Orleans Cottonmouth Kings at the **Spotted Cat** (623 Frenchmen St., 70116; https://www.spottedcatmusicclub.com) at 10pm.

- If it's Tuesday, head to the **Maple Leaf** (8316 Oak St., 70118; https://www.mapleleafbar.com) for the world-renowned Rebirth Brass Band at 10pm. (This one is essential if it's your first time.)

- If it's Wednesday, catch the Shotgun Jazz Band at the **Spotted Cat** (623 Frenchmen St., 70116; https://www.spottedcatmusicclub.com) at 6pm.

- If it's Thursday, head to **Rock 'n' Bowl** (3016 S Carrollton Ave., 70118; https://www.rocknbowl.com) for Zydeco Thursday, or catch the Soul Rebels at **Le Bon Temps Roule** (4801 Magazine St., 70115; https://lbtrnola.com) at 11pm.

- If it's Friday, look for Kermit Ruffins at **The Blue Nile** (532 Frenchmen St., 70116; https://www.bluenilelive.com) at 10pm (closer to 11pm, really).

- On a Saturday, do not miss the **Preservation Hall All Stars** (726 St Peter St., 70116; https://www.preservationhall.com) at 8pm.

Sunday is usually the night we come into town, in which case we head to d.b.a. on Frenchmen, preferring to keep it close to home (as we've mentioned, Lamothe House is right around the corner from Frenchmen). A great option is to check out the Palmetto Bug Stompers at d.b.a. (618 Frenchmen St., 70116; https://dbaneworleans.com) at 6pm. Alternately, if you have a lot of energy you could head out to the Maple Leaf (8316 Oak St., 70118; https://www.mapleleafbar.com) to see Walter "Wolfman" Washington with Joe Krown at 8pm.

These are merely suggestions; for tons more ideas, see our entry below under Music, Bars and the Rest.

First-timers' Long Weekend Jaunt

Day One
Morning

Breakfast at Cafe Du Monde.

Stroll on the Riverwalk on the Mississippi River.

Amble around Jackson Square and St. Louis Cathedral, then walk over to the French Market and explore the flea market.

Afternoon

Get a muffuletta lunch from Central Grocery (temporarily closed—consider Frank's as an alternative) and enjoy it in nearby Latrobe Park. (Wash it down with a spicy Bloody Mary from the adjacent Gazebo Cafe).

Stroll down Royal Street, lined with art galleries, *al fresco* musicians, and good restaurants.

Have a cocktail at historic Napoleon House. (The Pimm's Cup is the signature.)

Visit the New Orleans Jazz Museum at the Old U.S. Mint. (The Museum's afternoon lecture/performance series, led by rangers of the New Orleans Jazz National Historical Park, is also well-worth attending.)

Evening

Have dinner at Mr. B's Bistro. (The Hotel Monteleone's Carousel Bar is right across the street. A cocktail there is a signature New Orleans experience. Try a Sazerac or a Milk Punch.)

Your choice of evening music.

Day Two
Morning

Have "breakfast at Brennan's."

Hop the St. Charles streetcar over to the Garden District to explore Lafayette Cemetery No. 1 and do our Garden District Walk.

Take a break for a drink at Commander's Palace or the Columns Hotel.

Afternoon

Have lunch at Acme Oyster House.

Stroll down Bourbon Street, stopping at Marie Laveau's House of Voodoo and ending at Lafitte's Blacksmith Shop for a drink. (Consider picking up a Lucky Dog and daiquiri for the road.)

Evening

Have dinner at Muriel's for French Quarter ambience and New Orleans classics, or for something (way) less formal, Clover Grill on Bourbon for delicious burgers.

Your choice of evening music.

Day Three
Morning

Have breakfast at Cafe Beignet on Royal Street.

Tour the Backstreet Cultural Museum in Treme.

Visit Congo Square in Louis Armstrong Park, the birthplace of jazz.

Afternoon

Have lunch at Li'l Dizzy's.

Walk up Esplanade Avenue, enjoying the colorful and distinctive houses. Visit Degas House, where the great French artist lived during Reconstruction.

Dinner

Enjoy the Caribbean-influenced flavors of Compere Lapin.

Your choice of evening music.

FROM BLUES TO JAZZ: A NEW ORLEANS-BASED SOUTHERN ROAD TRIP ON THE BLUES HIGHWAY (2 WEEK ITINERARY)

Day One (Memphis):
Morning

Tour Sun Studios, one of the birthplaces of rock 'n' roll.

Afternoon

Have lunch at the the Four Way, for soul food and Civil Rights history. Tour the Stax Museum of American Soul Music.

Evening

Have dinner at Rendezvous for BBQ, then hit Beale Street clubs.

Day Two (Memphis):
Morning

Have breakfast at the Arcade, Memphis's oldest restaurant, then tour Graceland.

Afternoon

Have lunch at Marlowe's for some Elvis-approved BBQ.

Tour the Memphis Rock 'n' Soul Museum.

Evening

Catch the march of the Peabody Ducks at 5pm, if you missed their 11am perambulation.

Drive or hop a cab/Uber out to Wild Bill's for a true juke joint experience.

Day Three (New Orleans):
Morning

Time to drive from Memphis to New Orleans. Grab a breakfast bar, coffee, and hit the road.

On the way, do the Money Road/Robert Johnson's gravesite detour in Greenwood, Mississippi, as described in the "Delta Exploring" section above.

Afternoon

Pull off the road for lunch at Mr. D's Old Country Store in Lorman, Mississippi.

Evening

Pull into New Orleans and check in to Lamothe House. Dinner at Adolfo's on Frenchmen Street.

Depending on what night it is, pick your evening music. (See our guide in the New Orleans section, below).

Day Four (New Orleans):
Morning

Breakfast at Cafe Du Monde.

Stroll on the Riverwalk on the Mississippi River.

Amble around Jackson Square and St. Louis Cathedral, then walk over to the French Market and explore the flea market.

Afternoon

Get a muffuletta lunch from Central Grocery (temporarily closed—consider Frank's as an alternative) and enjoy it in nearby Latrobe Park. (Wash it down with a spicy Bloody Mary from the adjacent Gazebo Cafe).

Stroll down Royal Street, lined with art galleries, *al fresco* musicians, and good restaurants.

Have a cocktail at historic Napoleon House. (The Pimm's Cup is the signature.)

Visit the New Orleans Jazz Museum at the Old U.S. Mint. (The Museum's afternoon lecture/performance series, led by rangers of the New Orleans Jazz National Historical Park, is also well-worth attending.)

Evening

Have dinner at Mr. B's Bistro. (The Hotel Monteleone's Carousel Bar is right across the street. A cocktail there is a signature New Orleans experience. Try a Sazerac or a Milk Punch.)

Your choice of evening music. (If it is a Tuesday, don't miss the Rebirth Brass Band at the Maple Leaf.)

Day Five (New Orleans):
Morning

Have "breakfast at Brennan's."

Hop the St. Charles streetcar over to the Garden District to explore Lafayette Cemetery No. 1 and do our "Garden District Walk."

Afternoon

Take a break for a drink at Commander's Palace or the Columns Hotel.

Have lunch at Acme Oyster House.

Stroll down Bourbon Street, stopping at Marie Laveau's House of Voodoo and ending at Lafitte's Blacksmith Shop for a drink. (Consider picking up a Lucky Dog and daiquiri for the road.)

Evening

Have dinner at Muriel's for French Quarter ambience and New Orleans classics. Or, if you're more footloose, try Clover Grill on Bourbon for delicious burgers.

Your choice of evening music.

Day Six (New Orleans):
Morning

Have breakfast at Cafe Beignet on Royal Street.

Tour the Backstreet Cultural Museum in Treme.

Visit Congo Square in Louis Armstrong Park, the birthplace of jazz.

Afternoon

Have lunch at Li'l Dizzy's.

Walk up Esplanade Avenue, enjoying the colorful and distinctive houses. Visit Degas House, where the great French artist lived during Reconstruction.

Evening

Enjoy the Caribbean-influenced flavors of Compere Lapin.

Your choice of music. (If it is a Thursday, don't miss Zydeco night at Rock'n'Bowl. Or, to keep with the Treme theme, head to Kermit's Treme Mother-in-Law Lounge.)

Day Seven (New Orleans):
Morning

Have breakfast at Croissant D'Or.

Tour the New Orleans Art Museum and Besthoff Sculpture Garden.

Afternoon

Eat lunch at Liuzza's by the Tracks.

Explore the Bayou the St. John neighborhood.

Evening

Have a classic Creole dinner at Dooky Chase's.

Your choice of music.

Day Eight (New Orleans):
Morning

Have breakfast at EnVie Cafe.

Attend a 10am Ranger Talk at the Jean Lafitte National Historical Park & Preserve French Quarter Visitor Center, or do our Royal Street Art Galleries/Historic Mansion Walk.

Have a Famous Frozen Irish Coffee at Molly's in the Market. Try to sit in the window.

Afternoon

Have lunch at Li'l Dizzy's.

Visit the Ogden Museum of Southern Art.

Evening

Have dinner at Cochon.

Your choice of music.

—or—

Let's assume this is a Sunday:

Go to Buffa's for jazz brunch.

Take part in a second line. Look for the Pigeon Town Steppers. The parade usually starts around 1p, often at the Big Man Lounge (2916 Louisiana Ave., 70115).

Day Nine (New Orleans):

Morning

Have breakfast at Elizabeth's Cafe.

Explore the neighborhood, using our Faubourg Marigny/Bywater walk as guide.

Afternoon

Have lunch at Frady's One-Stop Food Store.

Explore Dr. Bob's headquarters.

Have dinner at Bacchanal.

Evening

Choose your evening music. If you've been exploring the Bywater all day and it's a Thursday, consider extending your stay in the neighborhood by catching Corey Henry and the Treme Funktet at Vaughan's Lounge.

Day Ten (New Orleans):
Morning

Have breakfast at Meals From the Heart.

Take a Free Tours by Foot Voodoo Tour.

Afternoon

Take an afternoon trip over to Algiers. Have lunch at Dry Dock Cafe and Bar. While away the afternoon at the Old Point Bar, or visit the Algiers Folk Art Zone & Blues Museum. Watch the sunset from Algiers Point.

Evening

Have dinner at N7.

Your choice of live music.

Day Eleven (New Orleans):
Morning

Have breakfast at the Camellia Grill.

Explore one of the cemeteries in our "cemeteries" section.

Afternoon

Eat lunch at Mandina's.

Visit the New Orleans Pharmacy Museum.

Evening

Take a French Quarter Ghost Tour by Free Tours on Foot. Grab a bite beforehand, or if you're peckish afterwards and it's a Friday or Saturday evening, consider a late dinner at Port of Call.

For the final leg of our "From Blues to Jazz" trip, you have your choice:

OPTION 1: CLARKSDALE

Day Twelve (Clarksdale):
Morning/Afternoon

If you get an early enough start, consider stopping at the Whitney Plantation on your way to Clarksdale from New Orleans.

Next, head directly to the crossroads where Highway 61 meets 49, and have lunch at Abe's.

Tour the Delta Blues Museum.

Evening

Have dinner at Ground Zero Blues Club, and stay for live blues.

Day Thirteen (Clarksdale):
Morning

Have breakfast at Bluesberry Cafe, or Our Grandma's House of Pancakes.

Browse and shop at Cat Head Delta Blues and Folk Art.

Afternoon

Have lunch at Hick's Famous Hot Tamales.

Browse at the Hambone Art Gallery.

Head to the New Roxy for a drink.

Evening

Have dinner and a beer at Rust Restaurant in the Shack Up Inn, and stay for some live blues at the Juke Joint Chapel.

Head to Red's for a true juke joint experience.

OPTION 2: NASHVILLE

Day Twelve (Nashville)
Morning/Afternoon

Drive the eight hours from New Orleans to Nashville.

Evening

Head to Tootsies Orchid Lounge

Day Thirteen (Nashville)
Morning

Visit the Ryman Auditorium.

Lunch

Have lunch at Broadway Brewhouse.

Visit the Country Music Hall of Fame.

Evening

Have dinner at Jack's Bar-B-Que.

Head to Robert's Western World.

OPTION 3: ACADIANA, AKA CAJUN COUNTRY

Day Twelve (Breaux Bridge)
Morning

Make your way to Breaux Bridge, Louisiana from New Orleans.

Check into Maison des Lion.

Afternoon

Get lunch at Glenda's Creole Kitchen Restaurant.

Visit the Living History Museum and Folklife Park at the Vermillion Performance Center.

Evening

Have dinner at Poche's Market, Restaurant & Smokehouse.

If it's a Saturday, head to La Poussiere Cajun Dancehall.

Day Thirteen (Breaux Bridge)
Morning

Take the Cajun Country Swamp Tours.

Afternoon/Evening

Have lunch at Johnson's Boucaniere

If it's a Sunday, head out to Whiskey River Landing (zydeco dancing and food trucks) or Cajun Country Lounge & Dancehall (live Cajun music and BBQ).

SITES AND MUSEUMS

HISTORIC BUILDINGS

Napoleon House
500 Chartres St.
New Orleans, LA 70130

It says something about New Orleans that an entry under "Historic Buildings" could just as easily be listed under "bars/restaurants," and vice versa. Today Napoleon House is an atmospheric place for a bite and/or a drink, but it was once the home of the fifth mayor of New Orleans, Nicholas Girod, who served from 1812-1815. Drop in for a cocktail: the house's signature is the Pimm's Cup, which legend has it is their own invention. (At the very least, Napoleon House put the drink on the map.) This is also a solid place for jambalaya and muffuletta. Today, the kitchen is run by the Ralph Brennan group, which represents the current generation of the storied Brennan family of NOLA restaurateurs. Enjoy the archways and the grandly aged, worn walls with their yellowing portraits which seem to drip history. Or you could relax in the palm-tree-graced courtyard. In 1821, this house was actually earmarked to be the home in exile of Napoleon himself: Mayor Girod was a sympathizer of the deposed emperor, who was then languishing on the island of St. Helena—an ignoble end for the very man, you'll recall, who sold Louisiana to the United States in 1803. Girod devised a scheme to rescue him and bring him to New Orleans, but Napoleon died right before the plan could be put into play. All in all, Napoleon House is a quintessential New Orleans experience, where time seems to bend.

Cost and Hours: W-Th, Su 11a-9p, F-Sa 11a-10p, closed M-Tu; $$;

Tel: (504) 524-9752

https://www.napoleonhouse.com

Lafitte's Blacksmith Shop
941 Bourbon St. (Bourbon & St. Philip)
New Orleans, LA 70116

Lafitte's is another bar that demands to be placed under the "historic buildings" section. Dating from 1772, Lafitte's is the oldest bar in the Quarter, and, legend has it, the onetime hideout of French pirates. Jean Lafitte and his mateys, including his brother Pierre, operated a blacksmith shop here as a front for their extensive trade in black market contraband. While the bar's website confirms that this property was indeed the New Orleans base for the Lafitte Brothers' Barataria Bay smuggling operation, it goes on to caution that, "Like most New Orleans legends, Lafitte's Blacksmith Shop is a gumbo of truth and French, Spanish, African, Cajun and American embellishments."

By the way, did you know that Jean Lafitte and his Baratarians pretty much won the Battle of New Orleans single-handedly, defending the city and routing the Brits for General Jackson? That's if you believe Cecil B. DeMille's picture "The Buccaneer" (1938). (In reality, the pirates played a relatively minor role.)

If you catch Lafitte's when the ambience is right—candlelit in the twilight, not too crowded, perhaps sitting in the window—you'll feel the magic. As you enjoy your frosty Abita—one of the coldest beers in town, in fact—be sure to note the soft bricks reinforced with timber, a construction form used by early settlers. If you're there in the small hours, you may even see the ghost of an unknown woman in black…or even the ghosts of Lafitte himself and his pirate crew. (However, if you also see flying pink elephants, it's just that you've had too many daiquiris.)

Speaking of which, we have actually not yet been brave enough to try their signature Voodoo Daiquiri—the purple one. You just know there's gonna be so much sugar. Plus, we're not huge daiquiri fans in the first place. However, one of these days—if we start our Bourbon Stroll at Lafitte's instead of ending it here, as per our usual custom—maybe we'll get one for the road.

Cost and Hours: Everyday 10a-3a; $;
http://www.lafittesblacksmithshop.com/Homepage.html

Degas House
2306 Esplanade Ave.
New Orleans, LA 70119

The great French Impressionist artist Edgar Degas lived here in 1872-3, during Reconstruction. The house has been turned into a fascinating museum, and the grounds contain a lovely garden. (For much more on Degas House, see our "Treme/Esplanade Avenue Walk" section.)

Cost and Hours: Edgar Degas House Creole Impressionist Tours happen everyday at 10:30a and 1:45p, $29/person; there's also a Creole Breakfast and Tour combo offered everyday: breakfast is served from 9a-10a, $50 per person, reservations required; there's a Sa and Su brunch available by reservation; Drawing and painting classes are also available;

Tel: (504) 821-5009;

info@degashouse.com; https://www.degashouse.com)

Faulkner House
624 Pirates Alley

New Orleans, LA 70116

Faulkner House is down Pirate's Alley just off Jackson Square. Faulkner lived here in the '20s and wrote his first novel, *Soldiers' Pay*, here. Today, it's a fine little bookstore, and the perfect place to pick up whatever Faulkner volumes you're missing.

Hours: Everyday 10a-5p;

Tel: (504) 524-2940;

https://faulknerhousebooks.com

Hermann-Grima House
820 St Louis St.
New Orleans, LA 70112

At Hermann-Grima House, built in 1831, the grounds have been restored to show what life was like for a prosperous Creole family in the years from 1830 to 1860, the Golden Age of New Orleans. ("Golden Age" for people like the Hermann-Grimas, at least. Recall that the city made its money in the trade of slaves and cotton. It wasn't exactly a Golden Age if you were a slave.) It's an opulent, sumptuous historic Creole mansion. The Women's Exchange, which owns the mansion, has gone to great lengths to accurately recreate the lifestyle of a wealthy 19th-century Creole family.

On the day we visited, the house was re-enacting the funeral of the Widow Grima, which they do every October. The house was dressed as it was at her wake in 1850, replete with black wreath on the door. We got a vivid sense of the mourning customs of a wealthy Creole family. As the museum's website reminds us, death was a key part of the southern Victorian experience, what with yellow fever and cholera. Fans of the late Anne Rice will be interested to know that the Hermann-Grima House was an inspiration for her—she modeled a home in her novel *Feast of all Saints* after it. The house is said to be quite haunted, naturally—by the spirit of Widow Grima, for one.

Cost and Hours: Open 6 Days a Week 10a–4p; Closed Tu, Tours 10a, 11a, 1p, 2p, and 3p (no 12p tours); Adults $15, Children aged 8-18 $12 (under age 8 free), Seniors aged 65 and over $12;

Tel: (504) 274-0750;

http://www.hgghh.org

Beauregard-Keyes House
1113 Chartres St.
New Orleans, Louisiana 70116

A fascinating visit, the Beauregard-Keyes House, a 19th-century mansion established in 1826, was once the home of Confederate general P.G.T. Beauregard. After the Civil War, Beauregard became the president of the New Orleans railroad; interestingly, he also became a leader of the Equal Rights Unification Movement.

As part of your visit you'll see the exterior of the slave quarters, on the second story of the structures behind the house: the slaves worked in the kitchen and courtyard below. Joseph Le Carpentier, the wealthy French Creole gent who originally built the house, was an auctioneer...and a part of his trade was auctioning slaves. (As an interesting side note, if you visit the slavery museum at the Whitney Plantation: the plantation was owned during the slavery era by the Heydel family. When the Heydels sold their slaves, Le Carpentier was their auctioneer.)

Starting in 1904, the Beauregard-Keyes House was owned for a period by the Giacona family, wine and liquor merchants from Sicily. They attended "St. Mary's Italian Church"—otherwise known as the cathedral-basilica of the Old Ursuline Convent—which is still directly across the street, and which happens to be the oldest building in the Mississippi River Valley. The church was then at the center of Italian life in the French Quarter.

It was in these years that a massacre took place at the house. It seems the Sicilian Black Hand, a sect of the New Orleans mafia, was starting to lean on the Giaconas. Pietro Giacona invited five of the key members around to the house for dinner...then stood up in the middle of the meal and blew them away.

Later, this was the home of Frances Parkinson Keyes, from 1945 until her death in 1970. Ms. Keyes, the author of 51 books including, most famously, *Dinner At Antoine's* and *The Chess Players*, made General Beauregard a character in many of her books. "The Chess Players" loosely fictionalizes the life of chess champion Paul Morphy, who lived in this house until 1833, when he was five and his family moved out. Ms. Keyes turned the first floor of the old slave dwelling in back into her studio, which you'll tour.

Of course, this house is extremely haunted. Civil War soldiers are frequently seen, thought to be spirits of men who died on the battlefield fighting alongside General Beauregard—it's thought their spirits latched onto his person, or one of his objects, when they died. After all, the general's ghost himself is often seen.

Be sure to stroll the garden after the tour, which is landscaped in the same sun pattern as Jackson Square—itself modeled on Louis XIV's gardens at Versailles.

Cost and Hours: Open for tours M-Sa from 10a-3p, tours begin at the top of every hour and last 45 minutes, last tour at 3p, closed Su; Adult $10, Senior Citizen $9.00, Student $9, Military $7.50, Children 12 and under $4, Children under 6 free;

Tel: (504) 523-7257;

https://www.bkhouse.org

1850 House
523 St Ann St. #3318
New Orleans, Louisiana 70116

The 1850 House is an apartment in the Lower Pontalba building, one of the two iconic apartment buildings that flank Jackson Square. A visit here offers a fascinating time-machine ride back to the town's glory days. (Again, glory days for the town's wealthy: the non-wealthy weren't having such a glorious time of it). A visit here lets you experience what it would have been like to enjoy your own wrought-iron balcony overlooking St. Louis Cathedral in antebellum New Orleans, "the most prosperous period in the city's history."

Cost and Hours: Tu-Su 9:30a-4p, closed M; Adults $5, Students, seniors, military $4, Children 6 and under free;
https://louisianastatemuseum.org/museum/1850-house

Madame John's Legacy
632 Dumaine St.
New Orleans, Louisiana 70116

Madame John's Legacy, built in 1788, is one of the last remaining 18th-century structures in town. You can see this French colonial house in the film "Interview with a Vampire." As of this writing, it is closed for restoration. We eagerly await the day it's reopened to the public.

Perseverance Society Hall
1644 Villere St.
New Orleans, LA 70116

You can't go inside this building as it is currently closed to the public, but jazz lovers might like to make a pilgrimage to see the exterior, as it still looks very much the way it did a century ago. La Société de la Perseverance, a mutual aid society formed by Creoles of color in 1853, built this dance hall in the 1880s. The social dimension of these Black mutual aid societies can't be overstated: they were key to the early development of jazz. Throughout Treme and the Seventh Ward in the 1910s, society halls like this one hosted dances where many future jazz legends cut their teeth, including Freddie Keppard, Joe "King" Oliver, Sidney Bechet, Henry "Kid" Rena, "Big Eye" Louis Nelson, "Wooden" Joe Nicholas, Buddy Petit, Chris Kelly, Sam Morgan, and Isidore Barbarin. According to earwitnesses, Buddy Bolden played so loud in Perseverance Hall they feared he'd "blow his brains out." From the mid-20th century until recent years, it's been used as a church.

According to WWOZ's "A Closer Walk" website, "A renovation in the 1920s added the current Spanish Mission style façade. The interior of the hall is decorated with wainscoting from the 1880s and 1920s. A second story camelback added in the 1920s was removed after suffering damage from Hurricane Katrina." In 2021, Hurricane Ida substantially damaged back areas of the building that were in the process of being renovated at the time. WWOZ concludes that "Pastor [Harold A.] Lewis is raising funds to rebuild it, and hopes to make the church available as a multipurpose event space for the neighborhood, much as the Perseverance Society Hall was originally."

To donate, go to https://www.louisianalandmarks.org/perserverance-hall.

Mt. Moriah Missionary
147 Millaudon St.

New Orleans, LA 70118

Mahalia Jackson sang in this church located in Black Pearl, a historically Black neighborhood nestled in the western bend of the Mississippi, out near Audubon park and the Uptown/Carrollton 'hood.

Tel: (504) 866-2257;
https://www.facebook.com/pages/Mount-Moriah-Missionary-Baptist-Church/118191814897545

Jelly Roll Morton House
1443 Frenchmen St.
New Orleans LA 70116

In the Seventh Ward, this charming red Creole house is where Jelly Roll Morton grew up. Morton was a treasure of New Orleans music: a pioneer and innovator. The house is not open to the public, but still finds itself visited by music-loving pilgrims from around the world. (If you ever want to hear some music to really curl your hair, seek out the recordings Morton made for Alan Lomax and the Library of Congress in 1938. Songs like "The Murder Ballad" and "Make Me a Pallet on the Floor" make it clear there's nothing new about the controversial lyrics of N.W.A or 2 Live Crew. In fact, Jelly Roll makes them sound rather tame.)

St. Augustine Church
1210 Governor Nicholls St.
New Orleans, LA 70116

Treme, the country's oldest African-American neighborhood, is also the oldest Black Catholic parish in the nation. This parish congregated at St. Augustine Church, built by free people of color on land donated by the Ursuline Sisters and dedicated in 1842. That was the same year that Henriette Delille, a free woman of color, and Juliette Gaudin, a Cuban, founded the Congregation of the Sisters of the Holy Family, under the counsel of French immigrants. These remarkable women knelt in St. Augustine and proclaimed it their mission to work for slaves, orphan girls, the poor, the uneducated, the sick, and the elderly among the free people of color.

Thus, and rather remarkably (it wasn't even legal at the time), St. Augustine became a place where free people of color, whites, a "smattering of ethnic folk," and slaves worshipped under the same roof. Each group had their own pew they'd purchased; in what the church's historical material describes as "an unprecedented political and religious move," the colored members also bought the two outer side-aisle pews and "gave those pews to the slaves as their exclusive place of worship." (The pews you'll see are the originals).

The upshot of all of this was that St. Augustine was the most integrated church in the country. The church should be appreciated on an aesthetic level, as well, for its art and architecture. Enjoy the centuries-old pink marble altar, the "Eye of God" skylight, the paintings depicting the Stations of the Cross.

Do not neglect to visit the Tomb of the Unknown Slave, located outside the church. This shrine consisting of grave crosses, chains, and shackles is dedicated "to the memory of the nameless, faceless, turfless Africans who met an untimely death in Faubourg Treme." As a plaque near the Tomb attests, "This Saint Augustine/Treme shrine honors all slaves buried throughout the United States and those slaves in particular who lie beneath the ground of Treme in unmarked, unknown graves. There is no doubt that the campus of Saint Augustine Church sits astride the blood, sweat, tears and some of the mortal remains of unknown slaves from Africa and local American Indian slaves who either met with fatal treachery, and were therefore buried quickly and secretly, or were buried hastily and at random because of yellow fever and other plagues."

The Gospel Jazz Mass held every Sunday at St. Augustine is a renowned NOLA experience. Also, Satchmo Summer Jazz Mass is held here in August in conjunction with Satchmo Summerfest, a festival that pays tribute to Louis Armstrong (see our entry under "festivals"). According to the church's website, "during the jazz mass special musicians like the Treme Brass Band join our Saint Augustine Soulful Voices for an extra special Sunday mass."

(We visited the church during Tremé Fall Festival, when its doors are open to the public; Gospel Jazz Mass is held every Sunday 10a-12p, rosary followed by mass W 5p; 504-525-5934; The church's restoration fund-raising campaign is in need of any assistance you can give, especially in the wake of damage from Hurricane Ida; https://staugchurch.org)

Our Lady of Guadalupe Church and International Shrine to St. Jude
411 N Rampart St.
New Orleans, LA 70112

Built in 1826, this landmark of African-American Catholicism is actually the oldest still- standing church in New Orleans. (What of St. Louis Cathedral, you say? It first went up in 1718, but was destroyed in the Great New Orleans Fire of 1788; the Spanish rebuilt in 1789, though the version we see today is largely a rebuild completed during the 1850's). Per Wikipedia, Our Lady of Guadalupe was built right across the street from St. Louis Cemeteries #1 and #2 so as to be a mortuary chapel for victims of yellow fever. Like St. Augustine, Our Lady also hosts a famous Gospel Jazz Mass.

(The church is open M-Sa 6:30a-5p, Su 6a-7p, Jazz Mass Su 9:30a, 1:30p; 504-525-1827; https://judeshrine.com)

Alphonse Picou residence
1601 Ursulines Ave.
New Orleans, LA 70116

Alphonse Picou (1878-1961) played in the Tuxedo Brass Band, Papa Celestin Brass Band and Excelsior Brass Band. All these bands played at the Paddock Lounge on Bourbon Street in the '40s and '50s, the precursor to the tourist-oriented clubs that work the strip today. Picou's house is not open to the public, but it's fun to visit this landmark and read the plaque.

Jack Laine residence
2405 Chartres St.
New Orleans, LA 70117

While walking to Bacchanal, we passed the home of Papa Jack Laine (1873-1966), leader of the Reliance Brass Band, which featured many of the great first generation of New Orleans musicians. Again, the house is not open to the public, but it's nice to drop by and pay your respects.

Danny Barker's birthplace
1027 Chartres St.

New Orleans, LA 70116

This is the address of the boyhood home of Danny Barker, the great banjoist and guitarist (1909-1994). He ranged far and wide in his youth, but from the '60s to his death in '94, Barker and his wife, the great singer Blue Lu, lived in town and were apostles of the great NOLA traditions. (Go and listen to his version of "St. James Infirmary.") Today, the building is condos, but the developers were good enough to name them after Barker.

William Burroughs' house
509 Wagner St.
New Orleans, LA 70114 (Algiers)

The great writer William S. Burroughs lived at this house in Algiers in 1949, when Jack Kerouac and Neal Cassady swung by on the legendary road-trip across America that Kerouac chronicled in *On the Road*. Kerouac wrote about their time here: they only got across the river to hang out on Canal Street and bet on horses, though Kerouac would've loved to have checked out the jazz scene. Mostly, they hung around the house. This is a pilgrimage stop for Burroughs and Kerouac fans: the house with the wraparound porch also featured in Burroughs' first novel, *Junkie*.

SHOPS

FAB, Frenchmen Art & Books
600 Frenchmen St.
New Orleans, LA 70116

FAB in its original incarnation was not only a cool, if completely shambolic, bookstore: it was also an anchor of the neighborhood. Its proprietor, Otis Fennell, was something of the mayor of the block, often to be seen sitting outside on the corner. Its haphazard stacks also reflected Otis's proclivities, including the gay books section. FAB is still a bookstore, thankfully (presum-ably, someone could have popped a Starbucks in there). The current version (which reportedly has the blessing of Otis himself), if less funky, is much more of a functioning bookstore—and there's still clearly a locally-oriented curatorial mind at work here. You'll find fascinating books on art, music, and culture. We met the new proprietor, David Zalkind, and he seems like a really swell guy. He presides over a beautifully curated selection of locally-themed books, and is an exponent of the local, independent culture we support. The shop occasionally hosts top live musicians such as Jason Marsalis.

Hours: M-W 12p-8p, Th-Su 12p-10p;
Tel: (504) 302-1772;
https://frenchmenartandbooks.com

(See more about FAB below where we discuss changes around Frenchman Street. We address the events of 2019 and the Young Fellaz brass band.)

Louisiana Music Factory
421 Frenchmen St.
New Orleans, LA 70116

Louisiana Music Factory is a great local record shop, unbeatable for its extensive collection of local music. We once met the great Trombone Shorty here, in November of 2017. He was picking up some tunes in order to bone up in preparation for Fats Domino's Second Line.

Hours: Open every day 11a-6p except for W, when it's closed;
Tel: (504) 586-1094;
https://www.louisianamusicfactory.com

Faulkner House
624 Pirate's Alley
New Orleans, LA 70116

We never leave town without a book or two from Faulkner House. Joanne, the lady who runs the place, can usually be counted on—particularly if you're buying a book penned by or concerned with Faulkner—to turn to her favorite page in the book you've selected and read aloud a key passage. She did that when Scott bought "Absalom! Absalom!" (the passage had to do with a steamboat coming into New Orleans), and another time with a Eudora Welty book on Faulkner he'd picked out. We can't remember the passage she read from that one, but we remember her comment: "Isn't that so Eudora?" (Also see our entry above under "Historic Buildings.")

Hours: Everyday 10a-5p;
Tel: (504) 524-2940;
https://faulknerhousebooks.com

Crescent City Books
240 Chartres St.
New Orleans, LA 70130

Crescent City Books is a lovely independent book shop.

Hours: Open seven days a week 11a-7p;
Tel: (504) 524-4997;
books@crescentcitybooks.com

Unique Boutique Grocery
129 Royal St.
New Orleans, LA 70130

The Unique Grocery has some of the best prices for bottles of wine in the Quarter. It's conveniently located right off Canal.

Cost and hours: Everyday 7a to 12a; $; 504-586-0102

...AND MISCELLANEOUS...

The Singing Oak
City Park

Locals have told us that their favorite thing about living in New Orleans is actually the Southern live oaks. One of the best places to experience them is in City Park, along Bayou St. John. Between Wisner Blvd and the Big Lake, look for the Singing Oak. Artist Jim Hart made this gorgeous oak tree into the Singing Oak by hanging from its boughs wind-chime-like aluminum tubes tuned to the pentatonic scale, "the same scale used in West African music, gospel hymns and New Orleans jazz." For a stirring interlude to your trip, sit under the oak, listening to the melodies the wind plays and gazing out over the Big Lake.

MUSIC AND MARDI GRAS INDIAN HISTORY

Congo Square
701 N Rampart St.
New Orleans, LA 70116

Visit Congo Square in Armstrong Park to drink in the vibrations here at the birthplace of jazz and funk. In the late 1740s on Sunday afternoons, Congo Square was a meeting place and open market run by enslaved peoples, as well as free people of color, from Africa and the Caribbean. The relatively permissive French allowed their slaves to dance, sing, and drum here, thereby preserving their West African culture—an expression of freedom that still echoes, as Wynton Marsalis says. This is "ground zero" for all the unique New Orleans traditions: jazz and rhythm and blues, Mardi Gras Indians, Second Line parades—they all developed out of these African expressions. By 1803, the year of the Haitian revolution's success and the Louisiana purchase, Congo Square was already famous for these celebrations.

As an interesting aside: historian Bruce Raeburn details the regional distinctions of the African drumming which could be heard in Congo Square. The French brought in Senegambian slaves, who brought a swinging beat; the Spanish brought slaves from Congo, who contributed the polyrhythmic style we most associate with West Africa. (Raeburn further reminds us that Native Americans and their drumming traditions were here before any of them.)

Congo Square is an open space in the southern corner of Armstrong Park, which is open every day from dawn to dusk *(8a-6p)*. There are historical markers, beautiful sculptures, and grand oak trees to enjoy here and in the rest of the park.

New Orleans Jazz Museum in the Old U.S. Mint
400 Esplanade Ave.
New Orleans, Louisiana 70116

Located in the Old U.S. Mint, the New Orleans Jazz Museum is a tremendously curated collection. You'll see Louis Armstrong's first cornet, as well as various special exhibits. When we were there, we saw paintings and photos commemorating the musicians of the Preservation Hall Jazz Band such as Lucien Barbarin, as well as a remembrance of the great traditional jazz collector and historian William "Bill" Russell. This is where we first encountered one of our favorite quotes, said by the late Darryl "Little Jazz" Adams, alto saxophonist and bandleader at Preservation Hall: "If I don't make somebody cry—to be straight-up honest with you—I haven't done my job. If I don't make you try to reach the sky, I haven't done my job." (This has been Karolyn's standard for how she rates a gig ever since.)

The Museum's afternoon lecture/performance series, often led by rangers of the New Orleans Jazz National Historical Park, is also well-worth attending. Browse around the exhibits of the old mint as well, while you're here. This building once minted coins for the United States, the Confederacy, and the short-lived "Republic of Louisiana."

Cost and Hours: Tu-Su 9a-4p, closed M; Adults $8, students, seniors, military $6, children 6 and under free;
Tel: (504) 568-6993;

https://louisianastatemuseum.org/museum/new-orleans-jazz-museum-old-us-mint

Treme's Petit Jazz Museum
1500 Governor Nicholls St.
New Orleans, LA 70116

Personally curated by Al Jackson, a local music historian, this museum, which is indeed as petit as advertised, "promises," in the words of its website, "to provide an insider's glimpse of the influences, legends, and historical events that gave rise to the music that has kept this community's, and the world's, feet tapping since 1895." It's a personal collection of Jackson's paintings, photographs, and other artifacts. As he shows you around, he has several CD players stationed around the room to provide soundtracks to his commentary, bringing the various exhibits to life.

Jackson might even ask you to sit down and play a little piano to begin your visit. Scott attempted to summon his memory of Scott Joplin, on whose music he cut his teeth when just a piano-lesson-taking youth. After a few half-remembered bars of "Maple Leaf Rag" and "The Entertainer," we got the tour of the museum's two rooms.

After tracing the origins of string and rhythm instruments back to Africa, the exhibits herald relatively unsung musicians of African descent, including 19th-century Creole classical/opera composers like Louis Moreau Gottschalk (1829–1869), a virtuoso pianist, and Edmond Dédé (1829-1901), a violinist. Jackson explores the relationship of Haiti (then St. Domingue, a French colony), both pre- and post-revolution, to the development of New Orleans music. The opera-loving French, for example, taught their slaves to play classical music.

He covers 19th-century brass bands like Excelsior (which featured Theogene Baquet, Alphonse Picou, and Isidore Barbarin) and Onward (featuring Barbarin, George Baquet, and King Oliver) and focuses especially on Bunk Johnson (1879?-1949), who influenced Louis Armstrong. Jackson gives attention to the Dew Drop Inn, a now-vanished hotel, restaurant, and performance venue where a lot of great early r&b/rock 'n' roll singers started out. Little Richard, for example, recorded "Rip it Up" and "Ready Teddy" at the Dew Drop. The museum also remembers Joe's Cozy Corner, a storied Treme jazz club—today, it's a Turkish cafe called **Fatma's Cozy Corner** (1532 Ursulines Ave., 70116, 7a-3p daily), which is a good place to stop for a bite after your visit here is concluded.

The Petit Jazz Museum is a bit overpriced at $15 a head, but it's a worthwhile visit for anyone who'd like an "advanced" look at this neighborhood's world-historic musical history. Jackson is an informed guide and he takes the time to linger as long as you like at any exhibit and answer any questions you might have. We'll leave you with the words of the museum's site, which puts it well: "As America's oldest integrated neighborhood, Treme has always been an important center of African-American and Creole culture; New Orleans' beating heart for brass bands, Mardi Gras Indians, and of course, the jazz that is the life blood pulsing through the city."

W-F, tours at 1:30p, 2:30p, 3:30p and 4:30p; $15; no photos;
Tel: (504) 715-0332;
https://www.tremespetitjazzmuseum.com

Backstreet Cultural Museum
1116 Henriette Delille St.
New Orleans, LA 70116

Curated by the late Sylvester Francis, whom we were lucky enough to meet when we visited in 2013 (he passed away in 2020), this museum is a rich storehouse of African-American tradition in the heart of Treme. The Mardi Gras Indian tradition is a fascinating one wherein African-American "chiefs" spend the better part of the year carefully sewing beautiful, intricately detailed costumes of elaborate beadwork and feathers, in homage to the Native American tribes who once helped runaway slaves escape to freedom. "The Native Americans in New Orleans and the African Americans have a historic relationship that is displayed in the suits, spirit and traditions of the Mardi Gras Indians," a placard in Backstreet Cultural Museum reads. It's a fascinating example of "cultural appropriation"—and yet another illustration of the fact that American culture wouldn't have gotten very far without such appropriation.

Traditionally, the suit was only worn once, on Mardi Gras day itself, and then the whole process started again. The museum features one of the greatest collections anywhere of these costumes: a colorful eye-feast. (Sylvester Francis himself paraded with the Gentlemen of Leisure Social Aid & Pleasure Club in the '70s.)

You'll see suits worn by New Orleans cultural icon Allison "Big Chief Tootie" Montana (1922-2005). A lather by trade, he was Big Chief of the Yellow Pocahontas tribe in the '50s and was known as the "Chief of Chiefs" of all Mardi Gras Indians for over 50 years. Montana designed and built his innovative suits himself, introducing new ideas to the art of suit design, such as three-dimensional geometric designs and wide-spreading feathered crowns.

Perhaps most importantly, Montana is also credited as the leader who changed Mardi Gras Indian culture, so that whereas once the tribes fought with knives and guns, today they mock battle with their suits instead, competing with "skill and craftsmanship," and the victor is "the prettiest."

You'll also see exhibits on the history of traditional jazz funerals and second lines, and learn how jazz developed out of the syncopated music played by fraternal/societal brass marching bands. Being at the Backstreet Museum makes one think about the post-Katrina themes of rebirth, of keeping cultural traditions alive.

As we went to press, this invaluable museum was temporarily closed, attempting to recover from damages sustained in Hurricane Ida, and hoping to reopen temporarily at 1114 N. Villere Street. Hopefully they will have reopened by the time you visit. Follow their progress, and consider making a donation, at https://www.backstreetmuseum.org.

House of Dance and Feathers
1317 Tupelo St.
New Orleans, LA 70117

Located in the Lower Ninth Ward, this little museum-in-a-backyard-trailer is a "celebration of New Orleans street culture," the bulk of which is the late Ronald W. Lewis's personal collection of Mardi Gras Indian memorabilia and artifacts. Mr. Lewis passed away in 2020 while sick from Covid-19, but for many years he was the president of the Big Nine Social Aid & Pleasure Club; he also served as the Council Chief of the Choctaw Hunters, the King of Krewe de Vieux, and "a lifelong resident of the Lower Ninth Ward."

His collection is a feast for the eyes, with a special emphasis on the Skull & Bone Gangs tradition, a specifically Treme expression of Mardi Gras culture. (The Skull & Bone Gang go from door-to-door in the Treme in the small hours on Carnival Day to wake up the neighborhood and spread a message of peace, though they look like something out of a horror movie with their skulls, skeletons, and antler helmets.) Another one of the suits movingly depicts Mr. Lewis' sister's battle with cancer and her overcoming it.

Mr. Lewis wrote that he conceived of House of Dance & Feathers as not only a "celebration of the living culture of New Orleans and the Lower Ninth Ward," but also "an attempt to share this culture with the rest of the world and to pass on knowledge and traditions to the next generation." "Although you'll arrive a stranger," he liked to say, "you'll certainly leave as a friend!" We can say from personal experience how true this was. Though the museum was temporarily closed, it appears to be continuing as a tribute to his life.

Cost and Hours: Tours are flexible: give them a call at 1-504-957-2678 to ask about setting up a visit. The visit is free, but donations are greatly appreciated. Look also for the beautifully produced book Mr. Lewis co-authored about the museum.

Donald Harrison Sr. Museum and Guardians Institute
1930 Independence St.
New Orleans, Louisiana 70117

In the Upper 9th Ward, the compact Donald Harrison Sr. Museum showcases the "Afro-New Orleans" culture of Mardi Gras Indians, brass bands, and second-line parades. When we visited, we were greeted by Herreast Harrison, widow of Donald Harrison Sr., the Mardi Gras Indian chief to whom the museum is dedicated. Mrs. Harrison is also the mother of jazzman Donald Harrison Jr. She is, as Rebecca Solnit writes, a "cultural preserver and "dynamic force in the city." Also showing us around was Cherice Harrison-Nelson, Mrs. Harrison's daughter. It was a lovely experience to meet them.

On one level, the museum is a labor of love from Mrs. Harrison to her husband, a way of preserving and carrying on his legacy and mission. As Herreast told Solnit, "My late husband used to go into the schools. He felt that a lot of the young people who were being educated in the city of New Orleans had no idea what this tradition really means. He would go into the schools to inform them, and now we're trying to do the same thing here, in his memory."

You'll see Harrison Sr.'s personal collection of suits. Gazing upon these exquisite works of art, you'll believe that this Big Chief must have been "the prettiest."

Mrs. Harrison commented movingly to Solnit about the significance of Mardi Gras Indian culture, and we'll end this entry by quoting her here. (Ms. Harrison, we should say, prefers the term "masquerader" to "Mardi Gras Indian.") "But those groups remembered their cultural heritage and practiced it there [in New Orleans], that memory, they had this overarching memory of their pasts. And when they were there, they were free. And their spirits soared to the high heavens. They were themselves. In spite of limitations in every aspect of their lives. Where they should have felt like, 'we are nothing,' because you get brainwashed constantly about the fact that you're a nobody...but they didn't, they brought back. And now it's part of the world, that music."

Cost and Hours: Set up an appointment by email atinfo@guardiansinstitute.org, or by calling 504-214-6632, or completing the form in the "contact us" tab at http://www. guardiansinstitute.org/home.html. Donations are much appreciated.

Lower 9th Ward Living Museum
1235 Deslonde St.
New Orleans, LA 70117

The Lower 9th Ward was hard-hit by Hurricane Katrina and the subsequent failure of the levees—in fact, only one in five residents were ever able to return to their homes. This museum, which is also a community center, features an impressive collection of photographs which tell the story. Two newspaper photographs and their captions illustrate the racial divide of media coverage: one of a white man "surviving" by removing supplies from a shop without stopping at the cash register, and another of a Black man doing the exact same thing who's "stealing/looting."

The museum further documents the distressing history of the racism and violence of white residents of Algiers Point during Katrina. They would actually shoot at refugees from Katrina (mainly Black) who were trying to get over to Algiers Point for shelter.

The museum boasts terrific photos of Mardi Gras Indian culture. Look for the memorable view inside the home of a Mardi Gras Indian chief in 1988, which shows a young boy sitting at a sewing machine making bows, helping with the annual ritual of suit-making. Don't miss the bulletin board where people have posted moving thank-you's to the museum for keeping the story of the Lower 9th alive.

Cost and Hours: Tu-Su noon to 5p; closed M; Admission is free but donations appreciated;
Tel: (504) 220-3652;
https://www.leonatatefoundation.org/lower-9th-ward-living-museum

Handa Wanda's
2415 Dryades St.
New Orleans, LA 70113

WWOZ's listing for Handa Wanda's proclaims: "Home base of the Wild Magnolias, Handa Wanda's hosts the weekly Unified Mardi Gras Indian Practice." Indian Practice traditionally runs from the last Sunday in November and every following Sunday until the Sunday before Mardi Gras. For more information about the possibility of seeing a Mardi Gras Indian Practice, reach out at 504-813-3496 or 504-258-4361; or try messaging them at https://www.facebook.com/Handa-Wandas-625027771282391/.

Algiers Folk Art Zone & Blues Museum
207 Leboeuf St.
New Orleans, LA 70114

Across the river in Algiers Point, you'll find self-taught woodcarver and multi-media artist Charles Gillam's Algiers Folk Art Zone & Blues Museum. According to its website, "the Algiers Point destination features work that pays tribute to Louisiana's rich musical heritage and stands as one of the South's few 'living' folk art environments. Mixed-media statuary, poured concrete sculptural forms, and a small museum housing music memorabilia and works by noted self-taught artists are all located on the property. Highlights include pieces by Roy Ferdinand, Lonnie Holley, and Mr. Imagination as well as Gillam's own 'Blues Greats' series featuring the sculpted faces of Al Hirt, Pete Fountain, Memphis Minnie, and Clarence 'Gatemouth' Brown, among others."

Cost and Hours: Visit by appointment; fees may apply;
Tel: (504) 261-6231;
e-mail: gillamfolkart@yahoo.com; https://folkartzone.org

CEMETERIES

A visit to one of NOLA's "cities of the dead" is a must. After all, in the 19th century yellow fever, influenza, and cholera virtually turned the whole town into a Victorian necropolis. Just imagine: the yellow fever epidemic in 1832 was followed by another in 1833, where in one month alone a reported one thousand people died. That wasn't even the worst outbreak. (See below.) Of the myriad choices of cemeteries in town (there are over 40), which should you choose for your first experience? We'd make it Lafayette Cemetery No. 1, which dates back to 1833. (Note: many cemeteries are now closed unless you take a tour led by a licensed guide, due to vandalism.)

As you explore these cemeteries, look for the main types of New Orleans burials: above-ground mausoleums, walls of oven vaults, and coping graves.

The above-ground tombs really came into their own in the mid-19th century in the high days of the yellow fever epidemic, since they had the extra benefit of getting around the Catholic Church's prohibition on cremation. Survivors of the outbreaks were under the misguided impression that the cadavers were contagious, so they passed a law stating that a tomb had to be sealed for 366 days as soon as two new dead bodies moved in. This policy cleverly ensured that the deceased would be shut up inside the vault during a famously intense New Orleans summer. Under the blazing sun, the tombs were hot as ovens inside, and the cadavers would be naturally cremated.

What is the story with those exterior walls lined with what look like brick pizza ovens? Most of these were rented out to families to hold relatives who died while the family tomb happened to be sealed. The departed would rest in the wall until the balance of the 366 days had elapsed, when the family vault could be opened and they could join their ancestors. If the dead person's kin failed to pay the rent, he or she literally "got the shaft": a cemetery worker used a long pole to push the body to the back of the wall and into a shaft, where it fell ignominiously to the bottom of the vault.

Notice also the coping graves—small family plots surrounded and enclosed by short stone or marble walls, and filled in with soil, gravel, or marble chips. Along with delineating the family plot, they can have the added benefit of protecting the coffins from water levels.

Lafayette Cemetery No. 1
1400 Washington Ave.
New Orleans, LA 70130

To get here, hop on the St. Charles streetcar to the Garden District, sa-voring the architecture along the way. (See more about this cemetery in our Garden District walk, below.) Founded in 1833, by 1840 Lafayette Cemetery was fairly bursting at the seams, mostly with victims of yellow fever. In the worst outbreak, in 1853, yellow fever claimed 7,849 residents. As you stroll, appreciate the characteristic sculpture and above-ground tombs. See if you can find the youngest person to pass away (some were only a few days old), and the oldest. Look for Civil War veterans. As you come to the periphery, stroll along the wall and note the almost 500 oven vaults. Many movies have been shot here at Lafayette, including Neil Jordan's take on Anne Rice's *Interview with a Vampire* and Dennis Hopper's *Easy Rider*.

Cost and hours: M-F 7a-2:30p, Sa 7a-12p, Closed Su; free;

Tel: (504) 658-3781;

https://www.saveourcemeteries.org/cemeteries/cemeteries/lafayette-cemetery-no-1.html

St. Louis Cemetery No. 1
425 Basin St.
New Orleans, LA 70112

Another good option for your first cemetery experience is St. Louis Cemetery No. 1. However, we should add the caveat that the Archdiocese of New Orleans, in an effort to curb vandalism (no matter how well-meant), now requires all visitors be accompanied by a licensed tour guide. Opened in 1789, it is the oldest still-existing cemetery in NOLA, and probably the most famous. That's largely because it is the resting place of Marie Laveau, the legendary Voodoo priestess. As we indicated, her grave in the Glapion family crypt was so perpetually decorated with gifts and marked with x's or crosses by visitors that the Archdiocese finally implemented new security regulations to discourage pilgrimages and offerings to Laveau's tomb.

Though marking Marie Laveau's crypt is strictly forbidden, we should note in passing that x's do represent African tradition. As Michael Murphy writes, "The two crossed lines represent the intersection between the realm of the living and the realm of the spirit. The custom, unique to New Orleans, of drawing x's on grave markers is related to Haitian Vodou practice called kwasiyen. Signing with an X is used to establish contact with the lwa, or Vodou deities."

The Barbarin family, perhaps the foremost dynasty of traditional jazz, has a tomb here, dating back to the 19th-century. Today, it also serves as the New Orleans Musicians Tomb, providing musicians free burial—an idea conceived by Anna Ross Twichell. The first such burial was that of Lloyd Washington of the Ink Spots, on October 23, 2004. The late Sylvester Francis, of the Backstreet Cultural Museum, has been laid to rest here, as well. Glass artist Mitchell Gaudet cast the blue note you'll see atop the tomb, symbolizing the blue note that makes jazz. He forged the cross of iron you'll see, as well.

Several generations of Barbarins rest in this tomb, having passed the baton of jazz forth, from its first flowering to the present day. Patriarch Isidore Barbarin (1872-1960) is here: this was a man whom Louis Armstrong himself called "Pops." Isidore played trumpet and mellophone in the Excelsior Brass Band, and later in Papa Celestin's Tuxedo Brass Band and the Onward Brass Band, the most fabled bands in New Orleans from 1900 until the end of World War I. Isidore wasn't even recorded until late in life, playing with Bunk Johnson in 1945.

Three of Isidore's sons became drummers: Paul, Louis, and Lucien. Lucien is interred here in the family tomb, along with his son, trumpet player Charles. Isidore's daughter, Rose, also rests here.

If you'll allow us a bit of a digression, we thought we'd mention here that Rose gave birth to guitar legend Danny Barker ("My Indian Red"). Barker, it should be noted, "brought brass back" in the '70s when he founded the Fairview Brass Band. Fairview, in turn, inspired the Dirty Dozen Brass Band and the Soul Rebels. Dr. Michael White and drummer Herlin Riley, whom you can still see perform at Snug Harbor, both come out of Fairview. There's one more Fairview-related connection: in January 2020, Isidore's great-great-grandson Lucien (a popular name in this family) passed away, and joined his ancestors in this tomb. He was a trombonist who co-founded Fairview with Barker.

Other famous New Orleanians buried in St. Louis No. 1: Jean Etienne de Boré, an innovative sugar planter and the first mayor of New Orleans; Homer Plessy, who bravely if unsuccessfully challenged Louisiana's segregation laws as the plaintiff in the 1896 Plessy v. Ferguson Supreme Court decision; Benjamin Latrobe, one of America's first professional architects; Ernest N. 'Dutch' Morial, the first African-American mayor of New Orleans; and Paul Morphy, the greatest chess champion of his age.

Nicolas Cage, thinking of the future, has a pyramid tomb already erected here, for his own burial.

Lastly, look for tombs decorated by outsider artist Arthur Smith. You'll see his work at the Dorsey family tomb which holds his grandmother. This tomb is on the left of the cemetery gate, fourth grave in along the oven wall.

Cost and Hours: M-Sa 9a-3p, Su 9a-12p; $20 per person;
Tel: (504) 596-3050;
Book an offical tour at https://cemeterytourneworleans.com

St. Louis Cemetery No. 2
300 N Claiborne Ave.
New Orleans, LA 70119

Dating to 1820, St. Louis Cemetery No. 2 is just a few blocks away from No. 1, and is the final resting place of victims of pandemics and diseases, as well as soldiers and pirates. Alexander Milne, who is buried here, actually had his will engraved onto his tomb—so there would be no mistake about his wishes to found a boys' and a girls' orphanage with his fortune. Ernie K-Doe rest here, as does drummer Paul Barbarin, who passed away while second-lining in 1969. (Curious that he doesn't rest in the Barbarin tomb in No. 1, described above.) His tomb also includes Danny Barker and his wife, Louisa "Blue Lu" Barker. Also look for Oscar James Dunn, the United States' first African American Lieutenant Governor.

Cost and hours: As we went to press, St. Louis Cemetery No. 2 was closed to visitors and tours, due to vandalism and other issues.

St. Louis Cemetery No. 3
3421 Esplanade Ave.
New Orleans, LA 70119

Located in the Bayou St. John neighborhood, St. Louis Cemetery No. 3 was born in the 1840s when the epidemics of cholera, influenza, and yellow fever got too much for even St. Louis No. 2. The 1848 yellow fever outbreak left so many bodies in its wake that the city had to buy up this land, a former leper colony/cemetery, to have somewhere to bury them. The cemetery is the site of the dramatic Priests' Tomb, a large vault where the archdiocese buries priests whose families don't make other plans. This large cemetery (much bigger than its two sisters) boasts 5,000 mausoleums, 2,000 individual family crypts, 12 society tombs, and more than 3,000 oven vaults in the walls around the perimeter.

Cost and Hours: Gates are open M-Sa 8a to 4:30p, Su 8a-4p; free.

St. Roch Cemetery (Campo Santo) Nos. 1 & 2
1725 St Roch Ave.
New Orleans, LA 70119

Stroll the grounds of the St. Roch cemetery (or "campo santo") and you'll find the chapel of the National Shrine of St. Roch, the patron saint of miraculous cures, plague and pestilence (perhaps we could add Covid-19 to this list), and...dogs. Inside, you'll find a tiny room to the left of the altar. This little anteroom is full of "flowers, crutches, toys, glass eyes, braces and prosthetics of all kinds as a tribute to cures and hopes of future cures," as Chris Champagne puts it in his book *Secret New Orleans*.

Michael Murphy adds that this Healing Room, as it's come to be known, "has become one of the coolest, if lesser-known, spots in New Orleans. The small room is filled with tokens of thanks: plaques, abandoned leg braces, crutches, and plaster or cement statues of previously afflicted body parts; hands, hearts, brains, ears, and eyeballs healed through prayer at St. Roch's."

The chapel is currently in the midst of a restoration project, which may be completed by the time you visit. Even if the chapel is closed when you visit, you can still peep in through a barred window on the south, or river-side, side of the chapel.

What's the story behind the shrine? In 1867, Father P.L. Thevis, a German immigrant, promised God that if none of his parishioners died of the yellow fever then sweeping the city, he would build a chapel "to thank and honor St. Roch." Well, it seems that "Bronze John" (the virus's nickname) did indeed pass his flock by. When news of the "miracle" got out, the chapel became a pilgrimage site for all those in need of healing, who left behind "plaster feet, arms, hearts and crutches" as "tokens of hope and gratitude."

Champagne further notes that the cemetery is the site of a traditional Station of the Cross devotion on Good Friday; "legend has it that single women who come on that day to ask for St. Roch's assistance in finding a husband will be successful." We should mention that the ghost of a large dog haunts the grounds. It makes sense, considering St. Roch is the patron saint of pooches, as well.

Cost and hours: M-Th 8a-4:15p, F 8a-4p; Monthly healing masses in the St. Roch chapel are the first Friday of each month starting at 10a. Visitation of the chapel is the first Friday of each month from 11a to noon; free;

Tel: (504) 945-5961;

https://nolacatholiccemeteries.org/st-roch-cemetery-1

Charity Hospital Cemetery & Katrina Memorial
5056 Canal St.
New Orleans, LA 70119

Charity Hospital Cemetery's Katrina Memorial features six mausoleums that are the final resting place for unclaimed and unknown, but not unloved, victims of Hurricane Katrina. It's a moving place to pay your respects. In the words of a nurse from now-shuttered Charity Hospital, "It's so people don't forget — the bodies may have been removed, maybe, but the souls are still there." While you're here, walk the labyrinth-like pathway in the shape of a hurricane.

This site is a fitting place for the Katrina memorial, because Charity Hospital Cemetery was built atop a Potter's Field—a burial ground for the unclaimed and unknown victims of another age—of yellow fever, malaria, and influenza epidemics. Again, the land shortage comes into play: by 1848, so many had died from these epidemics that Charity Hospital had to purchase this land to create a new cemetery. It's one of the few cemeteries in town where the burials are below-ground: these tend to correlate with the poverty of the internees, and also with race. Black people are disproportionately buried in below-ground cemeteries. (Above-ground tombs were mainly for the wealthy and white.)

As for Charity Hospital itself: set up since 1736 to give medical care to the poor, it has been closed since sustaining heavy damage from Hurricane Katrina, and is rumored to be as haunted as the cemetery itself. The hospital is abandoned, you see, except for mysterious lighted windows—when there is no electricity. When we took a ghost tour that visited Charity Cemetery, at the end of the night our bus drove past the dark husk of the hospital's edifice—and we saw the lights for ourselves. Well, all we can say is that the occupants of the hospital and the cemetery should be revenants in at least one sense—that we never forget them, or the scandalous treatment of the indigent.

Cost and Hours: Hours vary, but the visit is free;

Tel: (225) 342-9500;

https://www.saveourcemeteries.org/cemeteries/cemeteries/charity-hospital-katrina-memorial-cemetery.html

Holt Cemetery
4901 Rosedale Dr. / 635 City Park Ave.
New Orleans, LA 70119

Officially dating to 1879 and created on the ground of a potter's field, Holt Cemetery is sometimes described as the town's "most eccentric" cemetery. That's because it gives families the freedom to design their loved ones' resting places themselves, giving the graves a homemade feel. It's an idiosyncratic cemetery in the sense that the graves are decorated with personal objects. However, as Catherine Smith writes, those who take the time to look closely beyond the ramshackle initial appearance will note that "Holt is a place where love is shown creatively and authentically." You'll see handmade and hand-lettered grave markers, cans of beer, rubber duckies, and stuffed animals. It's a moving visit.

In fact, the practices you'll see at Holt are actually extensions of traditional burial practices dating back to Africa. Objects are left for the dead to use in the spirit world. You'll see cracked pottery: in African tradition, as Michael Murphy writes, "the dishes and medicine bottles must be cracked so that the spirit inside the objects are released to serve the former owner in the next world." Look for the Zulu coconut decorating Ms. Thelma Lowe's grave: if you catch the golden coconut on Mardi Gras day, you've caught the most coveted prize of all. Also, look for the mailbox grave. We left a dollar, as there was already a stack of dollar bills. Take 'em across the river in heaven.

Amazingly, Buddy Bolden, the "Father of Jazz," is buried somewhere here in an unmarked grave—imagine that: a world-historical musical figure in an unmarked grave. Thankfully, both Bolden and the numberless war veterans beside whom he's buried are honored with monuments in the vicinity of their resting places, which you will easily find. Somewhere on the grounds of the cemetery also rest noted local musicians Jewell "Babe" Stovall and Jessie Hill.

Look for installations by grave decorator Arthur Smith, who considers his work "memorial chapels for all the dead of Holt Cemetery." Arthur's signatures include baby-bed railings and wire garden fencing topped with red shag carpet, or "a tangle of lawn chairs or bicycle wheels or even a large plastic owl."

As with Charity Hospital Cemetery, those buried here are poor and disproportionately Black, which also means they received below-ground burials. As we noted above, the city's famous above-ground tombs were mainly for those with means.

Cost and Hours: M-F 8a-2:30p; Sa closes at noon; closed Su; free;
Tel: (504) 658-3781;
https://www.saveourcemeteries.org/cemeteries/cemeteries/holt-cemetery.html

Cypress Grove Cemetery
120 City Park Ave. / 5190 Canal Blvd.
part of Greenwood Cemetery
5242 Canal Blvd. (where City Park Ave. meets Canal Blvd.)
New Orleans, LA 70124

Established in 1840 by the Firemen's Charitable and Benevolent Association, Cypress Grove Cemetery honors the firemen who "gave their courage and, sometimes, their lives to protect their neighbors." The cemetery also features the unique Chinese Tomb, dedicated in 1904. You may walk inside: note the fireplace and altar for burnt offerings and sacrifices.

Cypress Grove was initially built to handle the overflow from adjacent Greenwood Cemetery. As the cemetery's website notes, "In 1852, America was stricken with an epidemic of yellow fever. New Orleans, America's third largest city, was hit particularly hard. By 1853, over 8,000 in the city had expired from the disease." In Greenwood rests local character Ruthie the Duck Girl (Ruth Grace Moulon), famous for going about the French Quarter for five decades in roller skates, a fur coat, and a wedding dress, and with a webbed-footed friend or two in tow. John Kennedy Toole, who penned the ultimate book about New Orleans, *A Confederacy of Dunces*, is here as well.

Cost and hours: Everyday 8a-4p;

Tel: (504) 482-0233; free;

https://www.saveourcemeteries.org/cemeteries/cemeteries/cypress-grove-cemetery.html

Lake Lawn Metairie Cemetery
5100 Pontchartrain Blvd.
New Orleans, LA 70124

Lake Lawn Metairie Cemetery is vast—a former race track converted to a cemetery after the Civil War. As Fodor's notes, at Metairie you'll see everything from "Gothic crypts to Romanesque mausoleums to Egyptian pyramids." You almost need a car to get around here. We recommend stopping in to the office for a map first, and perhaps mention a few of the tombs you'd like to see. They will probably be able to circle these spots on the map.

The cemetery is worth a visit just to see the soul-stirring, lifelike Weeping Angel statue, a moving representation of grief, based on a Roman original. Look for her in the Charles Hyams tomb, located towards the southeast corner of the cemetery. Even if the doors are locked, you can see her through the plexiglass in the door. Hyams, we should say, helped create the Art Museum of New Orleans, in 1911.

You'll also find the tombs of trumpeter Al Hirt; Al Copeland, the Popeye's chicken king; and Angelo Brocato, the famed purveyor of ice cream and cannoli *Siciliani*. Louis Prima of "Pennies From Heaven" and "Just a Gigolo" fame is buried here, as is Ruth Udstad Fertel, founder of Ruth's Chris Steakhouse. For many years, Anne Rice had a tomb ready for the day it would become her own final resting place; Ms. Rice passed away in 2021.

General Beauregard—whose home, the Beauregard-Keyes House, you may visit: see our entry above—rests in the Army of Tennessee section. He started the Civil War when he ordered the first shots fired on Fort Sumter.

The Carmichael monument, decorated by statues of three playful, curious pups, reads "How Lucky I Was To Have Had Dogs Who Made Saying Goodbye So Hard."

Look for the 80-foot memorial to Mary Farrel, Daniel Moriarty's wife. The couple were self-made *nouveau riche*—looked down upon by the old-money rich. It's said Daniel built this tomb so tall so Mary can eternally look down on all the people who thought themselves superior to her.

Cost and Hours: Daily 8:30a-5p; free;
Tel: (504) 484-9008;
https://www.dignitymemorial.com/funeral-homes/new-orleans-la/lake-lawn-metairie-funeral-home/9785

Chevra Thilim Cemetery
5000 Iberville St.
New Orleans, LA 70119

Chevra Thillim is another of the rare in-ground cemeteries, in this case per Jewish burial traditions. For more information, contact Sandy Lassen at 504-782-7218.

Subjects for future research for us: **Masonic Cemetery** (400 City Park Ave., 70119), where Catherine Smith writes of its "large, elaborate, beautiful tombstones"; **Providence Memorial Park** (8200 Airline Dr., Metairie, 70003), where Mahalia Jackson rests; **Garden of Memories** (4900 Airline Hwy., Metairie, 70001), where Gram Parsons rests; and **Mount Olivet Cemetery** (4000 Norman Mayer Ave., 70122), where rests the great Henry Roeland "Roy" Byrd, better known as Professor Longhair or just "Fess." Shirley & Lee, who made some great New Orleans hits, rest here as well.

Saint Peter Street Cemetery (gone, but not forgotten)

Saint Peter, the city's first cemetery (1718-1780), exists now only as a memory. It's now buried under expanding construction, but if you are strolling in between the boundaries of N. Rampart (to the lakeside, or northerly), St. Peter (downriver, or easterly), Burgundy (riverside, or southerly), and Toulouse (upriver, or westerly) Streets, you're walking atop the souls who rest where this cemetery used to be.

As the Ghost City Tours website puts is, "prostitutes were known to kidnap men, snatch them from the street, haul them inside—then take their belongings and even murder them, depositing their bodies in the yards of their brothels. It's one of the reasons the backend of the French Quarter is considered to be so haunted, the forgotten souls of St. Peter's Street Cemetery just might be the reason for all of the paranormal phenomena." Hmm. Building right on top of burial grounds: wasn't that where they went wrong in *Poltergeist*?

ART AND HISTORY MUSEUMS

Ogden Museum of Southern Art
925 Camp St.
New Orleans, LA 70130

This funky museum in the Warehouse District boasts one of the truly great collections of Southern paintings and woodcarvings made by artists belonging to the self-taught (no formal training), outsider (outside of society due to isolation, incarceration, and/or mental illness), and visionary (received a vision from God) persuasions. You'll see work by Reverend Howard Finster, an intensely prolific painter of angels, leopards, UFOs, and clouds. You'll also see Roy Ferdinand's mixed media work chronicling street life in gritty NOLA hoods, Arthur Kern's unforgettably bizarre sculptures, and the wonderfully vivid, eye-awakening paintings of Marie Hull. The Ogden is also known for its Thursday after-hours parties, held once a month. As a personal note, we'll always think of the Ogden as the place we were when we got the news that Prince had died.

Cost and Hours: 10a– 5p seven days a week; Adults: $13.50, Seniors (65 and over): $11, Children (ages 5-17): $6.75, Children (under 5): Free, Students and Teachers (with ID): $11;

Tel: (504) 539-9650;

https://ogdenmuseum.org

New Orleans Art Museum and Besthoff Sculpture Garden
1 Collins Diboll Cir.
New Orleans, LA 70124

Located in beautiful City Park, the New Orleans Art Museum (NOMA) boasts an impressive collection. Look for local Louisiana art in the Louisiana Gallery. The 3rd floor boasts a fine collection of Native American/Pacific/Asian Art, whereas the 2nd floor is the place to find the Great Masters, Impressionists, and Cubists/Surrealists. Also look for eggs and other artworks by the Faberge family, as well as Will Ryman's "America," a big golden cabin made of wood, arrowheads, chains, shackles, corn, cotton, coal, candy, bullets, and iPhones.

On a beautiful day it's a wonderful experience to stroll the surrounding Besthoff Sculpture Gardens, where you'll see work by Robert Indiana, George Segal, and Anish Kapoor (whom we Chicagoans know for the "bean.") The museum's cafe is run by Ralph Brennan, scion of the great restaurant family.

Cost and Hours: Free on Wednesdays with a local zip code such as 70125. (10a–6p seven days a week; General admission: Adults: $15, Active Military with ID $10, Seniors $10, University Students with ID: $8;

Tel: (504) 658-4100;

https://noma.org

New Orleans Pharmacy Museum
514 Chartres St.
New Orleans, LA 70130

If you want the old, weird New Orleans, it doesn't get more redolently atmospheric than the New Orleans Pharmacy Museum. It's housed in a 1823 town house, the onetime business of the first licensed pharmacist in the United States, Louis J Dufilho Jr.

Before you go in, check out the front windows. Notice the colored liquids in large glass globes. These once warned travelers whether an epidemic was in progress (red liquid) or not (green or blue). (We would have had to have the red liquid out for the last couple years, due to the COVID-19 pandemic.)

Now step inside. You'll be transported back to the early 19th century, the days when pharmacies carried wonderful medicines like cocaine, heroin, and opium. You'll see Cocaine Toothache Drops ("Instantaneous cure!"), and learn that heroin was once prescribed as a painkiller, cough suppressant, and diarrhea treatment—and might have gotten its name because it made you feel "heroic." Opium was used to treat cholera. You'll learn about "patent medicines" sold at traveling medicine shows—made up mainly of alcohol and opiates. There are displays of special teas, tinctures, and potions—including love potions.

The museum features a re-created 19th-century physician's study, and a rare 1880s linen prescription file. A terrific display of antique spectacles illustrates the historical development of vision aids. A display of surgical instruments used during the Civil War is wince-inducing. And ladies, you can see how far gynecological instruments have advanced.

You'll also learn of the medicinal properties of absinthe, and that cocktails were considered good for you: they "render the heart stout and bold," as one contemporary account had it, even as—it must be conceded—they "fuddle the head."

In fact, it was a New Orleans pharmacist, Antoine Amédée Peychaud, who is credited with inventing "bitters," circa 1830: a blend of bitter herbs such as dandelion, peppermint, wormwood, and mild thistle, thought to help with everything from colds and respiratory ailments to diarrhea. Peychaud, a Creole with a background from Saint-Domingue, invented a drink using these bitters as a key ingredient: the Sazerac. After having your notions of a healthy regimen redefined at the Pharmacy Museum, consider stepping over to the Old Absinthe House in Pirate's Alley, or over to the Carousel Bar for a Sazerac (where they still use Peychaud's Bitters today). Drink your medicine: it's good for you!

Cost and hours: W-Sa 12p-5p, self-guided tour, no reservations, closed Su-Tu; $10/adults, $7/seniors 65+, students & military;
Tel: (504) 565-8027;
https://www.pharmacymuseum.org/home

Confederate Memorial Hall and Civil War Museum
929 Camp St.
New Orleans, LA 70130

Founded in 1881, this museum consigns Confederate artifacts of the antebellum and Civil War period to the place where they belong: indoors, inside a museum. In other words, part of the dead past. It houses Confederate flags, uniforms, weaponry, photographs, and tintypes. It's fascinating, yet we must say, some of the visitors seemed to savor the exhibits in a way that was a bit, well, unsavory.

Cost and hours: Tu-Sa 10a-4p, closed Su-M; Adults $10, children 7-14 $5, Children under 7 free;
Tel: (504) 523-4522;
https://confederatemuseum.com

New Orleans African-American Museum
1417-1418 Governor Nichols St.
New Orleans, LA 70116

We've been interested in visiting this museum located in the Tremé neighborhood ever since our first visit to town. Now it has finally reopened after years of restoration (though efforts to renovate the entirety of the campus remain ongoing). Its site proclaims that "The mission of the New Orleans African American Museum is to preserve the history and elevate the art, culture, and contributions of African Americans in New Orleans and the African Diaspora." Every third Saturday, museum entry is no charge, and vendors and artists attend to teach and sell their wares.

Cost and Hours: Th-Su 11a-4p, closed M-W; $20 self-guided tour, also offers a full day or half day Treme Experience;
Tel: (504) 218-8254;
https://www.noaam.org

National World War II Museum
945 Magazine St.
New Orleans, LA 70130

The foremost World War II Museum in the country, the massive National World War II Museum is a real feather in the city's cap. It was originally conceived as a D-Day Museum under the guidance of its founder, Dr. Stephen Ambrose, a scholar who made his home in New Orleans, but its scope has become increasingly all-embracing with a series of massively-funded expansions. It boasts a tremendous collection of oral histories, films, and artifacts. In fact, the museum is so vast, comprising five pavilions (with another coming soon) and theaters, that it could easily be an all-day experience—and, in fact, taking a whole day is recommended.

As you enter you are given a digital Dog Tag with a real service-member's story keyed to it, and throughout the museum there are stations where you may follow his or her story. (You can also go online later and learn more about your person by keying in the Dog Tag number.)

While you're in the entrance hall, gaze up at the suspended WWII aircraft. If you like that, the bulk of the airplane collection is in the US Freedom Pavilion. Then, be sure to see the replica of a Higgins Boat, built from the original plans by former employees of the Higgins factory and using original parts. The Higgins Boats were produced in New Orleans by Andrew Higgins, which is in fact the reason the museum itself is here. Eisenhower credited these crafts with having won the war, for their ability to land troops on beaches. In fact, at one point in the war, 92% of the vessels in the U.S. Navy were designed and/or built by Higgins Industries right here in NOLA.

Next, begin your tour by stepping into a '40s Pullman train car (stationary) and viewing a film evoking the experience of a young person going off to war. Speaking of films, the ticket desk really pushes the 4D film narrated and co-produced by Tom Hanks, "Beyond All Boundaries," and you may enjoy this immersive experience, but we found it more like a Disney thrill-ride than an illuminating look at the war. (Your seat shakes at one point, for example.) No disrespect to Mr. Hanks, but the film lasts nearly an hour and we would've rather used our time looking elsewhere.

In fact, we only had about half a day and we spent the bulk of our time in the initial Louisiana Memorial Pavilion. Still, the visit was a rich, thought-provoking experience. One of the first exhibits, for example, is about the likes of Charles Lindbergh and the isolationists at America First, who wanted to keep the U.S. out of the war. (Leading even the generally anti-war, such as ourselves, to wrestle with the idea that being anti-war isn't always the way to go, and being interventionist sometimes is). We didn't even get to the exhibits about the women of World War II or the Holocaust, nor did we go aboard the submarine (US Freedom Pavilion). All reasons to go back.

Cost and Hours: Daily 9a-5p; Adult $29.50, Senior (65+) $25.50, Student, military, and visitors with disabilities $18, WWII Veterans free, Beyond All Boundaries film $7, Final Mission: USS Tang Experience $7; visitors are strongly encouraged to pre-purchase timed tickets online if at all possible;
Tel: (504) 528-1944;

e-mail: info@nationalww2museum.org; https://www.nationalww2museum.org

RESTAURANTS

NOLA is the greatest food city in the world. (Care to debate?) That being the case, we thought we'd organize the "restaurants" section here in a slightly different way. There are certain foods a beginner simply must try. With that in mind, we offer the following "food for beginners" along with our recommendations for the best places to try these iconic New Orleans dishes.

Barbecue shrimp

In this classic Creole recipe, beautifully plump grilled or pan-fried shrimp arrive not in barbecue sauce, but rather bathed in a succulent, buttery, Worcestershire-and-pepper-spiked sauce.

Mr. B's Bistro (201 Royal St., or **Royal & Bienville**, 70130; Lunch W–Sa, 11:30a–2p, Dinner W–Su 5p–9p, Sunday Brunch 10:30a–2p, Closed M-Tu; $$; 504-523-2078; http://www.mrbsbistro.com) is one of our favorite places in the French Quarter. In our estimation, they serve the tastiest barbecue shrimp in town. Another "must" is the Gumbo Ya-Ya, and Karolyn heartily recommends the rabbit, as well. The waiters here are known to swoop down uncannily with another loaf of warm, crispy French bread right when you need it for roux-sopping purposes. Don't forget to make a reservation.

Pascal Manale's (838 Napoleon Ave., 70115; Tu-Sa 4:00p-9p, W-F 11:30a-9p; $$; 504-895-4877; https://pascalsmanale.com) invented barbecue shrimp—a veritable "genesis." A chronicler is tempted to add: hopefully, they looked upon what they had created, and said it was good.

Beignets

The French doughnuts without which no trip to New Orleans is complete.

Cafe du Monde (800 Decatur St., 70116; open every day 7:30a-11p; $; 800-772-2927; https://shop.cafedumonde.com). Whether it's your first time in town or your 50th, this great Creole institution is *the* classic place to get your beignets, along with their perfect soulmate, a cup of chicory-laced café au lait. The "original French Market coffee stand" has been dishing it up since 1862. We think they have it down by now. No one else does these basics quite like Cafe du Monde. You'll get a bit messy if you're eating these snowy pillows right: explosions of powdered sugar envelope you when you bite down. These treats are golden crisp on the outside, warm and dense—yet somehow also light and airy—on the inside. We drop by every visit—to paraphrase Dr. Johnson, the person who is tired of Cafe du Monde is tired of life. The magic hour is just before dawn, but really, any time is good.

Cafe Beignet (334 Royal St., 70130; daily 7a-5p; $; 504-500-4370; https://www.cafebeignet.com) Cafe Beignet on Royal Street is also a New Orleans tradition (if not quite as venerable as Cafe Du Monde, having only

242 | PFEIFFER, STEELE-PFEIFFER

opened up in 1990.) Enjoy your beignets and chicory-laced café au lait in this atmospheric take on a French Bistro. What feels like a deep cave is actually a converted 1800s carriage house. There's also a lovely courtyard. Pick up some "Slap Ya Mama" Cajun seasoning while you're here. This is one of four locations.

Morning Call (5101 Canal Boulevard, or Canal Boulevard and City Park Ave., 70124; Su-Th 7a-12a, F-Sa 7a-12:30a; $; 504-459-2086; https://www.facebook.com/leroyquigly/?ref=page_internal). If you've got a bike, or you're staying in the Bayou St. John neighborhood, get your beignets and café au lait at this new location of Morning Call, the second-most iconic beignet stand after Cafe du Monde. Morning Call started out in the French Market only a few years after its more famous competitor, but left for a Metairie location in 1974. Starting in 2012 they had a stand in City Park, but it closed. The good news is they've re-opened on Canal Boulevard, on the outskirts of City Park. So you can once again get your beignets and then, say head over to the New Orleans Art Museum.

Loretta's Authentic Pralines was founded over 35 years ago by Loretta S. Harrison, the first African-American woman to open a praline business. (Sadly, Ms. Harrison passed away in 2022.) If you want to take your beignet-eating experience to a new level, try their praline beignets: they're as scrumptious as all get-out. We like the crab beignet, as well. They have a stall in the French Market at #9 (Th-Su 9a-5p, Closed M, W), and their cafe is at 2101 North Rampart, 70116 (W-Sa 9a-4p, Closed Su-Tu). Website: https://lorettaspralines.com; 504-944-7068.

Breakfast (beyond beignets)

Buttermilk Drop Bakery (1781 N. Dorgenois St., 70119; M-Sa 6a-4p, Su 6a-3p; 504-252-4538; http://www.buttermilkdrop.com). Time was, we used to stop by the Buttermilk Drop Bakery on our way out of town, grabbing a donut breakfast for the road. These were the days when their head baker was Dwight Henry, who also starred in *Beasts of the Southern Wild*, with whom we once had our picture taken. He and the Buttermilk split up in 2014; last we heard, Mr. Henry had opened his own **Wink's** bakery in Gentilly, after opening places in the Quarter and the CBD that closed. Even without him, the Buttermilk Drop is still a 7th Ward institution and the signature drops themselves are bits of sugary heaven. Also, do not miss the sausage, egg, cheese, and donut sandwich. (Yes, you read that right.)

Brennan's (471 Royal St., 70130; Breakfast/Lunch Th-M 9a-2p, Dinner Th-Su 6-10p, Bubbles at Brennan's Happy Hour Th-Su 2-6p, M 9a-2p, Champagne Sabering in the Courtyard Th-Su 5p; $$$; 504-525-9711; https://www.brennansneworleans.com). Brennan's is the famous Creole restaurant near the entrance to the French Quarter; the classic ritual here is "Breakfast at Brennan's," which you must do once in your life. (Try not to worry about the price tag when you're doing Breakfast at Brennan's: it's meant to be a blowout.) It's also where Bananas Foster was invented. It's always a fun show when the old-school Creole places bring out this dish. They light it up for you tableside, setting afire the banana liqueur and dark rum; the flames burst into the air, and you can't help but "ooh." Do not miss the sherry-spiked turtle soup, either.

Camellia Grill (626 S. Carrollton Ave., 70118; M-Th 8a-7p, F-Su 8a-8p; 504-309-2679; http://camelliagrillnola.com). It's worth a trip to the Uptown neighborhood for breakfast or lunch at the Camellia Grill, an institution since 1946. The bow-tied, dryly funny waiters are iconic. The blender-whipped omelets are beautiful. Great burgers, too. However, the jam here is the pecan pie on the grill! Karolyn had a slice and her server said, "You want another piece of pecan pie?" She said she wasn't sure. He rephrased the question as a statement. How could she refuse?

Elizabeth's (601 Gallier St., 70117; Th-M 8a-2:30p; closed Tu-W; 504-944-9272; https://www.elizabethsrestaurantnola.com), is colorful and fun, a go-to spot in the Bywater. It's only open for breakfast, lunch and, on the weekends, brunch. "Real food done real good" is their motto, and they live up to it. Get the praline bacon! Also look for the waffle topped with sweet potato and duck hash with pepper jelly.

Meals From the Heart (1100 N Peters St #13, 70116; Everyday 10a-3:30p; $; 504-285-4036; https://mealsfromtheheartcafe.net). If you're tired of all the fried, heavy foods, pull up a stool at Meals From the Heart Cafe in the French Market. Don't let the gluten-free, healthy menu mislead your taste buds: this is not medicine. Their meals do make you feel good, though. We like to go for breakfast. If there's two of you, one of you should order the heavenly crab cake with poached egg (Crab Cake Passion). The other should order the pancakes. If you're on your own, consider going back two days in a row—or else order it all at once!

EnVie Cafe (1241 Decatur St., 70116; $; daily 7a-midnight; $; 504-524-3689; http://www.cafeenvie.com) is a favorite hangout of Andrei Codrescu, the local poet and NPR commentator. They offer hearty breakfasts, and you'll feel like a local eating at one of the outdoor tables.

Croissant d'Or (617 Ursulines Ave., 70116; M-F 7a-1p, Sa-Su 7a-3p, closed Tu; $; 504-524-4663; https://www.croissantdorpatisserie.com) is a hip breakfast spot. Enjoy coffee, quiche, and buttery croissant-based breakfast sandwiches in a lovely courtyard.

Chicken Bon Femme

Roasted chicken with cottage fries and bacon caramelized onions.

Look for this classic Creole dish at **Galatoire's** (209 Bourbon St., 70130; W-Sa 11:30a-9p, Su 12p-9p, closed M-Tu; $$$; 504-525-2021; https://www.galatoires.com).

Chicken Clemenceau

Clemenceau is a Creole favorite: chicken or shrimp in garlic sauce, peas, mushrooms, and brabant potatoes.

You can find both shrimp and chicken Clemenceau at **Galatoire's** (209 Bourbon St., 70130; W-Sa 11:30a-9p, Su 12p-9p, closed M-Tu; $$$; 504-525-2021; https://www.galatoires.com).

Scott had a delicious shrimp Clemenceau at **Arnaud's** Sunday Jazz Brunch (813 Bienville St., 70112; Dinner W-Sa 5:30p-9pm, Sunday Jazz Brunch 10a-1:30p, closed M-Tu; $$$; 504-523-5433; https://www.arnaudsrestaurant.com).

Crawfish Monica

Crawfish Monica has been a Jazz Fest staple for 40 years. The authors have actually never had the pleasure of trying it: it's one of those dishes we're always keeping an eye out for, but which has eluded us so far. Apparently, it is a scrumptious pasta dish featuring crawfish in a spicy cream sauce. You can find it at the **Kajun Kettle Foods** booth at Jazz Fest: Chef Pierre Hilzim named the dish for his wife.

Crawfish Étouffée

Smothered crawfish: crawfish tails, onions, green peppers and spices in a flavorful roux, served with steamed rice. Étouffée can also be made with shrimp.

The Gumbo Shop (630 St Peter St., 70116; Su-Th 11a-10p, F-Sa 11a-11p; 504-525-1486; $$; http://www.gumboshop.com) does an acceptable version of this classic. You can also find it also at **Galatoire's** (209 Bourbon St., 70130; W-Sa 11:30a-9p, Su 12p-9p, closed M-Tu; $$$; 504-525-2021; https://www.galatoires.com).

Fried Chicken

Some reckon **Willie Mae's Scotch House** (2401 St Ann St., 70119; M-Sa 11a-5p, closed Su; $$; 504-822-9503; https://williemaesnola.com) makes the best fried chicken in town, and some say **Fiorella's**. Though the latter's dependable location near the French Market has closed—and hadn't been run by the founding family since the late '90s, anyway—the original family has now opened an "original Fiorella's" in the Gentilly neighborhood (5325 Franklin Ave., 70122; M-Sa 11a-7p, closed Su; $; 504-309-0352; https://originalfiorellas.com).

There's also a great tradition of gas station fried chicken in New Orleans, which you can grab any time of day or night. Our favorite is **Key's Fuel Mart** (1139 N. Rampart St., 70116; always open; $; 504-301-4598; https://www.facebook.com/Keys-Fuel-Mart-146556205408924/), where we once picked up some scrumptious chicken at 1am.

This is also the only time Scott has ever been told, by a young man also awaiting some good grub, "Have you ever been told you look like a 25-year-old Johnny Depp?" He had to admit he had not. Karolyn didn't know whether to laugh more at the "25-year-old" bit, or the "Johnny Depp" assertion. (Scott: Ahem.)

McHardy's Chicken & Fixin' (1458 N Broad St., 70119; M-Sa 10a-10p, Su 10a-3p; $; 504-949-0000) deserves nods for its peppery fried chicken. The take-out only menu features classic soul food fixings to go with your chicken.

While these are all damn good, we have our top two contenders. As runner-up: **Lil' Dizzy's** (1500 Esplanade Ave., 70116; M-Sa 11a-3p, Closed Su; $; 504-766-8687; https://lildizzyscafe.net). Scrumptious fried chicken, and moreover, Lil' Dizzy's is a family experience. You don't need a family to go there, but when you leave, you will have one. Their food is made with the essentials of Southern cooking: butter and love.

We'd give the ultimate nod for best fried chicken (and best mac 'n' cheese! and best peach cobbler!) to the late, great Ms. Leah Chase, whose fried chicken recipe you can still taste at **Dooky Chase's** (2301 Orleans Ave., 70119; F 11a-3p and 5:30p-9p, Sa 5:30p-9p, Tu-Th 11a-3p, Closed Su-M; $$$; Call 504-821-0600 or 504-821-0535 for reservations, https://www.dookychaserestaurants.com).

In short, Lil' Dizzy's is a quick-serve eatery, whereas Dooky Chase's is a sit-down, white-table-cloth place—but you'll get some of the best fried chicken of your life at either.

Sotto voce: When we asked our cabbie once for his pick for the best fried chicken in town, he said Popeye's. We've yet to experiment with this option.

Gumbo
The official food of Louisiana.

Speaking of Ms. Leah Chase, the best gumbo we've ever had is her Gumbo Z'Herbes, served only on Holy Thursday. Legend has it that if you eat gumbo z'herbes on Holy Thursday, you will make as many new friends as there are greens in the gumbo. Ms. Chase's version includes nine: mustards, collards, red Swiss chard, beet tops, cabbage, carrot tops, spinach, kale, and watercress. Even if you're not in town on that special day, **Dooky Chase's** (2301 Orleans Ave., 70119; F 11a-3p and 5:30p-9p, Sa 5:30p-9p, Tu-Th 11a-3p, Closed

Su-M; Call 504-821-0600 or 504-821-0535 for reservations, https://www.
dookychaserestaurants.com) is still the place to start for gumbo. Chef Leah
famously slapped President Obama's hand when he reached for hot sauce.

Our second most beloved gumbo is the Gumbo Ya-Ya at **Mr. B's Bistro** (201 Royal St., 70130; Lunch W–Sa, 11:30a–2p, Dinner W–Su 5p–9p,
Sunday Brunch 10:30a–2p, Closed M-Tu; $$; 504-523-2078; http://www.
mrbsbistro.com).

A cup of the Creole gumbo at **Lil' Dizzy's** (1500 Esplanade Ave., 70116;
M-Sa 11a-3p, Closed Su; $; 504-766-8687; https://lildizzyscafe.net) will make
you happy. This restaurant is a classic institution of the Treme community.

Cochon (930 Tchoupitoulas St., 70130; Tu-Su 11a-10p, closed M; $$$;
504-588-2123; https://cochonrestaurant.com) serves up a delicious duck
& andouille gumbo.

Liuzza's By the Tracks (1518 N Lopez St; M–Sa 11a–8p, Closed Su except
when the Saints are playing, 504-218-7888; https://www.liuzzasbtt.com)
makes a spicy gumbo that has made lists of the spiciest dishes in the country.

The seafood gumbo at **Coop's Place** (1109 Decatur St., 70116; Th-M
11a-11p; Closed Tu-W; $$; 504-525-9053; https://www.coopsplace.net) is
good. (However, as we've said elsewhere, watch out for their $30 "market-
price" oyster po' boy.)

Ice Cream

Angelo Brocato (214 N. Carrollton Ave., 70119; Tu-Sa 10a-10p, Su 10a-9p,
closed M; 504-486-1465; https://www.angelobrocatoicecream.com). Since
1905, Angelo Brocato is the classic neighborhood Italian gelato parlor. This
town wouldn't be the same without their lemon ice and cannoli Siciliani.

Ice Cream 504 (2511 Jena St., 70115; M-Th 2p-8:30p, F-Sa 2p-9:30p,
Su 2p-8p; $; 504.266.2708; https://icecream504.com) We happened to drop
in here after a hot summer's afternoon second-lining. Their all-natural ice
cream was just the thing to cool us off, and the proprietor is a pip.

Italian

Irene's (529 Bienville St., 70130; Tu–Sa 5p-9:30p, closed Su-M; $$; 504-529-8811; https://irenesnola.com). Irene's is a wonderfully friendly, homey Italian restaurant, even in their new, more spacious location. It's as if a Sicilian grandma, perhaps Irene herself, is still whipping up the house-made tastes in the kitchen. We enjoyed the Oysters Irene: oysters with pancetta, pimento, and pecorino romano. The lasagne Bolognese with house-made pasta was everything Scott dreamed it would be. Consider pairing your meal with a nice Montepulciano d'Abruzzo. When we were there, complimentary bruschetta made for a nice lagniappe.

Adolfo's (611 Frenchmen St, 70117; Th-Sa 5:30p-9p; closed M-W; $$; 504-948-3800; https://www.facebook.com/profile.php?id=100063808125235; text 504-408-3253 for reservations (recommended). Adolfo's is a great Creole-Italian spot on Frenchman Street, almost hidden above the pocket-sized Apple Barrel club. Get the cannoli stuffed with crab, and don't miss Scott's favorite: steak with "ocean sauce." That dish should be in the dictionary next to the word "rich."

Mona Lisa (1212 Royal St., 70116; Th-M 5p-9p(ish), Closed Tu-W; $$; 504-522-6746; https://www.monalisaneworleans.com) is a cozy, atmospheric Italian place. When we were here, we made Crayola renditions of one another on the white paper tablecloth with the supplied crayons.

Mandina's (3800 Canal St., 70119; F-Sa 11a-9:30p, Su-Th 11a-9p; $$; 504-482-9179; https://mandinasrestaurant.com) was founded by an Italian immigrant, Sebastian Mandina, from Salaparuta, Sicily. Billy Sothern has this to say about the local importance of this Creole Italian institution in the book *Unfathomable City: A New Orleans Atlas*, "An old-fashioned cocktail, an appetizer of garlicky crab claws, and a plate of spaghetti and meatballs in a room full of judges, day laborers, and grandmas daily ensure the cultural survival of the city."

Paladar 511 (511 Marigny St., 70117; dinner every day 5:30p-9:30p, brunch Sa-Sunday 10a-2p; $$; 504-509-6782; https://www.paladar511.com. Paladar 511 comes highly recommended when you're in the Italian mood.

It's at the corner of Decatur and Marigny St., just across Elyisan Fields in the Marigny/Bywater.

Mosca's (4137 US-90, Westwego, 70094; F-Sa 5p-8:30p, W-Th 5p-8p; $$; 504-436-8950; https://moscasrestaurant.com). Mosca's is right outside New Orleans. You'll need to drive or Uber out here. Still, when Phil Rosenthal visited Mosca's on his TV show, it made us want to drive out to Westwego one day. We love the idea of getting the Oysters Mosca and putting it over your spaghetti Bolognese.

Jambalaya
The Fat Tuesday tradition.

To extend the plaudits for **Dooky Chase's** (2301 Orleans Ave., 70119; F 11a-3p and 5:30p-9p, Sa 5:30p-9p, Tu-Th 11a-3p, Closed Su-M; Call 504-821-0600 or 504-821-0535 for reservations, https://www.dookychaserestaurants.com), it should come as no surprise that their jambalaya is likewise the best we've ever had. It is chunky with shrimp and two different sausages—smoked and chaurice, both from Vaucresson.

The rabbit and sausage jambalaya at **Coop's Place** (1109 Decatur St., 70116; Th-M 11a-11p; Closed Tu-W; $$; 504-525-9053; https://www.coopsplace.net) is pretty tasty. (However, whenever we mention Coop's these days we always have to warn people to beware the "market price" oyster po' boy, after we got charged upwards of $30 for one sandwich. If you're gonna try it, be sure to ask how much it's going to be.)

King Cake
This crown-shaped dessert is a Fat Tuesday tradition

King Cake has a fascinating history: during Saturnalia, a winter solstice celebration of Saturn (the god of agriculture), the ancient Romans baked beans into cakes to celebrate the harvest. Whoever found the bean was named "king of the day." In the Middle Ages, Christianity appropriated this pagan tradition (as it did in so many cases) for the festival of the Epiphany, also known as Three Kings' Day (Jan. 6). You may eat King Cake then, or really at any point during Carnival Season—including Mardi Gras itself.

We'd recommend getting your King Cake from **Bywater Bakery** (3624 Dauphine St., 70117; Th-M 8a-3p, closed Tu-W;504-336-3336; https://www.bywaterbakery.com), **Angelo Brocato** (214 N. Carrollton Ave., 70119; Tu-Sa 10a-10p, Su 10a-9p, closed M; 504-486-1465; https://www.angelo-brocatoicecream.com), or **Loretta's Authentic Pralines** (locations at French Market #9, Th-Su 9a-5p, Closed M, W and 2101 North Rampart, 70116, W-Sa 9a-4p, Closed Su-Tu;504-944-7068; https://lorettaspralines.com.)

Late Night Eating
Each of these places will get you through when you find yourself peckish outside of normal dining hours, which just might happen.

Buffa's (1001 Esplanade Ave., 70116; Su-Th 11a-2a, F-Sa 11a-4a; $; 504-949-0038; https://www.buffasbar.com) is open damn late. They serve up tasty hot wings, burgers, and red beans 'n' rice.

Cafe du Monde (800 Decatur St., 70116; everyday 7:30a-11p; $; 800-772-2927; https://shop.cafedumonde.com) stays open until 11pm, should you ever need a late-night beignet.

Check Point Charlie's (501 Esplanade Ave., 70116; always open; $; 504-281-4847; https://www.facebook.com/Checkpoint-Charlies-1920820391513131/), open all night, is a punk-rock and blues dive bar—and we do mean "dive." It's a good place when you need a late-night burger to soak up a surfeit of alcoholic stimulants. They've got a pool table, and you can even do your laundry here.

Don't forget **Verti Marte** (1201 Royal St., 70116; open 24-7; $; 504-525-4767; https://vertimarte.net), which is always open. Get your All That Jazz at 3am, if you're so inclined.

Frenchmen Grocery & Deli (602 Frenchmen St., 70116; $; Su-W 11a-8p, Th 11a-11p, F-Sa 11a-2a; $; 504-655-3777). The Frenchmen Deli is always a reliable stop for your Abita/wine needs, and also offers po' boys, or actually Banh Mi—which, come to think of it, we suppose is a kind of Vietnamese po' boy. There's usually pork belly, chicken, and tofu. They're open especially late on Fridays and Saturdays, until 2am. During busy times, they have pre-made Banh Mi, egg rolls, and french fries in brown bags at the cash register, so you can just grab and go.

Clover Grill (900 Bourbon St, proudly open daily 24/7, $; 504-598-1010, https://www.clovergrill.com). Clover Grill's cheeseburgers are magic, somehow. It must have something to do with being cooked under hubcaps. Scott likes to load his up with bacon and jalapeños. Getting late-night grub here is a classic New Orleans experience.

Dat Dog (601 Frenchmen, 70119; Su-Th 11a-12a, F-Sa 11a-3a; $; 504-309-3362; https://www.datdog.com/frenchmen-street) began as a stand on Freret Street, but now they offer gourmet dogs on Frenchmen. Look for crawfish, alligator and duck sausage, as well as more standard dogs.

Port of Call (838 Esplanade Ave., 70116; Su-M, W-Th 12p-9p, F-Sa 12p-12a, closed Tu; $$; 504-523-0120; https://portofcallnola.com) is a cozy, dimly lit NOLA tradition. It's our go-to for hefty, 1/2 pound, delicious burgers—which come with a loaded baked potato, not fries. Their signature Monsoon cocktail will knock you out and have you headed to detox.

Lucky Dog (headquarter tel: 504-524-6010; http://www.luckydogsinc.com). Ignatius J. Reilly's favorite treat can be yours as well. We're talking about the Lucky Dog, the hot dog that's the classic NOLA taste since 1948. For the further uninitiated, Ignatius is the hero of *A Confederacy of Dunces*, set in New Orleans and the funniest book we've ever read. We read it aloud to each other to pass the time while driving on our first Southern road trip. (Karolyn does an amazing Ignatius—Scott will always hear his voice in the drawl to which she assigned him). Ignatius for a time operated one of the famous Lucky Dog carts—until he got the boot for eating his own supply! The iconic carts can be found throughout the French Quarter, but it's always a good bet you'll find one on Bourbon at any time of day or night. Scott likes his with chili and mustard.

Coop's Place (1109 Decatur St., 70116; Th-M 11a-11p; Closed Tu-W; $$; 504-525-9053; https://www.coopsplace.net), open until 11pm, is a solid bet for decent grub in the Quarter. (Like we said, watch out for that $30 "market-price" oyster po' boy.)

Muffuletta

Round sandwich made with Sicilian sesame bread, cold sliced meats, cheese, and olive salad

Central Grocery (923 Decatur St., 70116; temporarily closed; 504-523-1620; https://centralgrocery.com). Established in 1906, Central Grocery invented the muffaletta, and this is still the place to get your first one. As their site advises, each of their sandwiches is made up of "meats sliced in house, locally baked handmade bread and our family's Italian Olive Salad." Be forewarned: it's HUGE. Under regular conditions, they are open every-day from 9a to 5p. Currently, however, they are closed for repairs due to extensive damage caused by Hurricane Ida—and may be in the process of moving shop altogether, for the same reason.

If they're closed when you arrive, consider **Frank's Restaurant** (933 Decatur St., 70116; daily 10a-11:30p; $; 504-525-1602; http://www.franksnola.com/home2.html) as an alternative place to get you muffuletta. It's quite close to LaTrobe Park, as well, so you can still have your picnic there.

Verti Marte (1201 Royal St., 70116; open 24-7; $; 504-525-4767; https://vertimarte.net), the purveyors of Scott's favorite sammitch, the All That Jazz, also makes a proper muffuletta.

Another solid choice for your first muffuletta is **Napoleon House** (500 Chartres St., 70130; W-Th, Su 11a-9p, F-Sa 11a-10p, closed M-Tu; $$; 504-524-9752; https://www.napoleonhouse.com).

Old School

Antoine's (713 Saint Louis St., 70130; Th-M lunch 11a-2p, dinner 5p-9p, Su (brunch only) 10:30a-2p, closed Tu-W; $$$; 504-581-4422; https://antoines.com) is the oldest family-run restaurant in the United States, founded by the Alciatore family in 1840. You'll want the oysters Rockefeller—it's the invention of the house (see our "oysters" section). Also look for Oysters à la Foch (fried oysters with foie gras and Colbert sauce). The wonderful "pommes de terre souffles" (or, popularly, "Balloon Potatoes") are an Antoine's tradition, a French innovation which they made a hit on these shores.

Make sure to explore the back rooms after dinner: walking around is a good way to digest. It's like being transported back to 1840. In fact, the 1840 Room, as the restaurant's website notes, "replicates a fashionable dining room from that time and is also a museum of sorts, housing a Parisian cookbook circa 1659, and the restaurant's silver duck press among other treasures." Enjoy the photographs of successive generations of the Alciatore family.

Look for the rooms dedicated to memorializing the great New Orleans institution of Mardi Gras. As Antoine's website notes, "Three of our private rooms bear the names of Carnival krewes—Rex, Proteus, and 12th Night Revelers and our bar is named after the Krewe of Hermes…The walls are adorned with photos of royalty and memorabilia, including crowns and scepters of many years long past."

Then there's the Mystery Room. It "acquired its name due to Prohibition, the 18th Amendment prohibiting the sale of alcoholic drinks (from 1919 until 1933)…During this time, some would go through a door in the ladies' restroom to a secret room and exit with a coffee cup full of booze (in spite of the Blue Laws). The protocol phrase at table when asked from whence it came was: 'It's a mystery to me.' The name stuck and to this day, it's still the Mystery Room, nestled charmingly at the end of an interesting corridor. The room is dotted with souvenirs of famous restaurants around the world, including Groucho Marx's beret."

Finally, the legendary 165-foot long, 7-foot wide wine cellar holds approximately 25,000 bottles. Either before or after your visit, find the little window around the corner on Royal Street, which lets you peer into this wine connoisseur's heaven.

Tujague's (429 Decatur St., 70116; Brunch F 11a-2:30p, Sa-Su 10a-2:30p, Dinner W-Th, Su 5p-9p; F-Sa 5p-10p, closed M-Tu; $$$; 504) 525-8676; https://tujaguesrestaurant.com). Founded in 1856, Tujague's is the *second* oldest restaurant in New Orleans (after Antoine's). While we haven't yet had the pleasure of dining here, Scott had their beef brisket with Creole horseradish sauce at French Quarter Fest and can attest to its deliciousness.

Arnaud's (813 Bienville St., 70112; dinner W-Sa 5:30p-9pm, Sunday Jazz Brunch 10a-1:30p, closed M-Tu; $$$; 504-523-5433; https://www. arnaudsrestaurant.com) is another historic restaurant in the Quarter—since 1918!—where Creole food is paired with sweet live jazz provided by Jerry Embree's Gumbo Trio. Arnaud's Sunday Jazz Brunch, also presided over by Embree's combo, is a local tradition—and a lot of good fun. The trio goes from table to table. If you're like Scott (not always recommended), you might try to stump the brunch band with a request they wouldn't normally expect a tourist to know about. Nothing really all that obscure: perhaps ask 'em for Louis Armstrong's "West End Blues." (Scott: As I recall, I first asked Jerry's combo for some Danny Barker, which they didn't happen to have in their repertoire, but then they absolutely nailed an Armstrong deep cut.) Be sure to tip.

After you eat, don't miss the Mardi Gras Museum upstairs, which boasts a collection of jaw-dropping gowns and costumes.

(Also, don't forget there's a dress code at Arnaud's, and really at all of the old-school Creole restaurants. At the very least, don't wear t-shirts, gym shorts, or flip flops—you likely won't be admitted, in any case. For a place like this, Scott would usually wear a tie and jacket, Karolyn a dress.)

Oysters

You're in a shellfish culture when you're in the Crescent City. After all, you're right on the Gulf of Mexico. You simply must enjoy some cool and salty raw "ersters" on the half shell, as well as some of the characteristically local ways of cooking them—we especially like the charbroiled style. (You may have heard this rule of thumb that you should only eat oysters if you're visiting in a month with the letter "r": that is, September through April. A place like Casamento's closes during the summer, adhering to this rule about oyster season. Still, even during the off months, you'll likely be able to find good oysters.) We recommend the following.

While many tourists do pub crawls down Bourbon, we opt for an oyster crawl (our own invention).

You could start with the famous charbroiled oysters at **Drago's** (Hilton Riverside Hotel, 2 Poydras St., 70130; daily 12p-10p; $$; 504-584-3911; https://www.dragosrestaurant.com), which have been called "The Single Best Bite of Food in New Orleans." Truly, we're inclined to agree! These delicacies are covered in Parmesan cheese, butter, parsley, and garlic—and you are gonna need that New Orleans-style French bread to sop it up. If you sit at the bar, you can watch the cook forging the oysters in the fiery furnace of the grill, which occasionally explodes in a dramatic fireworks show. Watch him snatch a taste of heaven from the jaws of hell.

Then, you could walk over to **Luke** (333 Saint Charles Ave., 70130; daily 7a-10p, Happy Hour daily 3p-6p; $$; 504-378-2840; https://www. lukeneworleans.com), which models itself on an Alsatian brasserie—a good bet for raw oysters.

Next, head to **Felix's** (739 Iberville St., 70130; Su-Th 11a-9p, F-Sa 11a-10p; $; 504- 522-4440; https://www.felixs.com). When we visited, to our delight, our shucker plopped our half-dozen raw right down on the bar right in front of us, old-school style.

Three stops is good for a crawl, but we should note that right across the street from **Felix's** is **Acme Oyster House** (724 Iberville Street, near Canal & Bourbon, 70130; Thu-M 11a-10p, closed Tu-W; $; 504-522-5973; https://acmeoyster.com), a fun place to have your first oysters. We got a tray of raw and a platter of Oysters Rockefeller, as well. Still, there's almost always a line at Acme, whereas the food across the street at Felix's is just as good—some even say better.

Now we'll run down some of our other favorite oyster spots in town.

We quite like **Royal House Oyster Bar** (441 Royal St., 70130; Su-Th 11a-10p, F-Sa 11a- 11p; 504-528-2601; https://royalhouserestaurant.com), especially the balcony seating. We won't forget the time we enjoyed oysters and cocktails on the balcony as the beautiful playing of buskers Tanya & Dorise wafted over us from a nearby corner of Royal Street.

If you're in the Uptown neighborhood, **Casamento's** (4330 Magazine St., 70115; Th-Sa 11a-2p and 5:30p-9p, Su 4:30p-8:30p, closed M-W; $;

504-895-9761; https://www.casamentosrestaurant.com) is a classic oyster house, having been slinging "ersters" for over 100 years. Their oyster loaf is a speciality. (They close during June, July, and August, adhering to the notion of oyster season, which we respect.)

You can't forget **Pascal Manale's** (838 Napoleon Ave., 70115; Tu-Sa 4:00p-9p, W-F 11:30a-9p; $$; 504-895-4877; https://pascalsmanale.com) for oysters: they've got some of the plumpest and juiciest we've had. In fact, Fodor's reckons "the atmospheric old bar might be the best place in the city to slurp raw oysters." After 30-plus years at his trade, Thomas "Uptown T" Stewart is a master shucker. Belly up to his bar, down some of his freshly shucked oysters, and let him regale you with his stories.

If you find you like the charbroiled oysters you had at **Drago's**, you'll also dig the chargrilled oysters at **Neyow's Creole Cafe** (3332 Bienville, 70119; M-Th 11a-9p, F-Sa 11a-11p, Su11a-7p; $$; 504-827-5474; https://neworleans.neyows.com).

Cochon (930 Tchoupitoulas St., 70130; Tu-Su 11a-10p, closed M; $$$; 504-588-2123; https://cochonrestaurant.com) offers beautiful wood-fired oysters with chili garlic butter.

Antoine's (713 St Louis St., 70130; Th-M lunch 11a-2p, dinner: 5p-9p, Su (brunch only) 10:30a-2p, closed Tu-W; $$$; 504-581-4422; https://antoines.com) invented oysters Rockefeller in 1899. Why is the dish named after the richest American of the day? Because of the richness of the sauce, which is still a secret, but is thought to contain a puree of greens including spinach and parsley, along with all that good cheese, butter, and breadcrumbs. These delicacies are then baked or broiled.

Arnaud's (813 Bienville St., 70112; Dinner W-Sa 5:30p-9pm, Sunday Jazz Brunch 10a-1:30p, closed M-Tu; $$$; 504-523-5433; https://www.arnaudsrestaurant.com) is another venerable restaurant with a special oysters invention to call their own, Oysters Bienville: shrimp, mushrooms, green onions, herbs and seasonings in a white wine sauce.

Superior Seafood (4338 St. Charles Ave., 70115; Su 10a-10p, M-Th 11a-10p, F-Sa 11a-11p; $$; 504-293-3474; https://www.superiorseafoodnola.

com) presents a beautiful dozen, as does **Cooter Brown's Tavern & Oyster Bar** (509 S. Carrollton Ave., 70118; daily 11a-1a; $; 504-866-9104; http://www.cooterbrowns.com/#home).

Pizza

Favela Chic (525 Frenchmen St., 70116; Su-M 11a-12a, Tu 7p-12a, W-Th 11a-12a, F-Sa 11a-2a; $; 504-312-3912; https://favelachicnola.com) sells tasty slices and freshly made pies, as well. The walk-up window on the corner of Frenchmen/Chartres is a good spot to place a takeaway order. We find their pizza deeply satisfying after a late night of music venue hopping. A fine addition to the neighborhood. Pay in cash and you pay 10% less, we believe. Ruben's Taco Taqueria is here, as well.

Louisiana Pizza Kitchen (95 French Market Place, 70116; Su-M 12p-9p, Tu-Th 5p-9p, F-Sa 12p-9p; $; 504-522-9500; https://lapizzakitchenfq.com) Good pizza and hospitable staff.

Mona Lisa (1212 Royal St.,70116; Th-M 5p-9p(ish), Closed Tu-W; $$; 504-522-6746; https://www.monalisaneworleans.com) is a cozy Italian place where you can eat pizza while doodling on the white paper tablecloth.

Pizza Delicious (627 Piety St., 70117; Tu-Su 11:30a-9p, F-Sa 11:30a-10p, closed M; 504-676-8482; http://pizzadelicious.com) Some locals consider this pizza joint in the Bywater the best in town.

Po' Boys (also spelled Poor Boy or poboy)

Not just a sandwich, this beautiful mess features succulent fillings (meats, cheese, seafood), "dressed" with lettuce, tomato, mayonnaise, and pickles on New Orleans-style French Bread.

Where should you have your first po' boy? Talk about a hot topic. Let's just dive in. For their roast beef po' boy (hot and home-cooked!), Scott's vote goes to the **Parkway Bakery** (538 Hagan Ave., 70119; W-Su 10a-6p, closed M-Tu; 504-482-3047; https://parkwaypoorboys.com), though it's easiest to get there if you have a car. Their surf and turf po' boy, which unites the roast beef with fried gulf shrimp, is legendary. This joint has been a neighborhood landmark since it opened in 1911. They use the proper Leidenheimer Bakery bread, for one thing. You're gonna wind up with plenty of beautiful debris with that roast beef po' boy: that's the bits of the gravy that fall from your sandwich onto your plate. Scott like to scoop the debris up with Zapp's, the classic Louisiana kettle chips. That's about as NOLA as it gets.

On the other hand, another candidate for the best roast beef po' boy in town could also be **Frady's One-Stop Food Store** (3231 Dauphine St., 70117; M-F 7:30a-5p, Sa 9a-3p, Closed Su; $; 504-949-9688; https://www.facebook.com/Fradys-One-Stop-Food-Store-124292370952193/) in the Bywater. (Surely there can only be one best, you say? You see the problem we're running into here.) Andy J. Forest even wrote a song about this beloved neighborhood joint: "They have everything you need, at the corner of Piety and Dauphine." While absorbed in the task of "getting outside" a po' boy from Frady's, Scott has been known to holler out, "debris me!" Karolyn loves Frady's because you can get a half po' boy. Her preference: oyster. Grab an Abita and sit outside with the likes of Dr. Bob and other community characters. Frady's is definitely a local joint. We believe they're cash only.

If you're in the Quarter, **Verti Marte** (1201 Royal St., 70116; open 24-7; $; 504-525-4767; https://vertimarte.net) features a signature po' boy known as the All that Jazz—the world's mightiest sandwich. Yes, you read that right: Scott has been known to proclaim the All that Jazz the greatest sammitch in the world. He's been known to become expansive on the subject. (Scott: I'm tempted to say there is scarcely a "mot juste" for it. Rather, it must be experienced.) It is comprised of shrimp, turkey, ham, cheeses, mushrooms and, let us not forget, the "top secret" WOW sauce. Truly a thing of beauty. Karolyn, for her part, swears by the Verti Marte's oyster po' boy. They deliver, as well.

Speaking of which, Karolyn also loves the oyster po' boy at **Lil' Dizzy's** (1500 Esplanade Ave., 70116; M-Sa 11a-3p, Closed Su; $; 504-766-8687; https://lildizzyscafe.net), when available.

If you are in the mood for more gourmet, non-traditional tastes, **Killer PoBoys** (811 Conti St., 70112; M-Th 12p-8p, F-Sa 10a-12a, Su 10a-10p; $; 504-252-6745; http://www.killerpoboys.com) in the back of the Erin Rose bar is a must. (They also have a "Big" standalone location at 219 Dauphine

St., 70112; W-M 11a-6p, Closed Tu; $; 504-462-2731; http://www.killer-poboys.com)

Liuzza's by the Tracks (1518 N Lopez St; M–Sa 11a–8p, Closed Su except when the Saints are playing, $$; 504-218-7888; https://www.liuzzasbtt.com) features a barbecue shrimp po' boy—as delicious as it is unique. We've heard that Bourbon House (144 Bourbon St., 70130; F-Sa 11a-10p, Su-Th 11a-9p; $$; 504-522-0111; https://www.bourbonhouse.com) does a nice barbecue shrimp po' boy, as well.

Now, when we are at French Quarter Fest, **Walker's Southern Style BBQ** (10828 Hayne Blvd., 70127; W-F 10:30a-2p or 'til sold out, Closed Sa-Tu; $; 504-241-8227; https://cochondelaitpoboys.com), usually located out in New Orleans East, serves up a Cochon de Lait Po-Boy that is to die for. What is cochon de lait, you ask? It's a suckling pig—what you're eating, it must be faced, is a pit-roasted piglet, which was still recently at its mother's teat. Incredibly tasty, it must be said.

Some swear by **Johnny's PoBoy** (511 Saint Louis St., 70130; Everyday 8a-4:30p; $; 504-524-8129; https://www.facebook.com/johnnyspoboys/?ref=page_internal) in the Quarter, while others go wild for the shrimp po' boy at **Guy's** (5259 Magazine St., 70115; M-Sa 11a-4p, closed Su; $; 504-891-5025; https://www.facebook.com/guyspoboysnola/) in Uptown. Speaking of that neighborhood, **Mahony's Po-boys & Seafood** (3454 Magazine St., 70115; Su-W 11a-6p, Th-Sa 11a-9; $; 504-899-3374 https://mahonyspoboys.com) serves 'em up big, while **Domilise's** (5240 Annunciation St.; 70115; M-F 10a-6:30p, Sa 10:30a-7p, Closed Su; $; 504-899-9126; https://www.domilisespoboys.com) is a po' boy landmark. The list could go on and on.

In fact, we've got to mention one more. **Bevi Seafood Co.** (236 N Carrollton Ave., 70119; Tu-Sa 11a-8p, Su-M 11a-4p; $; 504-488-7503; http://beviseafoodco.com) makes ultra-stuffed po' boys: bigger than your head. Scott likes the "Peacemaker," which is surf 'n' turf style: shrimp and roast beef. Karolyn goes for the oyster po' boy. Whichever one you get, you'll wind up with tons of debris (have your Zapp's ready for scooping). Bevi is also known for their freshly boiled crawfish. Chat with the waitstaff and leave room for ice cream and cannoli at Angelo Brocato's, right next door.

Pompano Meuniere

Seasoned white fish. Meuniere refers to both the sauce and also the method of preparation, which involves dredging the fish with flour prior to cooking.

This is a classic French recipe that Julie Child popularized in the United States, though her version called for sole, not pompano, as the fish. **Arnaud's** (813 Bienville St., 70112; Dinner W-Sa 5:30p-9pm, Sunday Jazz Brunch 10a-1:30p, closed M-Tu; $$$; 504-523-5433; https://www.arnaud-srestaurant.com) boasts of their famous Creole Meunière Sauce, which they serve over crisply fried fillet.

Pralines

Pronounced "prah-lines," this delicious candy consists of pecans, milk, sugar, and butter

The **New Orleans School of Cooking** (524 St Louis St.) in St. Louis Square is a good bet for these sweet treats, but our favorite is **Loretta's Authentic Pralines**. Loretta's was founded over 35 years ago by Loretta S. Harrison, the first African-American woman to open a praline business. (Sadly, Ms. Harrison passed away in 2022.) Her pralines are rich and delicious; try her praline beignets to experience two great tastes going great together. They have a stall in the French Market at #9 (Th-Su 9a-5p, Closed M, W), and their cafe is at 2101 North Rampart, 70116 (W-Sa 9a-4p, Closed Su-Tu). Website: https://lorettaspralines.com; 504-944-7068.

Red Beans and Rice

The tradition in NOLA is to eat red beans and rice on Monday. A small thing, but a thread in the tapestry of the culture we love. Monday was laundry day, and you'd put on a pot of red beans to simmer all day while you washed your clothes and linens. Scott: When we were young, decades ago, an old friend and I used to try our hand at making red beans and rice using an all-day recipe while we'd watch movies on VHS. I always think of him when I eat red beans. When I first moved to Chicago, this buddy's mom would occasionally send me a homemade kit for the making of red beans, complete with a bag full of spices. That was all many years before either of us ever visited New Orleans and had "the real thing."

Mandina's (3800 Canal St., 70119; F-Sa 11a-9:30p, Su-Th 11a-9p; $$; 504-482-9179; https://mandinasrestaurant.com) was founded by an Italian immigrant, Sebastian Mandina, from Salaparuta, Sicily, so it makes sense that their red beans and rice features Italian sausage.

Liuzza's by the Tracks (1518 N Lopez St; M–Sa 11a–8p, Closed Su except when the Saints are playing, 504-218-7888; https://www.liuzzasbtt.com) serves delicious red beans and rice, and **Neyow's Creole Cafe** (3332 Bienville, 70119; M-Th 11a-9p, F-Sa 11a-11p, Su 11a-7p; $$; 504-827-5474; https://neworleans.neyows.com) makes a nice plate, as well. Consider washing the red beans down with a Bow Wow cocktail. Their sautéed crab claws are tasty, too.

Lil' Dizzy's (1500 Esplanade Ave., 70116; M-Sa 11a-3p, Closed Su; $; 504-766-8687; https://lildizzyscafe.net) red beans and rice will never let you down.

Scott likes the red beans and rice at **Acme Oyster House** in the Quarter (724 Iberville St., 70130; Thu-M 11a-10p, closed Tu-W; $; 504-522-5973; https://acmeoyster.com). They particularly remind him of the kind he and his pal made as young guys.

A word should be said about the tradition of free red beans and rice on Mondays. Bars like **Harry's Corner** (900 Chartres St., 70116; Every day 10a-3a; 504-524-1107; https://www.facebook.com/Harrys-Corner-139022506152999/) adhere to this tradition. Theirs are made by one our favorite bartenders, Paul, and they're great.

Also look for free Monday red beans at **Kermit's Tremé Mother-in-Law Lounge** (1500 N Claiborne Ave., 70116; 504-814-1819; https://www.facebook.com/Ruffinsbbq/). You might even get a neckbone!

Sandwiches (as a discrete category from Po' Boys)

Stein's Market and Deli (2207 Magazine St., 70130; Tu-F 8a-5p, Sa-Su 9a-5p, Closed M; $; 504-527-0771; https://steinsdeli.com) is the best place for a sammitch in all of NOLA, according to Mason Hereford from Turkey and the Wolf (see below). If the owner of the competition says your food is the best, you know it has to be damn good.

Mason Hereford and Lauren Holton are the owners and chefs at **Turkey and the Wolf** (739 Jackson Ave., 70130; W-M 11a-4p, "as in we're open everyday but Tuesday"; $; 504-218-7428; http://www.turkeyandthewolf.com), where high jinks abound in the form of whimsical sandwiches and cocktails. The fried bologna sandwich is indeed a kind of masterpiece. The Mama Tried burger ("two all beef patties, special sauce, lettuce, cheese, pickles, onions, tomatoes, all on a not sesame seed bun") is delicious, as well. (Fast-food homages is part of what they do here.) Karolyn still craves this burger and is often caught day-dreaming of its sheer perfection. There's also—of all things—a vegetarian reuben made with collard greens. When Phil Rosenthal visited, he proclaimed this latter the best vegetarian sandwich he'd ever tried.

Sauce Piquante with chicken, shrimp, or wild game

Piquante is basically a Cajun version of Creole sauce, based in stewed tomatoes and the "Holy Trinity" (diced onion, celery and bell pepper).

Look for sauce piquante on dishes throughout Iberia Parish, such as in the cities of Lafayette and New Iberia. It's tomato-based, usually using not only stewed or crushed tomatoes but tomato sauce as well, and then throwing in the "Holy Trinity" (diced onion, celery and bell pepper) cooked in a roux, along with garlic and spices. You'll find it on chicken and seafood as well as game meat like rabbit, alligator, venison, and duck. It's usually served over rice.

Shrimp and Grits

Two Louisiana favorites together make for a classic pair

Commander's Palace (1403 Washington Place, 70130; lunch Th-F 11:30a-depends on season, dinner M-W 5:30p-depends, Th-F 6p-depends; jazz brunch with live jazz Sa 11a-2:30p, Su 10a-2:30p; 504-899-8221; https://www.commanderspalace.com) is famous for their shrimp and grits.

The "Shrimp and Gris Gris Grits" from **Gris Gris** (1800 Magazine St., 70130; Th 11a-9p, F-Sa 11a-10pm, Su-M 11a-9p, Closed Tu-W, Brunch every day, red beans & rice on Mondays; $$; 504-272-0241; https://grisgrisnola.com/gris-gris-1) is fast becoming a local favorite.

Shrimp/Chicken Creole

As the name implies, this is shrimp or chicken simmered in a creole sauce with stewed tomatoes, over steamed rice.

Shrimp Creole can be found at any good Creole restaurant, with the greatest being **Dooky Chase's** (2301 Orleans Ave., 70119; F 11a-3p and 5:30p-9p, Sa 5:30p-9p, Tu-Th 11a-3p, Closed Su-M; $$; Call 504-821-0600 or 504-821-0535 for reservations, https://www.dookychaserestaurants.com).

The **Gumbo Shop** (630 St Peter St., 70116; Su-Th 11a-10p, F-Sa 11a-11p; 504-525-1486; $$; http://www.gumboshop.com) does an acceptable version.
Both chicken and shrimp Creole can be found at **Galatoire's** (209 Bourbon St., 70130; W-Sa 11:30a-9p, Su 12p-9p, closed M-Tu; $$$; 504-525-2021; https://www.galatoires.com).

Smothered Chicken

This scrumptious dish is served with rice and creamed spinach at **Neyow's Creole Cafe** (3332 Bienville, 70119; M-Th 11a-9p, F-Sa 11a-11p, Su 11a-7p; $$; 504-827-5474; https://neworleans.neyows.com).

Turtle Soup
A local Creole/Cajun classic

A bowl of sherry-spiked turtle soup will make you happy. We'd recommend your first taste of this classic come from **Brennan's** (471 Royal St., 70130; Breakfast/Lunch Th-M 9a-2p, Dinner Th-Su 6-10p, Bubbles at Brennan's Happy Hour Th-Su 2-6p, M 9a-2p, Champagne Sabering in the Courtyard Th-Su 5p; $$$; 504-525-9711; https://www.brennansneworleans.com) or **Commander's Palace** (1403 Washington Place, 70130; lunch Th-F 11:30a-depends on season, dinner M-W 5:30p-depends, Th-F 6p-depends; jazz brunch with live jazz Sa 11a-2:30p, Su 10a-2:30p; 504-899-8221; https://www.commanderspalace.com).

Vaucresson Sausage Co.

Vaucresson sausage is a classic in local Creole cuisine, the go-to encased meat for area restaurants, as well as for home chefs cooking for their families. As Ian McNulty says of Vaucresson's classic Creole chaurice, it's "a pork/beef blend with layered flavors and a peppery bite that's sliced into gumbo, blended into burgers or served on its own." Vaucresson is the only food vendor to be included in every single Jazz Fest from the beginning—and it was the sausage of choice for Leah Chase, of Dooky Chase's. Scott had their Creole hot sausage po-boy at French Quarter Fest, and it made his day—if not his life. Aside from the hot sausage, look for the alligator sausage po-boy, as well.

Although the longtime home of Vaucresson Sausage on the corner of St. Bernard Avenue and North Roman was shuttered for a time, we learned of an encouraging development as we were going to press: as we write, workers are redeveloping the site into what will be a combination restaurant, meat market, and affordable apartment building. Edgar Chase IV, the current chef of Dooky Chase's, will be a partner in the new venture. We couldn't be more chuffed about this great next step for this historic Black-owned business.

Vietnamese/Cajun

Maypop (611 O'Keefe Ave., 70113; M 4p-9p, Th 4p-9p, F 4p-9:30p, Sa 5p-9:30p, Su 5p-9p, Happy Hour Weekdays 4p-6p (excluding Saints Game Days), closed Tu-W; $$; 504-518-6345; https://www.maypoprestaurant.com; reservations recommended). Maypop is where chef Michael Gullota (former *chef de cuisine* of **August**) serves up traditional favorites (shrimp and grits, gumbo, jambalaya) with a Southeast Asian twist. Also, look for **MoPho** (514 City Park Ave., 70119, https://www.mophonola.com) Gullota's original restaurant, a pho/po' boy joint.

Lilly's Cafe (1813 Magazine St., 70130; M-Th 11a-9p, F-Sa 11a-9p, Closed Su; $; 504-599-9999; https://www.facebook.com/LillysCafe/). Lilly's is known as a terrific spot for pho, but what's really got us intrigued is the spring rolls with Ponchatoula strawberries ("Lilly's Rolls").

Bywater Brew Pub (3000 Royal St., 70117; M 4p-9p, F-Su noon-9p, Closed Tu-Th; $$; 504-766-8118; https://www.bywaterbrewpub.com). Come to the Bywater Brew Pub for house-made brews and Viet-Cajun grub from the Chef Anh Luu, "born and raised in the Vietnamese Community of New Orleans." This is a good place to try ya-ka-mein, a local Creole/Asian favorite, reminiscent of pho or ramen but with a distinct seasoning. Only in New Orleans! (The dish is said to have magical pick-me-up qualities after a big night. We can see how this could be so.) You've also got to try the crawfish étouffée nachos. If you're there on a Monday, trivia starts at 7p.

The Best of the Rest

Muriel's
801 Chartres St.
New Orleans, LA 70116

For French Quarter ambience and New Orleans classics, Muriel's Jackson Square is one of our favorite restaurants. As Karolyn says, Muriel's could slide by on name and history like some restaurants, but they don't. The food is delectable. Ah, those crawfish and goat-cheese crepes! Karolyn's pecan-crusted drum was scrumptious. Some say Muriel's is also the most haunted restaurant in NOLA—in fact, they set a table nightly with bread and wine for their "friendly" ghost, Pierre Antoine. From their website: "Pierre Antoine Lepardi Jourdan is still with us today in spiritual form on the same piece of property that is now Muriel's. His ghost doesn't appear in human form, but instead as a glimmer of sparkly light wandering around the lounge." After you eat, explore the blood-red Seance Lounge on the second floor (historically, this was the slave quarters)—sadly, this area was where Mr. Antoine committed suicide, after losing his beloved mansion, which Muriel's once was, in a poker game. We think you'll like the sarcophagi. The upstairs balconies overlook Jackson Square, and we went out and had a good look at the atmospheric square awash in shadows, lamp-lit in the night.

If you can't get a reservation at Muriel's, several Ghost Tours pop in.

Cost and Hours: Dinner Su-Th 5p-9:30p, F-Sap-10p; Sunday Jazz Brunch 10:30a-2p; $$$;
Tel: (504) 568-1885;
https://muriels.com

Dooky Chase's Restaurant
2301 Orleans Ave.
New Orleans, LA 70119

We've talked about Dooky Chase's a lot up above, but we had to give them their own entry as well. The late, great Leah Chase established the restaurant with her husband in 1941, the eponymous Dooky for whom the restaurant is the namesake. Ms. Chase was nothing less than the Queen of Creole Cuisine—as the restaurant's website puts it, "Through the vision of Leah Chase, the barroom and sandwich shop grew into a sit-down restaurant wrapped within a cultural environment of African-American art and Creole cooking." After Chef Leah passed in 2019, her family has taken her reins and continues her legacy.

There's incredibly rich history here. Dooky Chase's food literally fueled the civil rights movement and social change. "Before the United States Supreme Court reversed its 1896 decision, *Plessy v. Ferguson*, Dooky Chase's Restaurant had become the hot spot for discussing issues of civil and economic rights in the African-American community in New Orleans and throughout the country. Thurgood Marshall along with local attorneys such as A.P. Tureaud, Lionel Collins, Ernest 'Dutch' Morial, and Revius O. Ortique, Jr. and later freedom fighters such as Reverend A.L. Davis, Reverend Avery Alexander, Oretha Castle Haley, Rudy Lombard, Virginia Durr, and Jerome Smith propelled civil rights and protests in the courts and on the streets of New Orleans. In the 1960s, Martin Luther King, Jr. and others would join these local leaders for strategy sessions and dialogue over meals in the upstairs meeting room at Dooky's."

The restaurant also features a beautiful collection of African-American art—a collection so good, in fact, that a museum that only featured this collection would be well worth a visit. The paintings are beautifully displayed in the main dining room, as well as in the Victorian Room and the Gold Room. Mrs. Chase's favorite room may have been this latter. "Mrs. Chase proudly describes the art displayed in the Gold Room, as her 'Salon Collection,' as the pieces displayed range from folk art, to works that serve to personally inspire her, challenge or broaden the perspectives of others, or give the viewer a moment of reflection."

In 2017, we got to experience her legendary Holy Thursday dinner, one of the great pleasures of our lives. (See the "gumbo" entry for our breathless description of the Gumbo Z'Herbes, which is only available on Holy Thursday.) We got to see her making the rounds after dinner service, happily greeting everyone at age 94. It's a memory we'll always cherish.

Cost and Hours: F 11a-3p and 5:30p-9p, Sa 5:30p-9p, Tu-Th 11a-3p, Closed Su-M; $$$; Call: (504) 821-0600 or (504) 821-0535 for reservations; https://www.dookychaserestaurants.com)

Bayona
430 Dauphine St.
New Orleans, LA 70112

Bayona's chef is Susan Spicer, one of the inspirations for the character of Janette Desautel on the important TV show "Treme." Don't miss the smoked duck "PB & J," one of the house signatures. The ever-changing menu is internationally inspired and seasonal. When we were there, the salmon cakes and pappardelle turned out to be one of our favorite tastes of the entire trip. The crouton with Capriole goat cheese (crafted by hand in Greenville, Indiana) was quite tasty, as well. For your apertif, sip a Kir Royale.

Cost and hours: Dinner Hours Tu-Sa 5p-9p, Lunch Hours Th-Sa 11:30a-1:30p, Closed Su-M; $$$; Tel: (504) 525-4455; Reservations recommended. https://www.bayona.com

Atchafalaya
901 Louisiana Ave.
New Orleans, LA 70115

With our first visit, Atchafalaya fast became one of our favorite new restaurants. Karolyn had the red fish in curry sauce with spinach and sweet potatoes, and it was one of our Top 5 tastes of the trip.

Brunch Th–M 10a–2:30p, Happy Hour Th–M 3p–5:30p, Dinner Th– M 5:30p–9p, Closed Tu & W;
Tel: (504) 891-9626;
e-mail: info@atchafalayarestaurant.com;
https://www.atchafalayarestaurant.com

Upperline (permanently closed)

The Upperline is now permanently closed, but you know what? We're gonna leave our entry for it in place, to preserve it in our memory. When we visited, Scott had the slow-roasted half duckling with garlic port sauce. This dish was featured on a 2011 episode of "The Best Thing I Ever Ate," and now Scott knows why: it just might go on his list, as well. The taste filled his whole body with pleasure. The local favorite dish of fried green tomatoes with shrimp rémoulade sauce—two great tastes that go great together—was actually invented here at the Upperline, back in '92. We also fondly recall their spicy P&J Oysters St. Claude. The night we were there, we got to meet JoAnn Clevenger, the proprietor, who made the walls of the restaurant into a gallery of her wonderful, personal art collection. Now 83, she has moved on to the next chapter in her life—Upperline, and her art collection, will be sold. She, and her restaurant, will be missed.

Compere Lapin
535 Tchoupitoulas St.
New Orleans, LA 70130

Nina Compton's Compere Lapin is one of our favorite restaurants in this town. She grew up on the island of Saint Lucia, and her food is a delightful amalgam of her life experiences and education in the Caribbean and its cuisines and culture, blended with the tastes of Louisiana, France, and Italy. Karolyn loves the curried goat with sweet potato gnocchi and cashews—in fact, it's her second-best taste in the world. (For her first, see our entry for August, below). We can also vouch for the scialatielli with shrimp and run-down sauce, the conch croquettes with pickled pineapple tartar sauce, and the spiced pig ears with smoked aioli. Absolutely next-level nosh. We always go with an order of the daily selection of chilled oysters, which sometimes come from the Alabama Gulf Coast. Compere Lapin's cocktail program, presided over by Abigail Gullo, is second to none.

Cost and Hours: Su 5:30p-9p, W-Th 5:30p-9p, F-Sa 5:30p-10p, Closed M-Tu; $$;
Tel: (504) 599-2119; Reservations recommended.
http://comperelapin.com;

Cafe Amelie
912 Royal St.
New Orleans, LA 70116

In a city of lovely courtyards, Cafe Amelie's 150-year-old Princess of Monaco Courtyard must rank among the loveliest. Karolyn started with the Ponchatoula strawberry salad with baby arugula, goat cheese, pine nuts, and strawberry balsamic dressing: it sent her into a rhapsody. Scott went with the beet and goat cheese salad, also very nice. Scott's appetizer of cajun country poutine (oven fries, mozzarella, and cochon) was so flavorful that even Karolyn—usually unmoved by the genius of poutine as a dish—went back for a second fork. This was a Louisiana twist on a dish Scott had learned to dig in Montreal. Karolyn's entree was oven-roasted wild Atlantic salmon with horseradish cream, while Scott went with the dreamy seasonally-inspired chef's pasta, which on this day featured crawfish, cherry tomatoes, and spinach in a light cream sauce. For dessert, the creole cream cheesecake with Ponchatoula strawberries sent Karolyn into yet another strawberry rhapsody, after she'd just recovered from the salad. If you're in the mood for fresh and seasonally inspired cuisine, look no further than Cafe Amelie.

Cost and Hours: Cafe-style brunch Th-Su 10a-3p, Dinner F 6-9p Closed M-W; $$;
Tel: (504) 412-8065;
https://cafeamelie.com

August
301 Tchoupitoulas St.
New Orleans, LA 70130

August's signature handmade potato gnocchi with Louisiana blue crab and black truffle is Karolyn's favorite taste *in the world*. That's right: in the whole world. We always go for the Friday "prix fixe" lunch, a great deal—to which we add an order of the amazing gnocchi. (As we went to press, August's lunch service has been suspended. Check their website to see if it returns.) Aside from the gnocchi, the menu tends to change: in the past we've enjoyed everything from crawfish bisque to slow-cooked guinea hen. A plate of rustic pâté or cooked seasonal root-veg can make you feel like you're on a picnic in the French countryside—except you're actually eating in an elegant 19th-century French-Creole building.

Cost and hours: Dinner W-Su 5p-10p, closed M-Tu; $$$;
Tel: (504) 299-9777;
https://www.restaurantaugust.com; Reservations recommended.

Orleans Grapevine Wine Bar & Bistro
720 Orleans Ave.
New Orleans, LA 70116

You can't beat bacon happy hour in a lovingly restored building dating back to 1808. We hear you saying, you intrigue me—what is this bacon happy hour? Why, it's where you get a bucket of bacon with your glass or bottle of wine. Bacon and wine, yay! We should note this was a pre-Covid tradition: it's unclear whether it's still in place. Even if it's not, this is an excellent wine bar with some wonderful selections and a kitchen.

Cost and Hours: Th-Su 4p-10p, closed M-W; Bacon Happy Hour (4p-6p & 10p-12 midnight);
Tel: (504) 523-1930;
https://orleansgrapevine.com

Café Reconcile
1631 Oretha Castle Haley Blvd.
New Orleans, LA 70113

As their website puts it, Café Reconcile is a "Nonprofit daytime eatery serving Southern staples cooked by at-risk youth receiving job training." We always like to support these kind of endeavors.

Cost and Hours: Tu-Fr lunch 11a–2:30p, closed Sa-M;

Tel: (504) 568-115;

https://www.cafereconcile.org

N7
1117 Montegut St.
New Orleans, Louisiana 70117

A very cool "hidden" wine bar, N7 is the vision of filmmaker Aaron Walker and chef Yuki Yamaguchi (a couple). N7 is meant to evoke a roadside farmhouse restaurant along France's Highway N7, the French equivalent of Route 66. The food is French bistro fare with a Japanese influence (not to mention a French New Wave influence, judging from the great movie posters that adorn the interior: Aaron is a cinephile, and it shows). We like to eat outside here.

On one of the nights we visited, an appetizer of hamachi carpaccio proved to be Karolyn's favorite taste of the evening, while Wagyu beef was special for Scott. In both dishes, we could taste Chef Yamaguchi bringing the Japanese influence. On another occasion we enjoyed the duck à l'orange as well as grilled bok choy in blue cheese apple sauce, a rich and delicious taste. We recommend ending the meal with the soy sauce crème brûlée while sipping a bit of Calvados.

N7 is also lauded for their excellent wine list, including good European natural wines. On one visit we enjoyed a 2016 Pinot Blanc by Domaine Maurice Schoech in Alsace, on another a 2018 Bourguiel Cabernet Franc by Domaine de la Chanteleuserie in the Loire Valley.

Incidentally, if you've an evening to spare sometime, ask Karolyn about the legend of "Anna," the ghost of the little girl she maintains haunts N7. Anna is part of our personal mythology of the town. The gist of it: once, while sitting out on the terrace, we heard the silvery laughter of a little girl waft over us and, as Scott ordered squid in ink, we distinctly heard a little girl comment, "I don't want that." The thing is, there was no little girl on the grounds—which are behind a high wall on a somewhat deserted side-street, and children are barred at N7 in any case.

Karolyn once wrote a long e-mail to N7 about our paranormal experiences with Anna. It says something about the coolness of the place that Aaron, the co-owner, wrote her back, telling her about ghostly experiences the employees have had, and about how excavations for the restaurant unearthed children's toys. Did these once below to…Anna? On a later visit, Aaron came over after dinner and we shared ghost stories.

Actually, it just so happens we've got Karolyn here, so she can tell you more about it herself.

Karolyn: Ah, the times we've had here. We have named the ghost Anna, as an Italian family used to live on the estate prior to it being a restaurant, which was a tire shop before. The thing is, when you believe and you have a listening ear, the ghosts will come forth. Anna has come forth in so many ways and so many times there is no denying that N7 is truly haunted.

Cost and Hours: Dinner M-Th 5p-9p, F-Sa 5p-10p, Brunch F-Sa 11:30a-2:30p; $$;
no phone number;
https://www.n7nola.com; no one under age 18 admitted, reservations recommended (use the website).

Cochon
930 Tchoupitoulas St.
New Orleans, LA 70130

Cochon (meaning "pig" in French) features terrific Southern and Cajun cooking from Chef Donald Link. Aside from the delicious wood-fired oysters with chili garlic butter we mentioned above (in the oysters section), we also dig the boudin balls (especially Scott). Scott had Louisiana cochon with cabbage, cracklins and pickled peaches; Karolyn had rabbit and dumplings. We recommend both highly. Delicious sides include macaroni & cheese casserole and smothered greens. The duck and andouille gumbo should not be missed.

Cost and Hours: Tu-Su 11a-10p, closed M; $$$;

Tel: (504) 588-2123;

https://cochonrestaurant.com

Cochon Butcher
930 Tchoupitoulas St. b
New Orleans, LA 70130

Get your meat fix at this more casual spot from the folks who brought you the adjacent Cochon (listed above). We recommend the blood sausage, the boudin, and the Pig Mac—think Big Mac, but with pork sausage patties. We like the smoked turkey sandwich, as well. Cochon Butcher makes a good bet for lunch after you explore the World War II Museum.

Cost and Hours: Daily 11a-10p; $$;

Tel: (504) 588-7675;

https://cochonbutcher.com

GW Fins
808 Bienville St.
New Orleans, LA 70112

GW Fins is an excellent place for fresh seafood in the Quarter. For appetizers, we enjoyed the lobster ravioli and pork belly with watermelon. Scott had an entree of absolutely beautiful Louisiana Yellowfin tuna—seared rare.

Cost and hours: Su-Th 5p-9:30p, F-Sa 5p-10p; $$$;

Tel: (504) 581-3467;

https://gwfins.com; reservations recommended.

Saba
5757 Magazine St.
New Orleans, LA 70115

At Saba, you'll get Chef Alon Shaya's justly famous wood-fired, fresh-from-the-oven puffy pita bread: tear it open and watch the steam billow out. We came here for lunch. We started with lovely plates of salatim (cold salads and spreads), a staple of Israeli cuisine: wood-roasted asparagus with amba, tahini, and almonds; tabouleh in crushed pecans, freekeh, and avocado; and labneh with pink peppercorns, shallots, and mint. We supplemented these with orders of ikra (lox shmear) and lutenitsa (oven-fired peppers, tomatoes, and eggplant). We also got an order of the blue-crab hummus with sweet peas, lemon butter, and mint.

We can recommend two of the sandwiches on the menu: Safta's fried eggplant with caramelized tomato, whipped goat cheese, and local greens, and the oyster schnitzel sandwich with Yemenite curry, half-sour pickles, and sesame seeds.

We should add a note that Alon Shaya started his career over at **Shaya** (4213 Magazine St., 70115; $$$; 504-891-4213, Su-Th 12p-9p, F-Sa 12p-10p) but for various reasons broke out on his own. (They kept his name, somewhat controversially.) Before we knew the backstory, but after Chef Shaya had left, we dined at Shaya and, honestly, had a wonderful meal. They've kept the puffy pita bread and a lot of Alon Shaya's other signature dishes. The roasted cauliflower was memorable: an entire head of cauliflower, charred and tasty. The slow-cooked lamb with whipped feta, pecan, and blueberry tabouleh was heavenly.

Cost and hours: W-Th 4:30p-9p, F 11a-2:30p, 4:30p-10p, Sa 10a-2:30p, 4:30p-10p, Su 10a-2:30p, 4:30p-9p, closed M-Tu; $$;
Tel: (504)324-7770; Reservations accepted.
https://eatwithsaba.com;

14 Parishes Jamaican Restaurant
8227 Oak St.
New Orleans, LA 70118

We've had the delicious jerk pork and jerk chicken from 14 Parishes at various festivals around town, including Tremé Fall Festival and French Quarter Fest, where their food was one of our favorite tastes of the many we had. Aside from the location above, also look for them if you're over at Pythian Market at 234 Loyola Ave., 70112.

Cost and hours: Tu-Th 4p-9p, F-Sa 11a-10p, Su Brunch 11a-3p, closed M; $$;
Tel: (504) 264-7457;
https://www.14parishes.com

Silk Road
2483 Royal St.
New Orleans, LA 70117

Silk Road is a neat combination Indian/Asian Creole restaurant/wine & cheese bazaar/b&b. (On Sundays and Mondays, food is provided by the Mexican Delicious pop-up restaurant.)

Cost and hours: Daily 3p-9p, Tu-Sa Silk Road dine-in & carry out, Su-M Mexican Delicious Pop Up; $$;
Tel: (504) 494-8307;
https://www.silkroadnola.com

Commander's Palace
1403 Washington Place
New Orleans, LA 70130

Commander's Palace is known as "the masterpiece" of Ella Brennan, the matriarch of the Brennan family of restaurateurs. It's also famously the home of 25-cent martinis at lunchtime (with the purchase of an entree: limit three, sots!). Signatures here include sherry-spiked turtle soup, Cajun cochon de lait, and shrimp and grits. Commander's Palace is right across the street from Lafayette Cemetery No. 1. Their jazz brunch is a signature NOLA experience.

Cost and hours: Lunch Th-Fr 11:30a-last seating varies by season, Dinner M-W 5:30p-depends, Th-F 6p-depends; jazz brunch with live jazz Sa 11a-2:30p, Su 10a-2:30p; $$;
Tel: (504) 899-8221;
https://www.commanderspalace.com

The **St. Roch Market** (2381 St. Claude Ave., 70117) gathers up excellent food vendors under one roof and gives you a chance to sample their wares.

Cost and Hours: Su-Th 7a-9p, F-Sa 7a-10p, Coffee 7a-7p, Food 11a-Close (with some vendors offering earlier breakfast), bar 11a-Close; $;
Tel: (504) 267-0388;
https://www.strochmarket.com

We first tried **Fete au Fete's** (3501 Jourdan Rd., 70126) food at their booth at the St. Roch Market. Scott had their Nola Trio Sampler, which, along with a crawfish poutine of which he still dreams, was comprised of creamy shrimp and grits and delicious red beans & rice. They no longer have a booth at the market, but they've now got their own place—as well as a food truck.

Cost and hours: Th 2p-8p, F-Sa 11a- 8p, Su 11a-7p, closed M-W;
Tel: (504-475-7979);
https://feteaufete.com

J C Deli & Grocery
63 French Market Pl.
New Orleans, LA 70116

The home of "the coldest beer in the world?," as the sign outside asks/proclaims. (The question mark is presumably there to avoid lawsuits from someone who found an even colder one elsewhere.) We can attest that J C Deli is a good, convenient place where we always drop by to pick up a few of "the coldest." You'll always find a selection of beers swimming in an ice-packed bath in huge coolers; these are the very frostiest. If you don't see what you want, there's more selection in the refrigerators. They also have a kitchen and make fare such as sandwiches, ramen, and shrimp fried rice.

Cost and hours: Everyday 6a to 6p; $;
Tel: (504) 522-2961

Fatma's Cozy Corner
1532 Ursulines Ave.
New Orleans, LA 70116

Fatma's makes yummy Turkish cuisine in the Treme. This cafe is indeed a cozy spot, a real neighborhood hangout. It's located in the building that was once Joe's Cozy Corner, the storied Treme jazz club.

Cost and hours: Everyday 7a-3p; $;
Tel: (504) 266-2791;
https://www.fatmascozycorners.com

MRB Bar & Kitchen
515 St Philip St.
New Orleans, LA 70116

MRB offers soul/comfort food, live music, cocktails/craft beer, and art in the Quarter. (And big screen TVs with sports, if that's your bag.) (Note that this is not our recommended "Mr. B's," but "MRB.")

Cost and hours: Everyday 9a-4a; $$;
Tel: (504) 524-2558;
https://mrbnola.com

Palm & Pine
308 N Rampart St.
New Orleans, LA 70112

Palm & Pine is great little spot for seafood, meat, and twists on area favorites, as well as those of the Caribbean, Mexico, and Central America. They proudly source their seasonal ingredients from local farms.

Cost and hours: Th Dinner 5:30p-9p, F-Sa Dinner 5:30p-11p, Late Nite 11p-1a, Su Brunch 10:30a-2p, Dinner 5:30p-9p, M Dinner 5:30p-9p, closed Tu-W; $$;
Tel: (504) 814-6200;
https://www.palmandpinenola.com

Toups' Meatery
845 North Carrollton Ave.
New Orleans, LA 70119

Toups' is, as the name would suggest, a great place for meat. Chef Isaac Toups grew up in Cajun Country. He went on to get years of classical culinary education and fine dining experience, which he now applies to offering his take on Cajun classics like cracklins, characuterie, and lamb neck.

Cost and Hours: M-F Lunch 11a-3p M-F Happy Hour 3p-5p, Sat Brunch 11a-3p, Su Brunch 10a-3p, Dinner Su-Th 5p-10p, F-Sa 5p-11p; $$;
Tel: (504) 252-4999;
http://toupsmeatery.com

Station 6 Seafood & Oyster Bar
105 Metairie-Hammond Hwy,
Bucktown, LA 70005

Located up by Lake Pontchartrain, Station 6 is one of the best spots for oysters, seafood gumbo, and bread pudding.

Cost and Hours: Tu-Th 5p-9p, F-Sa 4p-9p, closed Su-M; $$;
Tel: (504) 345-2936; No reservations.
https://www.station6nola.com

Music, Bars and the Rest

We'll start this section by listing live music venues, before we get into some of our favorite bars. The line between the two is porous. Suffice it to say that nearly everywhere you can hear live music, you can also get a drink. To a large extent, the converse is also true. Some of the gigs we've listed have cover charges; some do not. For more information on cover charges, consult the venue.

Music

 "If I don't make somebody cry—to be straight-up honest with you—I haven't done my job. If I don't make you try to reach the sky, I haven't done my job." —*the late Darryl "Little Jazz" Adams, alto saxophonist and bandleader at Preservation Hall*

Though you may cry at the gig, New Orleans music is fundamentally about feeling good. It's about having a good time *despite* the blues, as Jon Cleary puts it. It's about living life at a kind of joyous high.

Spend most of your time on Frenchmen Street. It's lined with one top music venue after another. That said, we wouldn't be completely forthright if we didn't acknowledge some changes happening there, and perhaps this is the place.

Frenchmen is occasionally plagued these days by bullshit. The Willie's Chicken that took the place of the venerable soul food joint the Praline Connection is a tacky, crass place that lowers the cultural level of the street. It belongs over on Bourbon. More and more, the street is being reduced to a tourist party street, which saddens us—if you want that, go to Bourbon. We're live-and-let-live: there's a place for clueless tourists who won't be reading this book. Again, that's Bourbon (or, better yet, go straight to Harrah's Casino and stay there). Frenchmen is supposed to be a street for people who want to get in touch with the culture.

Right, and what is the deal with those moronic three-wheeled neon-lit Batmobile-like vehicles blasting house music that sometimes plague Frenchmen now? What the hell are those things? Take it to Bourbon. Harrumph.

Also, we mentioned up above how much we love hearing the stentorian sounds of a brass band playing on the corner of Frenchmen/Chartres from our porch at LaMothe House, calling us down into the street. We have to mention some unfortunate developments in that regard, as well. The brass bands were displaced from their usual corner when Dat Dog occupied the lot where they used to play. (Not that we have anything against Dat Dog, a good local encased meats purveyor.) The Young Fellaz Brass Band is one of the bands that typically played on the corner, and their displacement caused them to take up a position across the street in front of FAB Books, which culminated in an unfortunate incident in 2019 where David Zalkind, the bookstore's proprietor, felt he had no choice but to call the cops on them.

This was all very disturbing to us when we learned of it: brass bands playing on the street, of course, is the very essence of New Orleans culture. On closer examination it appears there's blame to be parceled around. Apparently Zalkind talked to the Young Fellaz about allowing a short set in front of his door, which is more than many local businesses would allow, and they initially agreed but then disregarded the deal. They carried right on playing, blocking the door and playing at such a volume that Zalkind couldn't even hear himself carrying on conversations with patrons.

When the cops came, they pinned and tased Eugene Grant, an autistic trumpeter who often performs with Lil Red and Big Bad at BMC—known around the neighborhood as Little Eugene, he's a really sweet guy whom we've met (he even photo-bombed one of our pictures). It's very easy to imagine him, though, not understanding/complying with the cops' orders—

and they should have been able to see he's cognitively disabled. It makes us sick to think of it. It seems fair to say that Zalkind, who is white, should have realized that calling the cops on Black street musicians can result in those musicians being killed. Still, as he's said, "If I knew that Little Eugene was going to be tackled, I wouldn't have made that phone call." He's clearly disturbed about that aspect of it.

Thankfully, Eugene is okay and still playing music (we saw him twice on our last visit in 2022, playing at BMC and in Jackson Square). Also, the last couple times we were there, in 2022, we could still hear the brass bands from our porch.

On closer examination we feel Zalkind's heart is in the right place, that he's a tolerant guy, understands the culture, and wants to coexist. Apparently he'd tried everything short of calling the cops. In short, it's complicated. There are larger forces at play and it's going to take everyone's cooperation to sort it out. What's clear is the brass bands can never go. They *are* the culture, not that stupid Willie's.

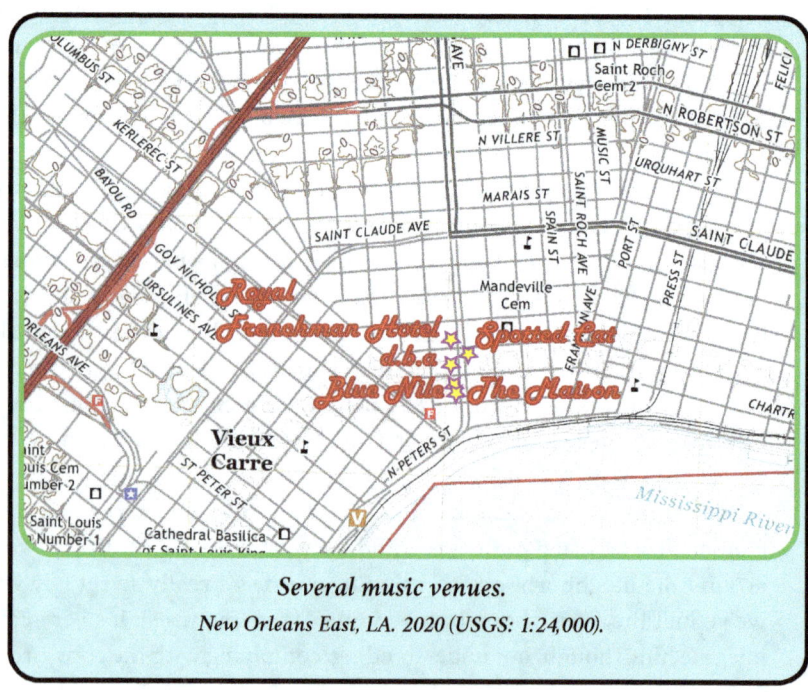

Several music venues.
New Orleans East, LA. 2020 (USGS: 1:24,000).

Okay, there's our harangue. It's not like we're the only one's worried about it. Hopefully, measures will be taken to save Frenchmen from becoming Bourbon Part II. If all this sounds like we're over Frenchmen, that's not the case. The magic is still there, if you're there at the right time and in the right place, to loosely paraphrase Dr. John.

On a Friday night, you can still just go up and down Frenchmen and see Kermit Ruffins at the **Blue Nile** (532 Frenchmen St., 70116; https://www.bluenilelive.com), Glen David Andrews at the **Royal Frenchmen Hotel** (700 Frenchmen St.; 70116; https://www.royalfrenchmenhotel.com/entertainment/live-performances), and Ashton Hines and his Big Easy Brawlers at **The Maison** (508 Frenchmen St., 70116; https://maisonfrenchmen.com). Here, then, are our picks for your best musical bets, on and off Frenchmen.

Be sure to supplement these tips by checking WWOZ's Livewire Music Calendar (https://www.wwoz.org/calendar/livewire-music). It gives the most current and accurate information about live music. Here's our best bets:

Trombonist and singer Glen David Andrews, the "Crown Prince of Treme," can be found at the **Royal Frenchman Hotel and Bar** (700 Frenchmen St.; 70116; https://www.royalfrenchmenhotel.com/entertainment/live-performances) at 10pm on Saturdays. (When he's in town, at least. He's often on the road on tour, these days.) His gospel-inspired bellow can be heard all the way down Frenchmen. When he really gets grooving, it's "the Hottest Saturday Night in Town."

The **Apple Barrel** (609 Frenchmen St., 70116; https://www.facebook.com/profile.php?id=100038284283503) is a pocket-sized club that provides a concentrated, outsized intensity of musical experience. Over the years, we've seen everyone from nonagenarian cornet great Jack Fine to red-hot up-and-coming rock 'n' roller Jack Sledge.

If you're in town on a Friday, see Ashton Hines and the Big Easy Brawlers at **The Maison** (508 Frenchmen St., 70116; https://maisonfrenchmen.com) at 10pm. Hines was our introduction to NOLA music when, on our very first visit, we stepped into the Maison to find him singing the curious refrain, "damn, damn damn damn, that white girl's got a big ol' butt." The phrase became rather a catchphrase with us.

Speaking of **The Maison** (508 Frenchmen St., 70116; https://maison-frenchmen.com), they offer an excellent series of free Sunday afternoon traditional jazz concerts in the spring and fall called Nickel-a-Dance. Nickel-a-Dance features top-flight bands and attracts an attentive audience who are there to listen. In short, this series gives this music the respectful showcase it deserves. Previous concerts have featured Shannon Powell & His New Orleans Jazz All-Stars, Joe Goldberg & The Function, Mari Watanabe & Her Chosen Few Jazz Band, and Tom Fischer & The West End Rhythm Kings. The shows start early, too: 4-7pm.

Tin Men is always fun: they tout themselves as America's "premiere" sousaphone-washboard-guitar trio, and they're probably right. The band features noted local singer-songwriter Alex McMurray, Frenchmen Street fixture Washboard Chaz, and the New Orleans Nightcrawlers' Matt Perrine on sousaphone. Catch them at **d.b.a.** (618 Frenchmen St., 70116; https://dbaneworleans.com) on Wednesdays at 6pm.

For more Washboard Chaz, catch him with the Palmetto Bug Stompers at **d.b.a.** (618 Frenchmen St., 70116; https://dbaneworleans.com), at 6pm. This gig is a Sunday evening tradition for us.

A chance to hear John Boutté's spine-tingling rhythm and blues in person should not be missed. That's Mr. Boutte singing the great opening number over the credits of the HBO series *Treme*. His version of Sam Cooke's "A Change is Gonna Come" is inspiring: so inspiring, in fact, that it does in fact make Karolyn weep. He also sings great tunes like "Foot of Canal St." As a musician's musician, he insists that his audience listen, not gab. (In fact, posted signs insist upon it, and you will be asked to leave if you don't abide.) Catch him at **d.b.a.** (618 Frenchmen St., 70116; https://dbaneworleans.com) on Mondays at 7pm.

Catch rock 'n' soul musician Dana Abbott at **Cafe Negril** (606 Frenchmen St.; 70116; https://cafenegrilnola.com), Thursdays at 11pm. This club is also a good bet for reggae fans.

Walter "Wolfman" Washington: when the **Maple Leaf** (8316 Oak St., 70118; https://www.mapleleafbar.com) reopened after Hurricane Katrina, the first performer to take the stage was Walter "Wolfman" Washington. It's a testament to how much he means to this town that he would lead a show that was a symbolic rebirth. He and his killer band, the Roadmasters, can also be heard at **d.b.a.** (618 Frenchmen St., 70116; https://dbaneworleans. com) on Wednesdays at 9pm.

The Shotgun Jazz Band, led by the powerful Marla Dixon, plays tradi-tional New Orleans jazz as well as it can be done. See them at **The Spotted Cat** (623 Frenchmen St., 70116; https://www.spottedcatmusicclub.com), Wednesdays at 6pm. You can also see them occasionally at **The Maison** (508 Frenchmen St., 70116; https://maisonfrenchmen.com), Fridays at 7pm, or at **Three Muses** (536 Frenchmen St., 70116; https://www.3musesnola. com) on Saturday at 9pm. Dixon also leads the terrific, all-female Shake 'Em Up Jazz Band, which you can see at **The Spotted Cat** (623 Frenchmen St., 70116; https://www.spottedcatmusicclub.com) every other Saturday at 6pm.

On Friday evenings, don't miss Kermit Ruffins at **The Blue Nile** (532 Frenchmen St., 70116; https://www.bluenilelive.com). For decades, Kermit has upheld the great tradition of New Orleans jazz, preserving and passing on the culture. If you're lucky, he'll bring up James Winfield, a.k.a. the Sleep-ing Giant, a local R&B singer who made a record in the '60s, then worked as a mechanic for 40 years before making a return to music. Winfield will often get up onstage and do a few classic R&B numbers. He's a living link to those heady days when New Orleans rock was the finest in the land. Or Kermit might bring up Nayo Jones, one of the town's top singers. Some-times, he calls the ladies up for a dance party on the stage: Karolyn has been up there with Kermit on more than one occasion. The music usually gets rolling close to 11pm.

You have a number of options for catching Kermit, actually. A great spot to see him is at his own place, Kermit's **Treme Mother-In-Law Lounge** (1500 N Claiborne Ave., 70116; https://www.facebook.com/Ruffinsbbq/) on Sundays and Tuesdays at 6pm. For many years, he has also held down a legendary set on Thursday evenings at 6pm at **Bullet's Sports Bar** in Treme (2441 A.P. Tureaud St., 70119; https://www.neworleans.com/listing/bullets-sports-bar/33532/). A stop at Bullet's is a quintessential NOLA experience. There's a real sense of community. It's all very informal. The musicians wander around the club and greet people, or step outside if they feel like it.

The Sleeping Giant often sings a few songs. Somebody's little girl might get up and sing. Last time we were there, Jason Marsalis himself happened to be sitting in on vibraphone. (How great it is to see a musician whom people would pay big bucks to see at, say, the Blue Note in New York City, playing at the community tavern.) Occasionally the Tuesday evening gig is filled by Shamarr Allen, who's terrific. Plus, at both Mother-in-Law or Bullet's, there's always a chance someone will be cooking some barbecue! (What's more, there's free red beans and rice on Mondays at the Mother-in-Law.)

Speaking of the **Mother-in-Law Lounge**, the TBC Brass Band, an electrifying band, plays Tuesdays at 8pm.

And speaking of Kermit (again), for years he had a much-loved Thursday-night residency at **Vaughan's Lounge** (4229 Dauphine St., 70117; https://www.facebook.com/Vaughans-Lounge-472659709508376/), deep in the Bywater. Now, that slot is held down by Corey Henry and the Treme Funktet, who are making some history of their own. The music usually gets started around 10:30p.

And speaking of drummer and vibraphonist Jason Marsalis (as we were above), you can see him at **Snug Harbor** (626 Frenchmen St., 70116; https://snugjazz.com), an impeccable concert hall for a slightly more formal listening experience. Herlin Riley, John Mahoney, and Dr. Michael White also regularly play here. Check their website for current events.

A word should be said for **Bamboula's** (514 Frenchmen St., 70116; https://www.facebook.com/bamboulasbar/), a club we like because, starting as early as 11am and going all evening, they have a constant lineup of hot trad jazz, with nary any cover. (There are different schools of thought as to whether "no-cover" policies are actually good for the bands and/or Frenchmen Street—some feel requiring patrons to pay something to get into a club makes for more of a dedicated music audience—so do be sure to tip each band.)

The quintessential New Orleans musical experience has got to be the world-renowned Rebirth Brass Band at the **Maple Leaf** (8316 Oak St., 70118, or Carrollton-Riverbend/Oak St., in the Uptown neighborhood; https://www.mapleleafbar.com) on Tuesday nights at 10pm. They don't really get rolling until 11:00 p.m., but do try to get there early: the place is usually packed so tightly that on one occasion, Scott felt himself lifted up by the squeezing bodies around him, and his feet did not touch the ground again for some moments.

Catch former Glen David Andrews saxophonist James Martin at the the **Hotel Monteleone's Carousel Lounge** (214 Royal St., 70130; https://hotelmonteleone.com/entertainment/carousel-bar/) on Wednesdays at 8pm. Drumming for James is the excellent Derek Freeman, formerly with Kermit Ruffins.

We never miss the blues-rock-r&b stylings of Lil Red and Big Bad, put over with plenty of sass and oomph by Nancy "Lil' Red" Gros at **BMC Balcony Music Club** (1331 Decatur St., at the corner of Decatur and Esplanade, 70116; https://www.facebook.com/BMCneworleans/) on Fridays at 6:30pm. Lil' Red's talented daughter, Renee Gros, also performs, sometimes on Wednesdays at 5pm, sometimes on Saturday at 3pm.

King James & the Special Men is a band to look out for, though their live schedule is unclear at present: looks like they can sometimes be found at **BJ's Lounge** (4301 Burgundy St., 70117; https://www.facebook.com/bjs.bywater/). Other performers to look for under the Special Men Industries (their record label) umbrella are Alynda Segarra of Hurray For The Riff Raff, Louis Michot of Lost Bayou Ramblers, and Leyla McCalla of Carolina Chocolate Drops.

Andy J. Forest is one of our favorite bluesy singer-songwriters in town (and a great gent as well). See him on Tuesdays and Fridays from 4 to 6:30pm at **Spotted Cat** (623 Frenchmen St., 70116; https://www.spottedcatmusicclub.com). You can see the Andy J Forest Treeaux on occasional Sundays at 3pm at **BMC Balcony Music Club** (1331 Decatur St., 70116; https://www.facebook.com/BMCneworleans/). Andy can also be seen at **Madame Vic's** (1500 Elysian Fields, 70117; https://madamevics.com) with his band the Swamp Crawlers or with the Washboard Chaz Blues Trio, on Thursdays from 8 to 11pm.

You must get over to **Preservation Hall** (726 St Peter St., 70116; https://www.preservationhall.com), one of the most famous venues in the quarter.

Look for Maynard Chatters, or see the Preservation Hall All Stars featuring Shannon Powell at 8pm on Saturdays. Enjoy the relaxed intensity of the vibe, where the musicians sit back and listen to each other improvise, sometimes with eyes closed. You can see the joy flit across their faces when somebody plays something really sweet. Powell, the great drummer and the "King of Treme," is quick to tell the audience that if they're looking to hear "Dixieland," they're in "the wrong building." Here, he says emphatically, we play "traditional New Orleans jazz."

Little Freddie King is a great local bluesman: at 81 years young, Freddie is not to be missed. He plays often at **d.b.a.** (618 Frenchmen St., 70116; https://dbaneworleans.com), sometimes on Saturdays at 11pm, sometimes on Thursdays at 10pm. He can also sometimes by found at **BJ's Lounge** (4301 Burgundy St., 70117; https://www.facebook.com/bjs.bywater/) in the Bywater. (Rumor has it this venue also features free red beans & rice on Mondays).

Palm Court Jazz Cafe (1204 Decatur St., 70116; https://www.palmcourtjazzcafe.com) features regulars Lars Edegran on Wednesday evenings and Kevin Louis & the Palm Court Jazz Band featuring Topsy Chapman on Friday evenings, 7-11pm. Enjoy traditional jazz with a Creole dinner.

Three Muses (536 Frenchmen St., 70116; https://www.3musesnola.com) is an atmospheric club that often features the Kris Tokarski Quartet. The tasty food on offer includes tacos and charcuterie. Make reservations here: you only have the table for a pre-determined amount of time. Tokarski's beautiful piano can also sometimes be heard at **The Bombay Club** (830 Conti St., 70112; https://bombayclubneworleans.com) and on records with the Squirrel Nut Zippers.

Head over to the **Hi-Ho Lounge** (2239 St. Claude Ave., 70117; Su-Th 5p-1a, F 5p-2a, Sa 5p-4a), where there's a Bluegrass Pickin' Party on Mondays at 8pm. There might even find dishes from Velocity's Vittles or tacos from Liberacion NOLA, if you're lucky.

By the way, locals say the strip of St. Claude Avenue between Elysian Fields and St. Roch, on which the **Hi-Ho Lounge** is located, is in line to become the "new" Frenchmen Street, now that Frenchmen has been "discovered" and is sometimes too crowded (on top of the other facts we discussed above). Karolyn and I stopped into the Hi-Ho for drinks as Super Bowl Sunday 2022

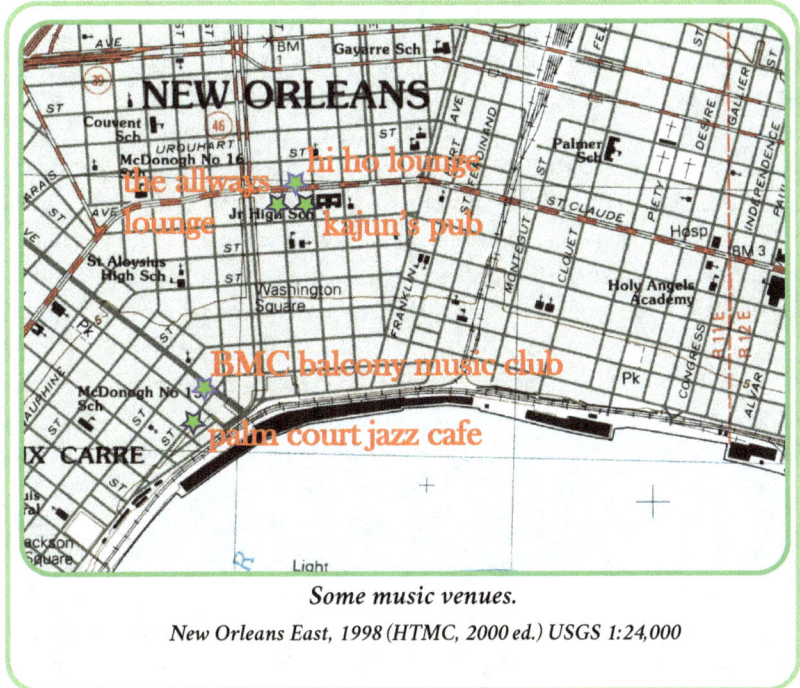

Some music venues.
New Orleans East, 1998 (HTMC, 2000 ed.) USGS 1:24,000

was kicking off. (We were waiting for the delightful 'tit Rex parade, which features floats made out of shoeboxes.) We met the super-friendly bartenders… who announced to us they were getting married soon. We also discovered a new bourbon, Larceny, to which they introduced us. We now purchase it often. (Hit us up for an endorsement deal, Larceny: we're ready to sell out.)

Aside from the Hi-Ho, this stretch of St. Claude is lined with clubs like the **Allways Lounge and Theatre** (2240 St. Claude Ave., 70117; https://theallwayslounge.net) and **Kajun's** (2256 St Claude Ave., 70117; http://www.kajunpub.com) (famous for its karaoke). **Siberia** (2227 St. Claude Ave., 70117) is permanently closed now: apparently, it was quite a place, a grunge/punk joint where something weird and funky always seemed to be happening, from burlesque to puppet shows. We mention Siberia here only because they were known for the Eastern European fare, like pierogis and kielbasa, they'd sell from a kitchen window. We wanted you to know the people behind that venture have started their own place, **Green Room Kukhnya** (1300 St. Bernard Ave., 70116; https://greenroomnola.com/menu).

In any case, explore the St. Claude corridor and feel like a local.

Don't miss zydeco Thursday at **Rock 'n' Bowl** (3016 S Carrollton Ave., 70118 in the Mid-City/Bayou St. John neighborhood—technically "Mid-City Lanes Rock 'n' Bowl"; https://www.rocknbowl.com). People come from all over south Louisiana to dance, in the tradition of the Saturday night dances that were once such a staple of Louisiana life. It's a real hoot! Don't worry if you really can't zydeco dance—one day, we may learn to do it properly ourselves, but for now it's just fun to spin around the dance floor amid the sea of humanity. Look out for Nathan & the Zydeco Cha-Chas or Geno Delafose & French Rockin' Boogie. Zydeco Thursdays generally go from 8-11pm. On another night, you might catch Jerry Embree playing swing.

Some Like It Hot is a thoroughly enjoyable traditional jazz combo, and the back room at **Buffa's** (1001 Esplanade Ave., 70116; https://www.buffasbar.com) is a homey and friendly place to see them. They're the regular band for Buffa's fun Traditional Jazz Brunch on Sundays at 12p and 2p.

The Gerald French Trio is an excellent jazz combo, led by Mr. French, an immaculate drummer. You can see them at **Mahogany Jazz Hall** (125 Chartres St., 70130; https://www.mjhnola.com) on Saturdays at 7pm. He also leads the modern iteration of perhaps the most venerable band in town, The Original Tuxedo Jazz Band. You can see them on Mondays from 8pm to midnight, also at the Mahogany.

One Eyed Jacks (615 Toulouse St., 70116; https://www.oneeyedjacks.net) is just a bit west of Jackson Square, between Royal and Chartres. They feature bands like the experimental Kirasu and the funk-rock Carly Myers' Yojimbo.

Check out the red-hot Hot 8 Brass Band at **Howlin' Wolf** (907 S Peters St., 70130; https://www.thehowlinwolf.com), Sundays at 10p.

See guitarist Carl LeBlanc, who's played with Sun Ra and the Preservation Hall Jazz Band, at **Dos Jefes Uptown Cigar Bar** (5535 Tchoupitoulas St., 70115, https://dosjefes.com), occasionally on Wednesdays at 9:30p. Dos Jefes also regularly features one of the town's top keyboard players, Joe Krown, on Wednesdays at 8:30p.

Antoine Diel & the Misfit Power is one of the town's most heralded jazz groups. They can be found at **Spotted Cat** (623 Frenchmen St., 70116; https://www.spottedcatmusicclub.com) at 9:30p, Wednesdays, and at **Buffa's** (1001 Esplanade Ave., 70116; https://www.buffasbar.com) at 8p, Mondays.

Local favorites the Brass-a-holics can be found at the **Jazz Playhouse** (300 Bourbon St., 70130; https://www.facebook.com/JazzPlayhouse/) at 8:30p, Thursdays. Also look for them at **Tipitina's** (501 Napoleon Ave., 70115; https://tipitinas.com), sometimes at the Free Fridays concert series.

The Soul Rebels bring the sounds of New Orleans far and wide with their national and international tours. When they're in town, catch them at **Le Bon Temps Roule** (4801 Magazine St., 70115; https://lbtrnola.com) at 11p, Thursdays, and also occasionally at **d.b.a.** (618 Frenchmen St., 70116; https://dbaneworleans.com).

Big Sam's Funky Nation, a funk/jazz/hip-hop/rock 'n' roll band led by Sammie "Big Sam" Williams that bills themselves as "the Big Easy's best-kept secret," can be found at **Howlin' Wolf** (907 S Peters St., 70130; https://www.thehowlinwolf.com) at 10p, Saturdays, and on occasion at **Broadside NOLA** (600 N. Broad, 70119; https://broadsidenola.com), a venue which also hosts live music, films, and more. Also look for another of Sam's projects, Funkin' it Up with Big Sam at **Jazz Playhouse** (300 Bourbon St., 70130; https://www.facebook.com/JazzPlayhouse/) at Wednesdays at 7p.

Deacon John, now 81, has been bringing the R&B party for decades. As his bio puts it, his band Deacon John & the Ivories, were the first rock 'n' rollers to play with the New Orleans Symphony in 1970. He has played at every single Jazz Fest. Don't miss any chance to see him.

Stanton Moore, a stellar drummer whose every gig is a joyous master class in percussion, co-founded the super-funky Galactic. They are often on national tour, but look for them if they're in town. Also catch the Stanton Moore Trio, who often play **The Maison** (508 Frenchmen St., 70116; https://maisonfrenchmen.com).

Paul Sanchez is a key local singer-songwriter whose most famous for his work with the band Cowboy Mouth. He's also made an album of the late Dan Baum's book *Nine Lives: Death and Life in New Orleans*. We caught him with his Rolling Road Show at French Quarter Fest in 2022.

BeauSoleil avec Michael Doucet is one of Lousiana's finest Cajun/Zydeco band. Look for them if they're in town. Last time we checked, they were on the road for their "one last time—au revoir" tour.

Nicholas Payton is one of NOLA's foremost musicians, currently holding down a residency at the Blue Note in New York. When he's in town, you might catch him playing trumpet and keyboard at **Tipitina's** (501 Napoleon Ave., 70115; https://tipitinas.com) and other joints.

The venerable Treme Brass Band, led by drummer Benny Jones, has a constantly rotating lineup that has at times featured Kermit Ruffins, James Andrews and the late, great Lionel Batiste. They can often be found at **Vaughan's** (4229 Dauphine St., 70117; https://www.facebook.com/Vaughans-Lounge-472659709508376/) on Fridays from 7-10p, and at **d.b.a.** (618 Frenchmen St., 70116; https://dbaneworleans.com) on Sundays at 9p.

The New Orleans Cottonmouth Kings play the **Spotted Cat** (623 Frenchmen St., 70116; https://www.spottedcatmusicclub.com) on Mondays at 10p. This band grew out of a split with the New Orleans Jazz Vipers, who feature Craig Klein on trombone and Joe Braun on alto saxophone, and who have their own regular gig at the **Spotted Cat** (623 Frenchmen St., 70116; https://www.spottedcatmusicclub.com)—in fact, the Vipers' gig is one of the longest-running residencies on Frenchmen Street. During the pandemic, they played regular on-line gigs at **St. Anna's Church** (1313 Esplanade Ave., 70116; https://stannanola.org).

One of Klein's other bands, the New Orleans Nightcrawlers, with sousaphone player Matt Perrine, recently won a grammy for best regional roots music album for *Atmosphere*, their first new album in 11 years. They often play at the **New Orleans Jazz Museum** (400 Esplanade Ave., 70116; https://louisianastatemuseum.org/museum/new-orleans-jazz-museum-old-us-mint) on Tuesdays.

For terrific traditional jazz, catch Tuba Skinny at **d.b.a.** (618 Frenchmen St., 70116; https://dbaneworleans.com) from 7-10p, Saturdays.

Aurora Nealand is a performer not to miss. Her own original music is playful, experimental, arty, and catchy. She also plays sax and sings with her trad jazz band the Royal Roses at **The Maison** (508 Frenchmen St., 70116; https://maisonfrenchmen.com) at 7p, Mondays. She gigs with the great pianist Tom McDermott at **Buffa's** (1001 Esplanade Ave., 70116; https://www.buffasbar.com) at 8pm on Thursdays. Watch out for her wild, fun rockabilly band Rory Danger and the Danger Dangers (she's Rory), who can occasionally be seen at **Tipitina's** (501 Napoleon Ave., 70115; https://tipitinas.com). We should also say, if we haven't said it before: when you go into Tip's, the tradition is to rub the head of the statue of the great Professor Longhair, which you'll see as you enter.

Also look for Meschiya Lake, a top-class singer, who sometimes plays with Tom McDermott at **Buffa's** (1001 Esplanade Ave., 70116; https://www.buffasbar.com) on Thursdays at 9p, where she can also be seen with My Favorite Trio (with partners-in-crime Tyler "Twerk" Thomson and Ben Polcer) on Monday evenings. Her top trad band The Little Big Horns has a regular gig at **Spotted Cat** (623 Frenchmen St., 70116; https://www.spottedcatmusicclub.com) on Tuesdays from 6-8p.

Trumpeter Jeremy Davenport plays at his namesake **Davenport Lounge in the Ritz-Carlton New Orleans** (921 Canal St., 70112; https://www.ritzcarlton.com/en/hotels/new-orleans/dining/davenport-lounge) beginning at 5:30p on Wednesdays and Thursdays, and 9p on both Fridays and Saturdays.

We've heard good things about rock 'n' rollers the Morning 40 Federation, who can be seen at **One Eyed Jacks** (615 Toulouse St., 70116; https://www.oneeyedjacks.net) and the **Maple Leaf** (8316 Oak St., 70118; https://www.mapleleafbar.com).

The Revivalists are a popular roots rock band. Look for them if they're in town. Their website is: https://therevivalists.com

Lastly, the **Trash Pile Concert Gallery** (2708 2nd St., 70113) is a new venue in Central City that hopes to bring "good vibes" to the city. We wish them all the best.

Bars

First, we'll list alphabetically some key drinks to try while you're in town, along with our favorite places to get 'em. Afterwards, we'll list some of our favorite bars, more generally speaking.

Absinthe

Tony Seville's Pirate's Alley Cafe and Old Absinthe House (622 Pirates Alley, 70116) You learned about absinthe's medicinal properties at the Pharmacy Museum; Tony Seville's Pirate's Alley Cafe and Old Absinthe House is a good place to try the medicine for yourself. It is located in Pirate's Alley, a historic, block-long passageway between St. Louis Cathedral and the Cabildo, right off Jackson Square. (Look for the famous lamppost). At night, the Jesus statue in nearby St. Anthony's garden throws spooky shadows onto the back wall of the cathedral. You're also treading in young William Faulkner's stomping grounds: he lived right next door in the '20s. (M-Th Noon to midnight, F-Su 10a-2a, https://www.piratesalleycafe.com/home.html).

Jean Lafitte's **Old Absinthe House** (240 Bourbon St., 70112) Since 1807, the Old Absinthe House is a terrifically atmospheric place on Bourbon. With a bar "in the round," it's one of Bourbon's soulful places. This was the outlaw Jean Lafitte's favorite watering hole. Legend has it (don't a lot of our entries start that way, in this town?) this is where Lafitte got together with Andrew Jackson during the War of 1812, and the two struck a deal whereby Lafitte and his pirates would help Jackson's forces stave off the British invasion in the Battle of New Orleans. This is a great place to sample absinthe Pernod, an elixir which has a strong effect. (M-W 9a-2a, Th 9a-3a F-Sa 9a-4a, Su 9a-3a; 504-523-3181; https://www.ruebourbon.com/old-absinthe-house)

Bloody Mary
vodka, tomato juice, other spices/condiments

Our favorite spot for a bloody in NOLA is the to-go window of the **Gazebo Cafe** (1018 Decatur St., 70116; M-Th 10a-6p, F-Su 9a-6p; 504-527-5000; https://gazebocafenola.com), Cajun or "Gazebo" style.

However, the very best one in town may be found at **Le Bon Temps Roule** (4801 Magazine St., 70115; open 24-7; 504-897-3448, https://lbtrnola.com). (They've also got free oysters on Friday!)

Mr. B's Bistro (201 Royal St., 70130; Lunch W–Sa, 11:30a–2p, Dinner W–Su 5p–9p, Sunday Brunch 10:30a–2p, Closed M–Tu; $$; 504-523-2078; http://www.mrbsbistro.com) serves up $1.50 Bloody Marys until 2 pm on weekdays, with purchase of an entree.

Three Muses (536 Frenchmen St., 70116; Th-Su 4p-10p, closed M-W; 504-252-4801; https://www.3musesnola.com) has a great one, too: we were standing at the bar with Kermit Ruffins one time, watching Glen David Andrews (as one does), and Kermit said their bloody was the best around—so good he wanted to put it in his wife's purse to take home.

Daiquiri
rum, citrus juice, and sugar

For your Bourbon Street stroll, a daiquiri is the appropriate sip. Hit up an **Original Daiquiris/Fat Tuesday** (633 Bourbon St., 70130; F-Sa 10a-2a, Su 10a-midnight, M-Th 11a-midnight; 504-524-5185; https://fattuesday.com). Consider an extra shot for added toxicity. **The Gazebo Cafe** (1018 Decatur St., 70116; M-Th 10a-6p, F-Su 9a-6p; 504-527-5000; https://gazebocafenola.com) offers an ice cream daiquiri.

French 75
gin, sparkling wine, syrup, lemon

The best place to sip this one is, as the name would suggest, the **French 75 Bar** in **Arnaud's** (813 Bienville St., 70112; W-Sa 5:30p-10:30p, Su 10a-2p, closed M-Tu; 504-523-5433; https://www.arnaudsrestaurant.com/bars/french-75/).

Hurricane

rum, fruit syrup, orange and lime juice

The Hurricane is the signature cocktail at **Pat O'Brien's** (624 Bourbon St., 70130; W, Th, Su noon-midnight, F-Sa noon-2a, closed M-Tu, piano lounge Th 4p-midnight, F-Sa 3p-1a; 504-525-4823; https://patobriens. com/new-orleans/) in the Quarter. Their pleasant courtyard is a nice place to enjoy one of these potions as you while away a sunny afternoon.

Milk Punch

brandy or bourbon, milk, sugar, and vanilla extract

This is Karolyn's favorite drink. For milk punch at its best, try **Carousel Bar at the Hotel Monteleone** (214 Royal St., 70130; everyday 11a-12a, live music W-Sa; 504-523-3341; https://hotelmonteleone.com/entertainment/ carousel-bar/), **21st Amendment Bar** (725 Iberville St., 70130; W-Th, Su 3p-11a, F-Sa 3p-12:30a, closed M-Tu; http://www.21stamendmentlalouisiane. com), and/or **Commander's Palace** (1403 Washington Place, 70130; lunch Th-F 11:30a-depends on season, dinner M-W 5:30p-depends, Th-F 6p-depends; jazz brunch with live jazz Sa 11a-2:30p, Su 10a-2:30p; 504-899-8221; https://www.commanderspalace.com).

We haven't tried it yet, but **Bourbon House** (144 Bourbon St., 70130; F-Sa 11a-10p, Su-Th 11a-9p; 504-522-0111; https://www.bourbonhouse. com) is reputed to pour a damn fine frozen milk punch. It's so rich it's even on the dessert menu!

Pimm's Cup

Pimm's No. 1 (gin-based liqueur), lemon juice, ginger ale

This gin-based refresher is the signature cocktail at **Napoleon House** (500 Chartres St., 70130)—a historic building where the drink may have actually been invented (or at the very least popularized). (See our entry under "historic buildings," above.) Get your first Pimm's Cup here, and nowhere else. (W-Th, Su 11a-9p, F-Sa 11a-10p, closed M-Tu; Tel: 504-524-9752 website: https://www.napoleonhouse.com)

Ramos Gin Fizz

gin, heavy cream, lemon and lime juice, simple syrup, club soda, orange blossom water, egg whites

The place to try this treat is **Bourbon "O"** (730 Bourbon St., 70116; everyday 1p-12a, live music everyday 4p-12a; 504-523-2222; https://www. bourbonorleans.com/eat-drink-jazz/bourbon-o-bar/). The bar sports a mechanical arm that shakes your Ramos Gin Fizz for several minutes on end, till it's just as fizzy as it should be.

Sazerac

rye whiskey (or cognac), Peychaud's bitters, Angostura bitters, absinthe

At the **Carousel Bar at the Hotel Monteleone** (214 Royal St., 70130; everyday 11a-12a, live music W-Sa; 504-523-3341; https://hotelmonteleone. com/entertainment/carousel-bar/), you sip your Sazerac and drift slowly in a circle, feeling slightly out-of-time, as if the ordinary rules have been suspended (that special New Orleans feeling we love).

Another place where they really do it right is, as the name would suggest, is the **Sazerac Bar**, a classic cocktail lounge in the **Roosevelt Hotel** (130 Roosevelt Way, 70112; F-Su 12p-1a, M-Th 2p-1a; 504-648-1200; https:// www.therooseveltneworleans.com/dining/the-sazerac-bar.html).
Broussard's Empire Bar (819 Conti St., 70130; W-Th 5p-8p, F-Sa 10a-8p, Su 10a-4p, Happy Hour W-Sa 3p-6p; closed M-Tu; 504-581-3866; https://broussards.com/menu/empire-bar/) in the Quarter is presided over by mixologist Paul Gustings, who makes a "proper Sazerac" with absinthe and cognac (rather than the more traditional rye whiskey).

Vieux Carre

Sazerac rye whiskey, Pierre Ferrand 1840 cognac, Berto red vermouth, benedictine, angostura and Peychaud's bitters

The Vieux Carre is the **Carousel Bar's** signature cocktail, invented by bartender Walter Bergeron in 1938. (214 Royal St., 70130; everyday 11a-12a, live music W-Sa; 504-523-3341; https://hotelmonteleone.com/entertainment/carousel-bar/).

Now, here are some of our favorite bars. You're likely to meet new friends at any of these places.

Let's start with our favorite cocktail bars. As has become evident by now, our very favorite is the **Carousel Bar at the Hotel Monteleone** (214 Royal St., 70130; everyday 11a-12a, live music W-Sa; 504-523-3341; https://hotelmonteleone.com/entertainment/carousel-bar/).

Other good bets: just across Canal from the Quarter, on the edge of the Central Business District, look for **Loa Bar in International House Hotel** (221 Camp St., 70130; everyday 4p-12a; 504-553-9550; https://www.ihhotel.com/loa-bar/idea). It's named for the spirits ("loa") in the voodoo religion—a sophisticated, relaxing place for some good cocktails.

A short walk up Canal brings you to the **Sazerac Bar**, the swanky cocktail lounge in the **Roosevelt Hotel** (130 Roosevelt Way, 70112; F-Su 12p-1a, M-Th 2p-1a; 504-648-1200; https://www.therooseveltneworleans.com/dining/the-sazerac-bar.html). Back in the Quarter, **French 75 Bar in Arnaud's** (813 Bienville St., 70112; W-Sa 5:30p-10:30p, Su 10a-2p, closed M-Tu; 504-523-5433; https://www.arnaudsrestaurant.com/bars/french-75/) is, as the name would indicate, the best place to try a French 75 cocktail, but their other drinks are special, too.

Swoop's (916 Lafayette St., 70113; opening summer 2022; 504-827-1655; https://www.swoopsnola.com) is the reincarnation of the now-closed **Starlight Lounge**, which made a Bananas Foster cocktail that tasted just like banana pancakes.

Cane & Table (1113 Decatur St., 70116; W-F 5p-10p, Sa-Su 11a-3p, 5p-10p, closed M-Tu; 504-581-1112; https://www.caneandtablenola.com), aside from being a great place for rum drinks, features small plates by noted chef Alfredo Nogueira.

At **Bar Tonique** (820 N. Rampart St., 70119; everyday 12p-2a or later; https://www.bartonique.com) you'll get excellent cocktails at reasonable prices. Try the "Corpse Reviver No. 2."

We've heard a lot about **Cure** (4905 Freret St., 70115; F-Sa 4p-1a, Su-Th 4p-11p; 504-302-2357; https://www.curenola.com) in the Freret neighborhood, and **Twelve Mile Limit** (500 S. Telemachus, 70119; M-Th 5p-12a, F 5p-2a, Sa 1p-2a, Su 10a-12a; 504-488-8114; https://twelvemilelimit.com) in the Mid-City neighborhood. Twelve Mile in particular is called "chill" by locals.

Those would be our best bets for dedicated cocktail bars. Now for the best of the rest.

The **R Bar** (technically, the Royal Street Inn) (1431 Royal St., 70116) This dive bar/neighborhood hangout in the Marigny is a true classic. Charles Bukowski stayed in a room upstairs. We never miss their Friday evening crawfish boil. Come on out: you're almost bound to get know some locals. It's a real community. Their Dark 'n' Stormy cocktail has gotten us in trouble on more than one occasion. (M-Th 3p-3a, F 3-to-5a, Sa noon to 5a, Su noon to 3a; (504) 948-7499; https://royalstreetinn.com).

Molly's in the Market (1107 Decatur St., 70116) One of our favorite spots to be in NOLA is the window of Molly's at the Market, sipping a Famous Frozen Irish Coffee (made with their signature "frozen house blend of liquor and cream"), watching life go by on Decatur Street and listening to the jukebox. There's nowhere we'd rather be. It's a legendary journalist hangout, a bit like New Orleans' answer to Chicago's Billy Goat Tavern or Old Town Ale House. (Every day 10a-6a; 504-525-5169; https://www. mollysatthemarket.net).

Erin Rose (811 Conti St., 70112) is Molly's "sister bar," and our second favorite place in all of NOLA for famous Frozen Irish Coffee. Also, look for Killer PoBoys in the back if you're up for a scrumptious sammitch. (Open 21 hours a day starting at 10a; 504-522-3573; http://www.erinrosebar.com).

Vaughan's Lounge (4229 Dauphine St., 70117) This warm and friendly bar deep in the Bywater is a true local spot. This is where Scott sipped his first Basil Hayden bourbon. It's also a venerable spot for good local, live music. Look for Corey Henry and the Treme Funktet on Thursdays at 10:30p. (Every day 12p-2a; 504-947-5562; https://www.facebook.com/ Vaughans-Lounge-472659709508376/).

Bacchanal Wine (600 Poland Ave., 70117). Enjoy this lovely outdoor Bywater wine bar not far from Vaughan's. You can sip your wine and eat bacon-wrapped dates stuffed with chorizo in a leafy patio while enjoying beautiful live music. The night we visited, we saw the terrific Mark Weliky Trio. Someone once said that the backyard of Bacchanal's, on an evening as the sun sets, might be the finest place to be in all of New Orleans. Whoever said that was correct. (M-Th 12p-10p, F-Su 12p-11p, Closed Tu unless there's a special event; live music M-Th 12p-3p & 6p-9p; F-Su 12p-3p & 7p-10p; 504-948-9111; http://www.bacchanalwine.com).

St. Roch Tavern (1200 St Roch Ave., 70117). In *New Orleans: The Underground Guide*, Michael Patrick Welch describes the St. Roch Tavern as "warmly lit, cheap and dirty, but cozy." There you have it. Drop by after exploring the St. Roch cemetery for a well-needed cold one, or after a bite at St. Roch market. Don't forget to explore the innards of the bar, especially on a quiet afternoon. The walls read like a palimpsest of past revelry. (Every day noon to 2:30a; 504-945-0194; https://www.facebook.com/StRochTavern/).

Bombay Club (830 Conti St., 70112) This is a classy-yet-friendly spot for drinks and/or dinner. The menu features good gulf seafood and cocktails, and your meal is accompanied by sweet live jazz if you're there on a Friday or Saturday. Look for the Kris Tokarski Trio. (Happy Hour Tu-Su 4p-7p, closed M, Bar Hours: Tu-Su 4p to 12a, closed M, Brunch Sa-Su 10a-3p, Dinner Tu-Su 4p to 11p; live music on F-Sa 8p-11p; 504-577-2237; https:// bombayclubneworleans.com).

Swirl Wine Bar & Market (3143 Ponce De Leon St., 70119). In the beautiful Bayou St. John neighborhood, Swirl is a friendly, community-member-owned wine bar and shop. (M 12p-8p, Tu-Th 11a-8p, F 11a-9p, Sa 11a-9p, food available Tu-Th 11a-7:30p, F-Sa 11a-8:30p; 504-304-0635; http://www.swirlnola.com).

Harry's Corner (900 Chartres St., 70116). Harry's Corner is one of our favorite watering holes in town. It boasts a fine jukebox and some of the friendliest bartenders around. Our friend Paul, for example, is a bartender who's also a tireless ambassador for local food and music. Harry's Corner still adheres to the great local tradition of free red beans and rice on Mondays; Paul, who makes them himself, will hardly countenance any protestations that you're already full, so belly up to the bar! He'll tell you all about the city that, in his own words, he's "so gay" for. (Every day 10a-3a; 504-524-1107;https://www.facebook.com/Harrys Corner-139022506152999/).

Gold Mine Saloon (701 Dauphine St., 70116). This is allegedly a cool writers' bar where Lawrence Ferlinghetti once held forth for poetry read-ing night. The one time we stopped in the guy at the door tried to shake us down, for reasons that made more sense to him than to us. We'll have to give it another try. Dave Brinks, son of the bar's owner, Barbara Bear, is the author of the post-Hurricane Katrina poem cycle *The Caveat Onus.* (F-M 6p-4a, Closed Tu-Th; 504-495-3538).

The Candlelight Lounge (925 N Robertson St., 70116), in the Treme, often features brass bands. (Daily 11 a.m. - til' whenevs; 504-525-4748; https://www.facebook.com/Candlelightlounge925/).

Fauborg Wines (2805 St Claude Ave., 70117). This shop/wine bar is known for their Wednesday evening free wine-tastings. (Open daily from 12p-7p, free wine tastings every W evening from 5p-7p; 504-342-2217; https://www.faubourgwines.com).

Pepp's Pub (706 Franklin Ave., 70117) Classic neighborhood bar, which bills themselves as "Dog friendly, people tolerant." That's the right balance. (everyday noon to 2a; 985-326-1975; https://www.peppspub.com.

Old Point Bar (545 Patterson Rd., Algiers Point, 70114) Take the Algiers Ferry over to Algiers Point. There you'll find the Old Point Bar, in the shadow of the Mississippi River levee. (Live music Th-Su, often rock 'n' roll, F after-noons feature piano music, Sunday evenings are jazz nights; 504-364-0950; http://www.oldpointbarnola.com/).

Dry Dock Cafe and Bar (133 Delaronde, Algiers Point, 70114) Go "over da river" for good red beans and rice, alligator po-boys, and fried catfish with hush puppies. (every day 11a-10p, https://www.facebook.com/profile.php?id=100039380724882).

Saturn Bar (3067 St. Claude Ave., 70117). A classic and beloved neighborhood dive bar. When it was sold in the wake of the coronavirus, many feared it would be gone for good. Word now comes that the new owners, who used to patronize the place as customers and loved it, are planning to reopen it just as it was. (Last we checked, it appears they are up and running. They were posting the following hours: M-Th 4p-12a, F 4p-1a, Sa-Su 2p-1a; 504-949-7532; https://www.thesaturnbar.com).

St. Claude Avenue bars

As we said up above, **St. Claude Avenue** between Elysian Fields and St. Roch is a place where you can "barhop like a local." If Frenchmen is getting too crass and/or crowded for you, stroll around here and see what you can find. One of our favorites is **Hi-Ho Lounge** (2239 St. Claude Ave., 70117; Su-Th 5p-1a, F 5p-2a, Sa 5p-4a). We write a lot more about St. Claude Avenue under the "Music" section above.

Tours and Festivals

Fanning out in a crescent shape, New Orleans lies along a bend in the Mississippi River (aka the "Big River"), which connected the city's music to the world. In this curving town, you should get used to thinking "upriver" when you mean essentially "west," with "downriver" being the rough equivalent of "east." "Lakeside" is a rough equivalent of "north," and "riverside" basically means "south." The best way to get oriented is to explore on foot. To that end, we thought we'd kick off the "tours" section by offering the following Self-guided Walks, each organized around a neighborhood.

We should note that the tourist information center, The French Quarter Visitor Center, is located at 419 Decatur Street; it also houses the New Orleans Jazz National Historical Park's visitors center, which moved here from its old location at the French Market's Dutch Alley.

Old Square ("Vieux Carre") and French Market Walk

 ...the mainly 18th-century French Quarter, or Vieux Carre, has been so suffused with literary associations that you can practically hear the echoes of clattering typewriters."—Jennifer Moses, New York Times

After enjoying a breakfast of beignets and cafe au lait at Cafe Du Monde (800 Decatur St., 70116; always open), stroll around Jackson Square.

Stand in the center of the square, under the statue of Andrew Jackson, who famously defeated the Brits at the Battle of New Orleans in the War of 1812. (He was also famously the scourge of Native Americans.) Breathe it all in. You're in the French Quarter, otherwise known as the Old Square ("Vieux Carre"), the "geographic and cultural heart of the city since the early 1700s," in the apt phrase deployed by Fodors. The Quarter is laid out in a grid pattern: its first two streets on the downriver side are named Iberville and Bienville, after the two founders of New Orleans.

At the top of the square you'll find the St. Louis Cathedral, the oldest continuously operating Catholic cathedral in the U.S., originally built in 1727 to honor Louis XIV, "the Sun King." That version was destroyed in the Great Fire of 1788; though the Spanish rebuilt in 1789, the version we see today is largely another rebuild done during the 1850's. As you amble through Jackson Square, notice the "rays" (walkways) shooting out of the center, modeled after the style of the Sun King's gardens in Versailles.

Spinning around the square, you'll take in the twin Spanish colonial-style buildings that flank the cathedral, the Cabildo on the left and the Presbytere to the right. These two buildings are among the few that remain from the era of Spanish rule.

The **Cabildo**, built between 1795 and 1799 as the Town Hall, was the site of the Louisiana Purchase in 1803, a transfer "which finalized the United States' acquisition of the Louisiana Territory and doubled the size of the fledgling nation," as the building's website puts it. Today, the Cabildo houses

Vieux Carre, New Orleans, LA.
New Orleans East, LA. 1939 (HTMC, 1939 ed.) 1:31,680.

a fine museum on Louisiana history (701 Chartres St., 70116; Tu–Su 9a–4p, closed M; Adults $10, Students, senior citizens, active military $8, Children 6 and under free; 504-568-6968 or 800-568-6968; https://louisianastate-museum.org/museum/cabildo).

The **Presbytere**, built to match its twin, is likewise a museum today, boasting excellent exhibits on Mardi Gras and Hurricane Katrina. (751 Chartres St., 70116;Tu–Su 9a–4p, closed M; Adults $7, Students, senior citizens, active military $6, Children 6 and under free; 504-568-6968 or 800-568-6968; https://louisianastatemuseum.org/museum/presbytere).

If you'd like to visit a site whence one of those clattering typewriters mentioned up above by Jennifer Moses would have rung out in the '20s—specifically, the one belonging to one William Faulkner—drop by **Faulkner House Books** (624 Pirates Alley, 70116) in Pirate's Alley between St. Louis Cathedral and the Cabildo. (Everyday 10a-5p; Tel: 504-524-2940; Website: https://faulknerhousebooks.com).

Enjoy the street musicians who will undoubtedly by busking in front of St. Louis Cathedral when you visit. Jamming in Jackson Square is how many of the town's best musicians, such as Kermit Ruffins, paid their dues.

Turn your attention to the twin sets of town houses flanking the square. These are the historic Upper and Lower Pontalba Buildings, built in the late 1840s by Joseph Pontalba, a planter. Admire their flowery cast-irony balcony railings. For a look inside the apartments of the Lower building, we recommend a visit to **The 1850 House** (see our entry under Historic Buildings). (523 St Ann St #3318; Tu-Su 9:30a-4p, closed M; Adults $5, Students, seniors, military $4, Children 6 and under free; Website: https://louisianastatemuseum.org/museum/1850-house

Leave Jackson Square and perambulate pleasantly along the Mississippi River for a spell. After all, you've followed it all this way, rolling down the Blues Highway. Standing on the concrete platform of Washington Artillery Park, directly across from Jackson Square, you'll have a great view. (The cannon you'll see was used in the Civil War.)

Now, stroll deeper into the **French Market**. This vast flea-and-farmers' market marks the beginning of the French Quarter (or the end, depending on which way you're coming). It stretches from **Cafe du Monde** at the upriver end to the flea market downriver. On the way, consider dropping by the to-go window of the **Gazebo Cafe** (1018 Decatur St., 70116; M-Th 10a-6p, F-Su 9a-6p) in Latrobe Park. We recommend a Bloody Mary, Cajun or "Gazebo" style. **Latrobe Park** is a lovely place to enjoy a drink (or to bring a picnic lunch, such as a muffuletta from nearby **Central Grocery**—or **Frank's**, if Central Grocery is closed). A musical combo is likely to be laying down some sweet blues nearby. Be on the lookout for chess master Jude Acers, who can sometimes be seen sitting in front of his chessboard, ready to take on any potential challenger. The fountain, on the edge of which you may now be sitting with your Bloody Mary, honors Benjamin Latrobe, America's first professional architect. He designed New Orleans' first waterworks. (He's buried in St. Louis Cemetery #1—something to keep in mind, should you get there.)

As you stroll through the French Market, keep in mind Fodors' unimprovable phrase, which describes it, circa 1791, as "once the stomping grounds of French trappers, seafood vendors, and rowdy sailors." In the Farmers' Market Pavilion, you'll walk past stall after stall of tempting snacks, fresh seafood, and produce. We recommend grabbing a gator on a stick! Note the stall called **Meals From the Heart Cafe** at #13 (everyday 10a-3:30p): it's a wonderful spot for a healthy breakfast. At #9, you'll see **Loretta's Authentic Pralines** (Th-Su 9a-5p, Closed M, W). If you don't try their praline beignets, you're truly missing out. We like the crab beignets, as well.

As you move into the vast flea market, goggle at the dense array of wares on offer, where if you look carefully you can find just about everything, from international crafts such as jewelry and masks, to locally-made books, CDs, and films. You might find a treasure-box full of great CDs.

Walk over to the **Old U.S. Mint** to tour the **New Orleans Jazz Museum** (400 Esplanade Ave., 70116; Tu-Su 9a-4p, closed M; $8; https://louisiana-statemuseum.org/museum/new-orleans-jazz-museum-old-us-mint). Once, this building minted coins for such entities as the United States, the Republic of Louisiana, and even the Confederacy. (Some of those made it, at least as of this writing, and some of them, thank god, did not.) Today, the Jazz Museum holds a terrific collection of artifacts, including Louis Armstrong's first cornet, and often boasts fascinating special exhibits. It also houses a performance venue operated in partnership with the New Orleans Jazz National Historical Park. Catching one of their "Ranger Talks," a combination performance/lecture, is informative and fun.

If you've worked up an appetite, grab an Abita and a muffuletta from **Central Grocery** (923 Decatur St., 70116; everyday 9a-5p, though they may be closed when you visit due to Hurricane Ida) or **Frank's** (933 Decatur St., 70116; daily 10a-11:30p). Stroll over to Latrobe Park to enjoy your picnic, if you haven't been there yet. Or even if you have.

Royal Street Art Galleries/Historic Mansion Walk

Stroll down Royal Street, our favorite street running through the Quarter, to enjoy art galleries, street musicians, and a great lineup of historic mansions.

Our walk starts at the "upriver," or westerly, end of the Quarter, towards Canal. As we walk, feel free to pop into any art gallery that strikes your eye.

A few of our favorites: **Frank Relle Photography** (910 Royal St.; 10a-6p daily; https://frankrelle.com). Relle specializes in beautifully evocative and otherworldly nighttime visions of Louisiana.

The **Craig Tracy Gallery** (827 Royal St., 70116; 10a-6p daily; www.craigtracy.com) showcases striking fine art bodypainting.

The **Hemmerling Gallery** used to be at 733 Royal St; it's no longer there, sadly enough: the new location is 477 SW Railroad Ave., Ponchatoula, LA 70454. We always used to pop in to see the work of the late folk artist William Hemmerling. His story moved us deeply: a white man, he loved Southern African-American culture. (He often painted a Black female figure he called "Sweet Olive.") He was apparently almost totally innocent of money and material things, and he didn't start painting until he was pushing 60. He went from penury to international celebration, before dying in 2009. His obituary notices, which were posted around the gallery, featured an unusual outpouring of personal love on the part of the obit writers. The gallery also showcased the work of Kalle' Siekkinen, a young protege of Hemmerling. We miss it on Royal Street. We include this writeup just in case you're ever out in Ponchatoula. If you are, check out their new digs.

Now for those historic mansions. First up on our stroll is **Rillieux-Waldhorn House** (343 Royal Street), a rare still-extent 18th-century Spanish colonial house, built between 1795 and 1800 for the great-grandfather of French Impressionist Edgar Degas. Love the wrought iron balconies.

Next stop, enjoy **LaTrobe's** (403 Royal St.). We can't improve on its website's own description: "Completed in 1822 as the Louisiana State Bank, Latrobe's is named after its Architect: Benjamin Henry Latrobe. Also known as the 'Father of American Architecture,' his contributions include: the US Capital, the Porticos of the White House, and the Baltimore Basilica, as well as the development of the Waterworks System of the United States in an effort to combat Yellow Fever." That's a pretty impressive résumé.

As you stroll through the 600 block, keep in mind that its nickname was "Governor's Row"—no fewer than five governors lived on this block over the years. The property that's now the **Court of Two Sisters Restaurant** (613 Royal) was home to Etienne de Perier, the second French royal governor of colonial Louisiana, way back in 1726. The present structure dates to 1832.

Next, enjoy the famous rounded cast-iron balconies of **LaBranche House** (700 Royal St.), built in the 1830s, curving around the corner of Royal and St. Peter streets, just behind the Cabildo. They've starred in many photographs seeking to evoke the iconic essence of the town. Is this house haunted, you ask? Naturally.

A few blocks down, you'll come to **Gallier House** (1132 Royal St.). Designed by New Orleans architect James Gallier in 1857, it's thought to be Anne Rice's model for Vampire Lestat's house.

Nearby is the **LaLaurie Mansion** (1140 Royal St), famously the "Haunted House of New Orleans" (though the version you see today was rebuilt in 1838, the original having been burnt down by angry New Orleanians in 1834). Owner Madame Lalaurie had to beat it out of town when townspeople discovered seven mutilated slaves she'd been keeping secreted away in captivity in one of the apartments to torture for her own amusement. This was beyond the pale, even for the white-supremacist USA. The house, it is said, has been haunted ever since. Many celebs have owned it over the years, including Nick Cage. While you're here, pop across the street to grab a sandwich at Verti Marte!

Also, keep an eye out for the wonderful street musicians. One of our favorites is violinist Tanya Huang, who was one half of the beloved, now retired, combo Tanya & Dorise, and who can be found "somewhere on Royal" on Friday and Saturday afternoons (in practice, usually at the corner of Royal and St. Louis, across from Royal Oyster House). You can also find the world-renowned Doreen Kitchens, who's played in the world's great halls but prefers to play in front of Rouse's (701 Royal), on Fridays or Sundays, starting around noon.

Garden District Walk

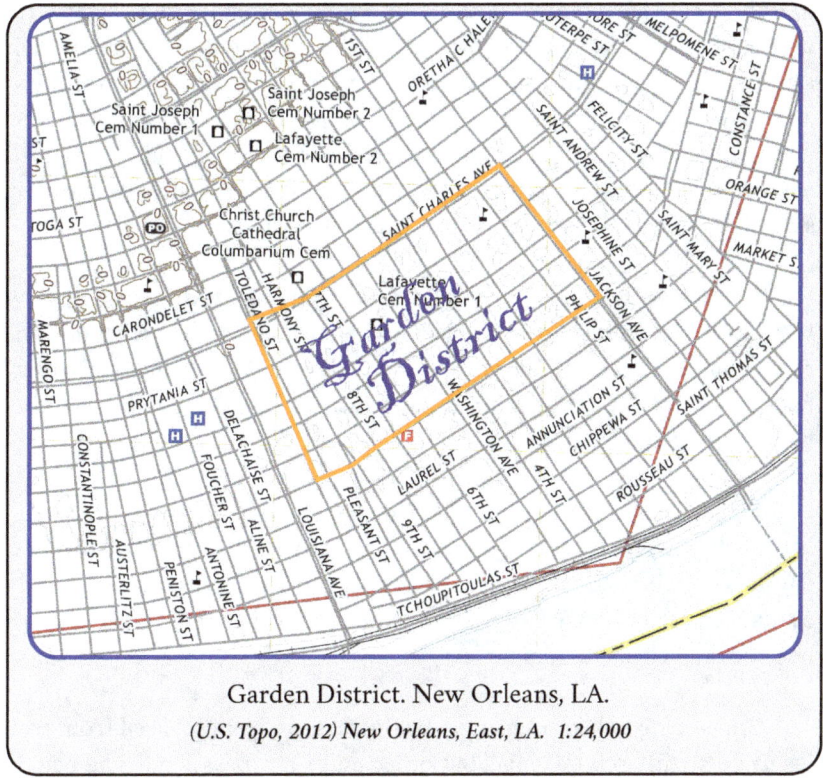

Garden District. New Orleans, LA.

(U.S. Topo, 2012) New Orleans, East, LA. 1:24,000

This walk takes you to the Garden District, a neighborhood of beautiful historic mansions and Lafayette Cemetery #1, ideal for your first visit to a City of the Dead. Start out at the base of Canal Street, where you'll catch the St. Charles streetcar to the Garden District. You're standing on the widest main street in the U.S. After the Louisiana Purchase in 1803, when the French sold Louisiana to America, Canal Street divided the city between the French Creole side to the east ("downriver") and the American side to the west ("upriver"). Canal Street's central median was "neutral ground" between the two, though American rule and culture was at odds with French (and Spanish) culture. To this day, all medians in the city are called "neutral ground."

Next, we're going to hop on the St. Charles streetcar (No. 12). Some like to get on where Canal meets Carondelet (which is Bourbon on the other side of Canal). Megan Romer helpfully writes: "The stop is on Carondelet, in front of the side windows of the Lady Foot Locker store that's right at the corner. You'll see the small yellow street sign marking it, and there's usually a group of people waiting right there." For whatever reason, however, we've always made it a habit to catch the trolley around the corner on St. Charles itself (when Royal crosses Canal, it becomes St. Charles). Just walk a little ways down St. Charles from Canal (you'll see Meyer the Hatter on the other side of the street) and you can't miss the street sign.

We agree with Romer's advice to download the GoMobile app (www. norta.com/GoMobile), from which you can buy tickets, view schedules and routes, and see the locations of trolleys in real time. We use it ourselves and have found it handy for taking the streetcar and the Algiers ferry. Other helpful tips listed by Romer:

• Single rides cost $1.25, but if you'd like to hop on and hop off the trolleys a few times, consider buying a Jazzy Pass for unlimited rides: A single-day pass costs $3, a three-day pass costs $9, a five-day pass costs $15, and a 31-day pass costs $55. Jazzy Passes can be used on any trolley line and city bus, too, as well as the Algiers ferry.

• Single-ride tickets and single-day passes can be purchased from trolley drivers with exact change, but other multi-day passes must be bought online, at Ticket Vending Machines found along Canal Street (*cash only*), at certain stores in the city, including all Walgreens, or via the GoMobile app.

Now then, let's assume you've sorted out your ticket and you've boarded the streetcar. You're on the oldest continuously operating street railway in the world—opened in 1835—rumbling towards the Garden District. Don't you feel like Tennessee Williams? We're going to hop off at Washington Street; as you approach this stop, pull the cord running above the windows. (Streets leading up to Washington include First, Second, Third, and Fourth Streets.)

First, we'll stroll a block south (i.e., towards the river) on Washington to explore Lafayette Cemetery #1. Stop at the corner of Washington Avenue and Prytania Street to read the sign welcoming you to the Garden District, "famous for its nineteenth century homes and gardens."

Stroll a little further down to the entrance of Lafayette Cemetery #1, first laid out in 1833. Many movies have been filmed here at Lafayette, including Neil Jordan's take on Anne Rice's *Interview with a Vampire* and Dennis Hopper's *Easy Rider*. By 1840 it was fairly bursting at the seams, mostly with victims of yellow fever. In the worst outbreak, in 1853, yellow fever claimed 7,849 residents. No wonder the city got the nickname "Necropolis" (city of the dead).

You'll begin by noticing the famous above-ground family tombs and vaults. The reason the town's cemeteries are above ground is often supposed to be because New Orleans is below sea level, and you don't want your loved ones washing away. The reason may in fact be that the French and Spanish started the tradition of above-ground cemeteries, and simply passed it on to their colonies, such as Louisiana/New Orleans. One more reason for the above-ground burials is land shortage: they ran out of land in which to bury people thanks to the massive amount of dead from, say, the Great Fire of 1788 and the yellow fever epidemic of 1853.

Look for Civil War veterans, and keep an eye out for poignant sculpture. See if you can find the youngest person to pass away (some were only a couple of days old), and the oldest. Notice also the coping graves—small family plots surrounded by short walls, filled in with soil or marble chips. As you come to the periphery, stroll along the almost 500 wall oven vaults. (See more on Lafayette Cemetery #1 in our section on "Cemeteries.")

Leave the cemetery and wander in an easterly direction down Prytania Street, which runs along its northern border. When appreciating Garden District architecture, look for the distinct "raised center-hall cottage," a classic Creole style which raises the home on brick piers and features a deep, columned front porch with a hall running down the center from front facade to rear. The neighborhood's also characterized by its Greek Revival mansions, a style popular in the South in the 1820s-1860s.

Walking down Prytania, you'll see some wonderful 19th-century mansions. We start with **Colonel Short's Villa** (1859) at the corner of Fourth Street, with its cornstalk fence; and **Briggs-Staub House** (1849) toward Third Street, the neighborhood's only Gothic Revival home. Toward Second you'll see Lonsdale House, a onetime Catholic chapel, and **Maddox House**, a Greek Revival mansion, with a five-bay expansion. On the corner of First and Prytania is **Bradish-Johnson**, today a private girls' school, and **Toby-Westfeldt**, a raised Greek Revival cottage.

When you come to First, hang a right and head southerly down the street. At Coliseum you'll see **Morris House** and **Carroll-Crawford House**, both 1869 (the latter is where *Toys in the Attic* was filmed), with their iron lace: romantic and Italianate. At 1239 First Street you'll see **Brevard House**, known familiarly as Anne Rice house—she lived there from 1989 to 2004. Built by James Calrow and Charles Pride in 1857, the house, which AnneRice.com calls "transitional" in style, contains both Greek Revival and Italianate elements. Its signature is the double galleries with Corinthian columns above and Ionic columns below, set between square pillars at the corners. **Payne House**—where Jefferson Davis died—is one block up, near the corner of Camp St.

Head back up First and take a detour down Coliseum for the heart of the Garden District. The **Italian Mansion** is at First and Coliseum—Trent Reznor's (of Nine Inch Nails) old crib. At Coliseum and Third you'll see **Robinson House**, the first house in town with indoor plumbing, and **Musson-Bell House**, built by Edgar Degas' uncle. Near Washington Street, you'll see **Nolan House**, where *The Curious Case of Benjamin Button* was filmed.

Gaze across the street upon **Commander's Palace**. If you're dressed up and it's around lunchtime, step over for lunch and a 25-cent martini. (Depending upon your taste, make it a Sidecar instead.) If you're not dressed up and it's off-hours, you may still enjoy a drink in the courtyard, with its verdant, palmy gardens.

Another great idea is to walk a little over half a mile down St. Charles to the **Columns Hotel** (3811 St. Charles), a wonderful place to have a drink on the porch and watch the streetcar rumble past. (The outdoor bar is open 4p-9p M-Th, 11:30a-11p F and Sa, and 11:30a to 9p Su.)

Faubourg Marigny/Bywater Walk

Founded in 1805, the Faubourg Marigny neighborhood, just to the east of the French Quarter, is one of the earliest neighborhoods in the city. The entire neighborhood was added to the National Register of Historic Places in 1974; in 1999 it was awarded a "Great Places in America" designation by the American Planning Association. We certainly consider it such.

Together with the Bywater, the next neighborhood to its immediate east, these are artists' neighborhoods—hubs of the creative spirit, aptly described by Fodor's as a "bohemian commingling of musical history and edgy alternative-arts scene." By day, the Marigny/Bywater is worth a stroll for the delightful architecture: by night, it's where the music is. This is a place where you can actually find streets named Desire and Music. This 9th Ward community was celebrated by Andy J. Forest in his song "Bywater," where he sings about living "deep down under" in this gritty 'hood. "Never a dull moment, I never feel alone."

We'll begin our walk at the corner of Frenchmen St. and Esplanade Ave., just behind the U.S. Mint, a bit below Decatur. You're at the tip of the Marigny Triangle formed by Frenchmen and Esplanade. Esplanade marks the western boundary of the Marigny, whereas one cool club after another runs up Frenchmen between Esplanade and Royal—the prime strip for live music. Locals worry the area becomes less of a local community with each year, more populated by transient out-of-towners, often knobheads—which is another reason to balance those tourists out with true music/culture travelers of the kind we hope are reading these words. For now, Frenchmen is still where we'd advise our kind of travelers to start for live music.

As author Lolis Elie aptly observed while strolling in the Marigny, the definition of a great city is one in which you can walk and discover stuff. It's in that spirit that we set out. Stroll up gorgeous, oak-lined Esplanade. Enjoy the beautiful, distinctive 19th-century mansions, such as **Gauche House** (704 Esplanade), right next to colorful Creole cottages and shotgun shacks. Looking at them, you can't help but be made happy. Why not walk up Esplanade at least to Rampart St. on the west side of the street, then come back down on the east side.

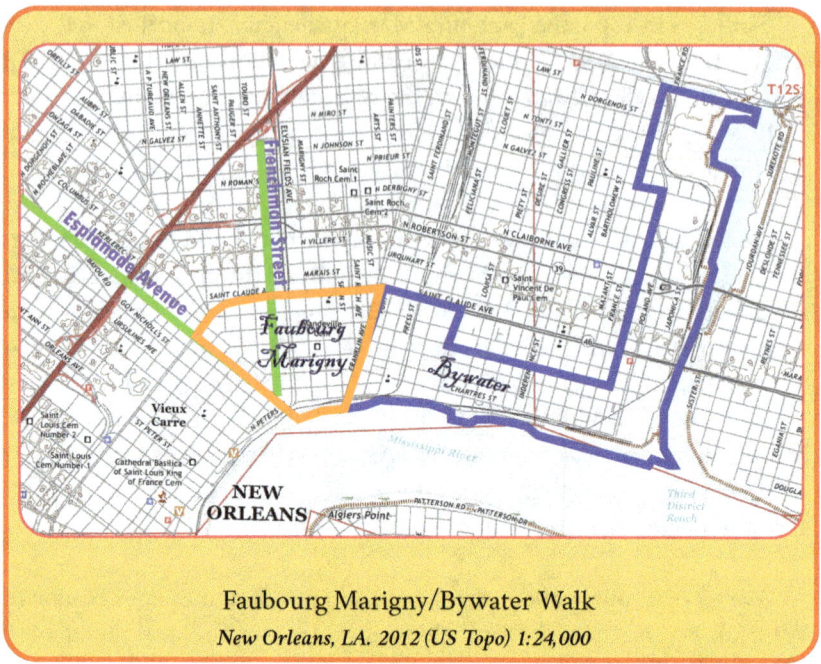

Faubourg Marigny/Bywater Walk
New Orleans, LA. 2012 (US Topo) 1:24,000

At Royal Street hang a left, passing neighborhood institution the "**R**" **Bar** (formally the Royal Street Inn) at 1431 Royal St. Keep walking until you hit Washington Park, then turn right and walk down Frenchmen. At Decatur, drop in on **Louisiana Music Factory**, a terrific record shop (421 Frenchmen St., 11a-6p every day except W, when they're closed). We once met Trombone Shorty here, picking up an armload of tunes so he could brush up in preparation for Fats Domino's second-line.

Now head back up Frenchmen a block, turn right at the corner and head down Chartres, crossing big Elysian Fields Avenue. At 2405 Chartres St., you'll come to the home of **Papa Jack Laine** (1873-1966), leader of the Reliance Brass Band. Many of the great first generation of New Orleans musicians played in that band. His house is not open to the public, but there's a plaque to read.

Keep walking. You'll pass the **New Orleans Center for Creative Arts** (2800 Chartres), the local arts-training center: a wonderful institution, renowned for their jazz, culinary arts, and acting departments, among others. When you cross Homar Plessy Way, you'll have crossed into the Bywater.

Keep going down Chartres to get to **Dr. Bob's Folk Art** (3027 Chartres St.), a wild and wooly place that's the studio, gallery and headquarters of the eponymous folk artist and local legend. It's open every day from 10a until… 4:20p! (Oh, that Dr. Bob.) Dr. Bob's signature paintings are brightly colored visions of Louisiana life (gators, juke joints, etc.), festooned and framed with Abita beer bottle caps. "Be Nice or Leave" is his credo, and it is also the legend you'll find emblazoned on his famous signs, which you'll see all over town. He also sculpts: dinosaurs guard the warehouse. Play "where's Ignatius": find the painting where the great man from *A Confederacy of Dunces* is pushing his Lucky Dog cart away from the Paradise Vendors garage, as well as the one where he's walking past his favorite place to go to the movies, the old Prytania theater.

If you'd like a slight detour, hang a left at Clouet Street and head up to Burgundy Street: you've come to the southern border of the St. Claude arts district, a neighborhood within the larger Bywater 'hood. Hang a right and keep walking down Burgundy. There are lovely galleries along the way. **Christopher Porché-West Galerie** (3201 Burgundy St) is one to look out for.

Or, since you've come this far, after visiting Dr. Bob's why not walk about another mile down Chartres to **Bacchanal** (600 Poland Ave.), a lovely wine bar with live music at the edge of the Bywater. Since you're down that way, **Vaughan's** (4229 Dauphine St), where Corey Henry and the Treme Funktet play on Thursday nights, is only a few blocks away. The No. 5 Marigny/Bywater bus also takes you to the end of the Bywater; its Chartres/Poland street drops you right at Bacchanal.

Treme/Esplanade Avenue Walk

Atop the French Quarter across N. Rampart, you'll find the Treme (pronounced trem-MAY), the country's oldest African-American neighborhood. This fertile hood is the cradle of jazz and second-line parades. It all began when Claude Treme sold his plantation to the city in 1810, creating the Crescent City's first subdivision. Treme, a Frenchman, broke up the plantation into large tracts of land and sold them off on a first-come, first-served basis. Many of those who bought were free people of color.

Doing a little hangin' in the Treme, watchin' people sashay, is one of the key experiences you can have in New Orleans. We'll enter the neighborhood at Esplanade and Rampart, where you should read the sign erected in its honor. It points out this was a diverse neighborhood—Europeans lived here alongside the majority of free people of color, and there were "craftsmen, artists, musicians, entrepreneurs, doctor and teachers."

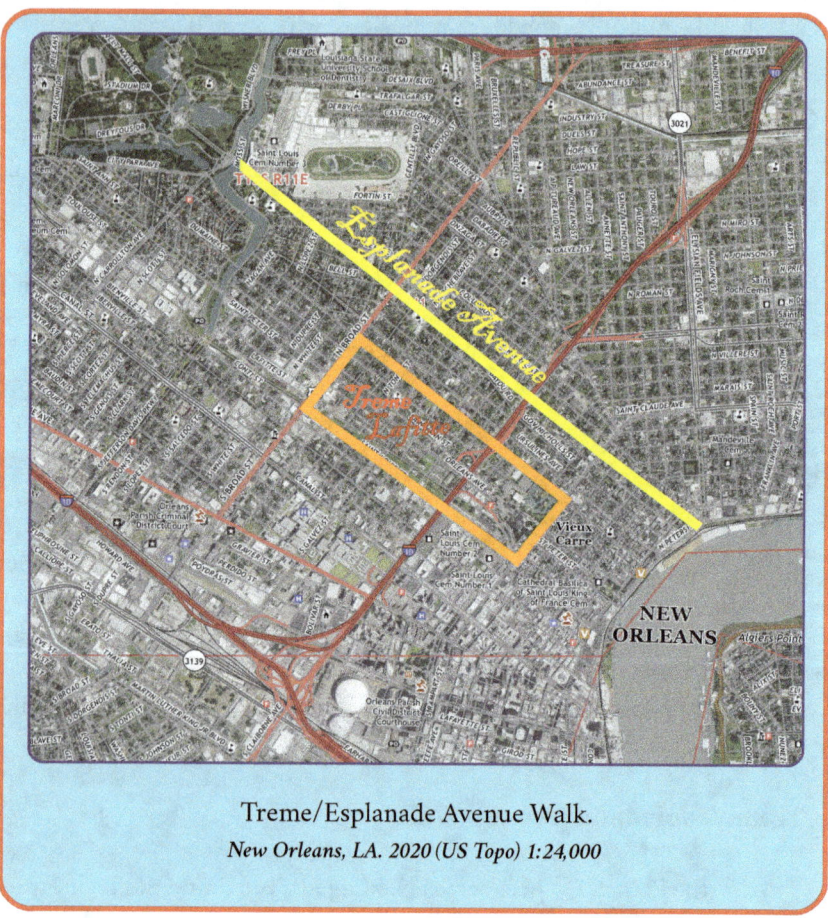

Treme/Esplanade Avenue Walk.
New Orleans, LA. 2020 (US Topo) 1:24,000

Walk up Esplanade a block and turn left on Henriette Delille. As you stroll, keep your eyes peeled for the neighborhood's unique Creole cottages. Many of these were designed and built by the free people of color who founded the neighborhood. You'll notice they're typically one to one-and-a-half stories tall and two rooms wide (two rooms deep, as well). Many feature gabled dormer windows. The facade will be symmetrical and have four openings, and the steeply pitched side-gabled roof will extend over the facade for protection from the elements. (The extension is called an abat-vent.) You might see a community garden as well: people "making groceries" the natural way.

Walk a few blocks over to the one-time site of the **Backstreet Cultural Museum** (1116 Henriette Delille St.), a small but mighty museum that houses a breathtaking collection of hand-sewn, beaded Mardi Gras Indians outfits. The Indians are a major facet of unique, local Black culture: this is the place to learn and celebrate their history. As we went to press, this invaluable museum was temporarily closed, attempting to recover from damages sustained in Hurricane Ida, and hoping to reopen temporarily at 1114 N. Villere Street. Hopefully they will have reopened by the time you visit. Follow their progress at https://www.backstreetmuseum.org.

Continue down Henriette until you come to Louis Armstrong Park. Walk around to the Rampart Street entrance. Stroll inside and find **Congo Square**, one of the most important, and perhaps even sacred, spots in Treme and New Orleans itself. It's the birthplace of jazz—in the 1740s, African and Caribbean slaves, as well as the free people of color who made up the majority of the neighborhood, preserved their culture on this spot with dancing, singing, and drumming celebrations. (See our entry below for more on Congo Square.)

What's more, right across the street is Cosimo Matassa's **J&M Recording Studios** (840 N Rampart St.), where Fats Domino and Little Richard recorded. It certainly counts as one of the birthplaces of rock 'n' roll. Today it's just a laundromat, but it's still a spiritual site, if you squint your eyes and use a bit of imagination. Not bad: two "birthplaces" within one city block. What's more, voodoo queen **Marie Laveau** had a home just a block away, right around the corner at 1020-1022 St. Ann, on the border between Treme and the Quarter.

Other neighborhood attractions include **St. Augustine Church** (1210 Governor Nicholls St., 70116), established by free people of color in 1841. Remarkably for the time period, they worshipped under the same roof as white people and slaves. (See our entry elsewhere.) The newly re-opened **New Orleans African American Museum** (1418 Governor Nicholls St.,

70116) promises to be of interest (Th-Su 11a-4p, $20 self-guided tour, also offers a full day or half day Treme Experience; 504-218-8254; https://www. noaam.org).

Treme's Petite Jazz Museum (1500 Governor Nicholls St., 70116) offers an advanced look at the city's music that goes beyond received notions, though this admittedly "petite" collection is slightly overpriced at $15 (W-F, tours at 1:30p, 2:30p, 3:30p and 4:30p; $15; 504-715-0332; https://www. tremespetitjazzmuseum.com).

Your best bets for food in the Treme? There can be no question that these would be **Dooky Chase's** for a sit-down meal (2301 Orleans Ave., 70119; F 11a-3p and 5:30p-9p, Sa 5:30p-9p, Tu-Th 11a-3p, Closed Su-M; Call 504-821-0600 or 504-821-0535 for reservations, https://www.dookychaserestaurants. com), and **Li'l Dizzy's** for casual-but-great fare (1500 Esplanade Ave; M-Sa 11a-3p, closed Su; 504-766-8687; https://lildizzyscafe.net).

For great music, head to Kermit's **Treme Mother-in-Law Lounge** (1500 N Claiborne Ave). You'll be buck-jumpin' and having fun. It's open every day at 4:20p (of course!) until whenever. (504-814-1819; https://www.facebook. com/Ruffinsbbq/).

Recall that we started our walk over at Esplanade and Rampart. If you're so inclined and you're back that way, we like to walk the "neutral ground" on beautiful oak-lined Esplanade all the way up to the Bayou St. John neighborhood. You could grab a bite at **Cafe Degas** (3127 Esplanade Ave; lunch served W & Th, 11a–3p, dinner served W–Su 5p–9:30p, brunch served F-Su 11a– 3p, closed M-Tu; 504-945-5635; https://cafedegas.com) or **Liuzza's by the Tracks** (1518 N Lopez St; M–Sa 11a–8p, Closed Su except when the Saints are playing, 504-218-7888; https://www.liuzzasbtt.com). As you walk, keep an eye peeled for eye-poppingly beautiful mansions such as the **Dufour-Baldwin House** (1859) at 1701 Esplanade.

Along the way, you could visit **Degas House** (2306 Esplanade Avenue). It's a museum as well as a B&B (and a wedding venue.) At least when we were there, you were able to look around the house and gardens on your own, though their Creole Impressionist Tours are highly regarded. Degas, the great French Impressionist, lived in the U.S. from 1872-1873, a sojourn that coincided with the Reconstruction era. The artist, whose mother and grandmother were born in New Orleans, made many famous paintings during his stay, including a study of his blind sister-in-law, "Portrait of Estelle"—you can see it at the New Orleans Museum of Art. In short, Degas House offers a compelling look at the passing of an era and of a way of life—that of the city's French-speaking Creoles.

There's a fascinating timeline which traces 19th-century art in the context of Louisiana and U.S. social history. Particularly relevant is the 1857 Dred Scott decision, which evolved out of fights over whether the massive Louisiana territory the U.S. had acquired in the Louisiana Purchase would be free or slave. The Missouri Compromise of 1820 had been intended to placate both sides, allowing the creation of Missouri as a slave state but making much of the rest of the territory free past a certain boundary. Scott sued for his freedom after being taken by his master across the boundary into freedom and back again, arguing he could no longer be a slave. The Supreme Court decision held that no Black, free or slave, could claim U.S. citizenship and that Congress could not prohibit slavery in U.S. territories.

Cost and Hours: Edgar Degas House Creole Impressionist Tours happen every day at 10:30a and 1:45p, $29/person; there's also a Creole Breakfast and Tour combo offered everyday: breakfast is served from 9a-10a, $50 per person, reservations required; there's a Sa and Su brunch available by reservation; Drawing and painting classes are also available; 504-821-5009; info@degashouse.com; https://www.degashouse.com)

Obligatory Bourbon Street Stroll

We've had visits to New Orleans when we never set foot on Bourbon—except to cross it. It disappoints us when people think New Orleans is all about Bourbon. That said, once a trip, typically, we do the obligatory Bourbon Street stroll, perambulating from one end to the other of that touristy honky-tonk strip, daiquiri in hand, and observing the human parade. We like to get our daiquiri from **Original Daiquiris/Fat Tuesday** (633 Bourbon), but the spots are legion.

You might meet some spring-break mentality dumb-asses; on the other hand, you might pop into a spot and discover a pocket of coolness, or see someone being themselves so unabashedly that it's rather inspiring. We once saw a woman walking down the street as nonchalant as could be—except she was painted silver from the neck down, and wearing only pasties and booty shorts. You'll see humanity at its best and its worst.

This walk is best done in the evening. (If you don't see hours listed for some of our suggestions below, just assume they'll be open when you want 'em.) Typically, we start on the Canal Street side of Bourbon and walk downriver.

As for cool, non-knobhead places for music and a drink along the way, there's **Bourbon House** (144 Bourbon St.), known for their excellent milk punch and BBQ shrimp po boy. **Jean Lafitte's Old Absinthe House** (240 Bourbon St.) is an atmospheric/historic place to try absinthe. The Jazz Playhouse (300 Bourbon St., 70130; https://www.facebook.com/JazzPlayhouse/) is a top venue for live music. **Bourbon "O"** (730 Bourbon St) is a hip place for a cocktail and live music. Get the Ramos Gin Fizz, but be patient: it takes the mechanical arm several minutes to shake properly. If you're doing the walk in the afternoon, and it's sunny, you can't beat a Hurricane in the courtyard of **Pat O'Brien's** (624 Bourbon St). **Fritzel's European Jazz Pub** (733 Bourbon St) is an atmospheric place to hear good traditional jazz.

We'd recommend dropping into **Marie Laveau's House of Voodoo** along the way. It's a legitimate outpost of voodoo culture (739 Bourbon; Daily 10a–10p, F-Sa 10a–12a, Reverend Zombie's psychic and spiritual readings offered daily 12p–8p, F/Sa 10a-10p).

Your main destination should be the place where we always wind up our stroll: the 18th-century **Lafitte's Blacksmith Shop** (941 Bourbon St), a one-time pirate hideout. Wikipedia puts it concisely: "Most likely built as a house in the 1770s during the Spanish colonial period, it is one of the oldest surviving structures in New Orleans." (See our entry elsewhere).

For late-night fare on Bourbon, **Clover Grill** can't be beat (900 Bourbon St, proudly open daily 24/7, 504-598-1010, https://www.clovergrill.com).

Here ends our self-guided walks. Now, for some guided tours we recommend.

New Orleans Voodoo Tour by Free Tours by Foot

New Orleans is famous for its voodoo 'n' hoodoo vibe. If you'd like a non-sensationalistic, non-Hollywood look at this African/Haitian religion, we'd recommend the Free Tours by Foot experience—the tour is "free," but you're expected to tip the guide at the end. You should, and you'll want to: they're well-informed and they make the subject come alive.

While the Roman catholic church conducted a decades-long campaign to present Catholicism as "legitimate" religion and voodoo as pagan heresy, voodoo is in fact a traditional Afro-Caribbean faith. "Voodoo offers a direct experience with the sacred that appeals to more and more people," according to Martha Ward, a professor of anthropology at UofNOLA. Today, people use voodoo to cure anxiety and depression and, as Michael Murphy writes, "to serve others and influence the outcome of life events through the connection with nature, spirits, and ancestors."

The tour begins in **Congo Square**. Located outside the city rampart (hence the name "Rampart Street"), from the late 17th century and into the 18th, Congo Square was the place where enslaved peoples from Africa and the Caribbean (as well as free people of color) gathered to express African culture, such as voodoo religious rituals. Code Noir, the laws governing Blacks in French colonial New Orleans, gave slaves more freedom than they'd enjoy under American rule, and slaves were given Sundays off to worship in the square.

The tour also stops at the **onetime home of Marie Laveau**, the Voodoo Queen of New Orleans (1020-22 Rue St. Anne), as well as at **Madame John's Legacy** (632 Dumaine), an 18th-century house that's one of the oldest extant structures in town. It shows you to the venerable **New Orleans Historic Voodoo Museum** (724 Dumaine St, everyday 10a-6p, $8 general admission, https://voodoomuseum.com). All the while, your guide discusses crucial voodoo-related historical subjects (the Haitian Rebellions, New Orleans' cemeteries vis-a-vis the Spirits of the Dead), and provides thoughtful analyses of the depiction of voodoo in popular culture and its historic and ongoing place in the city's culture.

The tour ends up at **Voodoo Authentica** (612 Dumaine St, M-Su 11a-7p, 504-522-2111; Email: info@voodooshop.com; https://www.voodooshop.com), which is not just a shop but is also a cultural and spiritual center—all employees are actual voodoo practitioners. This is where we'd recommend you get your voodoo dolls, Gris Gris bags, and potion oils. Scott likes to pick up a candle for "The Spirit of Writing" while he's here, and, for whatever reason, burning it does in fact seem to help him compose. Karolyn still carries her gris gris bag for self-confidence when she's feeling off.

They also offer rituals, readings, spiritual work & consultations—call 504-522-2111 between 11a and 7p if you'd like to talk about setting something up. Karolyn had a reading done by Juneaux the last time we were in town. She said it was far more personal and intimate than she'd thought it would be; she'd thought it would be very surface so that it could apply to anybody. Karolyn says: Instead, Juneaux provided facts from my life that he could not have possibly known—and not just the facts, but the feelings that go beyond the facts.

Take note of the "veve" outside of the store—this is a symbol that acts as a kind of lighthouse, or portal, to call the various Loa (spirits).

Cost and hours of New Orleans Voodoo Tour by Free Tours by Foot: Th-Su 10 am and 3p, reservation required. The tour meets at the **Archway to Armstrong Park** (701 N Rampart St) and lasts approximately 1.5 hours. You'll cover about a mile; Name-your-own-price. Book on the website at https://freetoursbyfoot.com/voodoo-tour/

French Market Walking Tour presented by the New Orleans Jazz National Historical Park

We were all set to highly recommend the walking tours conducted by the New Orleans Jazz National Historical Park and guided by a Ranger of the park, when we learned these walks are no longer offered. That said, they still offer Ranger Talks at the Jean Lafitte National Historical Park & Preserve French Quarter Visitor Center at 419 Decatur Street (itself worth a look for its exhibits) at 10am from Tuesday through Saturday. We recommend attending one of these talks. (Check out their calendar at https://www.nps. gov/jazz/planyourvisit/calendar.htm.)

We'll keep the following chronicle we'd prepared on the walking tour, as an example of what you might learn from one of the Ranger talks.

The Jazz National Historical Park's French Market walking tour reveals the seamy underbelly and history of this area which today's ambling tourists may scarcely countenance. It was once quite a rough stretch: sailors looking for women, good times, and/or trouble would go down into the French Market corridor, and sometimes they'd never come back.

The walk is also a survey of the roots of jazz and blues, a subject about which our Ranger was highly informed, explaining how what we think of as jazz was a fusion of gospel, blues, marching/military brass band music, opera, ragtime, and spirituals. It mixed all that with the polyphonic (i.e., lots of things going on at once) approach to rhythm and melody from Africa being played in Congo Square.

She carried a portable speaker on which she played us things like the trumpet solo with which Louis Armstrong kicked off "West End Blues." At that moment, Armstrong revolutionized jazz by inventing solo improvisation, transforming jazz into a mode of personal expression. Looked at that way, he is the inventor, or father, of free jazz: his innovation would eventually lead jazz away from dance music and towards the pure self-expression of Ornette Coleman.

She also memorably explained how Robert Johnson would bend the note when he sang, thereby creating notes that were not on the Western scale—that were actually *between* the notes on the Western scale. Our guide also made the point that the "tailgate" trombone style heard in trad jazz was "dirty" in its day: the kids liked it rough 'n' raw, just like today.

Ghost Tours

— Scott: It's all well and good to be rational; in fact, I recommend it. (Karolyn, on the other hand, as she herself says, lives for the irrational, unexplained lore.) However, don't be so rational that you can't enjoy a good ghost tour. Ghosts, after all, are as much a part of the atmospherics of New Orleans as the fog wafting down Pirate's Alley. It's a city that's haunted in so many ways.

— Karolyn: So let's talk about ghosts. I have no reservations about believing; Scott, on the other hand—well, let's just say skeptic is not a big enough word for it. Having said that, he and I, together and separately, have had incidents in New Orleans (*and in other places, such as Louisville, upstate New York, and around the world*) that we cannot explain. So why not just indulge?

Ghost & Graveyard Nighttime Bus Tour by Haunted History Tours

Sidney Smith's Haunted History Tours is one of the most venerable tour companies in town. This tour, which also goes by the name "Dead of Night Ghosts and Haunts Bus Tour," was a fun evening of visits to an interestingly curated selection of Cities of the Dead, though you don't enter most: in fact, the only one through which you stroll is **Charity Hospital Cemetery**, with its moving Katrina Memorial. (See our entry under the "Cemeteries" section.) You stand peering through the gates at others, as the guide regales you with their ghostly history. We stopped by **St. Louis Cemetery #3** and **Chevra Thilim Cemetery**, both fascinating (again, see our entries under "Cemeteries" for more). The latter is one of the rare in-ground cemeteries, in this case per Jewish burial traditions.

The tour memorably whisks you out to **Bayou St. John**, which is even more atmospheric at night. Alighting, you cross Magnolia Bridge on foot to the banks of the bayou, where voodoo priestesses and priests still hold ceremonies on St. John's Eve (June 23), the night before St. John's Feast. It's a celebration of the Summer Solstice, of Midsummer—the time of renewal and rebirth. This is all in the great tradition of Marie Laveau, who held city-wide voodoo rituals here, conjuring up and connecting with the spirits of the elders.

You then venture into **City Park** and listen to ghost stories under the Spanish moss. It is a rather unforgettable experience to be out among the beautiful (and haunted? you decide) oak groves in City Park in the dark of night, listening to ghost stories in the lagoon. Take photos to see how many spirits you can capture: orbs and light anomalies are commonly spotted when photographing "haunted" grounds. (Sure, there's probably an explanation for it. But what fun is that?)

A bit of history: in the 18th and 19th century, Bayou St. John was a vital trading route linking the Gulf of Mexico, Lake Pontchartrain, and the French Quarter. With all that schooner and barge traffic, you'd best believe there were plenty of deadly accidents—grist for the ghost mill. The traffic on this major commercial artery was controlled by one man, Jose Planas, "The King of the French Market": he owned all the surrounding land, you see. Indeed, some say his ghost still walks the bayou to this day.

Cost and hours: Tours go out at 7p and 9:30p everyday and last about two hours; tour departs from 740 Rampart. Age 13-64: $50;
Website: make reservations at https://www.tripadvisor.com/AttractionProductRev-iew-g60864-d15531042-Dead_of_Night_Ghosts_and_Haunts_Bus_Tour-New_Or-leans_Louisiana.html or https://hauntedhistorytours.com/our-tours/ghosts-haunts-bus-new-orleans/

French Quarter Ghost Tour by Free Tours by Foot

This was one of the first tours we took, and it spirits you to all the greatest hits: **LaLaurie House**, of course (see our entry), and the very haunted **Cornstalk Hotel**, as well as the adjacent **Andrew Jackson Hotel**—which has a quite haunted second floor, where we would later stay the night.

— Karolyn: The Jackson Hotel is extremely haunted, they say. Well, we stayed in the most haunted room; nothing happened and it was quite small (maybe that's why—there wasn't enough room for two guests of sizable girth and a ghost). Having said that, we did experience laughter inside the courtyard during our breakfast. It was not coming from the street, it was coming from the backyard, and it was children. If you know the history, five young boys were burned to death here in a fire in 1794, because it used to be a boarding school and orphanage. Not only did I hear it, so did Scott. He would not lie to me about this. This is the one thing that I have told him: if you lie about this the D-word is on the table.

The tour memorably winds up along the two alleys on either side of St. Louis Cathedral: **Pirate's Alley** and **Pere Antoine Alley**. Pirate's Alley is said to be haunted by everyone from pirate Jean Lafitte to William Faulkner, who lived there in the '20s. On the other side, the alley is named for the French priest Father Antoine, who preached at St. Louis Cathedral and baptized baby Marie Laveau in 1801. (Along with being a voodoo priestess, Laveau was also a devout Catholic all her life.) Pere Antoine was as beloved as he was unconventional, known as an advocate for prisoners and the enslaved. (That's truly doing the Lord's work, it seems to us.) His ghost can be found in the small hours, roaming the cathedral and both flanking alleyways, singing softly.

Our tour guide's final story told of another, earlier priest, Père Longuory, also unconventional and a champion of the poor. In the 1760s, Spain was in control of Louisiana. Certain sectors of French society refused to accept Spanish rule and conspired to overthrow it; in response the Spaniards had five plotting Frenchmen executed where Esplanade and Frenchmen Street meet. (In fact, Frenchmen Street was named in honor of these French martyrs.) The Spanish general who'd ordered the executions refused to allow these men traditional Catholic burial rites. Their grieving families appealed to Père Longuory, who preached at St. Louis Church (which was still a church then: it wouldn't become a cathedral until 1793).

Against all the odds, he managed to remove the rebels' bodies from under the eyes of the Spanish guard and bring them back to the church for a proper funeral mass; afterwards, and again miraculously, he breached Spanish security in the dark of night and led a funeral procession to the now-vanished St. Peter Street Cemetery to give the men a proper Catholic burial. Despite his singing hymns all the way, it's said the Spanish never heard or saw a thing.

It's all quite spooky by night (or early morning), and as our guide told the story, it almost felt as if we squinted hard enough, we could almost see Père Longuory leading his ghostly procession through the fog, singing softly as he proceeded on his mission. Many have seen and heard such things in these very environs over the years. If you happen to be haunting these alleys yourself as the long night turns into day, look for a monk wearing sandals and singing the hymn "Kyrie" as he makes his way from the cathedral down Pirate's Alley to St. Anthony's garden round back.

Cost and hours of French Quarter Ghost Tour by Free Tours by Foot: Daily at 7:30p, reservation required. The tour meets on the steps of the St. Louis Cathedral and lasts approximately 1.5-2 hours. You'll cover about a mile; Name-your-own-price. Book on the website at https://freetoursbyfoot.com/new-orleans-ghost-walking-tour/

Bloody Mary's Tour is very well-regarded, though we've not had the pleasure yet ourselves. A subject for further research. Should you care to try them out, here's the contact info: tel: 504-915-7774; e-mail: bloody-maryNOLA@gmail.com; website: https://www.bloodymarystours.com)

— Karolyn: Lastly, my feeling is that most ghosts, or spirits, or whatever you want to call them, are here because they want to be or are here because they can't leave. If you are kind to them they do not give off a bad vibe (I've never had an experience that made me feel uncomfortable, except in upstate New York, where a ghost told me to get out— mind you, I didn't get out, I stayed and looked around). But honestly, I think a lot of ghosts, especially the children, are just looking for a connection, like we all are. Why not make this opportunity a bridge and talk to them kindly. Ask if it's OK if you are speaking with them (to give them a little bit of control), and go with it.

Festivals

New Orleans loves a festival. In fact, there's probably a festival going on somewhere in town every week. Here are a few of our favorites.

New Orleans Jazz & Heritage Festival
Fair Grounds Race Course
1751 Gentilly Blvd.
New Orleans, LA 70119

Held over two weekends in late April/early May and popularly known as Jazz Fest, this event has become a cherished tradition, the annual time when New Orleanians gather on the fairgrounds to celebrate their heritage of music and food. In a sense it all began with Mahalia Jackson. At the first Jazz Fest in 1970, the Queen of Gospel was in Congo Square when she and Duke Ellington, no less, came upon the Eureka Brass Band leading a second-line through the grounds. George Wein, the founder and mastermind of Jazz Fest (who passed away in 2021), put a microphone in her face and bid her "Sing!" The rest is history.

Quint Davis helped Wein produce the fest, and a galvanizing appearance by Professor Longhair in 1971 put it on the map. After being called in 2020 and 2021 due to COVID, on what would have been its 50th and 51st anniversaries, Jazz Fest made a triumphant comeback in 2022. Aside from stages devoted to local, roots, and world music, there's also huge national rock and pop acts. A huge part of the fun is all the great Louisiana food vendors. Look for Prejean's pheasant quail andouille gumbo, Ms. Linda's ya-ka-mein, the Creole's Stuffed Bread from Lafayette, crawfish Monica from the Kajun Kettle Foods booth, and Vaucresson sausage, who've had a booth at every single fest. You'll need a Mango freeze, as well. Don't shirk the crafts booths, either, where local artisans display their wares.

Sure, it's touristy and expensive and hot. It's incredibly crowded: last time we were there, Scott attempted without much success to whittle his way into the Van Morrison crowd, while Karolyn helped a young girl who'd passed out. Whatever its shortcomings, though, it's still a great time, and it's cherished by most locals. We especially like the Blues Tent, where we've memorably seen great sets by the likes of Rhiannon Giddens and James Andrews and the Crescent City All Stars. The heart of it is still the celebration of Louisiana heritage envisioned by Wein and Davis. For the most ambience, enter at the Mystery Street gate (turn right off of Esplanade).

Cost and Hours: Held over two weekends for three or four days around each weekend. Tickets for single day admission on the 1st weekend or 2nd weekend are $80 in advance, $90 at the gate; tickets for three-day pass (1st weekend) go for $225 and a four-day pass (2nd weekend) are $275; there are also various even more expensive packages available.

Tel: (504) 410-4100;

https://www.nojazzfest.com

French Quarter Festival

French Quarter Fest is another great music 'n' food festival, held over three days in mid or late April. It has the benefit of being free, as well. Stages and stalls featuring local bands and food are arrayed throughout the Quarter, around the Mint, and in Woldenburg Park along the Mississippi.

You know the expression "embarrassment of riches": it could have been coined for this festival. Scott, who's loved stuffing his face since he was dandled on his mother's knee, was in heaven.

Here's the food we tried, all of which you should look out for: Cochon de lait po-boy (Walker's BBQ); jerk chicken dirty rice (Beaucoup Eats); crab beignet (Loretta's Pralines); jerk pork (14 Parishes); shrimp & andouille pie and creole crawfish pie (from the venerable NOLA institution Mrs. Wheat's Pies); alligator sausage kabob (TJ Gourmet); smoked duck & andouille gumbo (R'evolution); smothered rabbit po-boy (Voleo's Seafood); creole hot sausage po-boy (Vaucresson Sausage); crawfish étouffée (Galatoire's); nectar cream snoball (Plum Street Snoballs); crawfish bread pudding with étouffée sauce (The Bower); crawfish ravigote slider with crawfish boil pickles (Broussard's); yakinuku (Japanese grilled meats) po-boy and soft-shell crab po-boy (Ajun Cajun); mini steak sliders with BBQ butter (Ruth's Chris Steak House); veggie lentil sambusa (Addis Nola—Karolyn's favorite taste of the fest); whole hog platter and crawfish mac 'n' cheese (NOLA Crawfish King); and oyster pie (Patton's).

Now then. Let's also salute all the great musicians we saw throughout our days at the Fest, all of whom you should also try to see: Kermit Ruffins, Joe Krown, Paul Sanchez, Dirty Dozen Brass Band, Corey Henry, Palmetto Bug Stompers, NOLA Ragtime Orchestra featuring Lars Edegran, Hot 8 Brass Band, New Orleans Cottonmouth Kings, Sam Price & the True Believers, Original Pinettes Brass Band, Dwayne Dopsie and the Zydeco Hellraisers (our musical discovery of the fest—probably the best show we've seen since we first discovered Glen David Andrews), Smoking Time Jazz Club, James Martin Band, New Orleans Nightcrawlers, James Andrews, John Boutte, Washboard Chaz Blues Trio, and, last but never least, the great Little Freddie King.

Cost and hours: Ranging over three days in mid to late April, it's free; info@fqfi.org; Tel: (504) 522-5730;
https://frenchquarterfest.org

Mardi Gras

Well. This is the big one, isn't it? Typically, it brings in a cool million people a year. Carnival is actually an entire season, not just Fat Tuesday—which is actually the last day of the season. The season begins on January 6, the Festival of the Three Kings, aka the Feast of Epiphany, aka the Twelfth Night after Christmas: this is the day the three wise gents made it to JC to deliver their gifts. Fat Tuesday ("Mardi Gras" in French) itself, also known as Carnival Day, is the last day before Ash Wednesday or Lent (a period of fasting for Catholics). It's alway exactly 47 days before Easter; since Easter hops around, this means in practice it can fall anywhere from early February to early March.

We were in town in mid-February in 2022 to take part in Carnival festivities. It was cool to see the city festooned in purple, green, and gold. If you're going to enjoy Carnival, we recommend you observe it in the Faubourg Marigny/Bywater neighborhood. On Carnival Day itself (we'd left town by then), the **Societe de Sainte Anne** does their cherished stroll through this neighborhood, as they have done for over 50 years now. If you want to see them and their beautiful costumery, Doug MacCash advises, "If you stake out a spot on Royal Street near Esplanade by, say, 10 a.m., you'll probably catch it pass. To distinguish St. Anne from other marching groups, look for glinting standards [in the sense of the word meaning "flag"] made from hula hoops strung with fluttering ribbons. All hail!"

One reason to do this is to avoid the tractor-pulled floats that go down the major thoroughfares and which are led by krewes which range from Republican/fascist (Endymion, known as the Vegas of krewes; Bacchus, with which Rep. Steve Scalise, a 2020-election-denier/David Duke-wannabe, rides; and Orpheus, which allowed fascist commentator Laura Ingraham to ride) to the outright white supremacist (Knights of Chaos, which is a revived version of the white-supremacist Momus krewe; and Krewe d'Etat, a racist satirical krewe).

As a side note, we should add that of the historically white-supremacist krewes, Comus, Momus, and Proteus gave up parading rather than be forced to integrate, whereas Rex, to its credit, has certified publicly that times have changed and they no longer discriminate.

Enough of that, though. Let's get back to the joy. We caught the **Krewe du Vieux Parade**, which typically kicks off the parade season (there are 70 parades over the course of the season). Their theme in 2022 was Vaxxed and Confused, and the mule-drawn floats were as raunchy and satirical as can be, as per tradition. The masked, bespangled and outrageous costumery was something to see. Stentorian brass bands blew so sweet and loud, and numerous Sub-Krewes, all in their own regalia, some dancing, got involved. For their Queen, Krewe du Vieux crowned the wonderful Dr. Jennifer Avegno, the director of the city's Department of Health, who headed NOLA's tremendously successful anti-COVID measures. Her call for mask and vaccine mandates resulted in an exemplarily handling of the crisis. Tragically, she wasn't able to actually ride in the parade due to death threats.

"Throws," meaning stuff hurled by krewes from floats—like plastic to-go cups, plastic beads, blinking thingies, bespoke krewe doubloons, and, best of all, the signature throws (unique handmade items that are the trademark of each krewe)—are a huge part of the tradition. Poor Karolyn got beaned by a button hurled by the Krewe of Spank sub-krewe. We still have the button! It was quite a bacchanal. On another night, we caught the vivid Krewe Bohéme parade.

Our absolute favorite, though, was the **'tit Rex parade**, which we caught in the St. Claude corridor. All floats were made by artists or teachers out of shoeboxes! Beautifully crafted they were, these petite floats. Other krewes to look out for are the **Krewe du Jieux**, which combines African American and Jewish traditions, and the **Krewe of Barkus**, the pooch parade. There's even the **Box of Wine Krewe**, who celebrate Bacchus: god of wine, naturally.

The two major parades which take place on Mardi Gras itself are **Rex** and **Zulu**. The Rex krewe is named after Rex, "King of Carnival": you'll probably hear the beautiful "If Ever I Cease to Love," which has been the anthem of Rex—and New Orleans—ever since the first Rex parade of 1872, when it was played for guest of honor, Archduke Alexei Alexandrovich. This ladies' man from Russia was in New Orleans as part of his marathon US tour and had become smitten with British music-hall actress Lydia

Thompson, who also happened to be in town, and who sang the song in her popular operetta *Bluebeard*. Since the first Rex parade was set up essentially to entertain Alexandrovich, and "If Ever I Cease to Love" was supposed to be his favorite song (due to its association with his crush), it was used to serenade him. The rest is history: a different person is crowned as Rex, or King of Carnival, every year.

Speaking of tunes associated with Rex and Mardi Gras, we also like "Hail Rex! (The King Is On His Way)" by Edward James Gay and the Double Dealers.

The **Zulu Social Aid & Pleasure Club** is the other major krewe to parade on Mardi Gras itself. This historically Black krewe was set up in response to the white-supremacist krewes; it was also the first krewe to integrate. If you catch the Zulu golden nugget (a painted coconut), you've "won" Mardi Gras!

The most exhilarating aspect of the season is the Mardi Gras **Indian** tradition. These are the Black krewes with imaginary Indian tribe names (Wild Magnolias, Wild Tchoupitoulas, Yellow Pocahontas) who masquerade in tribute to actual tribes that once helped escaped slaves find freedom. They spend all year working on suits that they will only wear on Mardi Gras day and a few other special occasions—such as St. Joseph's Day and Super Sunday in March, and perhaps at Jazz Fest. As Carnival Day approaches, Big Chiefs throw all-day sewing sessions, working tirelessly to finish their masterpiece in time for Mardi Gras day, when Big Chiefs mock-battle with their suits to win the title of "the prettiest." The Mardi Gras Indians do not publish their parade routes, but we are told you can often see them around the Krewe of Zulu parade, sometimes at the corner of Claiborne and Orleans.

As for what to eat on Fat Tuesday, in New Orleans there's the King Cake tradition. (In Chicago, we get the paczki.) If you find the baby (a Christ symbol) in your slice it's good luck, and might even mean you're the king or queen of Carnival…but then you have to bring the cake next year. Jambalaya is the traditional dish to eat on Fat Tuesday itself.

Carnival, of course, goes back way before New Orleans, rooted as it is in ancient pre-Lenten debauchery. In New Orleans itself, Mardi Gras dates back to 1837. By 1856, the Mistick Krewe of Comus has established the tradition of the elaborate parade followed by a grand masquerade ball, with their beautiful gowns and Kings and Queens.

Here's what it's really all about, though. Rooted in the emancipation struggles of the Caribbean, Carnival embodies all the qualities we've been trying to highlight throughout this book: the African/European cultural mashup and the political/celebratory expression-of-the-oppressed. "Enslaved people in areas of the Caribbean, and specifically Trinidad, took elements of European masquerade balls and subverted them, using their own rituals and traditions to find freedom in adopting masquerade—or 'making mas'—and becoming different characters," says journalist Charlie Brinkhurst-Cuff. Sam Alexander of the Brazilian band Baque de Axe, put it well: "Carnival is reclaiming the streets. Carnival is doing everything that you're not allowed to do. Carnival is joy, it's celebration."

As we've indicated, Carnival Season can last anywhere from one to three months, all depending on when Easter falls. For all your Mardi Gras information, the best site is https://www.neworleans.com/events/holidays-seasonal/mardi-gras/. It contains a plethora of historical and practical articles.

Tremé Fall Festival
St. Augustine Catholic Church
1210 Governor Nicholls St.
New Orleans, LA 70115

The free Tremé Fall Festival takes place on the first weekend of October and celebrates the food, music and culture of Tremé, America's oldest African-American neighborhood. Enjoy the Samba Kids, who parade through the neighborhood and dance on stilts to the beat of African drums. The free Samba Kids program, part of Casa Samba, "teaches Samba drumming and stilt walking to support cultural enrichment and healthy activities for young people in the area," says Kortney Williams in the New Orleans Data News Weekly. (You might see stilt walkers in second line parades, as well.) Of course, the fest features a stage for music, as well as plenty of good food— we remember the yummy Jamaican food from 14 Parishes. The events take place around Saint Augustine Church. While you're in the neighborhood, don't forget to look around inside this historic church, established by free people of color in 1841 (see our entry elsewhere).

Cost and hours: Free over the first weekend in October;
Tel: (504) 525-5934;
https://hfta.org/fall-festival/2019-treme-fall-festival/#festival

Satchmo SummerFest
400 Esplanade Ave.
New Orleans, LA 70116

Taking place in late July-early August at the New Orleans Jazz Museum at the Old U.S. Mint, Satchmo SummerFest is, according to its website, "the premier American festival dedicated to the life, legacy, and music of New Orleans' native son, Louis 'Satchmo' Armstrong. It features live music, New Orleans' cuisine, and fascinating lectures about Louis Armstrong. Tickets also include access to the New Orleans Jazz Museum."

Cost and hours: Events take place over two days; $7 admission;
Tel: (504) 522-5730;
https://satchmosummerfest.org

Mid-City Bayou Boogaloo
Bayou St. John

Mid-City Bayou Boogaloo takes place in mid-May at various sites along Bayou St. John, and celebrates "music, food, art, community." In the past, the musical lineup has featured the North Mississippi All-Stars, New Orleans Nightcrawlers, Tank and the Bangas, and Cha Wa.

Cost and hours: On a weekend in mid-May, festival gates open at 4:30p on F, 10:30a Sa-Su; the fest runs till 9:30p on F-Sa and 8:30p on Su; Three-day general admission tickets are $45 if purchased early, single day tickets are also available;
https://thebayouboogaloo.com

Louisiana Cajun-Zydeco Festival
George and Joyce Wein Jazz & Heritage Center
701 N. Rampart St.
New Orleans , LA 70116

The Cajun-Zydeco fest happens in mid-July at the George and Joyce Wein Jazz & Heritage Center in Louis Armstrong Park, which carries on Jazz Fest founder George Wein's life's work of preserving Louisiana culture. It's two full days of life-affirming cajun-zydeco music.

Cost and hours: It happens on a weekend in mid-July from 11a-7p, and it's free.
https://www.jazzandheritage.org

Crescent City Blues & BBQ Fest
Lafayette Square Park
540 St. Charles Ave.
New Orleans, LA 70130

Held in Lafayette Square in mid-October, Crescent City Blues & BBQ Festival features fiery local and national blues acts and delicious smoked meat. What more could there to be life?

Cost and hours: It's free and takes place over three days in mid-October;
Tel: (504) 558-6100;
https://www.jazzandheritage.org/events/crescent-city-blues-bbq-festival/

New Orleans Film Festival
Various locations, including 900 Camp St.
New Orleans, LA 70130

Produced by the New Orleans Film Society, the New Orleans Film Festival is held in mid-October at venues from Canal Street Cinema and Prytania Theatre (Ignatius' favorite) to the Broadside. Its mission is to build a "vibrant film culture in the South." The festival programs local and national features and shorts, documentaries, and animation. There's a Second Line after the opening film.

Cost and Hours: All Access Pass for $330 for Non-Film Society members, though you can save $50 by buying early; individual tickets are presumably also available;
Tel: (504) 309-6633;
https://neworleansfilmsociety.org/festival

Now we're going to list two intriguing festivals that, while they haven't been held in a few years now, may yet raise their heads once more.

Mirliton Festival
700 Piety St.
New Orleans, LA 70177

The Mirliton Festival used to take place in November in Bywater: described as "delightfully mellow" by Michael Patrick Welch, the fest featured the creations of local chefs who had been challenged to make something yummy out of mirliton, a gourd much beloved in the Bywater neighborhood (also known as chayote). This fest began in 1989 and ran up until 2015 or 2106, so the mirliton must have something to recommend it. There was music, too, naturally. There's rumblings every now and then that the fest may return. Keep an eye on their FB page at https://www.facebook.com/MirlitonFestival/.

The Ponderosa Stomp Festival
Ace Hotel New Orleans
600 Carondelet St.
New Orleans, LA 70130

Though currently on hiatus, the Ponderosa Stomp Festival has been honoring the "unsung heroes" of garage, R&B, soul, rockabilly and country music for over 20 years now. Founded by Ira "Dr. Ike" Padnos, the fest is like some "record geek's wet dream" as Michael Patrick Welch put it in his book New Orleans: The Underground Guide. Over the years everyone from Roky Erikson to James Burton to William Bell and Teenie Hodges have played. Until the fest returns, check out their amazing project https://acloserwalknola.com site, produced in conjunction with WWOZ, which gives you amazing self-guided walks of important sites in NOLA music history.

Cost and hours: There hasn't been a Ponderosa Stomp Festival since 2017. However, keep checking their website at http://www.ponderosastomp.com: there's always a chance it'll come back.

Second Lining

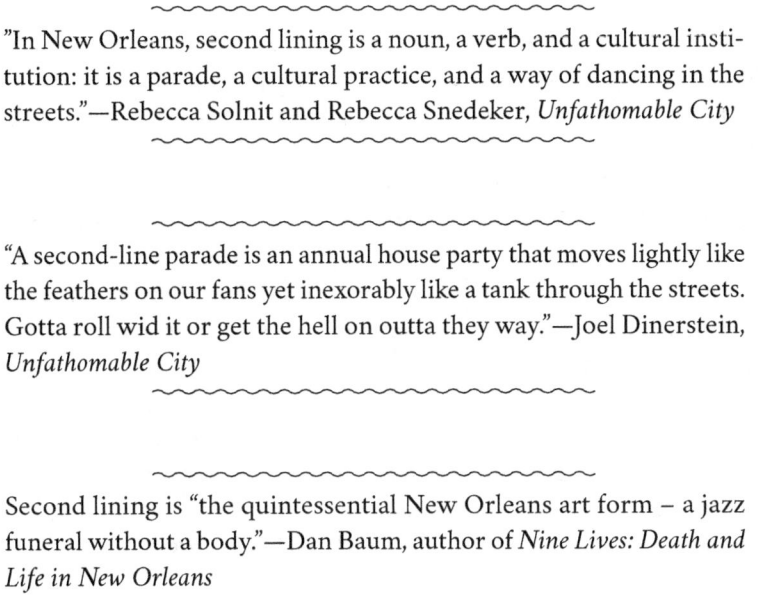

"In New Orleans, second lining is a noun, a verb, and a cultural institution: it is a parade, a cultural practice, and a way of dancing in the streets."—Rebecca Solnit and Rebecca Snedeker, *Unfathomable City*

"A second-line parade is an annual house party that moves lightly like the feathers on our fans yet inexorably like a tank through the streets. Gotta roll wid it or get the hell on outta they way."—Joel Dinerstein, *Unfathomable City*

Second lining is "the quintessential New Orleans art form – a jazz funeral without a body."—Dan Baum, author of *Nine Lives: Death and Life in New Orleans*

You've read a lot about this culture of liberation, but how can you see it in action, and not merely as a witness but as a participant? Participate in a second line parade! In fact, that's the very definition of the "second line"—it's the people like you joining in behind the parade. The brass band and the official paraders make up the "main line" or "first line." You'll enjoy the main line's colorful twirling parasols and flashy duds, as well as their cool moves, as you traipse along, taking in the carnival of life.

We participated in our first second line in 2014 under the auspices of the Prince of Wales Social Aid and Pleasure Club, a venerable Black mutual aid society (one of many such clubs, or krewes, in the Black community which are descendants of post-Civil War fraternal freedmen's societies.) Wikipedia notes that "membership benefits [in Social Aid & Pleasure Clubs] usually included a brass band for funerals and at least one public parade with music a year, so such societies became important in establishing the second line traditions." They are the second oldest parading club in the city, established in 1928 by dock and rail yard workers from the wharves and rail lines along Tchoupitoulas Street.

We've also second-lined with the Original Pigeon Town Steppers Social Aid and Pleasure Club on their annual Easter parade, in what's known as the "Pigeon Town" neighborhood (in Uptown/Carrollton).

Local musicians are forged in this street culture, the roots of which go all the way back to Congo Square. In particular, the second line dance style can be traced to the Square, the site of Sunday-afternoon African dance and drumming celebrations. There's usually folks barbecuing along the side of the road as well. Grab a sausage sammitch from a sidewalk chef and a beer from an eight-year-old.

In short, second lining is empowering as all get-out. It's freedom and ultimate pleasure. Freedom to dance however, freedom to think whatever. Freedom to laugh loud, dance hard, eat good, and party with strangers who may become friends. Take it to the streets and groove to the music.

Let's leave the second-to-last word on second lining to Joel Dinerstein of the Prince of Wales Social Aid and Pleasure Club (who, as a side note, is a professor and happens to be a white person who's been admitted into this historically Black krewe): "If a city is a circulatory system of its residents' energy—with streets like arteries and airwaves—then New Orleans is the city as dancing body, a place whose spirit is stomped into existence every Sunday."

Perhaps we should leave the very last word on the second line to the late Ronald W. Lewis, who was until his passing the curator of the House of Dance and Feathers, as well as serving as King of Krewe du Vieux (and as a member of the Krewe du Jieux). Second lines, wrote Mr. Lewis, "create a safe space for people from all walks of life to experience a moving festival of music, food, dance and song. For people who come to New Orleans from suburban places, the second line shows how to be together in shared spaces in the city, dancing together, rubbing shoulders alongside the band in the heat of the action, or walking along the edges at a leisurely pace and catching up with old friends and meeting new ones."

Second line parades jump off on Sunday afternoons. The Pigeon Toe Steppers parade usually starts around 1p at Big Man Lounge (2916 Louisiana Ave., 70115) and ends up at Merry-Go-Round Hall in Pigeon Town around 5p.

Prince of Wales usually kicks off at 1p at Carmouche's Rock Bottom Lounge (3801 Tchoupitoulas) and ends up back at Carmouche's at 5p.

For all your information about where and when to catch a second line parade while you're in town, your best resource is WWOZ's "Takin' it to the Streets" site: https://www.wwoz.org/programs/inthestreet.

Hotels

LaMothe House
621 Esplanade Ave.
New Orleans, LA 70116

Our home in New Orleans is the Lamothe House's "Marigny guest house," a beautiful Creole cottage built in the 1880s, which is just across the street from the main building, itself a historic mansion built in 1839. We always shoot for either room 401 or 409 in the guest house. Lamothe's location in the Marigny hood, just steps away from Frenchmen Street, is perfect for the music lover. While Lamothe House has three sister hotels (Inn on St. Ann, Inn on St. Peter, and Inn on Ursulines), we always stay here for the location, pool, and staff.

Tel. (504) 947-1161;
e-mail: lamothe@frenchquarterguesthouses.com;
https://www.frenchquarterguesthouses.com/our-hotels/lamothe-house;

Hotel Monteleone
214 Royal St.
New Orleans, LA 70130

With its beautiful 1886 Beaux-Arts façade (be sure to admire it on the way in), the famed "Grand Dame of the French Quarter" is our splurge stay. We once got an upgrade to the Ernest Hemingway Suite, for a reasonable fee. We had to reassure ourselves they hadn't made an error upon inspecting the room, whose French doors open right onto the rooftop pool, and whose barroom has a chandelier. But no, they actually let the likes of us sleep there.

As its website notes, the Monteleone is a "favorite haunt of distinguished Southern authors." The guest book reads like a who's who of esteemed writers, Southern and non-Southern alike: Ernest Hemingway, Tennessee Williams, William Faulkner, Truman Capote, Anne Rice, Stephen Ambrose, and John Grisham all stayed here. In fact, in June of 1999 the hotel was designated an official literary landmark by the Friends of the Library Association, which is quite a distinction. (The Plaza and Algonquin in New York are the only other hotels in the United States that share this honor.)

Another thing about the Hotel Monteleone: as you may have already gleaned from our comments above, we consider the hotel's Carousel Bar a signature NOLA experience.

One more thing. In case you're willing to put your rationalist adult emotions aside for a bit (we always are), the Hotel Monteleone is also, according to its website, one of the most haunted hotels in the U.S.: "This haunted hotel has an elevator that stops on the wrong floor, leading a curious couple down a hallway that grows chilly and reveals the ghostly images of children playing." We always do a bit of ghost hunting when we're staying here…and even when we're not.

— Karolyn: Scott and I regularly explore the Queen Anne Ballroom which is on the second floor. We pretend we're staying there because, let's be honest, we can't afford it most of the time. (Summertime, though: that's when we can afford to stay there. Give it a shot.) Anyhow, go to the Queen Anne Ballroom on the second floor and try the door. You'll find a true ballroom, suitable for, oh, I don't know, weddings or conventions etc. etc. However, if you pretend like you know what you're doing, no one will bother you. We've been several times. We've had several encounters there with a young boy we call Danny. The last time I used my camera there, not only did I record some sort of shadowy figure pass through on a video, it also drained my camera completely, even though I had just charged it—after all, it was Halloween in New Orleans and I wanted as many pictures as I could get of all the costumes. Danny! When we went over to Bourbon "O" for Scott's Ramos Gin Fizz, I asked if they happened to have a charger for my camera. They did not. I told them what happened, and the bartender shrugged and said "It *is* the Hotel Monteleone."

Tel: (504) 523-3341;
e-mail: www.hotelmonteleone.com;
https://hotelmonteleone.com

Karolyn's Tip Jar

- Cafe Du Monde is cash only. There's a "to go" line around the side, for takeout.

- Reserve your tickets for Preservation Hall in advance. The VIP seats are worth it.

- Be sure to dress up for Commander's Palace. Really, you should assume you'll have to dress nicely for reservations at any of the old-school Creole restaurants.

- If you're going to spend the day at the National World War II Museum, take your lunch break at nearby Cochon Butcher. (This worked at least in pre-Covid times, when you received a small clip-on button with your ticket which allowed for re-entry. Confirm at ticket desk.)

- Many of the higher-end restaurants run excellent fixed-price lunch specials throughout the week. Restaurant August's Friday afternoon special is particularly good—add an order of the blue crab gnocchi (unfortunately, lunch serve at August is temporary suspended). Bayona used to have a fixed-price lunch, as well. Even if they don't, going to a nice restaurant for lunch almost always gets you a cheaper meal, same quality food and service.

- Don't miss the R Bar's Friday evening crawfish boil. Tip the chef. Buy a drink. In off-season, they do shrimp boils, jambalaya or even a Mexican night.

- If you're in town for Holy Thursday, don't miss the Holy Thursday meal at Dooky Chase's. Make your reservations way in advance, though.

- For second lining, look to WWOZ's Takin' it to the Streets site for a complete schedule (https://www.wwoz.org/programs/inthestreet). Come hungry and thirsty, because a six year-old will sell you a Hurricane and a hot dog. Note that second lines sometimes do not run in the highest dog days of summer: it's just too hot.

- Mr. B's Bistro serves up $1.50 Bloody Marys until 2p on weekdays with purchase of an entree!

- Some of the best music you'll see will be on the streets, especially Royal Street. Look for Tanya Huang, late of beloved, and now retired, combo Tanya & Dorise, "somewhere on Royal Street" on Friday or Saturday afternoons (usually on the corner with Royal House oyster restaurant). You can also find the world-renowned Doreen Kitchens, who's played in the world's great halls but prefers to play on Royal in front of Rouse's (701 Royal), on Fridays or Sundays, around noon.

- When exploring graveyards, bring a gift for the musician, politician, historian, author, etc. whose grave you are visiting. He or she might like a beer, some whisky, or some smokes.

- If you can't get into Lamothe House, they do have three sister hotels under their French Quarter Guest Houses umbrella (though they don't have pools): Inn on St. Ann, Inn on St. Peter, and Inn on Ursulines.

- Lastly, if you just can't get to New Orleans to try some of their classic dishes, check out the websites of some of the restaurants we've listed above for recipes. Mr. B's Bistro's website (http://www.mrbsbistro.com) features their recipe for barbecue shrimp, and Muriel's (https://muriels.com) has a recipe for their goat cheese crepes.

CHAPTER IX

Extra Credit:

St. Louis, Missouri;

Hannibal, Missouri; and Davenport, Iowa

These three towns can easily be linked when you're burning down Highway 61. We don't have formal itineraries for them, but we do have some ideas as to what you should do and see when you're there.

ST. LOUIS, MISSOURI

"Straddling the crossroads of the Blues Highway north and the Mother Road, Route 66, west, St. Louis has seen a lot of people pass through. Jazz and bluesmen were among those who came by as they made their way north during the 'Great Migration.' St. Louis learned from these musicians and added a few of its own ingredients to the musical melting pot of Highway 61."—Richard Knight, *The Blues Highway: New Orleans to Chicago*

In the St. Louis of the turn of the 20th century, Scott Joplin was the equivalent of a modern pop star, and ragtime was the hot music of the day. Joplin's "Maple Leaf Rag" was a blockbuster circa 1904, selling reams of sheet music. A decade later, pianist Jelly Roll Morton hit town and began stomping with his New Orleans style, playing ragtime as well as light opera. His great rival W.C. Handy, though not living in the namesake city at the time, dropped "St. Louis Blues" in 1914, one of the most iconic songs in all of jazz, and which enshrined the town's name in the music lover's imagination. (It's been called "the jazzman's Hamlet.") Other great St. Louis ragtime composers/players of the day were Tom Turpin, Louis Chauvin, Artie Matthews, and George Reynolds, who live on in their compositions even if they never recorded.

While Knight notes that "East St. Louis is the real home of St. Louis blues," he concedes that there's little in that neighborhood now for music lovers. On our visit, we found good blues and food in the Soulard and Tower Grove hoods. And don't miss a visit to City Museum.

Sites and Museums

City Museum
750 N 16th St.
St. Louis, MO 63103

— Scott: City Museum must be one of the craziest, and most delightful, places in the world. The only other place I've seen which may be even half as playfully weird as the City Museum is the Ho Chi Minh Museum, in Hanoi, though Gaudi's unfinished Sagrada Familia cathedral in Barcelona is another such monument to an eccentric and singular vision. Says the St. Louis Post-Dispatch: "[The late] Bob Cassilly opened City Museum in 1997 in an abandoned shoe factory with his former wife, Gail Cassilly. Their first mission statement: 'To reawaken the childlike imagination, joy and sense of wonder in all of us.'" Even its fence is fanciful: in fact, the serpentine wall is the very first part Cassilly sculpted.

We'd recommend starting on the rooftop, which holds a panoply of wonders. There's a 1940s Ferris wheel that they hoisted up, piece by piece. A school bus is perched vertiginously on the edge of the roof, looking as it it's about to spill over the side of the building. You can climb in and look through the bus door, which hangs open, and imagine plummeting down to the parking lot. (There's a grate over the opening: like a lot of City Museum, it's meant to give the thrill of danger without actually being dangerous). An airplane is part of MonstroCity, a "jungle gym in the sky." Cassilly's praying mantis sculpture presides over all this fun.

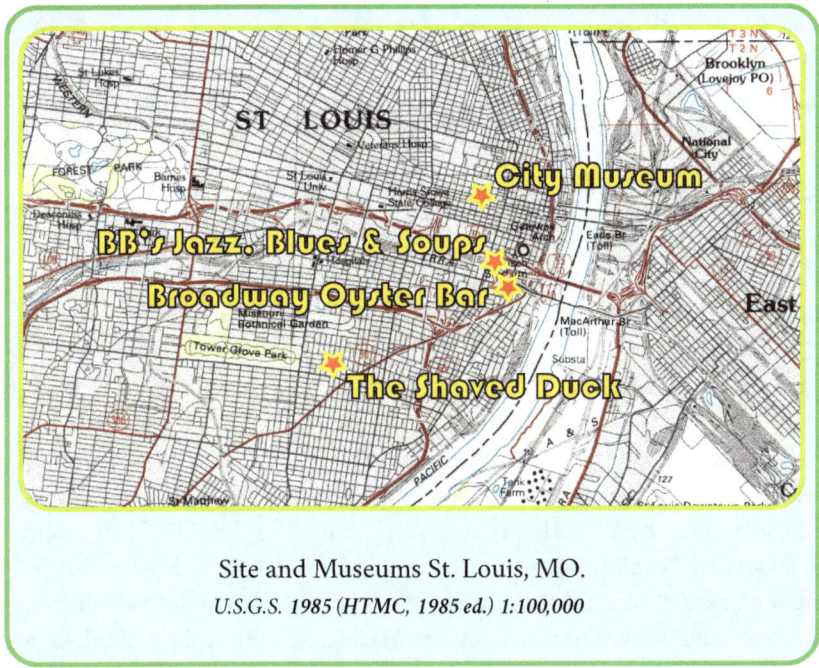

Site and Museums St. Louis, MO.
U.S.G.S. 1985 (HTMC, 1985 ed.) 1:100,000

"[Bob] Cassilly built City Museum with salvaged remnants from St. Louis' rich architectural history," wrote Diane Toroian Keaggy in the St. Louis Post-Dispatch. Indeed, inside Scott found all manner of salvaged architectural elements, such as cornices of a demolished historic building from Chicago's LaSalle street.

There's a World Aquarium, with the likes of stingrays, sharks and sea turtles, as well as the legendary "Puking Pig," a rather phallic character who is perpetually filling with water, tipping over and upchucking a torrent of water into the pond.

You can slide from the roof all the way down into the caves, as Scott did. Be sure to explore these Enchanted Tunnels and Caves, hand carved by Cassilly and crew. There's a wonder around every turn. Indeed, as Scott explored, he passed many an entranced groups of kids. It's like Alice in Wonderland come to life. The visionary Cassilly, who died in 2011, dreamed of creating a "warehouse of fun" out of an old shoe factory, and he did it—the City Museum is as if a child dreamed the most wonderful fort they could have ever imagined, and it came true.

Cost and hours: Su-Th 10a-6p, F-Sa 10a-10p; tickets at the gate: $20.00 (plus tax) ages 3 years and up (children age 2 and under admitted free). Online in Advance: $18.00 (plus tax) ages 3 years and up (children age 2 and under admitted free), guests may purchase $8 rooftop add-on at the gate;
Tel. (314) 231-2489;

https://www.citymuseum.org

National Blues Museum
615 Washington Ave.
St. Louis, MO 63101

We've seen a lot of music museums, and while this one isn't the foremost among them, it is still very much worth a visit for the blues lover. You'll see sheet music by W.C. Handy and, yes, "Maple Leaf Rag" by Scott Joplin. You'll also find exhibits for relatively unsung figures, such as Mickey Rogers' hat: a placard reads that Rogers "spent his youth straddling the Delta and Chicago," and he used to jam at Silvio's in Chicago with Hubert Sumlin and Howlin' Wolf. Elsewhere, there's a tribute to Big George Brock, who grew up near Clarksdale—one of our favorite towns. To its credit, the National Blues Museum highlights early blueswomen. "Mamie Smith and her Jazz Hounds' 1920 smash hit 'Crazy Blues' was the first blues recording by an African-American vocalist," reads one exhibit. It's got interactive touch-screen stations and video tutorials which guide you toward making music of your own, using percussion instruments provided. Learning to play jug band music was fun. Karolyn proved a natural on the spoons. (Scott's bid to rock the "bones" was not as successful.) At another touch screen you get to play a little guided blues piano (the virtual keys you're meant to press light up), while also learning about great pianists representing regional styles: Roosevelt Sykes (St. Louis); Little Brother Montgomery (Mississippi); Memphis Slim (Memphis, naturally); Otis Spann (Chicago); Count Basie (Kansas City); and Amos Milburn (California).

Cost and hours: Every day 12p-5p; Adult $15, Seniors, Veterans & Active Military $12, College Students, Children 5 and over $10, Members & Children under 5 Free; Tel. (314) 231-2489; https://nationalbluesmuseum.org

Scott Joplin House
2658 Delmar Blvd.
St. Louis, MO 63103

A state historic site, this house on Delmar Boulevard (then Morgan Street) is where Scott Joplin moved in 1900 after his "Maple Leaf Rag" had become the *fin de siecle* equivalent of a Top 40 hit. Your present writer, Scott, learned to play piano through playing Scott Joplin songs; I never thought I'd actually stand outside his house. Joplin "remains the undisputed king of ragtime piano and penned classics such as 'Maple Leaf Rag,' 'The Entertainer' and 'Easy Winners' while living in St. Louis," writes Richard Knight. Joplin's publisher, Stark, sold sheet music as fast as a modern record label could hope to sell compact discs (or the streaming equivalent).

Cost and hours: March through October: 10 a-4 p, M-Sa., closed Su.; closed November through January; February: 10 a-4 p, Tu-Sa., closed Su. and M; Tour Times: 10a, 11a, 12 p, 1 p, 2p, and 3, Tour cost: 18-Adults: $6 6-17: $4, Group Adult: $5, Group Youth: $3

Cathedral Basilica of St. Louis
4431 Lindell Blvd
St. Louis, MO 63108

The word "awesome" should be used with the utmost discretion. Few things in life are, in fact, awesome. One such thing is the gorgeous Cathedral Basilica of St. Louis, which happens to boast the world's largest collection of mosaics. If you can't make it to St. Mark's in Venice, the Byzantine basilica is, seriously, in contention with it for the adjective "eye-popping." Inside, it's a divine vision of glowing gold. Byzantine craftsmen perfected that gold background effect by baking gold leaf into the tiny tesserae, says Rick Steves—tesserae being the small cubes of colored stone or glass which make up mosaics. Steves was describing St. Mark's, but the craftsmen who created the mosaics for the St. Louis basilica were surely equally masters of their craft. The textures and colors reminded Scott of the sensory experience of strolling through great European churches. The bishop's chair or 'cathedra' is on the west side of the sanctuary dominated by the white marble figure of Christ crucified. (It is this chair that makes this church a cathedral.) The large structure over the main altar is the 'baldacchino' whose top dome imitates the main exterior dome of the Cathedral. Make sure to gaze up at the Central Dome, featuring such scenes as "the woman of the Apocalypse" (South side) and "Elias taken up to heaven in the fiery chariot: (West side).

Cost and hours: Every day 7a-5p for self-guided touring; Guided tours by appointment typically available during weekdays between 10a-3p, Sunday Tours following the completion of noon Mass are open to the public and do not require reservations;

Tel: (314) 373-8241;

cathedralstl.org

Restaurants

Broadway Oyster Bar
736 S Broadway St.
St. Louis, MO 63102

In the Soulard neighborhood, this cozy spot is inspired by Delta juke joints and the city of New Orleans, thus bringing together two of our favorite atmospheres. Enjoy the alligator sausage & shrimp cheesecake, the char-grilled oysters, and the Prince Edward Island mussels.

BB's Jazz, Blues and Soups
700 S Broadway St.
St. Louis, MO 63102

Next door to the Broadway Oyster Bar, the venerable BB's Jazz, Blues and Soups is a St. Louis institution, long known for hosting the town's best blues and jazz. In *The Blues Highway*, Richard Knight calls BB's the "most respected of Soulard's venues." We tried the soups, which were indeed delicious—Karolyn had a sweet potato soup and Scott had a saliva- inducing shrimp bisque. BB's is also as good a place as any to try toasted ravioli, a St. Louis staple. For the live blues accompanying the soups, we caught Joe Metzka, who jammed. He has a sweet touch on the guitar.

Frazer's Restaurant and Lounge
1811 Pestalozzi St.
St. Louis, MO 63118

Tipped off by a local, we discovered this excellent restaurant right down the street from the Venice Cafe. The menu features daily specials based on whatever's fresh, especially seafood. On the day we visited, that meant tasty blackened swordfish, slaw and red beans 'n' rice. We had oysters, as well. Hey, this crew never turns down oysters!

Pappy's Smokehouse
3106 Olive St.
St. Louis, MO 63103

Long venerated for its Memphis-style BBQ, Pappy's ribs are slow-smoked with brown sugar dry rub. Scott recommends the platter of ribs and burnt ends. If you're up for it, try a rather unique side: deep-fried corn on the cob!

The Shaved Duck
2900 Virginia Ave.
St. Louis, MO 63118

Over in the Tower Grove hood, The Shaved Duck is a joint that's all about "bbq, folk & soul." We still salivate when we think of the duck confit, which is evoked nicely by the menu's description: "Thigh slowly poached in duck fat, served over greens in cider molasses with grilled bread." Karolyn, a connoisseur of mac 'n' cheese, gives her seal of approval to the Shaved Duck's "famous" version of one of her most beloved dishes. Quite simply, the food here will make you happy.

Schlafly Tap Room
2100 Locust St.
St. Louis, MO 63103

Scott enjoyed a piping hot Shepherd's pie and a brew here.

Music, Bars, and the Rest

Venice Cafe
1903 Pestalozzi St.
St. Louis, MO 63118

This funky spot in the Soulard hood is a great spot for live music. It didn't surprise us to find out that the wild 'n' weird world of the Venice Cafe was co-created by some of the same eccentric visionaries who worked on the one-of-a-kind City Museum. Enjoy your beer amid fanciful, colorful mosaics and sculptures by Sharon von Senden and owner Jeff Lockheed. Sculptor Bob Cassilly, who created the City Museum, liked their work so much that he asked them to make some pieces for him to put in his museum. In turn, Cassilly gave the Venice Cafe a few of his fun and funky sculptures—check out the big frog. With the stage thus set, the fact that you also get to enjoy live music is a lagniappe. You can even watch the music from the rafters, so to speak, if you go up to the mezzanine.

BB's Jazz, Blues and Soups
700 S Broadway St.
St. Louis, MO 63102

See entry above.

HANNIBAL, MISSOURI

We passed through Hannibal, famous for being Mark Twain's hometown, on our way from St. Louis to Davenport. We scrambled up the banks of the Mississippi, from which point we could survey a well-known former brothel—it's still got a red light affixed to the wall. (Taverns with upstairs brothels were apparently a big draw for river travelers in the '20s, and Hannibal had a hopping vice district.) For many decades, this particular bordello had been converted into Lula Belle's restaurant and b&b, sadly closed now (and then the Riverside restaurant, which has since also closed.) The building is said to be quite haunted, naturally; hopefully, someone will open something new there soon. In the meantime, it's worth a stop to knock around in Twain's boyhood haunts, a bit like walking in Shakespeare's footsteps along the Thames.

Finn's Food and Spirits
214 N Main St.
Hannibal, MO 63401

On the main street of town, we dropped in at Finn's and had a good catfish hoagie and onion rings.

DAVENPORT, IOWA

In the 1920s, jazz musicians used to come up the Mississippi River on steamboats all the way from New Orleans, stopping off at ports like Davenport, giving the city its own musical heritage. We enjoyed our time in this one-quarter of the Quad Cities (the other three towns are Bettendorf on the Iowa side of the Mississippi, and Rock Island and Moline on the Illinois side). You can pick up Highway 61 down along the riverbank.

Sites and Museums

Bix Beiderbecke Museum and World Archives
129 N Main St
Davenport, IA 52801

This museum is a real feather in Davenport's cap. It is everything a dedicated museum should be: focused, personal and illuminating, with a good collection of artifacts. It is concise but rich in detail, and you come away knowing a lot more about Bix Beiderbecke and his brief, but brilliant, life and times. Born in 1903, Bix Beiderbecke was a native son of Davenport, a great cornetist and one of jazz's true innovators.

We start with an exhibit on The Coliseum Ballroom, popularly known as "the Col." Opened in 1914 and still extant a few blocks away from the museum (though now closed), it was once a great local jazz hall where the likes of Duke Ellington and Louis Armstrong played.

Next we come to an exhibit on young Bix's sojourns into Chicago. Note an original banner from Chicago's Royal Gardens Orchestra. A teenage Bix would sneak into clubs like that. When we took a "Jazz, Blues & Beyond" tour in Chicago, our hometown, we passed the original site of Royal (later Lincoln) Gardens on 31st Street on the South Side. It was one of the "Black and Tan Clubs," where, even in the early '20s, Blacks and whites were free to mingle, dance and listen to music. The likes of Joe "King" Oliver's Creole Jazz Band, featuring New Orleans' own Louis Armstrong, kept 'em dancing. Elsewhere in the museum, Hoagy Carmichael testifies to the effect seeing Armstrong had on young Bix: "Bix was on his feet, his eyes popping...Every note Louis hit was perfection." On other occasions, teenage Bix would sneak into speakeasies like the Friar's Inn to hear "hot jazz," occasionally jamming with the band that would become the New Orleans Rhythm Kings.

Study the instructive timeline. 1920, in particular, stands out as a big year for jazz and blues: King Oliver formed the Creole Jazz Band in Chicago, Mamie Smith launched the "blues craze" with her recording of "The Crazy Blues," and Charlie Parker was born.

Find the exhibit for Beiderbecke and Frank Trumbauer ("Tram"), showing the two men at the Arcadia Ballroom in St. Louis in 1925. They went on to play together in the legendary Jean Goldkette Orchestra at Hudson Lake, an Indiana resort, in the summer of '26. A placard commemorates "the best Jean Goldkette band ever": Bix on cornet, Tram on saxophone and Pee Wee Russell on clarinet. Talk about hot!

Have a look at Chauncey Moore's Conga Drum. A placard reads: "The Goldkette drummer owned this painted conga drum and was a serious student of African drumming. He is credited with recording the first drum solo in 1923."

Be sure to check the mirror that shows the back of Eddie Condon's mandolin: you'll see his secret compartment for hiding a bottle of whiskey! Condon, a young banjo player, became one of Bix's great friends.

The museum's exhibits also spotlight great musicians like Red Nichols (who is called the *second* most influential cornetist, after Bix), trombonist Miff

Mole, Eddie Lang (the "father of jazz guitar"), virtuoso violinist Joe Venuti, bass saxophonist Adrian Rollini, and trombonist/singer Jack Teagarden.

An exhibit commemorates Bix's "masterpieces," the recordings he made in New York in 1927 and 1928 with old friends like Trumbauer and the Paul Whiteman Orchestra. Sadly, Bix had very little time left. Tram's enduring friendship with Bix is perhaps the key theme wending through the museum. He always tried to help his friend during Bix's brief but brilliant life. Indeed, at the museum's final stop, an exhibit about Bix's new apartment in New York—where he died in 1931 at the age of 27 from some combination of pneumonia, edema and chronic alcoholism—we are told that when Bix died, Tram said, "I was always there for him. Why didn't he call me?"

Restaurants

The 11th Street Precinct Bar & Grill
2108 E 11th Street & 1107 Mound St.
Davenport, Iowa 52803

Over in the Village of East Davenport, the 11th Street boasts that they have "the best onion rings in town," and we can attest that they were pretty damn good.

Wide River Winery Village of East Davenport
1128 Mound St.
Davenport, Iowa 52803

Knocking around in the Village of East Davenport, we came upon a winery. In Iowa. Yes, Iowa. The hostess was very nice indeed, though the wines we tasted were rather too sweet for our palettes. Still, stop in and see what you think.

Antonella's Restaurant
112 W 3rd St.
Davenport, Iowa 52801

There are still days when Scott thinks wistfully of Antonella's Sicilian style pizza, and sighs.

CHAPTER X.

Extra Credit: Nashville

If you want a side trip from Highway 61, consider Nashville, another center of American roots music. It's about an eight-hour drive to Nashville from New Orleans, or about three hours from Memphis. When you're in Nashville, Lower Broadway—a.k.a Honky Tonk Row—is the place to be. Grab a Bud Light and get into the spirit of things.

PLANNING YOUR TIME: ITINERARIES

Day One
Morning/Afternoon

Drive the eight hours from New Orleans to Nashville.

Evening

Head to Tootsies Orchid Lounge.

Day Two
Morning

Tour the Ryman Auditorium.

Lunch

Grab a bite at Broadway Brewhouse.

Visit the Country Music Hall of Fame.

Evening

Dinner at Jack's Bar-B-Que will fill you up. Head to Robert's Western World.

SITES AND MUSEUMS

Ryman Auditorium
116 Rep. John Lewis Way N.
Nashville, TN 37219

No trip to Nashville is complete without a stroll around the curving oak pews in the legendary Ryman Auditorium, est. 1892—"the mother church of country music." The backstage tour culminates in your standing in the wings of the Ryman stage itself. Talk about a goose-bumps moment—you can't help but think of all those who have trod these boards before!

Check out the great origin story of the Ryman. The nutshell version, from its website: "According to legend, Thomas Ryman was fed up with Sam Jones' preaching against drinking and gambling, so he and a few friends went to Jones' tent revival to raise a ruckus. But something in Jones' speech affected Ryman so deeply that he repented his sins and vowed to build Jones a great tabernacle so that he would never again have to preach under a tent in Nashville."

While the Ryman is associated with country music, it had a storied history even before it became the home of the Grand Ole Opry. Over the years, the boards of its stage have been trod by purveyors of opera, theater, comedy, magic shows, and more. It was also a venue for speeches and lectures. Hellen Keller and her teacher Anne Sullivan spoke here…on the virtues of socialism. "We are successful so far as we help each other," said Keller from the stage of the Ryman. "My teacher has given me an opportunity to live and work, and that is what people with five senses should give each other. We can and must help each other. That's why I am a socialist."

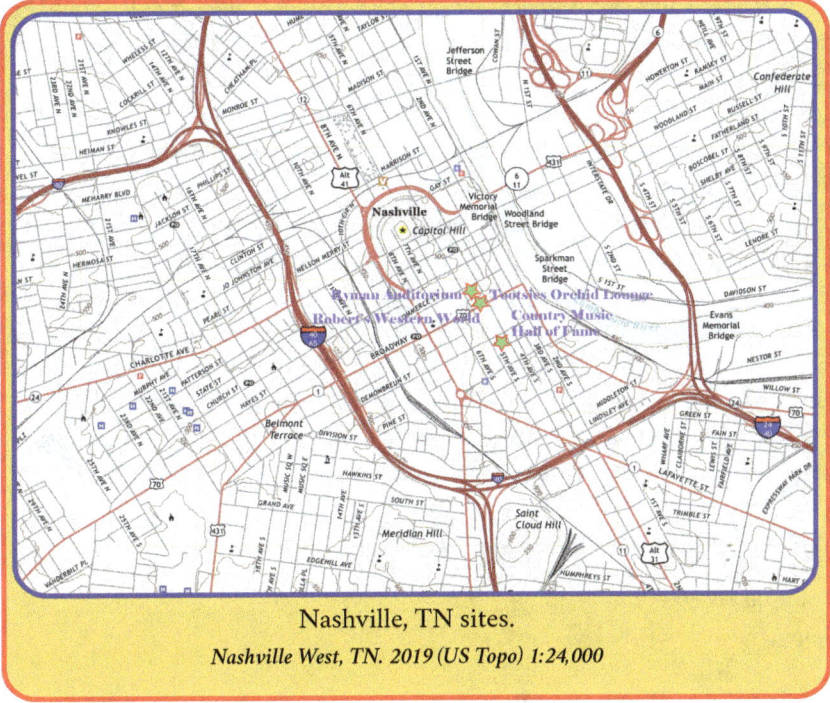

Nashville, TN sites.

Nashville West, TN. 2019 (US Topo) 1:24,000

The Ryman boasts a museum of fascinating exhibits. You'll learn, for example, that Minnie Pearl was not a real person but a character created by the actress Sarah Ophelia Colley, and that an actress still appears in Minnie Pearl garb at the Opry, despite Colley's death—it was her wish that the character never die. An exhibit for Hank Williams notes that he got a standing ovation and six encores at his first appearance on the Grand Ole Opry in 1949: no one else has even come close since. You'll see Webb Pierce's guitar. Pierce ("In the Jailhouse Now," "There Stands the Glass") was one of the most popular honky-tonkers of the '50s, known for his amazing Nudie suits.

Speaking of Nudie suits, you'll see some great ones at the museum. These were the glittering, embroidered works of art decorated with colorful birds and flowers created by Nudie Cohn, and worn by the likes of Elvis Presley, Marty Robbins, and Graham Parsons (his famously featured pills, syringes, and pot leaves.)

You'll see an exhibit for the groundbreaking *Johnny Cash Show*, which featured guests such as Bob Dylan, Joni Mitchell, The Who, Derek & the Dominos, and Stevie Wonder. The 1971 special "Johnny Cash on Campus" episode showed Cash engaging with college students and addressing the "generation gap" and youth culture. On display are missing lyrics for "What is Truth?," which he wrote especially for that episode. Cash had Pete Seeger on, even though the network balked at featuring the anti-war Seeger. Louis Armstrong was a guest, playing Jimmie Rodgers' "Blue Yodel #9."

Outside the Ryman, note a marker for "The Birth of Bluegrass" in '45. Said birth was midwifed by Bill Monroe, who brought together Lester Flatt on guitar and Earl Scruggs on banjo (along with Chubby Wise on fiddle and Howard Watts on bass). With Monroe on mandolin, these men created this new musical form when they took the stage as "The Original Bluegrass Band."

Cost and hours: Visit anytime between 9a and 4p every day with ticket; about $25.00 for adults, about $16 for children age 4 to 11;
Tel. (615) 889-3060;

https://ryman.com

Country Music Hall of Fame
222 Rep. John Lewis Way S.
Nashville, TN 37203

This museum is eye-opening for what you'll learn about country's tangled roots, which date back to the British Isles. British settlers brought their folksongs and fiddle tunes with them as they sailed westward to the New World, songs of "shipwrecks, floods, bandits, and murderers" and ballads like "Barbara Allen," sounding its timeless theme of romantic love.

Once in America, these roots got mixed up with the music of other immigrants and also with that of African-Americans. To its credit, the museum strongly emphasizes this latter theme. "Since Colonial times, African Americans have strongly influenced country music," declares one exhibit. Black and white players "sometimes worked together in the same rural stringbands." One of our favorite photographs depicts two African-American soldiers of the Spanish-American War with guitars. These Buffalo Soldiers, says a placard, "helped popularize the guitar."

Complicating our preconceptions even more, much of the music we think of as being born in the Southern hills was actually often created by Northern professionals fabricating folk-sounding songs, and played in tent shows and/or by blackface minstrels on fiddles and homemade banjos.

Interesting and/or revelatory items in this collection for which to be on the lookout include an early 1900s Minstrel Show Guide; Cindy Walker's decoupage typewriter, with which she composed hits for Eddy Arnold, Jim Reeves, Ernest Tubbs, and many others; Merle Travis's guitar; and Nathan Turk's bespoke suits for Buck Owens and the Buckaroos, icons of Westernwear. Check out a poster for Glen Campbell, along with John Wayne and Kim Darby, in *True Grit*: "the strangest trio ever to track a killer." Campbell acted in other pictures as well, playing a guitarist in Steve McQueen's band in *Baby, The Rain Must Fall*.

And speaking of Buck Owens, don't miss an interesting exhibit for the one town almost as famous in country lore as Nashville: Bakersfield, California, which produced such hit acts as not only Owens and the Buckaroos, but also Merle Haggard and the Strangers. Located near the southern end of the San Joaquin Valley, Bakersfield is the seat of Kern County, "one of America's leading producers of cotton, grapes, citrus, almonds, and oil." Beginning in the '30s, its orchards and oilfields lured displaced workers from the South, Southwest and Midwest who'd been buffeted by the Dust Bowl and the Great Depression. As a placard notes, "Some of these migrants and their children—disparaged as 'Okies' by other residents—became the creators of Bakersfield's best-known export: country music." By 1960, Bakersfield was challenging Nashville for chart supremacy.

The museum even boasts the black Pontiac Firebird Trans Am from *Smokey and the Bandit II*. If you're like us, this triggers a memory of the Springsteen lyric, "Even Burt Reynolds in a black Trans Am..."

Finally, stand in the circular atrium itself and spin slowly, gazing upon the plaques for all of the inductees into the Country Music Hall of Fame. Ask yourself, "Will the circle be unbroken?"

Cost and hours: 9a-5p every day, entries timed ever 15 minutes; about $28.00 for adults, about $18 for youth for the basic admission; for $20 more per ticket, you can now add a Historic RCA Studio B Tour (this would be interesting) or a tour of poster-makers Hatch Printers; for a whopping $67.95 (adult) or $52.95 (youth), you can get the whole package.

Tel. (615) 889-3060;

https://ryman.com

Ernest Tubb Record Shop
417 Broadway
Nashville, TN 37203

Established in 1947, this record shop devoted to country was founded by Ernest Tubb, one of the cats who developed the genre. (His big hit was "Walking the Floor Over You.") He also nurtured talent through his own Midnight Jamboree radio show, which broadcast before a live audience immediately after the Grand Ole Opry on station WSM and showcased for the most part deserving young hopefuls and their latest record releases. The Midnight Jamboree continues to this day, WSM's second-longest continuous broadcast. At the record shop, while you're filling the holes in your country collection, check out the display TV which perpetually shows a video of the great Leon Rhodes and Buddy Charleton of Tubb's band the Texas Troubadours, playing on *The Ernest Tubb Show* of the mid-60s. You'll also see the great Pete Drake's steel guitar. Drake played on jams like Charlie Rich's "Behind Closed Doors," Bob Dylan's "Lay Lady Lay" and Tammy Wynette's "Stand by Your Man," among many others.

Andrew Jackson's Hermitage
4580 Rachel's Lane
Hermitage, TN 37076

We overheard a local, Michael Oates Palmer, recommend a visit to Andrew Jackson's mansion, located 20 minutes outside of Nashville. Quoth Mr. Palmer, it "is crazy fascinating, including watching it as a case study in museums trying to adapt to the general consensus that the once vaunted inhabitant of the place was an awful human being." It's open Th-M from 9a to 6p, with the adult tour price of $24.

Betty Boots
321 Broadway
Nashville, TN 37203

A women's western-wear store, which boasts of being the only such shop in the country.

Parnassus Books
3900 Hillsboro Pike #14
Nashville, TN 37215

This is author Ann Patchett's bookstore, which we've heard is lovely. It's open M to Sa from 10a-6p and on Su from 12p-6p.

RESTAURANTS

Jack's Bar-B-Que on Broadway
416 Broadway
Nashville, TN 37203

This full-service BBQ buffet offers a beautiful spread of soul. You'll end up with plates of ribs, chicken, beans, potato salad, mac 'n' cheese, and corn bread. There are six sauces to choose from, everything from Tennessee Original to Music City White Sauce to "XXX-911" (judging by that name, you know it's got a kick!).

Arnold's Country Chicken
605 8th Avenue South
Nashville, TN 37023

Arnold's Country Kitchen's motto is "home-cooking since 1982." Some say that Arnold's might well be the best "meat and three" joint in the South. That's a cafeteria-style diner where you pick your meat, then pick your three sides. Special meats and sides vary from day-to-day, while other staples are available every day. There's always a choice of vegetables and starches like mac 'n' cheese or spaghetti. You'll want some cornbread and sweet tea to mop it all up and wash it down. Arnold's was also John Prine's favorite restaurant in the whole world.

Hattie B's
(Locations throughout Nashville)

Hot chicken is a Nashville specialty, and Hattie B's is famous for their fiery fried yardbird.

Prince's Hot Chicken Shack South
5814 Nolensville Pike #110
Nashville, TN 37211

One of the original hot chicken spots features eight flavors, everything from plain, to light mild, to hot, to XXX hot. We've been warned not to go hotter than "mild"—but Scott takes that as a challenge.

Biscuit Love in the Gulch
316 11th Ave S.
Nashville, TN 37203

A beloved local breakfast place, but get there early to avoid the line.

Husk
37 Rutledge St.
Nashville, TN 37210

A farm-to-table restaurant which insists on all fresh, local Southern ingredients.

Wendell Smith's Restaurant
407 53rd Ave N
Nashville, TN 37209

Another contender for the best meat and three spot in Nashville. This one's been around 65 years and counting and is much beloved by locals.

Martin's Bar-B-Que Joint
410 4th Avenue S
Nashville, TN 37201

"West Tennessee's legendary whole-hog BBQ tradition is the cornerstone of Martin's Bar-B-Que Joint," proclaims this joint, whose site goes on to explain that a fresh hog goes on their pit every day for the next day. Everything's cooked fresh, and their goal is to run out of food on the same day it's prepared.

Rolf and Daughters
700 Taylor Street
Nashville, TN 37208

A seasonal-ingredients-based restaurant featuring Italian and Asian influences.

The City House
1222 4th Avenue N
Nashville, TN 37208

A rustic, seasonal Italian place featuring gourmet pizzas.

Broadway Brewhouse
317 Broadway
Nashville, TN 37201

Craft beers and pub grub on Broadway.

MUSIC, BARS AND THE REST

Tootsies Orchid Lounge
422 Broadway
Nashville, TN 37203

Tootsies (no apostrophe) is a name that rings out in honky-tonk lore—and is a mecca for country fans. Since the Grand Ole Opry was "dry," performers used to nip across the alley from the Ryman to Tootsies to wet their whistles. (You can, literally, walk in their footsteps—check out the footsteps painted onto the sidewalk outside.) Tootsies is historic, and the stories are legion of country legends who have stood on its stage or drank at the bar. Jon Langford has referred to Tootsies as some kind of great "country music mausoleum" with its wall of pictures under "layers of nicotine snot." We always like to study this "Wall of Fame," the yellowing, framed pictures on the walls, and in fact seeing it when he first came to America inspired Langford to paint his own well-known portraits of honky-tonk icons. Scanning the wall, you'll see the likes of Roy Acuff with Howdy Forrester, a fiddler in Acuff's Smoky Mountain Boys. There are record covers, as well: here is Martha Carson's "A Talk With the Lord"; there is "I'll Take The Dog" by Jean Shepard and Ray Pillow.

Whenever we visit Tootsies we're impressed by how, after playing a song, the band will give props to the songwriter and/or singer who created it. We remember the night the band played a Keith Whitley song and then made sure to talk about him several times afterwards. There's a real sense of tradition.

A tip: Tootsies' 3rd floor is a rockin' spot that not every one knows about. You'll find stairs leading up to the 3rd floor on the side of the building.'

Tel: (615) 726-0463

Tootsies.net

Robert's Western World
416B Broadway
Nashville, TN 37203

Many years ago BR5-49 was the house band at Robert's Western World, a band Karolyn saw play many times in Chicago. Today it's Brazilbilly, who play "traditional country music with a Latin flair," led by "Brazilian hillbilly" Jesse Lee Jones, who also owns the place. The walls are adorned with posters featuring pro-Brazilbilly rockabilly girls as well as shelves of cowboy boots, which you can buy.

Tel: (615) 244-9552

robertswesternworld.com

Pinewood Social
33 Peabody St.

Nashville, TN 37210

Pinewood features good food and an expansive bar—and also a bowling alley.

Tel: (615) 751-8111

https:www.pinewoodsocial.com

Nashville is also home to a tradition of songwriters' clubs, which makes sense for a town to which many singer/songwriters move in the hopes of getting their big break in the music business. Both of the following venues are examples of such, and are tops for live music.

The Bluebird Cafe
4104 Hillsboro Pike
Nashville, TN 37215

Songwriters such as Cowboy Junkies, Willie Nelson, Kris Kristofferson, Taylor Swift, and Garth Brooks have all graced the Bluebird Cafe stage— often, when they were just getting started—and they return to play even as superstars. Swift, for one, was discovered here. However, the heart of what the Bluebird does is to support up-and-coming songwriters, which it does through showcases such as an open mic night on Mondays, writers' night on Sundays, and in-the-round nights from Tuesday through Saturday. They also feature a healthy menu (in Nashville!) and beer and wine.

Tel: (615) 383-1461

https://bluebirdcafe.com

The Listening Room Cafe
618 4th Avenue South
Nashville, TN 37210

Original live songs are the main attraction here: it's asked that table conversations be kept to a whisper. This venue's pride is the meticulous sound quality of the room, the better to showcase the musicians and the music. While you listen, you can order from a full menu of quality food and drink.

Tel: (615) 259-3600

CHAPTER XI.

Chicago, Illinois

Ah, Chicago—our hometown. The first thing we should tell you is that, as a blues town, the old days are gone. Suffice it to say that if you've read the chapter "Juke Joint Blues (Chicago 1977)" in Peter Guralnick's essential book *Lost Highway: Journeys and Arrivals of American Musicians*, you won't find any of those clubs still in operation. Florence's Lounge, the Expressway Lounge, Theresa's, the Flamingo Club, the Queen Bee I and II, Ma Bea's, the Golden Slipper, Big Duke's, the 1815 Club, Silvio's, even Wise Fools Pub—they're all gone now. Even an effort to revive the old Checkerboard Lounge expired in 2015.

Pioneering blues and jazz record labels like Bruce Iglauer's Alligator and (the late, great) Bob Koester's Delmark are still here and plugging on, but other historic labels like Chess and Vee Jay are gone—and have been for nearly 50 years.

Today, the music that once could be heard ringing out on the West and South Sides is now heard and consumed mainly by connoisseurs on the North Side, although when Lee's Unleaded Blues was still going on the South Side as recently as a decade ago, it attracted locals as well as U of C students. Perhaps someone will revive it.

All that said, Chicago is still a happening blues town. Before we get to that, let's start with a roll call of the original G.O.A.T.s ("greatest of all time") of Chicago blues, almost all dead now.

First there were the pioneers: Memphis Minnie (b. 1897), Tampa Red (1903), Sunnyland Slim (1906), and Big Bill Broonzy (1893).

Then there was the second, and arguably the greatest, generation: Muddy Waters (b. 1913) (the "Father of Chicago Blues"), Howlin' Wolf (1910), Willie Dixon (1915), Sonny Boys Williamson I (1914) and II (1912), Johnny Shines (1915) and Elmore James (1918).

Of the third generation of great Chicago blues players, the ones born in the '20s and '30s, a few are still with us. Buddy Guy (b. 1936), the most important living Chicago bluesman, is still going strong. Billy Boy Arnold (1935) still blows his harp. Tail Dragger Jones is a great Chicago bluesman who's still doing it at the age of 82. We were lucky enough to see the great West Side guitarist Jimmy Johnson a few years ago at B.L.U.E.S. on Halsted. Born in 1928, he was a mere 90 when we saw him. He was still playing weekly gigs up to the age of 93; the great man finally passed away in 2022.

Let's pause, then, for a roll call of the members of that generation no longer with us, please: Big Walter Horton (b. 1921), Eddie Taylor (1923), Jimmy Reed (1925), Otis Spann (1924 or 1930), Koko Taylor (1928), Little Walter (1930), Earl Hooker (1930), Otis Rush (1934), Magic Sam (1937), Eddy Clearwater (1935), Hubert Sumlin (1931), and Lonnie Brooks (1933).

To bring it all back to the present day, the spark of the blues is not dead in Chicago. At any weekend at Rosa's, you'll find musicians keeping the spirit alive. Toranzo Cannon, in his mid-50s, is a fiery guitarist and upholder of the Chicago way. Melvin Taylor is still keeping it real. Nellie "Tiger" Travis is out there doing her thing, and Billy Branch and the Sons of Blues are still among the foremost exponents of the blues. As you'll see below, there are a host of clubs and festivals and institutions keeping the living blues going.

SITES AND MUSEUMS

Willie Dixon's Blues Heaven Foundation
2120 S. Michigan Ave.
Chicago, IL 60616

Immortalized by the Rolling Stones in (instrumental) song, 2120 S. Michigan Avenue is, of course, where the building that housed Chess records stood, and still stands. (The Stones recorded the track here, in fact.) The building is now named in honor of Willie Dixon, who wrote most of the iconic Chess songs everyone knows and loves (except the Chuck Berry ones—Chuck wrote his own). Think "Hoochie Coochie Man," "My Babe," "Wang Dang Doodle," "Backdoor Man," "Little Red Rooster," and on and on. He produced and arranged them as well, and he was also the house bassist and the A & R (artists & repertoire) man, to boot.

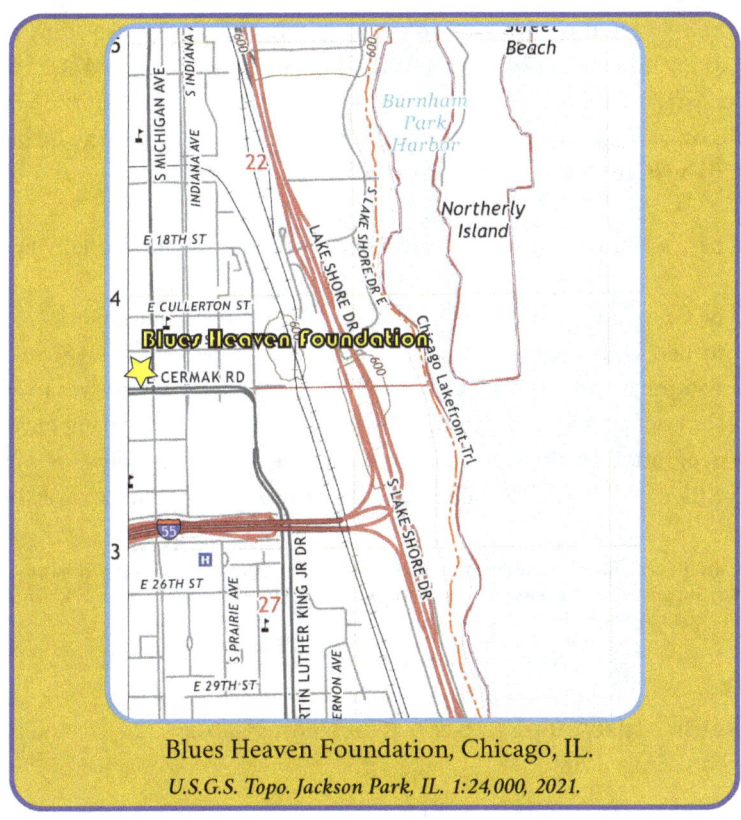

Blues Heaven Foundation, Chicago, IL.
U.S.G.S. Topo. Jackson Park, IL. 1:24,000, 2021.

Chess is one of the handful of places that can legitimately make a claim to being one of the birthplaces of rock 'n' roll, Berry having recorded "Johnny B. Goode" here. Founded and run by brothers Leonard and Phil Chess, Chess Records produced quite simply some of the most influential music of all time, particularly in the '50s. (See more on Chess in our report from the Jazz, Blues & Beyond bus tour below.) To tread these boards and scurry up the uneven stairway is to breathe in that rarified air where Muddy Waters, Etta James, Koko Taylor, Jimmy Rogers, Howlin' Wolf, Chuck Berry, and Bo Diddley worked their magic. (Scott's been twice.)

Your visit includes an introductory video, after which you can knock about and look at some exhibits: a guitar signed by Buddy Guy here, Koko Taylor's dress there. The wall of "Life Cast Portraits" of blues icons' heads is striking, including one of Taj Mahal that caught our eye. Guitars that once spoke, wept and stung now hang quietly in one of the old rehearsal rooms. You'll see Willlie Dixon's handwritten lyrics to "You Need to Be Loved" (this is the one from which Zep lifted "Whole Lotta Love"). Note the brick from Maxwell Street, the "birthplace of Chicago blues." There's also some great photos including Muddy and Willie at their peak—the Muddy Waters Band of the early '50s was certainly one of the greatest bands ever: Little Walter Jacobs on harp, Dixon on bass, Jimmy Rogers on guitar, Otis Spann on piano, and "Baby Face" Leroy Foster or Elgin Evans on drums.

There's a Blues Garden outside where concerts are occasionally held.

The Foundation's site's testimonial says, "Believing that his work was not yet finished, Dixon devoted much of his time in the 60's, 70's and 80's to the organization he founded, Blues Heaven Foundation. His vision was to allow the echoes of great American Blues to continue to develop, to encourage a new generation of blues greats and to provide for the on-going welfare of senior Blues musicians." The Foundation still awards a scholarship every year.

Cost and hours: Tours are offered from Th-Sa at 12, 1, 2, and 3p; Reservations required; Suggested donations for tour $20 per adult, $10 for youth (ages 5-17); Tel. (312) 808-1286;

https://www.bluesheaven.com/home.html

Dusable Museum of African American History
740 East 56th Place

Chicago, IL 60637

The Dusable is America's oldest independent Africa-American museum. Karolyn takes her South Side students on field trips here. Make sure to explore all wings and floors.

Cost and hours: W-Su 11a-4p, closed M and Tu; tickets are timed entry; $12.50 per local adult, $14.50 for non-resident adult; $4 for Chicago youth (ages 6-11), $5 for non-Chicago youth;

Tel. (773) 947-0600;

https://www.dusablemuseum.org

Chicago History Museum
1601 North Clark Street
Chicago, IL 60614

This museum is fascinating in terms of Chicago history generally, with a good set of blues exhibits featuring the important blues photography of Raeburn Flerlage. Recently, they featured a special 'Amplified: Chicago Blues' exhibit curated by the excellent Joy Bivins. Check out the museum's terrific online exhibit, *Sweet Home Chicago: Blues and African-American Life* (https://artsandculture.google.com/story/lQWBwTKL0sTsIw). The museum is kid friendly, as well.

Cost and hours: Tu 9:30a-8p, W-Sa 9:30a-4:30p, Su 12p-5-, closed M; $19 adult, $17 for seniors, $17 for students (aged 19-22); free for Chicago youth (18 and under);
Tel. (312) 642-4600;

https://www.chicagohistory.org

RESTAURANTS

Our favorite Chicago restaurants could comprise a book in and of itself, and we've talked about doing just that. (*Around the World in 80 Chicago Restaurants:* don't knick our idea.) Here's a few of our best bets and personal favorites, sticking to the BBQ/soul food theme.

Lem's BBQ 311
311 E 75th St.
Chicago, IL 60619

Lem's is a South Side classic, where the Lemons brothers, Bruce and Myles, have been serving up their famous rib tips and hot links since 1954. Lem's is home to the original glass aquarium smoker, an icon of the Chicago way of BBQ.

Su-Th, Noon to 10p, Fri & Sa: Noon-11p

Uncle J's
502 E 47th St.
Chicago, IL 60653

The "J" stands for "John." Uncle J's is another great tips-and-links spot, which they smoke in the classic aquarium smoker.

M-Th noon to 9p, F-Sa 1p to 11:30a

Bro-N-Laws
3820 W. Chicago Ave.
Chicago, IL 60651

A community-oriented barbecue spot, their motto is "where food is good in the hood." Brothers-in-law Ken Johnson and Gary Smith uphold the barbecue tradition in the West Side/Humboldt Park, a tradition they stress is rooted in the South. They recommend you bring a friend and split the chicken. They're also known for their Chicago ribs.

Mon and Sun 1pm-8pm; Tues-Sat 11 am-12 am
Tel. (773) 227-8344

Leon's BBQ
4550 S. Archer Ave.
Chicago, IL 60632

The venerable Leon's is another great aquarium smoker spot. Tips, hot links, and buckets of shrimp are the staples here. Counter-service takeout is the way to go. They've also got a location at 3309 E.106 St. Chicago.

Mon 10am-10pm; Tues-Sat 11am-10pm; Sun 11am-12am

Tel. (773) 247-4171

https://www.theoriginalleoansbbq.com

Honky Tonk BBQ
1213 West 18th St.
Chicago, IL 60608

In Pilsen, Honky Tonk features barbecue (chicken, ribs, pork) with live honky-tonk music. What more could you ask?

Mon-closed; Tues-Sun11am-10pm

Tel. (312) 226-7427

https://www.honkytonkbbqchicago.com

Smoque BBQ
3800 N. Pulaski Rd.
Chicago, IL 60641

This is our best bet for North side barbecue. With its Texas-style brisket, Smoque frequently wins the Chicago Reader's best barbecue award in their year-end "best in town" poll, and we tend to agree. Karolyn says their chicken "melts." She also advises that when asked which two sides you want with your platter, get two sides of mac 'n' cheese.

Mon-Closed; Tues-Wed, Sun11am-8pm;Fri-Sat11am-9am

Tel. (773) 545-7427

https://www.smoquebbq.com

Big Jones
5347 N. Clark St.
Chicago, IL 60640

Big Jones is an excellent New Orleans-themed Southern restaurant, known around town for its house-made aesthetic and Chef Paul Fehribach's commitment to "heritage and heirloom crops and livestock breeds" and traditional farming methods. At one time they even featured Gumbo Ya-Ya, Scott's favorite dish from Mr. B's Bistro in NOLA. Over the years, we've enjoyed many memorable dishes. "Eggs New Orleans" was Ponchartrain blue crab cakes with poached eggs, popovers, and bearnaise sauce. Alligator over cheesy grits made for a happy dish, and black-eyed pea fritters were a real treat. On another occasion, Scott enjoyed the gumbo a la Treme with filé powder (sassafras), preparatory to a main course of spaghetti & oxtails. Karolyn, for her part, thrilled to Chef Fehribach's gumbo-fat fried chicken: his regular recipe with the bonus of being fried in gumbo skimmings. Sides like red beans and rice and mac 'n cheese are solid, and their sweet potato pie is delicious. When on the menu, their jalapeño cornbread in a skillet is a spicy-mild sensation. As for their beignets, decent as they are, they don't quite get it. (Beignets may be one dish for which you really do have to be in NOLA.) During the pandemic, Big Jones was the first restaurant we supported, getting a generous to-go order with all the fixings for a reasonable price: fried chicken, greens, red beans 'n' rice, mac 'n' cheese, etc. It fed us for days.

Mon-Thurs-11am-3pm, 5pm-9pm; Fri 11am-3pm, 5pm-10pm; Sat 9am-10pm, Sun 9am-9pm

Tel. (773) 275-5725

https://www.bigjoneschicago.com

Twin Anchors Restaurant & Tavern
1655 North Sedgwick St.
Chicago, IL 60614

Since 1932, Twin Anchors' ribs have been a favorite in the Old Town neighborhood. (As they proudly claim, they've been doling out Chicago's finest pork baby back ribs, mild or zesty, for nearly a century.) Frank Sinatra dug this joint. They're also well-known for their battered codfish fry and their slow-roasted chicken.

While you're in Old Town, you could walk a few blocks around the corner and hit up Roger Ebert's old stomping grounds, the Old Town Ale House (219 W. North Avenue). Aside from being a classic journalists' tavern, this was a hangout for Second City folks like Bill Murray and John Belushi, as well.

Mon-Fri 4:30pm-10pm; Sat-Sun 12pm-10pm

Tel. (312) 266-1616

Https://www.twinanchorsribs.com

Josephine's Southern Cooking
436 E. 79th St.
Chicago, IL 60619

Formerly known as Captain's Hard Time Dining, Josephine's is Chicago's oldest Black woman-owned soul food restaurant. The menu boasts favorites like chicken 'n' waffles and short ribs. And yes, they have mac 'n' cheese. From their website: "Mother Josephine Wade's Josephine's Southern Cooking, situated in Chicago's working-class neighborhood of Chatham, has been a pillar in the community for more than 30 years. Josephine, with her southern charm and determination to create a better future for her people, established a home for political figures looking for words of wisdom, encouragement, and prayers. Josephine's was also a safe haven for at-risk youth and a place where those looking for a job could find employment, but above all, it was the place to come and have a fantastic, down-home, southern meal." They serve breakfast, lunch and dinner, as well as a late-night menu until 2am on Friday/Saturday. Closed Monday.

Tel. (773) 487-2900

https://josephinescooking.net

Daley's Restaurant
6257 S. Cottage Groave Ave.
Chicago, IL 60637

Scott went to Daley's, one of the oldest still-extant restaurants in Chicago—the place is over 100 years old now—with some friends about 20 years ago. He remembers sitting in a booth by the plate-glass windows. It's a soul food place much beloved by the local community. Daley's features staples like biscuits, smothered chicken, patty melts, and awesome chicken 'n' waffles. It's also two blocks away from where Karolyn teaches.

Daily 6am-4pm

Tel. (773) 643-6670

https://www.daleysrestaurant.com

MacArthur's Restaurant
5412 W. Madison St.
Chicago, IL 60644

MacArthur's is a meat and two cafeteria on the South Side with rotating daily specials. Belly up to the steam table for fare such as ham hocks (*Saturday*) or smothered pork chops (*Sunday*). Also look for buffet fried chicken most days of the week, and sides like greens, mac 'n' cheese, red beans, cabbage, and mashed potatoes, and desserts like peach cobbler and banana pudding. The most popular option for MacArthur's diners is takeout.

Daily 7am-10:45 pm

Tel. (773) 261-2316

https://www.macarthursrestaurant.com

Pearl's Place
3901 S. Michigan Ave.
Chicago, IL 60653

In Bronzeville, Pearl's Place is where you get "down home Southern cooking." This restaurant offers a buffet as well as cooked-to-order items, and on weekends there's an all-you-can-eat brunch buffet. They're justifiably proud of their fried chicken, catfish, salmon croquettes, and barbecue ribs, as well as sides like mac 'n' cheese and collards. They also offer homemade peach cobbler and sweet potato pie.

Daily 8am-7pm

Tel. (773) 285-1700

https://www.pearlsplacerestaurant.com

St. Restaurant #2 Country Kitchens
727 E. 87th
Chicago, IL 60619

St. Restaurant #2 Country Kitchens is a two-steam-table cafeteria where you'll find good comfort food staples. Their FB page attests, "A historical landmark in the black community, we sell heart food! We believe what comes from the heart reaches the heart. A family that eats together stays together." Look for chitterlings, neck bones, oxtails, smothered pork chops and chicken, among other tasty treats, as well as the usual classic sides: greens, candied yams, mac 'n' cheese, and spaghetti.

Tues-Sun 8am-8pm; Closed Monday

Tel. (773) 962-0700

https://www.countrykitchenrestaraunts.com

Manny's Deli
1141 S Jefferson St.
Chicago, IL 60607

Manny's offers enormous sammitches on the South Side. Their reuben is a beautiful thing to behold—and even better to taste.

Tues-Sat 7am-8pm; Sun-8am-3pm; Mon 7am-3pm
Tel. (312) 939-2855
https://mannysdeli.com

Pequod's Pizza
2207 N Clybourn Ave.
Chicago, IL 60614

Carmelized crust, baby! Lunch specials include a personal pan, making it a nice date spot. Also, if you're with a vegetarian.

Mon-Sat 11am-2 am; Sun 11am-midnight
Tel. (773) 327-1512
https://pequodspizza.com

Piece Pizzeria & Brewery
1927 W North Ave.
Chicago, IL 60622

Piece is a terrific (and terrifically popular) pizzeria and brewpub in Wicker Park. Get the white sausage and mushroom, says our connoisseur buddy Stephen Kropp.

Mon-Wed 11am-10:30pm; Thurs 11am-11pm; Sat 11am-12:30am;Sun 11am-10pm
Tel. (773) 772-4422
https://www.piecechicago.com

Steak N Egger
1174 W Cermak Rd.
Chicago, IL 60608

Where they "doze but never close" since 1955. The Steak N Egger is a classic South Side diner, open 24/7. They now have six locations in addition to the one above.

Daily 24 hrs
Tel. (312) 226-5444
https://www.steaknegger.com

Kopi, a Traveler's Cafe
5317 N Clark St.
Chicago, IL 60640

Kopi Cafe is a place that will always be close to our hearts, as this is where we first met. The owner Al Rose wound up being the man who officiated our wedding. Located in hip and happening Andersonville, Kopi is a vegetarian's paradise. But don't be put off by "vegetarian only": their quesadillas, the spicy salsa verde Pizza de Chucho and the falafel burrito de Calle Rosiers are delicious and hearty. You can also split a bottle or carafe of wine, or just get a glass. They've got delicious coffee, as well. The Cafe Loco ("Kopi house blend coffee with a shot of Tequila AND Kahlua. Whipped cream. BAM!") is definitely worth savoring in those long winter months. If you're up for an apertif, have an Absinthe Verte ("this is the real stuff served in the traditional style with a sugar cube atop an absinthe spoon.") If you want to shop, Al's partner Rhonda Welbel has a shop in the back featuring clothing and jewelry and other knickknacks from around the world. Karolyn says her wares are beautiful; "Scott never forgets to get me earrings there for my birthday." (One more thing: the carrot cake is so good: moist, with a cream cheese frosting and walnuts in the frosting rather than interspersed through the cake. Karolyn prefers it that way.)
Mon-Sun 10am-7pm
Tel. (773) 989-5674
https://kopicafechicago.com

The Hopleaf
5148 N Clark St.
Chicago, IL 60640

Also in Andersonville, the Hopleaf is a great independent venue with a wide selection of Belgian beers. They've got a top collection of sour reds, lambics, such as gueuze and kriek, and farmhouse ales like saison and grisette. Though renowned for their beer, they also have a good wine list. The food is amazing, led by their mussels and frites Belgian-style (in beer) and, when in season, smelt. The duck reuben has been supplanted by a brisket variety, but it's still damn good. They don't take reservations, nor do they allow children—even with parents. (Leave 'em at home). The Hopleaf was hit hard by the pandemic, but it held on and survived—and we're lucky it did. It's Scott's go-to place for Kwak, for example—an elixir you can't find just anywhere.

Daily 5pm-10pm
Tel. (773) 334-9851
https://www.hopleaf.com

Spoken Cafe
1812 W Montrose Ave.
Chicago, IL 60613

The owners of this terrific cafe are from Southern Louisiana. Featuring Acadian Cajun specials, it's a breakfast/lunch place that's committed to fresh ingredients and sustainable/seasonable food practices. We highly recommend the Acadian-style cheesy grits. The grocery items are excellent—try all of the pickled stuff.

Tues-Sun 7am-2 pm; Mon-Closed
Tel. (773) 769-2000
https://www.spokenchicago.com

Luella's Southern Kitchen
4609 N Lincoln Ave.
Chicago, IL 60625

Luella's is an acclaimed new Southern/New Orleans style restaurant.

Mon-Tues Closed; Wed-Fri 5pm-9pm; Sat and Sun 10am-3pm, 5pm-9pm
Tel. (773) 961-8196
https://www.luellassouthernkitchen.com

MUSIC, BARS AND THE REST

Rosa's Lounge
3420 W Armitage Ave.
Chicago, IL 60647

Our favorite blues club in town, run since 1984 by blues lover Tony Mangiullo, who moved to Chicago from Italy in 1978 to follow said love. His mama came along, and she is the titular Rosa. (Scott used to run off posters for Tony when he would come into CopyMax, the copy shop where Scott worked as a clerk in the '90s.) At Rosa's you'll see some of the finest local blues acts like Toranzo Cannon, Nick Moss, Carl Weathersby, John Primer & the Real Deal Blues Band, and Billy Flynn. To reiterate, Tony does it all for the love of the blues, and he's not stopping anytime soon.

Sun-Mon Closed; Tues-Fri 8pm-2am; Sat 8pm-3am
Tel (773) 342-0452
https://www.rosaslounge.com

B.L.U.E.S. on Halsted
2519 N Halsted St.
Chicago, IL 60614

A cool, intimate North Side club, just down the street from Kingston Mines, B.L.U.E.S. on Halsted is where original Maxwell Street stalwarts like Riler "Ice Man" Robinson once played. As Toranzo Cannon, who holds down a Thursday night slot, points out, a lot of the '30s generation played here: Lonnie Brooks, Koko Taylor, Billy Boy Arnold, Otis Rush, Eddy Clearwater. On one memorable night, we saw their generational peer, Jimmy Johnson, take the stage. Born in Holly Springs, Mississippi, Jimmy Johnson hit Chicago in 1950 and played South and West Side clubs in their heyday. In fact, he was still playing weekly gigs and shows at the age of 93, before passing away in 2022. Scott will always remember how Johnson's high-pitched voice sent shivers up his spine. As you look around the room, enjoy the photographs of the likes of Shemekia Copeland, Otis Rush, Robert Cray, and Honeyboy Edwards in action, much of it by Raeburn Flerlage. (There's a display case showcasing his work.) They even have Chicago blues pioneer Sunnyland Slim's piano! This is the place that most reminds Karolyn of the Beale Street clubs: it has the grit and the grumble you want.

Mon-Tues-Closed; Wed-Fri, Sun 8pm-2am; Sat 8pm-3am

Tel (773) 528-1012

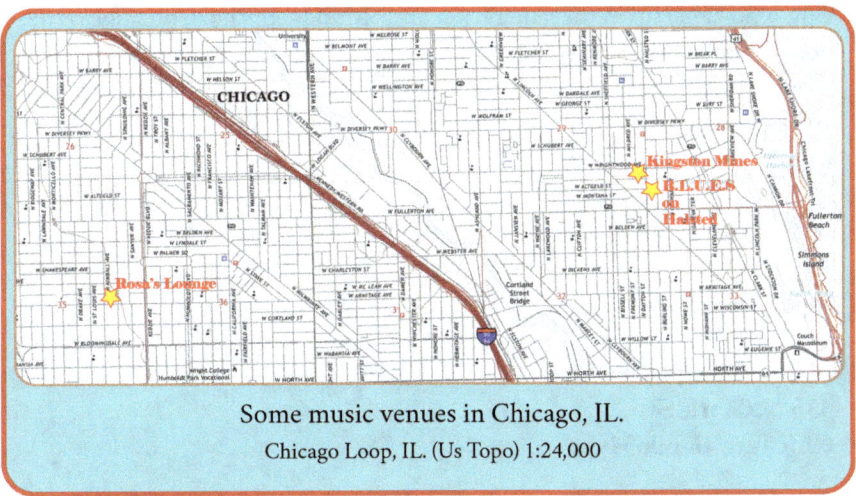

Some music venues in Chicago, IL.

Chicago Loop, IL. (Us Topo) 1:24,000

Kingston Mines
2548 N Halsted St.
Chicago, IL 60614

Kingston Mines was the pioneering North Side blues club. The proprietor, the great Lenin "Doc" Pelligrino, died in 2018 at the age of 92. His motto: "Illegitimus non carborundum": Don't let the bastards grind you down. On one memorable night, we saw noted Chicago harp player Sugar Blue sitting in with the Joanna Connor Blues Band, featuring Connor's blazing guitar. Kingston Mines features two stages and two separate bands a night: on the night we were there, Connor played an acoustic set on the first and then moved to the second stage for her electric set. Fun fact: Karolyn was in a Morrissey video shot at Kingston Mines. Look it up online, if you dare!

Thurs-Fri 7am-4am; Sat 7pm-5am

Tel (773) 477-4646

https://www.kingstonmines.com

Buddy Guy's Legends
700 S. Wabash Ave.

Chicago, IL 60605

Buddy Guy is one of the last of the great Chicago bluesmen born in the '30s, who came up in the generation after Muddy. In short, he's one of the greatest and most influential guitarists alive, a man from whom both Eric Clapton and Jimi Hendrix learned a few tricks. Every January Mr. Guy plays 16 shows at his club: Scott got to see one of these shows some 21 or 22 years ago. There's also Southern and Cajun food available.

Wed-Fri 11am-2am; Sat noon-3am; Sun noon-2am; Mon-Tues 5pm-2am
Tel (312) 427-1190
https://www.buddyguy.com

Blue Chicago on Clark
536 N Clark St.
Chicago, IL 60654

Blue Chicago features local greats like Gloria Shannon, who can be seen playing with Mike Wheeler. They're known for their commitment to featuring female vocalists. In a helpful article "Where to Hear the Blues: Juke Joints, Dive Bars and Historic Venues," Idoia Gkikas writes, "At Blue Chicago in the River North district, bands perform on a platform the size of an area rug. It's a welcoming, down-home atmosphere with no extravagance, just great music – the late greats Koko Taylor and Magic Slim performed here – seven nights a week."
Sun-Fri 8pm-1:30am; Sat 8pm-2:30pm
Tel (312) 661-0100
https://www.bluechicago.com

House of Blues
329 N. Dearborn St.
Chicago, IL 60654

Memorably located at the base of the Marina Towers (the "corn cob" buildings), this is not strictly a blues club. (We've seen Elvis Costello there.) Still, jazz and blues fans would enjoy getting their souls saved at Gospel Brunch. This event reminded us a bit of "The Last Waltz," where they served Thanksgiving dinner at the Winterland: long tables set out in front of the stage in a beautiful theater. The food is tasty southern fare. You grab a plate and serve yourself from various buffet stations. Fried chicken, biscuits and gravy, mac 'n' cheese, pretty much everything you could want. It's produced in bulk quantities, of course, but still pretty good, and the funky ambience is blues-drenched ("In Blues We Trust" reads the legend over an arch in the lobby.) In the bar, look for glowing reliefs of blues and rock legends in the ceiling, as well as folk art depicting Delta Blues Gods.

Tue- Closed; Mon-Sun 5 pm-11pm
Tel (312) 923-2007
https://www.houseofblues.com/chicago

The Green Mill
4802 N Broadway St.
Chicago, IL 60640

The Green Mill is located in the Uptown neighborhood, which in the Jazz Age '20s was the roaring entertainment district—Chicago's Times Square. Now going on 115 years old, the Green Mill is still Chicago's coolest jazz club. It's the speakeasy where Al Capone used to hang during the Prohibition era, and there's even an escape tunnel under the bar. We got to hear the Ben Allison Quartet there one night, with the stellar Jeremy Pelt on trumpet. On Wednesday nights, look for the Alfonso Ponticelli Trio, Chicago's premier Gypsy-jazz band. On Friday nights look for Chris Foreman, one of our town's top organists. (It's rumored that on some nights there are even organ duels between the instrument behind the bar and the one on stage.) Also look for the Fat Babies, one of Chicago's most joyous vintage jazz combos. Lastly, look for Stella, the statue in the corner—she's named for "Stella by Starlight." By the way, if you want to chat with your friends, go next door to the Mexican restaurant. Green Mill gives chitchat the side-eye. You're here to listen to the music.

Sun-Thurs 4pm-1:11am; Fri 4pm-2am; Sat 1pm-2am
Tel (773) 878-5552
https://www.greenmilljazz.com

The Empty Bottle
1035 N Western Ave.
Chicago, IL 60622

Scott used to attend Bloodshot Records showcases at the Empty Bottle in the '90s. This Ukrainian Village joint has long been a great dive club for alt-country, indie rock, and forward-thinking jazz. Ken Vandermark, one of Chicago's top avant-jazz saxophonists, had a residency here for some time. You used to be able to get a bottle of wine to go.

Daily 5pm-2am
Tel (773) 276-3600
https://www.emptybottle.com

Winter's Jazz Club
River East Club
465 N McClurg Ct.
Chicago, IL

The Leroy Jones Quintet from New Orleans frequently plays at this elegant cabaret.
Daily 8am-midnight
Tel (312) 344-1270
https://www.wintersjazzclub.com

Martyrs'
3855 N. Lincoln Ave.
Chicago, IL 60613

Martyrs' frequently features New Orleans bands: we've seen Rebirth Brass Band here, on which occasion both Karolyn and Scott were invited up onstage to do some impromptu shouting/singing. Other NOLA acts we seen here: Shamarr Allen and Bonerama. Martyrs' also has the benefit of being just down the street from our apartment. They often use the parking lot next door for outdoor Sunday afternoon shows, a tradition that started during the pandemic.

Mon-Fri 6pm-midnight; Sat 6pm-1 am; Sun Closed

Tel (773) 404-9494

https://www.martyrslive.com

FitzGerald's Nightclub
6615 Roosevelt Rd.
Berwyn, IL 60402

In the Berwyn suburb of Chicago, a roughly 30-minute drive from the North Side but well worth it, you'll find FitzGerald's. It frequently hosts New Orleans and roots-rock bands. We've seen Glen David Andrews and Kermit Ruffins here: Karolyn even jumped onstage with Kermit and the band for a mass ladies' dance. In the '90s, Scott saw the Bottlerockets here. FitzGerald's is inaugurating new festivals such as the Berwyn Blues Festival in September, as well as continuing with the long-running American Music Festival in early July. The great news is that FitzGerald's now hosts Babygold Barbecue, a restaurant that is getting high marks for its delicious barbecue. If barbecue is not your thing, there's the "World Largest Pizza Slice" place next door—they're open late. Parking is easy along the side streets.

Mon-Closed; Tues-Sat 7pm-2am; Sun 5pm-2am

Tel (708) 788-2118

https://fitzgeraldsnightclub.com

Space in Evanston
1245 Chicago Ave.
Evanston, Illinois 60202

In the northern suburb of Evanston, Space also hosts New Orleans bands. We've seen Glen David Andrews and Kermit Ruffins here as well. Get tickets early, because it often sells out. If you're seeing Glen David in the winter, don't be surprised to find yourself slippin' and slidin' through the streets in a second line. Don't forget your coat and your white hankie!

Mon-Sat 7pm-midnight; Sun 7pm-11pm

Tel (847) 492-8860

https://www.evanstonspace.com

The Hideout
1354 W Wabansia Ave.
Chicago,IL 60642

One of the great music clubs in Chicago, the Hideout is tucked into an industrial area near a Home Depot. This is where Scott has seen the likes of Robbie Fulks and Jon Langford. Singer Kelly Hogan once served him a drink the day after he had just seen her sing with Neko Case in concert. They also host annual festivals such as a SXSW showcase and a World Music Festival.

Mon-Fri-4pm-2am; Sat 6pm-3am; Sun Closed
Tel (773)227-4433
https://www.hideoutchicago.com

Old Town School of Folk Music
4544 N. Lincoln Ave.
Chicago, IL 60625

This school has been going since 1957, and the intimate concert hall here is a beautiful sounding room. Scott's seen Richard Thompson here on a few memorable occasions, including getting to sit in on a guitar workshop he conducted. We've seen Greil Marcus give talks here, as well, including one in which he appeared with Jon Langford and Sally Timms. We saw Fountains of Wayne's Adam Schlesinger there, a few years before he sadly died of Covid. They've recently expanded across the street. They host an outdoor Square Roots festival in July, where Scott once saw Patti Smith.

Mon-Thurs 3pm-9:30pm; Fri Closed; Sat Noon-5pm; Sun Closed
Tel (773) 728-6000
https://www.oldtownschool.org

The Victor Bar
4011 N Damen Ave.
Chicago, IL 60618

For a bit of grandeur, stop by the Victor cocktail bar just north of Irving Park on Damen. There are no televisions, so if you wanna watch a sports game don't come here. It will sweep you away to a Paris of the past with modern-style cocktails. If it's on the menu, try the Nighthawk, a beautifully crafted cocktail with Cynar 70, vanilla, whole egg, Xocolatl mole bitters and coffee sprinkled on top. Their Sazerac is nice, as well.

Daily 5pm-2am
Tel (773) 360-7049
https://thevictorbarchicago.com

The Promontory
5311 S. Lake Park Ave.
Chicago, IL 60615

The Promontory is a good South Side venue. Glen David Andrews once brought us a memorable New Orleans-in-Chicago evening here. You can get dinner there. Parking on the South Side can be difficult so be sure to either (a) take public transportation (*don't*) or (b) leave plenty of time to find parking.

If you're down that way to go to the Promontory, a great place for a burger and a brew is the **Woodlawn Tap**, popularly known as **Jimmy's** (1172 E 55th St). New owner Matt has made slight changes to the menu, which now includes cheese curds and a house salad. However, the greasy cheeseburger and fries are still the winner, and the grumble still lives here. They also feature a smoky beet reuben to appease the veg in your group. Be prepared: cash only. There is an ATM. Jimmy's also features Sunday Night Jazz.

Wed-Sun-4:30pm-9:30pm; Mon-Tues Closed
Tel (312) 801-2100
https://www.promontorychicago.com

We're also going to list a few clubs you should know about, even if they don't necessarily feature roots music. If you're in town and looking for live music or a nip, these are the places to be.

Estelle's (2013 W. North Avenue) was, in the '90s, a classic seedy dive down the street from where Scott lived in Wicker Park/Bucktown, right near the six-point Milwaukee, North and Damen intersection. There was an open mic night that brought out all sorts of Felliniesque characters. It's been refurbished now and swanked up, but it's still (barely) recognizable from what it was in the '90s. (Kind of like the neighborhood itself.) They gave up the grit for the grandeur, but the grumblings of the past still seep through the walls. Estelle's features late night food service. Right downstairs is **Subterranean** (2011 W North Ave.), another venerable neighborhood staple where live music can be heard ringing out.

A walk several blocks down Damen to Division Street will bring you to the **Rainbo Club** (1150 N. Damen), one of the classic Wicker Park dives bars. Liz Phair took the photo on the cover of Exile in Guyville in the photo booth there. Head a block or two east on Division Street and you'll get to **Phyllis Musical Inn** (1800 W. Division St.) the longest running club in the neighborhood, with live punk ringing out, now and forever.

Schuba's Tavern (3159 N. Southport) has a very nice live music venue in the back room, specializing in alt-country and indie rock. Scott has seen the Mekons and Sally Timms here over the years. Karolyn saw BR549 from Nashville here back in the '90s. It was built in 1900 by Schlitz, and they still sell that elixir at a good rate.

The Wild Hare (3530 N. Lincoln) is a good place for live reggae. Scott had some fun here in the early 2000s. Side note: if you're there during a Cubs game, be prepared to deal with non-locals.

Reggie's Rock Club (2105 S. State) is a punk rock and death metal club on the South Side, not far from Chinatown; in fact, it's just a few blocks from Chess Records, i.e. Willie Dixon's Blues Heaven. There's also **Lincoln Hall** (2424 N. Lincoln Ave.), where we've seen the Mekons and Trombone Shorty. It used to be a coffee shop Karolyn frequented in college, where you could get dollar cups of coffee with free refills and a CD selection. Across the street was Wax Trax where the likes of Billy Corgan and Eddie Vedder could be spotted.

Thalia Hall (1807 S. Allport St.) is located in an historic 1892 building in Pilsen modeled after the Prague opera house. Reopened and restored beginning in 2013, Thalia is now a venue for music as well as a community center and art gallery.

Then there's the **Vic** (3145 N. Sheffield).
— Scott: Baby, what are your memories of the Vic?

— Karolyn: That could get me in trouble. Mom, stop reading now. That was my second job in Chicago, bartending and meeting some of the great friends who are still in my life. Also, hobnobbing with the likes of the Charlatans, Ned's Atomic Dustbin, and Blur. Also, getting kicked in the nose at a Nitzer Ebb concert.

— Scott: I once dropped my glasses in a mosh pit there. Had to crawl through people's legs to find them. Miraculously, they were unscathed.

More recently we both saw Trombone Shorty there. These days, we prefer the balcony to the mosh pit.

There is the **Caberet Metro** (3730 North Clark Street) where Scott's seen Neko Case and Wild Flag. Karolyn saw Midnight Oil, Flaming Lips, and Blur there, back in the day. If you're in the mood to dance, downstairs from the Metro is **Smart Bar** (also 3730 North Clark).

There's also the grand ballroom the **Aragon** (1106 W. Lawrence) in Uptown, where Scott saw Nirvana in late '93, nearing the end of Cobain's life. (If driving, parking is roughly $40.) If you're standing in line waiting for the doors to open, food trucks normally park outside under the El tracks. Hence, don't drive: the El lets you off right there. Appreciate the Aragon's architecture: see more in Scott's report from the Jazz, Blues & Beyond tour below.

Across Broadway is the **Riviera** (4746 N Racine Ave.)—this is where Scott first saw Bob Dylan, in '94. Popularly known as the Riv, Scott also saw P.J. Harvey here. Wilco does a winter residency here every year. Karolyn's first concert at the Riv was seeing EMF. It would have been a fantastic show, had she not been on crutches due to knee surgery. Thankfully, her friend Julie saved her. Sadly, the Riv no longer hosts live shows as often as they used to. When they do, the line extends around the corner down Lawrence Avenue.

There's the **Park West** (322 W Armitage Ave), where Scott once saw Lucinda Williams from right below the lip of the stage.

The **Chicago Theater** (175 N. State St.) in the loop is one of the most beautiful, ornate theaters you'll ever see. You feel like you're in Versailles, which makes sense since the grand lobby was modeled after the Royal Chapel at Louis XIV's famous palace. We've seen Elvis Costello there multiple times over the decades.

We'll stop there, for now. There are countless other venues, as well, from palaces to storefronts. You get the idea. You won't have to go far to hear live music.

TOURS AND FESTIVALS

Chicago Blues Festival
Millennium Park
201 E. Randolph St.
Chicago, IL 60601

An international event, this free festival, now held throughout Millennium Park in early June, is the signature event in any blues lover's calendar in Chicago, and a real feather in our cap. It's one example of the city indeed honoring its heritage and showing how it continues to live today. Over the years we've been lucky enough to catch many memorable performances at Blues Fest, including a double bill with Dr. John and Aaron Neville, as well as acts such as Toranzo Cannon, our great Clarksdale discovery Christone "Kingfish" Ingram, and Eden Brent, among many more. Yes, it's hot. Make a plan before going, because it will be hot and it will be crowded. Enjoy seeing the kids playing in Crown Fountain as you stroll over to the festival.

Chicago Blues Boot Camp
Trading 4s Concert Series
430 S. Michigan Ave.
Chicago, IL 60605

An intriguing project, these camps take place in conjunction with Blues Fest under the auspices of the Chicago Blues Network. Says their FB page, "At Chicago Blues Camp, we take advantage of every Blues musician, club, and festival this city has to offer to provide the ultimate authentic Blues experience – Chicago style. There will be no shortage of learning and jamming throughout your five days of pure electric, urban Chicago Blues. Taught by Chicago Blues professionals, our course offerings in guitar, bass and 'harp' will teach you the classic blues styles of Muddy Waters, Buddy Guy, and Little Walter as well as contemporary developments by today's artists. Whether the blues is in your blood or you're looking to join the scene for the first time, you'll fit right in.

The camp also puts on a bi-weekly "Trading 4s" concert series featuring their faculty, which went virtual during the pandemic.

Logan Center Bluesfest
Reva and David Logan Center for the Arts
915 E 60th St.
Chicago, IL 60637

This new festival taking place in mid-October looks promising, "set up to celebrate the city's long and majestic history in the blues," it bills itself as a "three-day festival honoring the South Side roots of the blues tradition with conversations & presentations providing unique critical discourse of the blues—alongside a rich roster of headliner concerts and hands-on workshops." We've attended presentations at the host venue, the Reva and David Logan Center, which is on the University of Chicago campus, and they are always top quality.

Before the pandemic, Logan Center Bluesfest was to feature a concert by Elvin Bishop's Big Fun Trio, workshops with Fruteland Jackson (whom we met on our Jazz, Blues & Beyond tour back in 2013) and Fernando Jones, and a "Bringing Blues Back to the South Side" showcase hosted by Billy Branch and featuring Jimmy Johnson, Eddy Clearwater, Corky Siegel, Lil' Ed and Melody Angel. Sounds great.

The Logan Center also features a program called Second Monday Blues, which "features Chicago's world-class musicians and emerging blues stars. A live interview precedes each concert, moderated by the series' three-time, Grammy-nominated curator and host, Billy Branch. Relax with a glass of wine or cup of tea in Café Logan's intimate setting while getting up close and personal with local musicians and delving deeper into Chicago blues."

Taste of Chicago

This food-and-music festival, held annually down on the lakefront in Grant Park in July, is probably the closest Chicago gets to New Orleans' French Quarter Fest. Musicians play and restaurants citywide set up food stands, where you can get a taste of their wares. Scott has seen favorites such as Elvis Costello and Alejandro Escovedo at Taste of Chicago. Again, it's hot.

Chicago Detours' Jazz, Blues & Beyond Bus Tour

Below, we offer: Scott's report in full on this recommended tour:

One fine Saturday morning Karolyn and I hopped aboard the "Jazz, Blues & Beyond Bus Tour" presented by Chicago Detours—a birthday present from her to me. I've found on my trips to Europe that walking in artists' footsteps enhances the experience of their art. For example, wandering in London through the pubs and lanes where Shakespeare trod, you get a sense of his stomping grounds, the spaces and distances that somehow informed his work. Our abstract conception of the artist's context becomes concrete, despite the passage of time. So it sounded like a real kick to walk in the footsteps of the greats in my own town, Chicago, tracing the paths of, say, Muddy Waters instead of Bill Shakespeare.

We'd gathered on a Saturday morning in 2013 at the Jazz Record Mart, the much-lamented downtown record shop, now a thing of memory, founded by Bob Koester, a great man of Chicago music who passed away in 2021 at the age of 88. We met our tour guide, Amanda Scotese. As we boarded the bus and pulled away from the curb, Amanda explained her theory of Chicago as a locus of "productive tension," a place where music sometimes brought people together without fully resolving certain underlying contradictions. In that sense, an alternate title for her tour could have been the "Jazz *versus* Blues tour." This was a debatable but thought-stimulating framework for thinking about jazz and blues in terms of oppositions: north (jazz) versus south (blues), head (jazz) versus heart (blues), mood (jazz) versus story (blues).

The bus featured built-in video screens like on an airplane, so that while we were in transit, Amanda showed us footage of the jazz and blues musicians she was setting in opposition. What contrasts could we hear in, say, Mahalia

Jackson versus Scott Joplin (spirituals versus ragtime)? People volunteered some good stuff: soulful versus jaunty, rural versus urban, on-the-beat versus syncopated. She further juxtaposed Charlie Parker against Muddy Waters, as the progenitors who led respectively to the post-rock/free-jazz stylings of Tortoise and the electric blues-rock of the White Stripes.

All the while we were shooting up north, bound for Uptown, a neighborhood I passed through twice a day for years on the "El" while commuting to work. Amanda explained that Uptown was at the outer edge of a Chicago that kept expanding: the neighborhood was so far flung—the "end of the line"—that folks in the '20s had to drive or take the streetcar to get out there. The Green Mill, for instance, which once took up a whole Uptown block, was a roadhouse, the term "roadhouse" indicating a place you had to drive to reach. Amanda showed us a hot clip of trailblazing Chicago drummer Gene Krupa's band with trumpeter Roy Eldridge and Anita O'Day singing "Let Me Off Uptown": not only a celebration of the neighborhood, it was also a very early integrated duet (circa 1941), playful with sexual innuendo.

As we neared our destination, making our way down Argyle, Amanda pointed out the building that once housed Essanay Studios, where Charlie Chaplin made his earliest films.

We alighted the bus and stood studying the Aragon. There were years when I admired it from an El car every weekday, and in fact I saw Nirvana there, shortly after moving to Chicago in '93. Now we gave it a Rick Steves-like analysis, admiring its Spanish façade and its swirling columns, the faces peering out of the crisscrossing brickwork, the decorative shields and scalloped shells. The Aragon was an exotic place for rural and working people who traveled great distances to come dancing in the big city. (Sometimes the bands were told to play faster, so boys and girls wouldn't dance too close.)

We strolled over to the corner of Broadway, from which vantage point we had before us the Riviera Theater, the Green Mill and the old Uptown Theater, this last shuttered since 1981. Amanda asked us to imagine the scene as it would have been at the height of the Jazz Age, circa 1926: this was Chicago's Times Square, a neighborhood of glittering ballrooms and movie palaces. It was the place to be. Squinting, you could almost see gangsters stepping out of gleaming cars.

We clambered back aboard the bus. It was time to head down to the South Side and Bronzeville, that historic African-American neighborhood.

As we rounded corners, Amanda pointed to the former site of Lincoln Gardens on 31st Street, one of the historic "Black and Tan Clubs"- integrated venues which welcomed Black and white people to mingle, dance and listen to music together. Joe "King" Oliver's Creole Jazz Band kept 'em dancing at such clubs in the early 20's. Those were the heady days when cats like Bix Biederbicke, a young white aspiring cornetist from Iowa, would take the train to Chicago to sneak into speakeasies to hear some "hot jazz," jamming with the New Orleans Rhythm Kings.

Speaking of the Rhythm Kings, it's interesting to note how important New Orleans musicians were to jazz innovation in Chicago—so many greats like Louis Armstrong and Mahalia Jackson came up north with the Great Migration. As our bus passed Olivet Baptist Church, itself a catalyst of the Great Migration and the oldest African-American Baptist church in Chicago, Amanda called the church a "key to the neighborhood."

As the bus rumbled down State Street between 31st and 35th, Amanda pointed out that this particular strip was once known as "The Stroll," a hot 'n' jumpin' stretch of nightclubs, ballrooms, and theaters that was also considered a bit of a vice district. (The mainstream culture of the day associated jazz with sleaze.) Today "the Stroll" is the mostly non-sleazy campus of the Illinois Institute of Technology.

We came to a stop at what was in 2013 an ACE Meyer Hardware Store (it's no longer a hardware store as of 2022),which was housed in the building that was once the Sunset Café, a very important "Black and Tan club" which showcased Louis Armstrong's big band. (It was later known as the Grand Terrace Cafe when it came under the partial auspices of Al Capone.) Cab Calloway and Earl "Fatha" Hines got their start here under Armstrong, before they were promoted to leading the band themselves. In fact, Hines would go on to lead the band at the Sunset/Grand Terrace Cafe for twelve years. On the way, Amanda had shown us a photograph of the Earl Hines-led band during this residency. It featured a young Sun Ra, no less!

We entered the store and headed towards the back. A few at a time we climbed a few wooden steps and stepped into a narrow, cluttered office. Lo! We realized that the office, looking out over the store floor as it did, had been built atop the stage—in a sense, we were treading the boards of the stage at the Sunset Café! The original murals that once formed the stage's backdrop were still there, visible around a duct and a piles of boxes. In one of them, a topless demon lady clawed the skin of a great drum. Clambering back down to the floor, we stood amidst aisles of hardware supplies, imagining the floor filled instead with tables draped in elegant white tablecloths.

Back aboard the bus, we passed Pilgrim Baptist Church, originally designed as a synagogue by no less than Louis Sullivan and Dankmar Adler, and built in 1890-1891. Pilgrim Baptist, known as the "heart of Bronzeville," was one of the birthplaces of gospel music in the 1930s, whenThomas A. Dorsey, the "Father of Gospel Music", was its musical director.

Next up for our merry bus: the "blues" part of the tour. That meant we had to talk about the Chicago Defender—in its day the country's most important Black newspaper—and the Great Migration. The newspaper was yet another catalyst for the mass Black exodus from the South to cities like Chicago, which hit its peak in the '40s and '50s. The Defender, widely read in the South, wrote about Chicago as a place of hope for African-Americans, a place where housing and jobs could be had. Many came up from the Mississippi Delta and brought the blues with them, plugging it it when they got here to create the hard, electric city blues style. "Blues is hopeful music," Studs Terkel was now telling us from the screens on our bus. "I may be down now, but I won't be down forever."

We rumbled up South Michigan Avenue, past historic "Motor Row," once a vibrant auto showroom and service-station district, past the great display windows which once proudly showed off this year's models from Ford, Buick, Cadillac and others. We trundled up Record Row, grinding to a stop at 2120 S. Michigan, an address that rings out in music history. From 1957 to 1965, this was Chess Records, today the home of Willie Dixon's Blues Heaven Foundation. To some, this is the "birthplace of rock & roll," Amanda told us, and quite right she was. This is where founding father Chuck Berry recorded, doing his own accelerated blues/country amalgam. After you've been through this book and visited Sun Records in Memphis, as well as the laundromat in New Orleans that once housed J&M Recording Studios, it's interesting to think about which has the strongest claim as "birthplace of rock & roll." Hopefully, we've made the point by now that when it comes to music, there is no single birthplace, but Chess is certainly one of the handful of spots that can legitimately make a claim to being a place where something that hadn't been done before was done. It's one of those very special crucibles of creativity and originality. Our tour didn't go inside the Chess Building. Amanda opined that there's nothing much to see there, which may be true, in a way. Still, as someone who's been inside twice, it's very much a worthwhile experience to stand on the same floorboards as Muddy Waters, Jimmy Rogers, Howlin' Wolf, Chuck Berry, Bo Diddley, and Willie Dixon.

The tour wound up with a trip to Maxwell Street, once ground zero for the Chicago Blues, from the '20s through the war years and beyond, up until the street's destruction in 2000. Maxwell Street was where Blacks who came up with the Great Migration started out, mixing in with the immigrant communities which also prospered here; this was where the blues were electrified, forming the sound that seeded the '60s British rock explosion, which in turn carried a version of this music to the world. Described by David Whiteis as a "carnival of the soul," the street was a place for the community to gather around music. (Maybe Millennium Park/Grant Park are the closest equivalents we have today in Chicago; nice as evenings there are—and they are lovely—it's hard to imagine that scene as anything but a shadow of something as vibrant and culturally significant as Maxwell Street). Every musician had his or her corner, such as Blind Arvella Gray, who now appeared on our video screens. Like the Stroll, the old vice district, the old Maxwell Street flea market is gone now, destroyed by a UIC expansion and gentrification and putatively moved to the intersection of Des Plaines and Roosevelt. However, one can still stop, as we did, east of Halsted on Maxwell to note a sculpture commemorating the days when the blues rang out here. The statue depicts a bluesman in top hat sitting on a box, his harp resting on a crate by his side.

We had one more treat in store: a harp lesson from Fruteland Jackson, a longtime local bluesman who hopped aboard our bus when it stopped at Maxwell Street. We blues travelers were each issued a harmonica, and Jackson, wielding an acoustic axe and a harmonica rack, taught us to play a basic 12-bar pattern. The trick: for the first bars you suck, and then you blow. As we rolled back to our starting point, the bus resounded with the sounds of blowing, sucking, "dumping" (that is, exhaling) and big, flourishing finishes. We even got to keep the harmonica!

Did I say one last treat? There was actually to be one more. When we came full circle back to Jazz Record Mart, Bob Koester, who founded the joint back in 1962, happened to be there. Mr. Koester, who as noted passed away in 2021 at the age of 88, was also the founder of Delmark records in 1953, the oldest jazz and blues independent record label in America. The great man stood listening as Amanda summed up our very eventful day.

I've had occasion to say it before: as long as I've lived in Chicago—30 years now—there's always something new to discover. And in a way, there's always something "past" to discover as well.

Now, the next time I'm on the El's red line trundling north, I can imagine I'm on a streetcar headed for Uptown.

[Chicago Detours is still in operation, though it's unclear from their website, https://chicagodetours.com, whether they still offer the above-mentioned tour. Why not give them a call at 312-350-1131 or e-mail them at info@chicagodetours.com to find out?]

HOTELS

Since Chicago's our home, we don't know much about its hotels, if that makes any sense. We had a good staycation at the historic downtown **Palmer House** (17 East Monroe Street). Even if you can't stay here, stop in for a drink: it's a true gem in Chicago's architectural history. (It briefly closed during the pandemic, which saddened us greatly, but now appears to be back.) The original version went up in 1871, only to go back down 13 days later in the Great Chicago Fire. "By the turn of the century," the hotel's site notes, "the Palmer House had become Chicago's liveliest social center, hosting a long list of prominent figures—including those ranging from U.S. presidents to Charles Dickens to Oscar Wilde." Mark Twain, too. Holabird & Roche's version of the Palmer House (its third incarnation) was completed in 1925, and is considered one of their triumphs. A big thanks for the beauty of Palmer House must go to Bertha Honoré Palmer, Potter Palmer's wife. Her friendship with Monet led her to get in touch with her French roots by collecting French art, much of which now adorns the hotel. (In fact, it's guiding design motif is the French Empire period, 1800-1815).

The grand lobby features stunning paintings on the ceiling depicting Greek mythological subjects and tales. Pop into the Golden Empire Dining Room, established in 1925 and converted into an "entertainment epicenter" in 1933. It hosted legendary entertainers like Frank Sinatra, Judy Garland, Ella Fitzgerald, Harry Belafonte, Louis Armstrong, and Liberace. When we were there we had it to ourselves, so we got up on the stage and horsed around, adding our own names to this auspicious list.

The **Drake Hotel** (140 E Walton Pl.) is an opulent, historic hotel dating to 1920. In the roaring '20s you could find the likes of Bing Crosby, Walt Disney, George Gershwin, and Charles Lindbergh here; Marilyn Monroe and Joe Dimaggio smooched here, and carved their initials into the bar. We explored the Drake once: its corridors seem to wend endlessly past ball-rooms and meeting halls. The Drake is also known for **Coq d'Or**, its historic speakeasy downstairs. As its website writes, "On December 6th, 1933, the day after prohibition was repealed, Coq d'Or opened to the favor of thirsty patrons eager to purchase a 40 cent whiskey. In the 1940s it became a lo-cal hangout for reporters, politicians, and even some notorious characters, though it never lost the true Chicago crowd." Get the famous Bookbinder soup, the "Classic Drake red snapper soup"—you'll get a little crystal decanter of sherry on the side.

For our wedding we stayed at the **Ambassador Chicago**, once the **Public Hotel** (1301 N. State Pkwy.), where the historic Pump Room was. The Pump Room's completely remodeled past recognition now (and rechristened the Ambassador Room), but once it was the spot where all of Hollywood hung when they'd pass through town. Once upon a time, Booth One was where Sinatra, Bogie and Bacall, and Bette Davis all sat. It's still fun to be on the stomping grounds where it all happened. (That's what this book has been about.)

Winding It All Up (and Down)

— Scott: Well, there you have it. We hope you've enjoyed our rollicking tour through the American South and that we've been true to its great diversity. We hope we've shown that the "old, weird America" is still out there, if you know where to look. If we've done it right, you've come away seeing the region as a movable feast/party while also being inspired by the social protests and freedom struggles of the past to fight the forces of darkness and reaction today, who want to roll back all the hard-won changes we've been talking about. Look for us down the road, where we hope you'll be eating, dancing, partying and organizing your way into the triumphs of the future. We hope we've inspired you to get out there and given you plenty of ideas. All travel guides are aspirational in a certain sense. They represent a dream of future adventure, a bet that people are still good, and that there is still wonder just around every corner. We wrote this just as much to inspire future trips of our own, especially after the virus and in times as dark as these. In fact, we've made ourselves hungry just thinking and talking about it. Hon, do you have any last words for our readers?

— Karolyn: Don't be afraid to turn that corner and go off the beaten path. Some of the best experiences we've had are because we chose the road (and in some cases not really a road but a field disguised as a road) not taken. Get out of your comfort zone. Interact with locals. Learn. Listen. Grow.

Bibliography and Resources

LISTENING

15 Blues Albums To Own

1. King of the Delta Blues Singers—Robert Johnson
2. Howlin' Wolf (The Rocking Chair Album)—Howlin' Wolf
3. The Complete Plantation Recording—Muddy Waters
4. The Real Folk Blues—Muddy Waters
5. Hard Again—Muddy Waters
6. Founder of the Delta Blues—Charley Patton
7. Bumble Bee—Memphis Minnie
8. Live at the Regal—B.B. King
9. Blues is King—B.B. King
10. Right Place, Wrong Time—Otis Rush
11. The Essential Bessie Smith
12. Rediscovered—Mississippi John Hurt
13. The Essential Sonny Boy Williamson
14. Hooker—John Lee Hooker
15. Two Steps from the Blues—Bobby "Blue" Bland

25 Delta Blues Songs to Hear

1. Delta Blues—Son House
2. Clarksdale Moan—Son House
3. Traveling Riverside Blues—Robert Johnson
4. Cross Road Blues—Robert Johnson
5. Pony Blues—Charlie Patton
6. A Spoonful Blues—Charlie Patton
7. High Water Everywhere—Charlie Patton
8. Frankie—Mississipi John Hurt
9. Avalon Blues—Mississippi John Hurt
10. Yellow Bee—Bertha Lee
11. Knockin' a Jug—Louis Armstrong
12. Future Blues—Willie Brown
13. See That My Grave is Kept Clean—Blind Lemon Jefferson

14. My Home is the Delta—Otis Spann
15. MS Delta Blues—Jimmy Rodgers
16. Nelson Street Blues—Willie Love
17. Parchman Farm Blues—Bukka White
18. Down in the Delta—Super Chikan
19. Ice Storm Blues—Big Jack Johnson
20. Yellow Dog Blues—W.C. Handy
21. Devil Got My Woman—Skip James
22. Cypress Grove Blues—Skip James
23. A. & V. Blues—Mississippi Matilda
24. Highway 61 Blues—James "Son" Thomas
25. Burr Clover Farm Blues—Muddy Waters

5 North Mississippi Hill Country Blues Songs to Hear

1. Bad Luck Blues—R.L. Burnside
2. Tom Wilson's Place—R.L. Burnside
3. Holly Springs—Cedric Burnside Project
4. Junior's Place—Junior Kimbrough
5. She-Wolf—Jessie Mae Hemphill

20 City Blues Songs To Hear

1. Mannish Boy—Muddy Waters
2. Too Young to Know—Muddy Waters
3. Rollin' Stone—Muddy Waters
4. Hidden Charms—Howlin' Wolf
5. Smokestack Lightning—Howlin' Wolf
6. You Upset Me Baby—B.B. King
7. I'm a King Bee—Slim Harpo
8. Stop Breaking Down—Junior Wells
9. Jackson Town Blues—Eddie Taylor
10. Jackson Town Gal—Robert Nighthawk
11. Gulf Coast Blues—Bessie Smith
12. Bright Lights, Big City—Jimmy Reed
13. Take Out Some Insurance On Me Baby—Jimmy Reed
14. Let's Go To Town—Memphis Minnie
15. Your Funeral, My Trial—Sonny Boy Williamson II

16. One Bourbon, One Scotch, One Beer—John Lee Hooker
17. Wang Dang Doodle—Koko Taylor
18. It Takes Time—Otis Rush
19. Tore Up—Otis Rush
20. That's Where It's At—Johnnie Taylor

Those looking to learn about the blues might get a kick out of *Full Circle* by John Sinclair and His Blues Scholars (2012). Each song is a compact history of a great blues musician such as Bukka (Booker) White, some of which are told in their own voices as imagined by Sinclair.

Let's turn to New Orleans. The Meters are a quintessential NOLA band: Art Neville on keyboards and vocals, Cyril Neville on percussion and vocals, Leo Nocentelli on guitar, George Porter on bass, and Ziggy Modeliste on drums. As well as their own original hits, you'll hear them on many top Crescent City tunes, backing up the likes of Lee Dorsey, Dr. John, and Allen Toussaint. Listen to the compilation *Funkify Your Life: The Meters Anthology*, or look for albums like *Rejuvenation* and *Cissy Strut*.

Any self-respecting collection of New Orleans, or even American, music would include albums by Fats Domino (look for *Legendary Master Series*, *The Best of*, or *Fats Domino Jukebox: 20 Greatest Hits the Way You Originally Heard Them*), Professor Longhair (*'Fess: The Professor Longhair Anthology*, *Crawfish Fiesta*, *Rock 'n' Roll Gumbo*), *The Wild Tchoupitoulas* (self-titled debut album), Dr. John (*In The Right Place*, *Goin' Back to New Orleans*, *Gumbo*, *The Very Best of*) and Louis Armstrong (*Hot Fives and Sevens*, *Portrait of the Artist as a Young Man 1923-1934*).

We can understand if you boycott Spotify: Scott has done so in solidarity with Neil Young and Joni Mitchell ever since they took their stand. That said, *Up From the Streets: New Orleans: The City of Music* is a tremendous Spotify playlist that demonstrates the city's cultural syncretism. Among many others, you'll hear Kaleta & Super Yamba Band, Dr. Michael White, Kinfolk Brass Band, Papa Celestin and the Original Tuxedo Brass Band, Harry Belafonte, Herlin Riley, Ryan Kisor, Donald Harrison, Carl Allen, Mardi Gras Indians, Bill Summer, Claudio Monteverdi, Tom McDermott and Evan Christopher,

Preservation Hall Jazz Band, Emile Christian, Lovie Austin, Tommy Ladnier, Sweet Emma Barrett, Mahalia Jackson, John Handy, Geoff Bull, Jelly Roll Morton and his Red Hot Peppers, and Art Blakey & the Jazz Messengers.

VIEWING

The HBO series *Treme* (2010-2013), conceived by David Simon and Eric Overmyer (the team behind *The Wire*), is an indispensable primer for getting acquainted with the culture—and even the layout—of New Orleans. It follows a vivid cast of fictional characters as they rebuild and heal and begin again (or don't) in the years following Katrina. These are interwoven with real people and places, chefs and musicians, restaurants and clubs. The show deserves a special salute for being itself an act of preservation and curatorship of the city's heritage. When we started visiting New Orleans together, the show enriched our visits; in turn, our visits enriched our experience of the show.

Trouble The Water (2008) is a documentary about a young couple surviving Hurricane Katrina. *Flood Streets* (2011) likewise documents life in New Orleans in the hurricane's wake. *Five Days At Memorial* (2022) is a powerful dramatization of Sheri Fink's nonfiction book about the impossible decisions faced by the doctors and nurses at Memorial Hospital when the levees broke after Katrina.

When the Levees Broke (2006) is Spike Lee's heartbreaking, transcendent documentary on New Orleans and Katrina. It can make you angry, particularly at the oil industry, whose drilling operations and canals have destroyed so much of the delta marshland which once was the town's first line of defense against hurricanes, and at the Army Corps of Engineers, who built the slipshod levees. As always, it's the poor who primarily pay the price. In the end, though, the film's tone is more elegiac and haunted than angry, not least because of Terrence Blanchard's haunting music. Its vision of human resilience and of people who behaved bravely during the crisis—who helped others—is enough to restore your faith in humanity.

Mine (2009) is a moving documentary about the fate of beloved dogs in the wake of Katrina.

The Whole Gritty City (2013) documents endangered youth who find purpose by playing in marching bands, as well as their adult mentors, as they prepare for Mardi Gras.

Beasts of the Southern Wild (2013). Set in "the Bathtub," a bayou below the levee along the Gulf Coast of Louisiana, this fable stars Quvenzhane Wallis as the intrepid Hushpuppy, a little girl living in a kind of harmony and conflict with nature from which modernity has isolated most of us. Dwight Henry plays Wink, her irascible daddy. It's both a mythic allegory of Katrina, an environmental parable, and a memorable look at life lived off the grid of contemporary America.

Michael Murphy's *Up From the Streets: New Orleans: The City of Music* (2019) is a deeply felt survey of this singular town's musical history and contemporary scene. (This is not the same Michael Murphy who wrote the recommended Dat series of books, we should note.)

ReMastered: Devil at the Crossroads (2019), directed by Brian Oakes, is an atmospheric Robert Johnson documentary set at the crossroads, where myth, legend, and fact face off. The film does a good job of humanizing Johnson and showing the fears and traumas that may have motivated his behavior—causes that were less supernatural than social.

M for Mississippi: A Road Trip Through the Birthplace of the Blues (2008) is a documentary featuring Roger Stolle and Jeff Konkel as bemused characters tracking down their blues heroes. Konkel and Damien Blaylock directed.

READING

In terms of travel practicalities and inspiration, the following works are indispensable. We dip into them before every trip.

Steve Cheseborough, *Blues Traveling: The Holy Sites of Delta Blues* (2001)

Richard Knight, *The Blues Highway: New Orleans to Chicago* (2001)

Michael Murphy, *Dat series (Hear Dat, Eat Dat, Drink Dat, Fear Dat, All Dat)* (2014-2017)

Fodor's New Orleans

Susan Puckett, *Eat Drink Delta: A Hungry Traveler's Journey through the Soul of the South* (2013)

Rebecca Snedeker and Rebecca Solnit, *Unfathomable City: A New Orleans Atlas* (2013)

Michael Patrick Welch, *New Orleans: The Underground Guide* (2014)

The Mississippi Blues Trail: Your Guide to Uncovering the Mississippi Blues (2014), a special issue of Living Blues magazine by Scott Barretta, Amy Evans, and Melanie Young

Dave Hoekstra, *The People's Place Soul Food Restaurants and Reminiscences from the Civil Rights Era to Today* (2015)

John Kennedy Toole's *A Confederacy of Dunces* (1980) is the funniest book we've ever read, and essential reading when you're warming up for a visit to New Orleans.

To read more about Stax and Memphis soul, check out Robert Gordon's *Respect Yourself: Stax Records and the Soul Explosion* (2013) and *It Came From Memphis* (1995), as well as Peter Guralnick's *Sweet Soul Music: Rhythm and Blues and the Southern Dream of Freedom* (1986). Guralnick has written several of the classic books about American roots music: no self-respecting shelf of music tomes can be without the afore-mentioned title and the other two in the trilogy, *Lost Highway: Journeys* and *Arrivals of American Musicians* (1979) and *Feel Like Going: Portraits in Blues & Rock 'N' Roll Home* (1971).

Guralnick has also written the definitive books on Elvis Presley, *Last Train to Memphis: The Rise of Elvis Presley* (1994) and *Careless Love: The Unmaking of Elvis Presley* (1999), as well as the definitive account of Sam Phillips, the provocatively titled Sam Phillips: The Man Who Invented Rock 'n' Roll (2014).

For even more on Memphis, check out *Ghosts Behind the Sun: Splendor, Enigma & Death: Mondo Memphis Volume 1* (2011) by Tav Falco, of psychedelic rock band Panther Burns. It's is a wild read.

For more on Robert Johnson, we turn again to Guralnick and his Searching for *Robert Johnson: The Life and Legend of the "King of the Delta Blues Singers"* (1998). Greil Marcus's 1975 classic *Mystery Train: Images of America in Rock 'N' Roll Music* contains a chapter on Robert Johnson as an "ancestor" of rock 'n' roll. For many of us, reading this essay at the same time we were first getting into Johnson was fundamental in shaping the way we think about him.

Love in Vain: A Vision of Robert Johnson (1983), by Alan Greenberg, is a screenplay for an as yet un-produced film on Johnson; it's unbeatable as an introduction to the central and supporting real-life characters who made up the blues milieu of Johnson's era. Don't neglect to study the endnotes, which offer an indispensable factual history of each of the characters, and also serves as kind of discography. See if you can make a playlist of as many of the songs and artists mentioned as possible.

Our list of seminal books on the blues would further include the following.

Robert Palmer, *Deep Blues* (1981)

William Ferris, *Blues from the Delta: An Illustrated Documentary on the music and musicians of the Mississippi Delta* (1970)

Paul Oliver, *Screening the Blues: Aspects of the Blues Tradition* (1968)

Jim O'Neal and Amy van Singel, *The Voice of the Blues: Classic Interviews from Living Blues Magazine* (2002) (O'Neal and van Singel, at one time husband and wife, cofounded the seminal Living Blues magazine. O'Neal went on to operate Rooster and Stackhouse records, which were originally Clarksdale-based.)

David Whiteis, *Chicago Blues: Portraits and Stories* (2006)

Mike Rowe, *Chicago Blues* (1981)

APPENDIX A

ROBERT JOHNSON, EMMETT TILL, AND MEDGAR EVERS

We've talked a lot about the mythology of Robert Johnson in this book—the legend of the crossroads where Johnson sold his soul to the devil in the dead of night, in exchange for being able to play such otherworldly guitar. The historical Johnson *(1911-1938)* died at age 27 under mysterious circumstances, perhaps poisoned. Before his untimely death, he recorded 29 songs that would go on to become some of the most influential recordings in the history of American music. This is music so full of pain, high spirits, dark humor, and eerie poetry so as to seem almost inexplicable: one never gets to the bottom of these performances. When they were released as the King of the Delta Blues Singers albums, the first volume of which came out in 1961, they changed the lives of many musicians. A roll call of their names would begin with Bob Dylan, Eric Clapton, Keith Richards, and Robert Plant, just for starters. (And just think of all the lives they changed in turn).

While his music certainly didn't come out of nowhere, Johnson was a unique innovator both as a singer and as a guitarist. Over the course of his short life he rambled across the Delta. Retracing his steps, and even looking for the crossroads themselves, is a big part of any Delta exploration. (It's a bit like seeing the real-life places in the Holy Land that are the settings for the Biblical myths.)

Who was Emmett Till? The story begins in August of 1955, when 14-year-old Emmett, a Chicagoan visiting family in Money, Mississippi, went along with his cousin and some local boys to Bryant's Grocery and Meat Market to buy candy. There the boys encountered Carole Bryant, a white woman who was the wife of a man called Roy Bryant—the couple were co-owners of the store. Ms. Bryant accused Till of whistling at her, and propositioning her more generally.

In 2008, Ms. Bryant admitted that most of her story was false, especially the parts about Emmett's being fresh enough to take her by the hand and ask her out. Of course, the point isn't even that Till was innocent: he wouldn't have deserved his fate had he been "guilty." The point is that the allegations themselves were enough to get a young Black teenager killed in Jim Crow Mississippi.

The United States Civil Rights Trail's page entitled "Remembering Emmett Till" is well worth reading (https://civilrightstrail.com/experience/sumner/). It takes up the tale: "Rob Bryant made plans with his half-brother John William 'J.W.' Milam to wreak vengeance on Till... Roy, Carolyn and Milam took Till from his great-uncle's home in the early morning hours of August 28, 1955, and tied him up in the back of a pickup truck. After dropping off Carolyn and picking up two black men who worked for Roy, the men took Till to a barn in Drew, Mississippi, where they badly beat him. Till was also shot before the men threw his body into the Tallahatchie River, weighed down with a large fan blade they'd stolen from a cotton gin. Three days later, two boys fishing in the river discovered Till's nude and badly disfigured body. Till had been shot above his right ear, and his face had been beaten beyond recognition. The fan blade was secured around Till's neck with barbed wire."

You'll recall that earlier we recounted our experience visiting the historical marker at the funeral home in Tutwiler, Mississippi. While we were there, we took a photograph of the sign's text, and it explains what happened next: "On August 31, 1955, Woodrow Jackson prepared Emmett Till's body here at the Tutwiler Funeral Home, to return to Emmett's mother, Mamie Till-Mobley, in Chicago. Emmett's uncle...had to sign a document promising not to open the casket. Once the body reached Chicago, Mamie Till-Mobley defied that order, promising to show the world what was done to her son."

That last point is crucial, and the Civil Right Trail account expands on it. Ms. Till-Mobley "demanded an open-casket funeral so that attendees could see her son's mutilated body and understand the extent of the harm done to him. Photographs of Till's body were published in newspapers around the country, including two black publications, Jet and The Chicago Defender, and spurred public outrage at the treatment of blacks in the American South."

The marker in Tutwiler states the matter plainly: "The public outcry over the condition of Emmett's mutilated body is considered to be one of the main sparks that ignited the Civil Rights Movement."

What of the murder trial? "Roy Bryant and Milam were indicted for murder, and five attorneys from Sumner offered to defend the pair pro bono," relates "Remembering Emmett Till." The five-day trial took place in September 1955 in Sumner at the Tallahatchie County Courthouse. "Though the defense attempted to discredit Till's great-uncle Mose Wright by saying that he could not identify Bryant and Milam, Wright courageously testified that the two men had identified themselves to him and that he had seen Milam clearly. Wright's testimony marked the first time a black man had testified to the guilt of a white man in the state of Mississippi."

"On September 23, the all-white, all-male jury deliberated 67 minutes before acquitting Bryant and Milam. Jurors later admitted in interviews that although they knew Bryant and Milam were guilty of Till's murder, *they did not think imprisonment or the death penalty were appropriate punishments for white men who had killed a black man.*" [Emphasis ours.]

Bryant and Milam both later confessed to murdering Till in a magazine interview.

Today, you can visit several historical sites in Sumner and nearby Money associated with Till's unspeakable slaying, as well as the trial—from the former site of Bryant's Grocery & Meat Market in Money (a stop along the Mississippi Freedom Trail), to the Emmett Till Historic Intrepid Center in Glendora, housed in the cotton gin building from which Till's killers took the fan and wire used to weigh down his body before throwing it into the Tallahatchie River. Glendora also offers a bus tour, the Till Trail of Terror Tour.

You can also visit the site where Till's body was discovered in the Tallahatchie River. Though the historical marker designating this sacred site was shamefully vandalized in 2016 by multiple gunshots, the marker has since been replaced with money provided by the Emmett Till Interpretive Center in Sumner, located in the former Tallahatchie County Courthouse. (See our entry on the Center above, under Sites and Museums.)

Let's turn to Medgar Evers (1925–1963). As Mississippi's field secretary for the NAACP, Evers was a key civil rights activist of the '50s and early '60s. He was also a proud college graduate and a World War II veteran. Evers' efforts were particularly focused on integration of public facilities:

he made it his mission to challenge, and hopefully end, the rigid segregation of Mississippi society. In the wake of the Supreme Court's *Brown v. Board of Education* decision in 1954, which stated that segregated public schools were unconstitutional, Evers challenged the ongoing segregation of the University of Mississippi, a state-supported public institution, by applying to its law school. His work also encompassed fighting for voting rights and expanded economic opportunity for African-Americans.

While standing in his driveway in Jackson, Mississippi on June 12, 1963, Evers was assassinated by Byron de la Beckwith, a member of the White Citizens' Council. Decades passed. Beckwith was finally brought to justice...in 1994.

APPENDIX B

KAROLYN'S NEW ORLEANS CHECKLIST

100 Things to Do, in no particular order–Give yourself one point for each completed activity.

1. _____ Photo with a Lucky Dog vendor/cart. Bonus if you're eating a Lucky Dog.

2. _____ Dance at Spotted Cat. Bonus if video is posted on Facebook.

3. _____ Cocktail (*can be non-alcoholic*) at Carousel Bar. Bonus if you take a photo of yourself in the mirrors.

4. _____ Eat a beignet. Bonus if it is from Loretta's.

5. _____ Visit WWII Museum. Bonus if you need to return because it's too big for one afternoon.

6. _____ Ride the streetcar. Bonus if you ride it to the end.

7. _____ Walk around Garden District. Bonus if you find Anne Rice's House.

8. _____ Slurp a frozen Irish coffee from Erin Rose or Molly's in the Market. Bonus if you have it at both spots.

9. _____ Eat a po'boy from Verti Marte. Bonus if it's an All that Jazz.

10. _____ Dine at Dooky Chases's. Bonus if you bring back some chicken for me j/k.

11. _____ Walk along the Mighty Mississippi. Bonus if it's at sunrise/sunset.

12. _____ Stop by Faulkner House Books. Bonus if you buy a book.

13. _____ Go on a ghost tour. Bonus if photo taken proves spirits exist.

14. _____ Visit the Night Market on Frenchmen St. Bonus if you buy a souvenir.

15. _____ Listen to buskers play on Royal Street. Bonus if you tip them–you should. Double bonus if you buy their CD.

16. _____ Stroll down Bourbon St. Bonus if you sip a daiquiri while doing so. Double bonus if you don't spend more than an hour or two on it (*unless you're at Fritzel's for live jazz*).

17. _____ Eat red beans and rice. Bonus if you find out why they're served so often on Mondays. (*Note: Harry's Corner has free red beans and rice on Mondays made by bartender musical genius, Paul.*)

18. _____ Eat oysters any way. Bonus if you go to Felix's for raw ones or Drago's for char–grilled.

19. _____ Relax by hotel pool. Bonus if you wear a cute hat and drink a cocktail.

20. _____ Stroll through the French Market. Bonus if you eat alligator on a stick.

21. _____ Visit R-Bar. Bonus if you have the shot and beer special. Double bonus if you experience one of their community crawfish/shrimp boils or taco nights on Fridays.

22. _____ Go to Bullet's Sports Bar. Bonus if Uber driver asks, ***"You sure you wanna go there?"***

23. _____ Eat Kermit's BBQ/food at his Mother-in-Law Lounge. Bonus if he plays too.

24. _____ Dine at Mr. B's Bistro. Bonus if you eat BBQ shrimp. Double bonus if you need another loaf of bread to soak up the beautiful sauce.

25. _____ Eat macaroni and cheese at Lil Dizzy's. Bonus if you kiss the chef. (*I have.*)

26. _____ Try a Hurricane. Bonus if it's from Pat O'Brien's.

27. _____ Stay out after 10 p.m. Bonus if it's past midnight.

28. _____ Get a psychic reading. Bonus if it's from Voodoo Authentica.

29. _____ Experience a Jazz Brunch. Bonus if it's at Muriel's or Commander's Palace. Double bonus if you stump the band with a song request.

30. _____ Listen to the masters at Preservation Hall. Bonus if you get a VIP seat.

31. _____ Tour a cemetery. Bonus if you locate a famous New Orleanian.

32. _____ Sample absinthe. Bonus if you have more than one.

33. _____ Stop by LaFitte's Blacksmith Shop. Bonus if you have a purple drink. Double bonus if you get a seat by the window and people watch the day away.

34. _____ Walk around City Park and visit the New Orleans Museum of Art. Bonus if you have a picnic.

35. _____ Avoid the casino. Bonus if you avoid the casino. (*I know I said that twice.*)

36. _____ Pose with statue of Ignatius J. Reilly. Bonus if you've read Confederacy of Dunces.

37. _____ Explore the Bywater District. Bonus if you visit Dr. Bob's.

38. _____ Find and participate in a Second Line Parade. Bonus if you buy an adult beverage from a child under 10.

39. _____ Go on a food/history tour. Bonus if you try something you've never had before.

40. _____ Pop into the galleries on Royal Street. Bonus if you buy something. Double bonus if you buy an original piece of art.

41. _____ Sit in Jackson Park and revel in the beauty of the architecture surrounding you. Bonus if you drink chicory coffee and eat beignets from Cafe du Monde here.

42. _____ Visit the Ogden Museum of Southern Art. Bonus if you take the streetcar to get here.

43. _____ See Glen David Andrews perform. Bonus if you meet him. He's a swell guy.

44. _____ Go to Vaughan's for music. Bonus if it's on a Thursday night for Corey Henry.

45. _____ Sip a cocktail at The Columns Hotel. Bonus if you attempt to count the streetcars as they ramble by.

46. _____ Check out live music at Tipitina's. Bonus if you get yourself a t-shirt.

47. _____ Check out the legendary Rebirth Brass Band. Bonus if you find them at the Maple Leaf Bar.

48. _____ Visit Congo Square and explore Louis Armstrong Park and absorb the history. Bonus if you then go to Bar Tonique close by for a cocktail. (*Bloody Marys are great here*)

49. _____ Visit the Presbytere Museum. Bonus if you learn why all New Orleanians keep a hatchet in their attics.

50. _____ Have a meal and/or cocktail on a balcony. Bonus if you throw some beads to onlookers.

51. _____ Duck into all the music venues on Frenchmen St. Bonus if you also pop into BMC on Esplanade for Lil Red and Big Bad on a Friday night (*Note: this is not on Frenchmen, but across Esplanade from Frenchmen*).

52. _____ Have a burger at Port o Call. Bonus if you drink an entire Monsoon.

53. _____ Dine at Clover Grill on Bourbon St. Bonus if it's after midnight. Double bonus if anyone dances on the tables.

54. _____ Visit the Pharmacy Museum. Bonus if you don't shiver at the older methods doctors used during childbirth or lady exams.

55. _____ Visit Bourbon *"O"* for a cocktail and live music. Bonus if you get the Ramos Gin Fizz. Be patient. It takes the mechanical arm several minutes to shake properly.

56. _____ Sit under the Singing Oak in City Park. Bonus if you relax so much listening to the wind chimes you fall asleep.

57. _____ Dine at Liuzza's by the Track. Bonus if you have a BBQ shrimp po boy. Double bonus if you find out what character from the TV show Treme ate his last meal here.

THE GRIT, THE GRUMBLE AND THE GRANDEUR | 413

58. _____ Purchase a meal from a street vendor on/off of Frenchmen St. Bonus if it is right outside someone's front door.

59. _____ Visit Louisiana Music Factory. Bonus if you purchase some music to take home. Double bonus if you run into Trombone Shorty here. Happened to us!

60. _____ Indulge in some Angelo Brocato's ice cream. Bonus if you also grab a cannoli. Double bonus if you had lunch at Bevi Seafood next door first and saved room.

61. _____ Catch Washboard Chaz at dba or elsewhere. Bonus if he's playing with the Tin Men, Palmetto Bug Stompers, or The Blues Trio.

62. _____ Visit the US Mint Jazz Museum. Bonus if you can locate the musician who stated the following: *"If I don't make somebody cry–to be straight up honest with you–I haven't done my job."*

63. _____ Make your way to Frady's One Stop Shop in the Bywater for lunch. Bonus if you get the roast beef po'boy with debris and don't dribble it on your shirt. *(Cash only).*

64. _____ Attend a burlesque show. Bonus if you are selected to perform with the entertainment on stage.

65. _____ Visit the Beauregard-Keyes House. Bonus if you experience the ghost.

66. _____ Go to Latrobe Park and sit by the fountains. Bonus if you grab a muffuletta from Central Grocery across the street and eat it there while listening to the jazz.

67. _____ Dine at August for an upscale Friday lunch *(prix fixe)*. Bonus if you also order the blue crab gnocchi with black truffles as an appetizer. Double bonus if you lick the plate. I do every time. Best thing I've ever eaten.

68. _____ Attend a 10am Ranger Talk at the Jean Lafitte National Historical Park & Preserve French Quarter Visitor Center. Bonus if you learn something new!

69. _____ Visit the Lower 9th Ward Living Museum. Bonus if you also find Fats Domino's house in this neighborhood.

70. _____ Visit the Backstreet Cultural Museum. Bonus if you make a small donation.

71. _____ Sip wine and eat cheese under the stars at Bacchanal. Bonus if your husband convinces you to walk there when you should have taken an Uber.

72. _____ Take the ferry to Algiers Point. Bonus if you have a drink at the Old Point Bar.

73. _____ Check out Walter "the Wolfman" Washington at dba or Maple Leaf. Bonus if you get on his VIP list for his next show.

74. _____ Have a Bloody Mary at Le Bon Temps Roule. Bonus if you think this may be the best Bloody Mary you've ever had.

75. _____ Visit Degas House. Bonus if you stroll up and down Esplanade and marvel at the trees and homes. Double bonus if you stop for a moment and pay your respects at St. Anne's Episcopal Church's memorial wall to those lost to violence over the past 10 years or so. Sadly, the wall continues to grow...

76. _____ Purchase a Jazzy Pass. Bonus if you utilize it each day.

77. _____ Try Ms. Linda's Ya-Ka-Mein. Bonus if you meet the chef herself. Double bonus if it's your hangover cure.

78. _____ Visit N7 for a fantastic dinner. Bonus if you can get any of the staff to talk about who haunts the grounds.

79. _____ Rent bicycles and explore the city. Bonus if you get lost but don't care because it's just so gorgeous.

80. _____ Grab a cocktail at the upstairs bar at Muriel's. Bonus if you have dinner here as well. Double bonus if you happen to encounter their ghost.

81. _____ Indulge your sweet tooth at Bywater Bakery. Bonus if Washboard Chaz is playing outside for your entertainment.

82. _____ Pen your perfect portrait on the paper tablecloth while eating pizza at Mona Lisa. Bonus if you read their daily joke posted on their window.

83. _____ Dine at Brennan's for Breakfast. It's a tradition. Bonus if you get Bananas Foster. Double bonus if your bill is over 200 bucks for two. Ours was. But we also swam in champagne and cocktails.

84. _____ Get your "healthy" on at Meals from the Heart Cafe in the French Market. Bonus if you sit at the counter and chat with the workers.

85. _____ Visit the Katrina Memorial. No bonus here. Just be sure to pay your respects.

86. _____ Take a Free Tours by Foot Voodoo Tour. Bonus if you learn that Hollywood has completely manipulated the religion. Double bonus if you tip your guide well–you should.

87. _____ Stroll through The Treme neighborhood. Bonus if you pop into establishments such as The Candlelight Lounge and talk to the locals.

88. _____ Visit St. Roch Market and choose your poison. I like the pho, while Scott loved the trio of New Orleans classics. Bonus if you also pop into St. Roch Cemetery. Double bonus if you grab a drink at St. Roch Tavern.

89. _____ Get out of the city and head to Whitney Plantation. Bonus if you come away with a better understanding as to why this is the most important plantation of them all.

90. _____ Prove you're smart at Bywater Brew Pub's trivia night (Mondays). Bonus if you win. Double bonus if you order the crawfish etouffee nachos.

91. _____ Get your hat on at Meyer the Hatter! Bonus if you run into any of the many celebrities who purchase their hats there (Elvis Costello, Kermit Ruffins, Cyril Neville to name a few).

92. _____ Go for something completely different and dine at Mediterranean restaurant, Saba. Bonus if you continuously order the puffy pita bread knowing that it will spoil your appetite, but don't care cause it's just so damn good.

93. _____ Continue with something different and dine at Ethiopian restaurant, Addis. Bonus if you get a sambusa and then order more.

94. _____ Take a break during WWII Museum and grab lunch at Cochon Butcher. Bonus if you get the Le Pig Mac.

95. _____ Locate and snap a photo of one of the many graffiti paintings in the Bywater. Bonus if you locate a Bansky.

96. _____ Make your groceries at Rouse's. Bonus if you say "I'm going to make my groceries rather than I'm going grocery shopping."

97. _____ Grab a snoball at Plum Street Snoball on a hot day. Bonus if you add cream.

98. _____ Dine at Chef Nina Compton's Compere Lapin. Bonus if you get the Curried Goat with Sweet Potato Gnocchi.

99. _____ Get that Gator! Go on a swamp tour. Bonus if it is eco-friendly.

100. _____ Return if you have not completed this list. Bonus if you take me with you next time.